Breaking the Political Glass Ceiling

Second Edition

Why has the integration of women into Congress been so slow? Is there a "political glass ceiling" for women? Although women use the same strategic calculations as men to decide when to run, the decision regarding *where* to run is something else. While redistricting has increasingly protected incumbents, it also has the unintended consequence of shaping the opportunities for female candidates. The political geography and socio-economic profile of districts that elect women differ substantially from districts that elect men. With data on over 10,000 elections and 30,000 candidates from 1916 to the present, Palmer and Simon explore how strategy and the power of incumbency affect women's decisions to run for office.

Breaking the Political Glass Ceiling is the most comprehensive analysis of women in congressional elections available. The Second Edition is fully updated to reflect the pivotal 2006 midterm elections, including Nancy Pelosi's rise to Speaker of the House, Hillary Clinton's bid for the presidency, and a record number of women serving as committee chairs. Additionally, the authors have created a website, found at politicsandwomen.com, to highlight key features of the book and provide updates throughout the election cycle.

Barbara Palmer is Assistant Professor of Government and Affiliated Faculty in the Women and Politics Institute at American University.

Dennis Simon is Altshuler Distinguished Teaching Professor in the Political Science Department at Southern Methodist University.

Women in American Politics series
edited by Karen O'Connor

Madam President: Women Blazing the Leadership Trail
Eleanor Clift and Tom Brazaitis

Breaking the Political Glass Ceiling:
Women and Congressional Elections, First Edition
Barbara Palmer and Dennis Simon

Breaking the Political Glass Ceiling

Women and Congressional Elections

Second Edition

Barbara Palmer and Dennis Simon

Routledge
Taylor & Francis Group

NEW YORK AND LONDON

First published 2006
by Routledge
This edition published 2008
by Routledge
270 Madison Ave, New York, NY 10016

Simultaneously published in the UK
by Routledge
2 Park Square, Milton Park, Abingdon, Oxon OX14 4RN

Routledge is an imprint of the Taylor & Francis Group, an informa business

© 2006, 2008 Taylor & Francis

Typeset in Minion by
RefineCatch Limited, Bungay, Suffolk
Printed and bound in the United States of America on acid-free paper by
Edwards Brothers, Inc.

Library of Congress Cataloging-in-Publication Data
Palmer, Barbara, 1967–
   Breaking the political glass ceiling : women and congressional elections / Barbara Palmer,
Dennis Simon.—2nd ed.
      p. cm.—(Women in American politics)
   Includes bibiographical references.
   ISBN 978–0–415–96470–8 (hardback : alk. paper)—ISBN 978–0–415–96473–9
(pbk. : alk paper)—ISBN 978–0–203–93211–7 (ebook)   1. Women in politics—United States.
Simon, Dennis Michael.   Title.
   HQ1236.5.U6P35   2008
   324.9730082—dc22
   2007040845

ISBN10: 0–415–96470–9 (hbk)
ISBN10: 0–415–96473–3 (pbk)
ISBN10: 0–203–93211–0 (ebk)

ISBN13: 978–0–415–96470–8 (hbk)
ISBN13: 978–0–415–96473–9 (pbk)
ISBN13: 978–0–203–93211–7 (ebk)

Contents

For their years of understanding, support, and encouragement

To Mary Ann and Otto Palmer

Barbara Palmer

To Debbie, Jonathan, and Jennifer Simon
Valeria and Gary Simon and the memory of Michael Simon
Joan Roach and the memory of John Roach

Dennis Simon

Preface

This project began casually, with the academic equivalent of a water cooler conversation. In the fall of 1998, we were colleagues in the Department of Political Science at Southern Methodist University. Dennis Simon was teaching a course on congressional elections. He divided the House and Senate elections among the members of his class and required them to gather data on the party, background, and gender of the candidates. In looking over their work, he noticed that there were fourteen races in which a woman ran against another woman. At the drinking fountain one day, he mentioned these races to Barbara Palmer, whose expertise included women and politics, and asked whether she found it surprising. Our discussion of this "tidbit" about the 1998 midterm elections raised numerous questions about women in the electoral arena and congressional elections generally. Thus began a project that has spanned almost ten years and has included conference papers and journal articles, and has resulted in this book. We brought together two perspectives on politics in the United States and familiarity with two different bodies of literature. This project has been truly collaborative.

In the spring of 1999, the Research Council at Southern Methodist University awarded us a grant to begin the study. We used the funds primarily to hire research assistants to help in gathering and compiling what, in retrospect, turned out to be a staggering amount of data on House and Senate elections. We wish to thank those assistants who were recruited from Barbara's Women and Politics class at Southern Methodist University: Zhelia Bazleh, Diana Dorough, Cynthia Flores, Mandy Gough, Brooke Guest, Vanessa Hammond, Bernard Jones, Kristi Katsanis, Emily Katt, Albany Mitchell, Sheri Rogers, Heather Scott, Jessica Sheppard, Jennifer Sumrall, Andrea Swift, Natalie Thompson, Brenda Tutt, Amy Williams, and Kari Young. We owe a special expression of gratitude to those students who not only coded data but also "came back for more" to help us clean it and enter it into spreadsheets: Lindsay Abbate,

Erin Echols, Elizabeth Myers, and Steve Schulte. We suspect that their experience in "doing real political science" was a deciding factor in their choice to attend law school. We also would like to thank those students who worked with Barbara at American University, especially Amy Baumann, Meredith Hess, Cameo Kaisler, and Laura Pautz. Christine Carberry, of Southern Methodist University, was both expert and meticulous in preparing the index for both editions. We are grateful to her for unearthing a number of errors and omissions in the text. Our gratitude is also extended to Michael Kerns, Felisa Salvago-Keyes, Siân Findlay, Angela Chnapko and Amy Rodriguez at Taylor & Francis for their encouragement and guidance during the preparation, editing, and publication of the book.

We wish to thank all the panelists and discussants who offered critiques of our work over the years, especially those at numerous Southern Political Science Association Annual Meetings. At Southern Methodist University, we regularly vetted our ideas with Brad Carter, Valerie Hunt, Dennis Ippolito, Cal Jillson, Joe Kobylka, Harold Stanley, and Matthew Wilson. We also had frequent conversations with Carole Wilson of the University of Texas at Dallas. Susannah Shakow and Coke Stewart of Washington, D.C. provided much-needed proofreading and a fresh perspective to our work. We were extremely appreciative of the commentary and encouragement we received from David Broder of the *Washington Post*. For many reasons, we owe a tremendous debt of gratitude to Karen O'Connor, Director of the Women and Politics Institute at American University. Everyone's comments, questions, and encouragement proved most valuable, and we are grateful for their gift of collegiality.

1

Where We Were

Women of the 1950s

"Today, we have broken the marble ceiling," announced Representative Nancy Pelosi, after she was sworn in as the new Speaker of the U.S. House of Representatives on January 5, 2007. "It is a moment for which we have waited over 200 years. Never losing faith, we waited through the many years of struggle to achieve our rights . . . Never losing faith, we worked to redeem the promise of America, that all men and women are created equal."[1] After receiving the gavel and becoming the first woman to lead the House, Speaker Pelosi brought all of the children who had attended the ceremony up to the Speaker's chair, presenting a visual image of power rarely seen in American political history: a woman surrounded by children. Without doubt, her swearing in was a historic moment, but Speaker Pelosi leads a House that is only 16 percent female. The central question that motivates our book is why is the integration of women into Congress taking so long? Are women ever truly going to break the "political glass ceiling"?

A Snapshot: The Women of 1956

In 1956, sixteen women were elected to Congress, fifteen in the House and one in the Senate. The nation had elected President Dwight Eisenhower to a second term of office with 57.4 percent of the popular vote. Eisenhower's electoral appeal, however, was not sufficient to capture control of Congress. The Democrats enjoyed a 234–201 majority in the House of Representatives and a smaller, 49–47, majority in the Senate.[2] The national political agenda was crowded that year. President Eisenhower would address an international

---

[1] "Pelosi becomes first woman House speaker," CNN.com, January 5, 2007, http://www.cnn.com/2007/POLITICS/01/04/congress.rdp/index.html (accessed May 14, 2007).
[2] Alaska and Hawaii were not yet states, so the total number of senators was ninety-six.

crisis triggered in late 1956 by the British-French-Israeli invasion of the Suez Canal. The successful launch of Sputnik by the Soviets added to the anxiety about the ongoing Cold War and sparked a debate about the quality of education in the nation. The debate would ultimately lead to the National Defense Education Act in 1958. In September 1957, the effort to desegregate Central High School would force President Eisenhower to send federal troops to Little Rock, Arkansas.

The 85th Congress (1957 session) is noteworthy for two additional reasons. First, the election of 1956 was a high-water mark in the number of women elected to the House. Second, the 85th Congress enacted the Civil Rights Act of 1957, the first civil rights legislation passed by Congress since the Reconstruction era. Fourteen of the fifteen women in the House voted for the act, with Representative Iris Blitch (D-GA) casting the lone "nay" vote among them.

Nine of the women in the House were Democrats and six were Republicans. Senator Margaret Chase Smith (ME), the only woman in the Senate, was a Republican. Only one woman, Representative Martha Griffiths (D-MI), was a lawyer. Six were widows initially elected to succeed their deceased husbands. The most senior woman was Republican Edith Nourse Rogers of Massachusetts, a widow first elected in 1925; in 1957, she began serving her seventeenth term. Next in seniority was Republican Frances Bolton of Ohio, a philanthropist and, like Rogers, a widow. Bolton, first elected in 1940, began serving her tenth term. Another widow was West Virginia Democrat Maude Kee, who succeeded her husband, John. When Maude retired in 1964, her son, James, won the election to replace her.[3]

Many of these women would distinguish themselves as policy leaders in the House. Representative Martha Griffiths (D-MI) was a key force in passing the Civil Rights Act of 1964 and later became known as the "mother of the Equal Rights Amendment."[4] Representative Leonor Sullivan (D-MO) was a cosponsor of the Equal Pay Act of 1963 and an early advocate of consumer protection.[5] Representative Edith Green (D-OR) "left her mark on nearly every schooling bill enacted during her twenty years on Capitol Hill" and was the author and principle advocate of Title IX of the Educational Amendments of 1972.[6] Representative Gracie Pfost (D-ID), who became known as "Hell's Belle," was an opponent of private power companies and fought for federal intervention to manage the project planned for the Hell's Canyon branch of the Snake River.[7]

---

[3] Karen Foerstel, *Biographical Dictionary of Congressional Women* (Westport, Conn.: Greenwood Press, 1999), 144–45. Altogether, the Kee family held the seat from 1933 to 1973.

[4] Foerstel, 1999, 109–11.

[5] Foerstel, 1999, 263–65.

[6] Foerstel, 1999, 104.

[7] Foerstel, 1999, 218.

The Rules of the Game

In spite of the tremendous contributions of these women, that only fifteen were elected to the House in 1956 provides a vivid example that women had "a very small share, though a very large stake, in political power."[8] For women, entry into the inner world of politics was largely blocked. Specifically, women who were interested in politics faced numerous barriers, including cultural norms and gender stereotypes that limited their choices, little access to the "pipeline" or the hierarchy of political offices, and the politics of congressional redistricting.

Cultural Norms: A "Man's Game"

In the 1950s, women were socialized to view politics as a man's game, a game that was inconsistent with the gender roles to which women were assigned. As Jeane Kirkpatrick explained:

> Like men, women gain status for effective, responsible performance of culturally sanctioned roles. Any effort to perform roles assigned by the culture to the opposite sex is likely to result in a loss of status on the sex specific status ladder. The values on which women are expected to concentrate are those of affection, rectitude, well-being; the skills relevant to the pursuit of these values are those associated with nurturing, serving, and pleasing a family and community: homemaking, personal adornment, preparing and serving food, nursing the ill, comforting the downcast, aiding and pleasing a husband, caring for and educating the young. It is assumed furthermore that these activities will consume all a women's time, that to perform them well is both a full time and a life time job.[9]

Women attending college in the 1940s, for example, reported being cautioned about appearing too smart and earning top grades, because displays of intelligence endangered their social status on campus. Women were also reminded, typically by their parents and brothers, that pursuing a career would reduce their prospects for marriage and motherhood.[10] In 1950, only 23.9 percent of bachelor's degrees were awarded to women.[11] Traditional sex roles were widely accepted by men and women. In 1936, a Gallup Poll asked respondents whether a married woman should work if she had a husband capable of supporting her; 82 percent of the sample said, "No."[12] A similar

---

[8] Jeane Kirkpatrick, *Political Woman* (New York: Basic Books, 1974), 3.
[9] Kirkpatrick, 1974, 15.
[10] Mirra Komarovsky, "Cultural Contradictions and Sex Roles," *American Journal of Sociology* 52 (1946): 184–89.
[11] National Center for Education Statistics, http://nces.ed.gov (accessed August 1, 2005).
[12] *Gallup Poll, 1935–1971* (Wilmington, Del.: Scholarly Resources, 1973), 39.

question appeared in an October 1938 poll; 78 percent disapproved of married women entering the workforce. This included 81 percent of male respondents and 75 percent of female respondents.[13] Prior to World War II, the proportion of married women who worked outside the home was 14.7 percent. Labor shortages during the war drew married women in the workforce; by 1944, the proportion increased to 21.7 percent. In 1956, 29.0 percent of married women worked outside the home.[14] Working outside the home and pursuing a professional career represented a rejection of tradition, socialization, and conformity.

Also accepted was the norm that politics was the domain of men. A 1945 Gallup Poll reported that a majority of men and women disagreed with the statement that not enough "capable women are holding important jobs" in government.[15] In the 1950s, voter turnout among men was ten percentage points higher than among women.[16] One survey found that, compared to men, women were less likely to express a sense of involvement in politics; women had a lower sense of political efficacy and personal competence than men.[17] The political scientists conducting the survey reported that women who were married often refused to participate in the survey and referred "interviewers to their husbands as being the person in the family who pays attention to politics."[18] Moreover, these cultural norms about women and politics were slow to change. Indeed, as late as 1975, 48 percent of respondents in a survey conducted by the National Opinion Research Center agreed that "most men are better suited emotionally for politics than are most women."[19]

Against this cultural backdrop, it comes as no surprise that a "woman entering politics risks the social and psychological penalties so frequently associated with nonconformity. Disdain, internal conflicts, and failure are widely believed to be her likely rewards."[20] Entering the electoral arena was, therefore, an act of political and social courage. The example of Representative Coya Knutson (D-MN) poignantly illustrates that women with political ambitions were often punished. Knutson first ran for the House as a long shot in 1954, defeating a six-term incumbent Republican. During her campaign in the large rural district, she played the accordion and sang songs, in addition to criticizing the Eisenhower administration's agricultural policy.

---

[13] *Gallup Poll*, 1973, 131.
[14] U.S. Bureau of the Census, *Historical Statistics of the United States* (Washington, D.C.: U.S. Department of Commerce, Bureau of the Census, 1975), 133.
[15] *Gallup Poll*, 1973, 548–49.
[16] Angus Campbell, Philip Converse, Warren Miller, and Donald Stokes, *The American Voter* (Chicago: University of Chicago Press, 1960), 485.
[17] Campbell et al., 1960, 489–90.
[18] Campbell et al., 1960, 485.
[19] William Mayer, *The Changing American Mind* (Ann Arbor: University of Michigan Press, 1992), 394.
[20] Kirkpatrick, 1974, 15.

In 1958, Knutson was running for her third term. In response to Knutson's refusal to play along with the Democratic Party in their 1956 presidential endorsements, party leaders approached her husband, Andy, an alcoholic who physically abused her and her adopted son, to help sabotage her re-election campaign. At the prompting of party leaders, Andy wrote a letter to Coya, pleading that she return to Minnesota and give up her career in politics, complaining how their home life had deteriorated since she left for Washington, D.C. He also accused his wife of having an affair with one of her congressional staffers and threatened a $200,000 lawsuit. This infamous "Coya, Come Home" letter gained national media attention, and her Republican opponent ran on the slogan "A Big Man for a Man-Sized Job." She was defeated by fewer than 1,400 votes by Republican Odin Langin.[21] She was the only Democratic incumbent to lose that year.

Serving in political office could also be extremely unpleasant. Women in Congress often had to fight for access and positions, such as committee assignments, that would have rightfully been given to them had they been men.[22] For example, in 1949, Representative Reva Bosone, a Democrat from Utah, requested a seat on the House Interior Committee. When she approached Representative Jere Cooper (D-TN), the chair of the Ways and Means Committee who had the final say over assignments, he responded, "Oh, my. Oh, no. She'd be embarrassed because it would be embarrassing to be on the committee and discuss the sex of animals."[23] She shot back and said, "It would be refreshing to hear about animals' sex relationships compared to the perversions among human beings."[24] When Shirley Chisholm (D-NY) came to Washington, D.C., in 1968, she asked to be assigned to the Committee on Education and Labor. She was a former teacher with extensive experience in education policy while serving in the New York Assembly. Education was extremely important to her poor, black, Brooklyn district. The Democratic Party leadership in Congress, however, assigned her to the Agriculture Committee and the Subcommittee on Forestry and Rural Development. Outraged, she refused the assignment and took her case to Speaker of the House John McCormack (D-MA). He told her she should be a "good soldier," put her time in on the committee, and wait for a better assignment. Chisholm responded, "All my forty-three years I have been a good soldier. . . . The time is growing late, and I can't be a good

---

[21] Chuck Haga, " 'Come Home,' Coya Dies," *Minneapolis Star Tribune*, October 11, 1996, 1A; Leonard Inskip, "A Revival of Sorts for Minnesota's Knutson," *Minneapolis Star Tribune*, February 4, 1997, 11A; and Foerstel, 1999, 152–53. Another woman would not be elected to the House from the State of Minnesota until Democrat Betty McCollum in 2000.

[22] Sally Friedman, "House Committee Assignments of Women and Minority Newcomers, 1965–1994," *Legislative Studies Quarterly* 21 (1996): 73–81.

[23] Karen Foerstel and Herbert Foerstel, *Climbing the Hill: Gender Conflict in Congress* (Westport, Conn.: Praeger Press, 1996), 95.

[24] Fortunately, Cooper laughed and put her on the committee; Foerstel and Foerstel, 1996, 96.

soldier any longer."[25] She protested her committee assignment on the House floor, stating that "it would be hard to imagine an assignment that is less relevant to my background or to the needs of the predominantly black and Puerto Rican people who elected me," and was reassigned to the Veterans Affairs Committee.[26] It was not her first choice, but Chisholm did note, "There are a lot more veterans in my district than trees."[27] In 1973, Representative Pat Schroeder (D-CO) did receive an assignment on the committee of her choice, Armed Services, but the chair, F. Edward Hebert, a seventy-two-year-old Democrat from Louisiana, made it clear he did not want a woman on his committee. Hebert was also outraged that session because a newly elected African American, Representative Ron Dellums (D-CA), was assigned to his committee. Hebert announced that "women and blacks were worth only half of one 'regular' member," so Schroeder and Dellums were forced to share a chair during committee meetings.[28] An apt summary of the congressional ethos facing female members was provided by Representative Florence Dwyer (R-NJ), who served her first term in the 85th Congress (1957 session): "A Congresswoman must look like a girl, act like a lady, think like a man, speak on any given subject with authority and most of all work like a dog."[29]

Entry Professions and the Pipeline

One of the most prevalent explanations for the slow integration of women into Congress is "the pipeline theory." In American politics, there is a hierarchy of public office that functions as a career ladder for elected officials. A local office often serves as a springboard into the state legislature that, in turn, provides the requisite experience to run for the U.S. House of Representatives. Both the state legislature and the U.S. House serve as avenues to

---

[25] Shirley Chisholm, *Unbought and Unbossed: An Autobiography* (New York: Houghton Mifflin, 1970), 82–83.

[26] Chisholm, 1970, 84.

[27] After her speech on the House floor, several members told her that she had just committed political suicide; Chisholm, 1970, 84. She eventually did serve on the Education and Labor Committee and on the powerful House Rules Committee at the end of her congressional career; Marcy Kaptur, *Women of Congress: A Twentieth-Century Odyssey* (Washington, D.C.: CQ Press, 1996), 149.

[28] Pat Schroeder, *Twenty-four Years of House Work and the Place Is Still a Mess* (Kansas City, Mo.: Andrews McMeel, 1999), 41. Schroeder explained that she got the seat on the Armed Services Committee in the first place because of the pressure put on Hebert by Representative Wilbur Mills (D-AR), the head of the Committee on Committees. Normally, Hebert would have been able to veto Mills's decision to put Schroeder on the committee, but Mills pushed hard for Schroeder. Earlier that year, Mills was found "frolicking" in the Tidal Basin near the Jefferson Memorial with a stripper, Fannie Fox. Mills's support for Schroeder's appointment to the committee was an apparent attempt to appease his wife; Schroeder, 1999, 40. In January 1975, the House Democratic Caucus adopted numerous reforms, including a vote by secret ballot for committee chairs. In an act of poetic justice, Hebert lost and was removed as chair; *Congress and the Nation, 1973–1976* (Washington, D.C.: CQ Press, 1977), 13–14.

[29] Foerstel, 1999, 79.

statewide office, the most prominent of which are governorships and the U.S. Senate. Each successive office has a larger territorial jurisdiction, a larger constituency, and an increase in salary and prestige.[30] Before one can even enter this hierarchy, however, there are particular professions in the private sector that traditionally lead to political office, such as law and business. Although members of Congress come from a wide variety of career backgrounds, the most common by far is law. Those practicing in these professions typically form the "eligibility pool" of candidates for office. The pipeline theory maintains that once more women are in the eligibility pool, they will run for state and local office and then eventually "spill over" into Congress.

As table 1.1 reveals, very few of the fifty-five women elected to the House between 1916 and 1956 advanced to Congress through this traditional pipeline. The primary reason for this is that for most of American history, women were barred from entering many of the professions in the eligibility pool; the pipeline was blocked.[31] In 1956, only 3.5 percent of law degrees were awarded to women. Harvard Law School, for example, did not even admit women until 1950 and, despite skyrocketing applications, held the admissions rate for women between 3.0 and 4.0 percent until the 1970s.[32] Prior to 1970, less than 5 percent of lawyers were women.[33] Of the fifty-five women elected to the House between 1918 and 1956, only seven were lawyers.

Very few of these women had prior experience in lower-level political office. Six women had won election to local office, and nine had served in their state house of representatives. Representative Iris Blitch (D-GA) was the only woman to serve in the state senate and the only woman elected to both the lower and upper chambers of a state legislature. Democratic Representative Chase Going Woodhouse served Connecticut as Secretary of State and is the only woman of the fifty-five who had been elected to statewide office. Prior to pursuing a political career, she was an economics professor.[34]

---

[30] See for example Donald Matthews, *U.S. Senators and Their World* (Chapel Hill: University of North Carolina Press, 1960); Joseph Schlesinger, *Ambition and Politics: Political Careers in the United States* (Chicago: Rand McNally, 1966); David Canon, *Actors, Athletes and Astronauts* (Chicago: University of Chicago Press, 1990); and Wayne Francis and Lawrence Kenny, *Up the Political Ladder: Career Paths in U.S. Politics* (Thousand Oaks, Calif.: Sage, 2000).

[31] See for example Irene Diamond, *Sex Roles in the State House* (New Haven, Conn.: Yale University Press, 1977); Barbara Burrell, *A Woman's Place Is in the House: Campaigning for Congress in the Feminist Era* (Ann Arbor: University of Michigan Press, 1994); Susan Carroll, *Women as Candidates in American Politics* (Bloomington: Indiana University Press, 1994) M. Margaret Conway, Gertude Steurnagel, and David Ahern, *Women and Political Participation* (Washington, D.C.: CQ Press, 1997); Nancy McGlen and Karen O'Connor, *Women, Politics and American Society*, 2nd ed. (Upper Saddle River, N.J.: Prentice Hall, 1998); and M. Margaret Conway, *Political Participation in the United States*, 3rd ed. (Washington, D.C.: CQ Press, 2000).

[32] Cynthia Fuchs Epstein, *Women in Law*, 2nd ed. (Chicago: University of Illinois Press, 1993).

[33] Epstein, 1993, 4.

[34] Foerstel, 1999, 281.

Table 1.1 A Profile of the Fifty-five Women Elected to the House between 1916 and 1956

Background	Number of Women	Percent
Lawyer	7	12.7
Prior Elective Office Experience		
Elected to local office	6	10.9
Elected to state house of representatives	9	16.4
Elected to state senate	1	1.8
Elected to statewide office	1	1.8
Other Political Experience		
Served in appointed administrative office	10	18.2
Served in party organization	14	25.4
Lateral Entry		
Widows	21	38.2
No prior elective office experience	6	10.9

Because the pipeline was largely off-limits, women relied on other routes to gain experience.[35] As table 1.1 shows, ten of the fifty-five women, 18.2 percent, held administrative appointments, mostly at the local level, and fourteen, 25.4 percent, worked in some capacity for their political party. But even as volunteers in party organizations, women faced barriers. They were regularly confined to "expressive roles," while men assumed "instrumental roles;"[36] women hosted social events and were assigned "menial tasks associated with secretarial work," while men worked at recruiting candidates and managing campaigns.[37] Moon Landrieu, former mayor of New Orleans and father of U.S. Senator Mary Landrieu (D-LA), described this division of labor as "women do the lickin' and the stickin' while men plan the strategy."[38] In the late 1960s, Representative Patsy Mink (D-HI) pushed the Democratic National Committee to put more women in party leadership

---

[35] See for example Kirkpatrick, 1974; Susan Welch, "Recruitment of Women to Public Office," *Western Political Quarterly* 31 (1978): 372–80; and Raisa Deber, "The Fault Dear Brutus: Women as Congressional Candidates in Pennsylvania," *Journal of Politics* 44 (1982): 463–79.

[36] Diane Fowlkes, Jerry Perkins, and Sue Tolleson Rinehart, "Gender Roles and Party Roles," *American Political Science Review* 73 (1979): 772–80; and Edmond Constantini, "Political Women and Political Ambition: Closing the Gender Gap," *American Journal of Political Science* 34 (1990): 741–70.

[37] Conway, Steurnagel, and Ahern, 1997, 95.

[38] Conway, Steurnagel, and Ahern, 1997, 95.

and policy-making positions. She was confronted by another committee member, Edgar Berman, Vice President Hubert Humphrey's personal physician, who claimed that "if we had a menopausal woman President who had to make the decision of the Bay of Pigs," she would be "subject to the curious mental aberrations of that age group." [39] Mink demanded, and got, Berman's resignation from the committee. In response, he claimed he had been "crucified on the cross of women's liberation" and that her anger was "a typical example of an ordinarily controlled woman under the raging hormonal imbalance of the periodical lunar cycle." [40]

Because of such attitudes, the women who were elected to the House frequently gained their seats through "lateral entry," not through elective office or the party hierarchy. As table 1.1 reports, twenty-one of the fifty-five women elected to the House between 1916 and 1956 were congressional widows; they ran for the House seats held by their deceased husbands. Six other women won their seats without the benefit of holding prior elective or party office. Occasionally, these women capitalized upon their "celebrity status" to launch a successful campaign for office. In other words, they relied on prior name recognition and acclaim they had earned outside the political arena. [41] For example, prior to running for the House, Clare Boothe Luce (R-CT; see figure 1.1) was a writer for *Vogue* and *Vanity Fair*. In 1932, at the age of twenty-nine, she was named managing editor of *Vanity Fair*. A collection of her articles satirizing the social life of New York City was published in *Stuffed Shirts*. [42] She left the magazine two years later to work as a playwright and had several of her plays produced on Broadway, including *The Women, Kiss the Boys Goodbye,* and *Margin for Error*. [43] In 1935, she married Henry Luce, a founder and editor of *Time* magazine. Together, they developed *Life* magazine, which began publication in November 1936. In 1938, Luce's stepfather, Albert Austin (R-CT), won a seat in the House representing the 4th District of Connecticut. Two years later, Austin was defeated by Democrat LeRoy Downs. In 1942, having never run for political office, Luce won the Republican nomination and then defeated Downs. [44]

Helen Gahagan Douglas (D-CA; see figure 1.2) was a contemporary of Luce. At age twenty-one, she made her Broadway debut in *Dreams for Sale*, a

---

[39] Foerstel and Foerstel, 1996, 27.

[40] Foerstel and Foerstel, 1996, 27.

[41] Canon, 1990.

[42] Clare Boothe Luce, *Stuffed Shirts* (New York: Liveright, 1933).

[43] These plays were published by Random House in 1937, 1939, and 1940.

[44] In 1944, she was elected to a second term, defeating Democrat Margaret Connor by less than 1 percent of the vote. Luce declined to run again in 1946. After an eight-year hiatus from politics, Luce campaigned for Dwight Eisenhower in 1952. Thereafter, she became a fixture in Republican national politics. She served as ambassador to Italy from 1953 to 1957, co-chaired the 1964 campaign for U.S. Senator Barry Goldwater (R-AZ), and served two stints on the Foreign Intelligence Advisory Board (1973–1977 and 1982–1987). Just before her death in 1987, she was awarded the Presidential Medal of Freedom by President Ronald Reagan; Foerstal, 1999, 165–67.

Fig. 1.1 Representative Clare Boothe Luce was first elected to the House in 1942, having never run for office before. Photo courtesy of the Library of Congress.

play that won its author, Owen Davis, a Pulitzer Prize. A Broadway critic called her "ten of the twelve most beautiful women in the world."[45] Douglas also pursued a career as an opera singer. In 1931, she married the well-known and popular actor, Melvyn Douglas, and the couple left New York to pursue film careers in Hollywood. Helen appeared in one film. In the 1935 release entitled *She*, she played Queen Hash-A-Mo-Tep of Kor, a beautiful five-hundred-year-old queen of a lost arctic city who can only die if she falls in love.[46] The film lost $180,000 at the box office. According to critics, Douglas lacked "screen presence."[47] In Hollywood, Douglas became active

---

[45] Leonard Pitt, "Mrs. Deeds Goes to Washington," *Reviews in American History* 21(1993): 477–81, 477. See also Ingrid Winther Scobie, *Center Stage: Helen Gahagan Douglas, A Life* (New York: Oxford University Press, 1992); Foerstel, 1999, 73–75; and "Helen Gahagan Douglas: A Life," http://www.ou.edu/special/albertctr/archives/exhibit/hgdbio.htm (accessed June 13, 2005).

[46] *Internet Movie Data Base*, http://imdb.com/title/tt0026983/ (accessed June 13, 2005).

[47] *Internet Movie Data Base*, http://imdb.com/title/tt0026983/ (accessed June 13, 2005).

Fig. 1.2 Representative Helen Gahagan Douglas first ran for the House in 1944, after being encouraged by First Lady Eleanor Roosevelt. Photo courtesy of the Library of Congress.

in politics and testified before Congress on "the plight of migratory farm workers."[48] Her testimony attracted the attention of First Lady Eleanor Roosevelt. At Roosevelt's urging, Douglas became a candidate for Congress in 1944 when the retirement of Democrat Thomas Ford created an open seat in the 14th District of California. She won the election with 51.5 percent of the vote and was reelected in 1946 and 1948 by more comfortable margins. In 1950, Douglas won the Democratic nomination for the open Senate seat in California but was defeated by Republican Richard Nixon. As a member of the House, Douglas worked hard to emphasize her competence, in part, by "consciously playing down her beauty under conservative garb and hair

---

[48] Pitt, 1993, 478.

style."[49] During the 79th Congress (1945 and 1946 sessions), Douglas and Luce were colleagues in the House. Both of them had to contend with press coverage that tended to exaggerate personal rivalry between them.[50]

This attitude toward women who became involved in politics is reflected in the concluding chapter of *Political Life*, published in 1959 by Robert Lane, a political science professor at Yale. He explains:

> Broadly speaking, political affairs are considered by the culture to be somewhat peripheral to the female sphere of competence and proper concern. . . . [I]t is too seldom remembered in . . . American society that working girls and career women, and women who insistently serve the community in volunteer capacities, and women with extra-curricular interests of an absorbing kind are often borrowing their time and attention and capacity for relaxed play and love from their children to whom it rightfully belongs.[51]

John Lindsay, the mayor of New York City from 1966 to 1973, put it more bluntly: "Whatever women do, they do best after dark."[52] Thus, it should come as no surprise that many women who entered politics had very different career paths than their male counterparts.

The Politics of Redistricting

Potential female candidates for House seats also faced a more subtle barrier associated with the geography of congressional districts: malapportionment that favored rural districts. Prior to the early 1960s, most districts in the United States were malapportioned, in other words, most districts did not have equal populations.[53] According to the 1950 U.S. Census, if districts had

---

[49] Sara Alpern, "Center Stage: Helen Gahagan Douglas, A Life," *American Historical Review* 98 (1993): 967–68.

[50] Alpern, 1993, 967.

[51] Robert Lane, *Political Life* (Glencoe, Ill.: Free Press, 1959), 354–55. Lane goes on to intimate agreement with Abram Kardiner, who attributes the rise in juvenile delinquency and homosexuality to the feminist movement in his book, *Sex and Morality* (Indianapolis, Ind.: Bobbs-Merrill, 1954).

[52] Conway, Steuernagel, and Ahern, 1997, 95.

[53] After decades of dismissing malapportionment as a "political question," in 1962, the U.S. Supreme Court ruled in *Baker v. Carr* that a challenge to the apportionment of seats in the Tennessee General Assembly was a justiciable issue. The standard established by this landmark case is often described as the "one person, one vote" rule and held that disparities in population across legislative districts were unconstitutional. Once implemented, the decision reduced the dominance of representatives of underpopulated rural districts in many state legislatures. In 1964, the Supreme Court announced its decision in *Wesberry v. Sanders*, a case that challenged the congressional district boundaries in Georgia. Here, the Court applied the precedent from *Baker* and held that "construed in its historical context, the command of Article I, Section 2, that Representatives be chosen 'by the People of the several States' means that as nearly as is practicable one man's vote in a congressional election is to be worth as much as another's," 376 U.S. 1, 7.

been apportioned with equal populations, they would have approximately 349,000 residents.[54] The actual population of congressional districts, however, varied widely. In 1950, eighty-nine districts had less than 300,000 residents, and twenty-eight districts had less than 250,000 residents. There were also eighty-nine districts with populations exceeding 400,000, and twenty-eight with populations exceeding 450,000.[55]

This malapportionment created widespread disparities in representation that favored rural America. In essence, votes in less populated districts were "worth more" than the votes in highly populated districts. For example, the most populous constituency to elect a woman in 1956 was the 3rd District of Oregon, Democrat Edith Green's district. The 3rd District, with a population of 471,537, was a geographically small district that included the City of Portland. In contrast, the rural 4th District of Texas, represented by Democratic Speaker of the House Sam Rayburn, or "Mr. Sam," had 186,043 people. The value of an individual vote in the Texas 4th was over two-and-a-half times the value of an individual vote in Oregon's 3rd. In addition to diluting the voting power of minority groups residing in urban areas, the impact of this rural bias was to limit the number of urban districts, the kinds of districts in which the women of the 1950s were successful. In 1956, the median urban population of districts electing men was 58.2 percent. Twelve women had won their party's nomination but were defeated in the general election; the median urban population in those twelve districts was 54.0 percent. In contrast, the median urban population in those fifteen districts that had elected women was 87.1 percent. Most of the successful female candidates came from large cities: in addition to Green, Representative Frances Bolton (R-OH) was from Cleveland, Marguerite Church (R-IL) from Chicago, Kathryn Granahan (D-PA) from Philadelphia, Edna Kelly (D-NY) from New York City, and Leonor Sullivan (D-MO) from St. Louis. This suggests that women fared much better in urban districts. Malapportionment, however, constricted the number of these districts.

There were other apportionment issues that affected the electoral fate of women as well. Prior to the Supreme Court's decision in *Wesberry v. Sanders* in 1964, it was not unusual for a state gaining a seat in the reapportionment process to elect the new member at large for one or two elections until the state legislature got around to redrawing the district lines and eliminated the at-large seat. Of the fifty-five women elected between 1916 and 1956, eight were elected as at-large representatives. Only two, Representatives Isabella Greenway (D-AZ) and Caroline O'Day (D-NY), served more than one term

---

[54] Calculation of this target population excludes those at-large seats that have a statewide constituency and those states that are guaranteed one representative regardless of population (e.g., Vermont).

[55] Dennis Simon, "Electoral and Ideological Change in the South: The Case of the U.S. House of Representatives, 1952–2000" (paper presented at the Southern Political Science Association Annual Meeting, January 2004, New Orleans).

in the House. Two women, Representatives Jeannette Rankin (R-MT) and Winnifred Stanley (R-NY), left the House after redistricting dissolved their at-large seats.

After the 1960 U.S. Census and the Supreme Court's decisions in *Baker v. Carr* (1962) and *Wesberry*, states began a wave of redistricting in the 1960s, and several other women who were first elected between 1916 and 1956 fell victim to reapportionment. Some states lost seats and existing districts had to be dissolved, as was the case for Representative Kathryn Granahan's district (D-PA). As "compensation," Democratic leaders in Pennsylvania persuaded President John F. Kennedy to nominate Granahan for the post of U.S. treasurer.[56] In some cases, redistricting forced two incumbents to compete for a single seat. In 1968, to comply with *Wesberry*, Ohio enacted a redistricting plan that pitted Republican Representative Frances Bolton, who was seeking her sixteenth term in the House, against Democratic incumbent Charles Vanik. He defeated Bolton with 54.7 percent of the vote. Redistricting also forced incumbents of the same party to compete against each other. The 1968 redistricting plan in New York ended the career of Representative Edna Kelly when she had to run against fellow Democrat Emanuel Celler, chair of the House Judiciary Committee. In addition to enforced sex roles that limited their choices and the denial of access to the political pipeline, the success of some female candidates was often thwarted in the process of redistricting.

The Plan of the Book and Our Data

Our overview of the barriers faced by women in the mid-twentieth century reveals why so few were elected to the House and the Senate. The social and political culture was not amenable to female politicians. The preparatory professions and paths to public office were blocked. The geographic composition of House districts and the manipulation of those districts were additional challenges. Much has changed in American politics and culture. Our analysis is designed to examine the pace of women's integration into the electoral system since the 1950s. Chapter 2 provides an overview of the number of women running in primaries, winning primaries, and winning general elections for the House and Senate from 1956 to 2006. We also discuss the historical development of careerism in Congress. For most of the 19th century, members who served more than one or two terms were rare. But around 1916, when women were first beginning to run for Congress, the average length of service began to steadily climb; just as women were starting to enter the political arena, the path to success was becoming more and more arduous. Thus, careerism and incumbency provide the foundation for the "political glass ceiling."

---

[56] Her signature was on every dollar bill issued during her tenure as U.S. treasurer; Foerstel, 1999, 100.

We developed a data set that includes all elections to the U.S. House of Representatives from 1956 through 2006. Our major source for this "master file" is the *America Votes* series. For each district in each election year, we recorded the number of female candidates running for the Democratic and Republican nominations, the total number of candidates seeking each party's nomination, whether a woman won the Democratic or Republican nomination, and the outcome of the general election.[57] For each district, we also recorded the party and sex of the incumbent, whether the incumbent was seeking reelection, and the incumbent's share of the two-party vote in the prior election. Identifying the sex of candidates was done by examining the names listed in each district in the primary and general elections provided by *America Votes*. Occasionally, the sex of the candidate was not obvious from the name. While the most common questionable names were Pat, Lee, Terry, Leslie, and Robin (including Robin Hood), we also encountered the exotic Simone (no last name) and Echo in California. Other puzzlers included Kish, Avone, Twain, and Mattox. To investigate these unknowns, we consulted relevant editions of the *Almanac of American Politics* and the *Congressional Quarterly Weekly Report*. Quite often, the coverage in these sources provided information about the sex of the party nominees. For the more recent period (approximately 1974 onward), we conducted a Nexis search of newspaper coverage. In almost every case, we were able to find media coverage that revealed the sex of the candidates. Finally, if these methods provided no information, the name was excluded from our count of candidates. The total number of exclusions was less than 2 percent of all candidate names. Applying these procedures to electoral data from 1956 through 2006, we coded 11,301 House elections involving over 34,800 candidate names, and 895 Senate elections involving over 4,260 candidate names.

---

[57] For primary elections, this count includes those candidates who received votes in the party primary. This differs slightly from those counts based upon those who filed to run but withdrew before the actual primary balloting. In gathering these data, there are several special cases. The states of Connecticut, Utah, and Virginia employ a mixed system of conventions and primaries to nominate their congressional candidates. The nominating conventions are held first, with primaries scheduled only if there is a significant challenge to the designated convention nominee. In instances where there is no primary, we coded the gender of the nominees only because the number of candidates seeking the nomination at the convention is unknown. Louisiana is yet another special case. The state employs an open primary system in which candidates, regardless of party, run in a single primary. If a candidate wins an absolute majority of the primary vote, the candidate is elected to the House and there is no general election. For Louisiana, we coded the number of Democrats and Republicans (women and total) running in the initial primary. In instances where there was a general election, we followed the same conventions used with other states, noting, of course, instances in which the general election involved two candidates from the same party. Finally, there are states that have a primary runoff system. In these states, a candidate must win over fifty percent of the primary vote to obtain the party nomination. If no candidate wins over 50 percent, there is a runoff primary between the top two finishers. The winner of this runoff then becomes the party nominee. Our coding records the number of candidates (women and total) in the initial primary and the sex of the ultimate nominees.

In chapters 3 and 4, we turn to the question of political ambition and strategic behavior among women. Our focus in chapter 3 is the congressional widow. We explore why some widows simply served out the term of their deceased husbands while others chose to pursue congressional careers. Our analysis shows that there are systematic differences between these two groups of widows, including their ages when they first ran, their level of independent political experience, the region where they ran, and the era in which they were first elected to the House. To perform the analysis, we gathered biographical information on all women who served in the House between 1917 and 2007 from the *Biographical Directory of the American Congress;*[58] the *Biographical Directory of Congressional Women;*[59] *Congressional Women: Their Recruitment, Integration, and Behavior,* 2nd ed.;[60] and various editions of the *Almanac of American Politics.*[61] In addition to identifying whether a female member of the House was a widow, the database includes her party, her state, her congressional district, the date she was first elected to the House, her age when she was first elected to the House, her history of prior officeholding, and the number of terms she served in the House.

In chapter 4, we continue our study of political ambition and ask why some women pursue a career in the House while others leave the security of their seat and run for higher office. Our analysis shows that when faced with the opportunity to run for the Senate, women respond to the same strategic considerations as men. These considerations include the size of the state, the length of the representative's House career, whether the representative is a risk taker, and the probability of winning the Senate seat. For this analysis, we created a database where the unit of analysis is the opportunity of female incumbents in the House to run for the Senate from 1916 to 2004. The data are built from both our master file and our biographical file. We then use our analysis to speculate about the female House members who may make a run for the Senate. In addition, we discuss the female senators who may make a run for the presidency, with particular attention given to Senator Hillary Clinton. Together, chapters 3 and 4 suggest that women who pursue careers in the House or run for the Senate have exhibited the same forms of ambition and behave in the same strategic manner as their male counterparts.

We then turn, in chapter 5, to the competitive environment faced by House incumbents seeking reelection and explore whether this environment

---

[58] We use the 1971 and 1997 editions (Washington, D.C.: CQ Press) as well as the online version, http://bioguide.congress.gov/biosearch/biosearch.asp.

[59] Foerstel, 1999.

[60] Irwin Gertzog, *Congressional Women: Their Recruitment, Integration, and Behavior,* 2nd ed. (Westport, Conn.: Praeger Press, 1995).

[61] Information on the most recent widows was also compiled through various issues of *CQ Weekly,* from Lexis-Nexis searches, and from the Center for American Women and Politics.

is the same for men and women. Here, we rely upon our master file to perform an analysis that covers the period from 1956 to 2006.

We found that while female House incumbents are reelected at rates slightly higher than male House incumbents, these women face a more competitive environment. In other words, beneath the apparent equality of incumbency reelection rates, women have to work harder to keep their seats. We also show that the presence of a female incumbent draws more women into the electoral arena.

For the second edition of this book, we have added a new chapter that investigates another unexplored inequality: the tremendous gap between the number of Democratic women and Republican women in the House. In the 110th Congress (2007 session), Democratic women outnumbered Republican women fifty-one to twenty. In chapter 6, we disaggregate the number of women running in primaries, winning primaries, and winning general elections for the House and Senate by party, to explore the development of this party gap. For the last twenty years, the political glass ceiling has had a substantial partisan component.

Our results in chapter 5 show that female candidates tend to cluster in particular districts, and chapter 6 explores how party plays a role in the success of women candidates. Chapter 7 is designed to investigate why and how these two trends may be related. It turns out that districts electing women have distinctive features. In effect, there are "women-friendly" districts. We develop an "index of women-friendliness" and use it to examine electoral competition in swing and open districts. To conduct this phase of our analysis, we supplemented our master file with demographic data from the *Congressional District Data Set*[62] and *Congressional District Demographic and Political Data.*[63] Both databases are drawn from the U.S. Census. For the 1972–2000 period, we integrated twelve demographic measures representing the political geography of congressional districts into our master data file.

Chapter 8 summarizes our results and discusses the implications. Using the demographic data we compiled for 2002 through 2006, we assess the political fortunes of women in the upcoming election cycles given the redistricting regime in place until 2010 and provide a list of the nation's "best" and "worst" districts for women candidates. We ultimately conclude that while incumbency serves as the primary barrier for female candidates and has substantially slowed the integration of women into Congress, there is more to the story. Open seats can provide opportunities for women, but not all open seats are equally likely to elect women. In fact, a substantial proportion of congressional districts are still highly unlikely to elect female

---

[62] Created by Professor Scott Adler, http://socsci.colorado.edu/~esadler/districtdatawebsite/ CongressionalDistrictDatasetwebpage.htm.
[63] Created by Professor David Lublin, http://www.american.edu/dlublin/research/data/ data.html.

candidates. As it turns out, many of the districts that are the most likely to elect women candidates are currently held by male members of Congress. Thus, the "political glass ceiling" is a function of incumbency and district-level factors that have kept the integration of women into Congress at an achingly slow pace.

2

The Rise and Persistence of the Political Glass Ceiling

In the history of Congress, 215 women have served in the House, 139 Democrats (64.7 percent) and seventy-six Republicans (35.3 percent), and thirty-five women have served in the Senate, twenty-two Democrats (62.9 percent) and thirteen Republicans (37.1 percent).[1] Only three states have been represented by two women senators serving simultaneously: California, Maine, and Washington. One-third of all the women to serve in Congress are current members. In 2006, there were seventy-one women elected to the House and sixteen women elected to the Senate, making Congress 16.3 percent female.[2] Why is the integration of women into Congress taking so long? When will we have a Congress in which half the members are women?

The first woman to serve in Congress, Representative Jeannette Rankin (R-MT; see figure 2.1), was elected to the House in 1916, before women even had the constitutional right to vote.[3] Rankin was, however, active in the suffrage movement, and largely thanks to her efforts, Montana gave women the right to vote in 1914. Rankin became a candidate for the House two years later after her brother encouraged her. She ran because "there are hundreds of men to care for the nation's tariff and foreign policy and irrigation projects. But there isn't a single woman to look after the nation's greatest asset: its children."[4] Four days after taking her oath of office, she cast a vote

---

[1] These numbers are as of May 15, 2007.
[2] The number of women elected to the House includes Representative Juanita Millender-McDonald (D-CA), who died in April of 2007.
[3] See James Lopach and Jean Luckowski, *Jeannette Rankin: A Political Woman* (Boulder, Colo.: University Press of Colorado, 2005).
[4] Quoted from Karen Foerstel, *Biographical Dictionary of Congressional Women* (Westport, Conn.: Greenwood Press, 1999), 225.

Fig. 2.1 Representative Jeannette Rankin, the first woman to serve in Congress, ran in 1916 at the age of thirty-six. Photo courtesy of the Library of Congress.

that would cost her reelection. With fifty-five other members, she voted against the United States entering World War I. Two years later, with her vote against the war seen as a liability and her at-large district dissolved, she did not seek reelection to the House and instead ran for the Senate. She lost the Republican primary, but ran in the general election as a National Party candidate, coming in a distant third. During her term in the House, Rankin cosponsored the constitutional amendment granting women's suffrage, but it failed to pass the Senate in that session. Because she was not reelected in 1918, she was not a member of Congress when the amendment finally passed in 1920. She became actively involved in the peace movement and secretary for the National Consumers League, lobbying for child labor laws along with minimum-wage and maximum-hour legislation. In 1940, at the age of sixty, Rankin ran again for the House and won. But on December 8, 1941, the day after the bombing of Pearl Harbor, she cast the only vote against the United States' declaration of war against Japan. Once again, she decided not to run for reelection and continued her work as a peace activist.[5]

---

[5] Foerstel, 1999, 226–27. See also Marcy Kaptur, *Women of Congress: A Twentieth-Century Odyssey* (Washington, D.C.: CQ Press, 1996).

Rankin completed her House service as the only representative to oppose American entry into both World War I and World War II.[6]

The first woman to serve in the Senate was Rebecca Latimer Felton (D-GA), who was appointed in 1922 and served for two days, the shortest Senate career in history. Felton was also a strong advocate of women's rights and was especially interested in the plight of rural women, although at one point she did support lynching blacks "as a warning against suspected rapists."[7] After Felton's brief appearance, it would be ten years before another woman would serve in the Senate. Senator Hattie Caraway (D-AR) was first appointed in 1931 after the death of her husband and then was reelected twice. In her bid for her third term, she was defeated in the primary by J. William Fulbright, who would hold the seat for the next three decades and chair the Senate Foreign Relations Committee. During her tenure, she earned the nickname "Silent Hattie" because of her rare speeches on the Senate floor. She explained, "I haven't the heart to take a minute away from the men. The poor dears love it so."[8] Caraway was given the same desk on the Senate floor that Felton had used and remarked, "I guess they wanted as few of them contaminated as possible."[9] Caraway served almost her entire thirteen-year career as the only woman in the Senate.[10]

After these pioneers, the slow integration of women began. The growth in female candidates since 1916, however, has not been a slow, steady climb. Using our original data from 1956 to 2006, we show that consistent increases in the number of female candidates did not begin until the early 1970s. Since 1970 and for the next two decades, the number of women in the House would increase by one or two in a given election cycle. In the Senate, the integration was even slower. But in 1992, the "Year of the Woman," a record number of women candidates ran and won, doubling the number of women in the House and tripling the number of women in the Senate. Since then, the typical increase in the number of women in the House has been four or five. What explains these trends?

Our analysis in this chapter focuses on the power of incumbency. House and Senate incumbents are virtually unbeatable. They face little competition, and those who do face competition are likely to win in a "blow out." We show that the phenomenon of long-term career incumbents, however, is relatively recent. For the first one hundred years of congressional history, most members of Congress did not serve more than one or two terms. This

---

[6] For the next three decades after Rankin's initial victory, one or two women would typically be elected to the House. From 1940 to 1954, four or five women regularly served in the House during a given Congress.

[7] Foerstel, 1999, 87–89.

[8] Foerstel, 1999, 51.

[9] Foerstel, 1999, 51.

[10] During her tenure in the Senate, two other women would briefly serve after being appointed after the deaths of their husbands; Center for American Women and Politics, *Women in the U.S. Senate 1922–2005* (New Brunswick, N.J.: Rutgers University, 2005).

changed in the early part of the twentieth century, just as the first women began running. Our analysis thus illustrates the development of the political glass ceiling: the growth of careerism occurred just as women were entering the national political arena. And by the time social attitudes about the role of women began to change in the 1970s, the power of incumbency was well established. The political glass ceiling was firmly in place.

The Integration of Women into the House

Gaining a seat in Congress involves three distinct steps: (1) seeking the nomination of a party, which in the vast majority of instances means running in a primary; (2) winning the primary; and (3) winning the general election. All candidates, whether they are incumbents, challengers, or running in an open seat, must go through these steps in every election cycle. In essence, these are critical steps in the career pipeline discussed in chapter 1. Figure 2.2 provides an overview of the integration of women into the House from 1956 to 2006, showing the number of women running in primaries, winning primaries, and winning the general election.

Women and Elections to the House

As noted in chapter 1, the first year included in our data, 1956, marked a high point in the number of women candidates; it would not be reached again until 1972. In 1956, fifty-three women ran in primaries, twenty-nine women won primaries, and fifteen were elected to the House. By 1968, this dropped to forty women running in primaries, nineteen women winning primaries, and ten winning election to the House. One female House member commented, "There are three times as many whooping cranes as congresswomen. . . . While many things are being done to protect the rare, long-legged bird, nobody seems concerned about our being an endangered species."[11] These declines seem especially surprising given the events of the early 1960s. Women's rights were not a priority for President John F. Kennedy, but in 1961 he did create the Commission on the Status of Women and appointed former First Lady Eleanor Roosevelt to be its chair.[12] In 1963, Betty Friedan's *The Feminine Mystique* brought "the problem that has no name" to the attention of millions of American women, and she toured the

---

[11] Quoted from Karen Foerstel and Herbert Foerstel, *Climbing the Hill: Gender Conflict in Congress* (Westport, Conn.: Praeger Press, 1996), 25.

[12] It has been suggested that he created the commission in part because of pressure from labor unions that thought it would "siphon off pressure for an Equal Rights Amendment"; Jane Mansbridge, *Why We Lost the ERA* (Chicago: University of Chicago Press, 1986), 9–10. See also Cynthia Harrison, *On Account of Sex: The Politics of Women's Issues, 1945–1968* (Berkeley: University of California, 1988); Flora Davis, *Moving the Mountain: The Women's Movement in America since 1960* (New York: Simon & Schuster, 1991). In 1963, the commission released a report, *American Woman*, which provided an extensive account of the discrimination of women and made recommendations regarding paid maternity leave, federally subsidized child care, and more equitable divorce settlements; Davis, 1991, 37.

country talking about her book.[13] In 1964, Congress passed the landmark Civil Rights Act that banned segregation and discrimination in employment.[14] On September 7, 1968, a group of women lead by Jo Freeman and Shulamith Firestone protested the Miss America pageant in Atlantic City, New Jersey, and received national news coverage; this would be "the first time the mass media gave headline coverage to the new feminist movement."[15] At the same time, however, the integration of women into the House was slowing down.

These trends would change, however, in 1972. The early 1970s mark the beginning of a new era in the number of female candidates in House elections.[16] Between 1970 and 1974, the number of women running in primaries jumped from 42 to 105, the number of women winning primaries increased from 24 to 43, and the number of women winning the general election went from 12 to 18. The timing of this new era coincides with the dawn of the Women's Movement, marking the beginning of changing attitudes toward women as candidates and officeholders. "[L]ike most social movements, the women's movement seemed to burst onto the political scene with little warning."[17] As Jo Freeman explained, "Within the short space of a few months the movement went from a struggling new idea to a national phenomenon."[18] In 1970, new women's rights organizations were forming at a rate faster than anyone could count.[19] Membership in the

---

[13] Davis, 1991.

[14] The word "sex" as an illegal category of discrimination was added at the last minute by Representative Howard Smith (D-VA). The prevailing wisdom is that he did this in order to make the bill too radical and ensure its failure; Davis, 1991, 38–45. But the female members of Congress took the amendment very seriously, and this strategy to kill the legislation was ultimately unsuccessful. In 1966, the executive director of the Equal Employment Opportunity Commission, Herman Edelsberg, publicly stated that he had no intention of enforcing the provision. As far as he was concerned, "[M]en were entitled to female-secretaries"; quoted from Jo Freeman, *The Politics of Women's Liberation* (New York: David McKay Co, 1975), 54.

[15] Judith Hole and Ellen Levine, *Rebirth of Feminism* (New York: Quadrangle Books, 1971), 123. The press coverage itself is an interesting study of the media's ability to frame issues and influence perception. At the protest, demonstrators had set up a "freedom trashcan" and were encouraged to throw in things that represented traditional images of femininity, including high heels, curling irons, girdles, and bras. The coverage of the protest suggested that the women actually burned bras, leading to the term "bra-burners"; Hole and Levine, 1971, 123–24, 228–30.

[16] When viewed historically, 1972 represents a "critical moment." It is analogous to the 1963–1964 period in the politics of race in the United States; Edward Carmines and James Stimson, *Issue Evolution: Race and the Transformation of American Politics* (Princeton, N.J.: Princeton University Press, 1989). See Dennis Simon and Barbara Palmer, "Gender, Party, and Political Change: The Evolution of a Democratic Advantage," APSAnet eSymposium, "An Open Boundaries Workshop: Women in Politics in a Comparative Perspective," *PS Online* 37 (2004): http://www.apsanet.org/imgtest/EvolutionDemocraticAdvan-Palmer.pdf (accessed July 15, 2005).

[17] Ann Costain, *Inviting Women's Rebellion: A Political Process Interpretation of the Women's Movement* (Baltimore: Johns Hopkins University Press, 1992), 1.

[18] Freeman, 1975, 150.

[19] Freeman, 1975, 147–48.

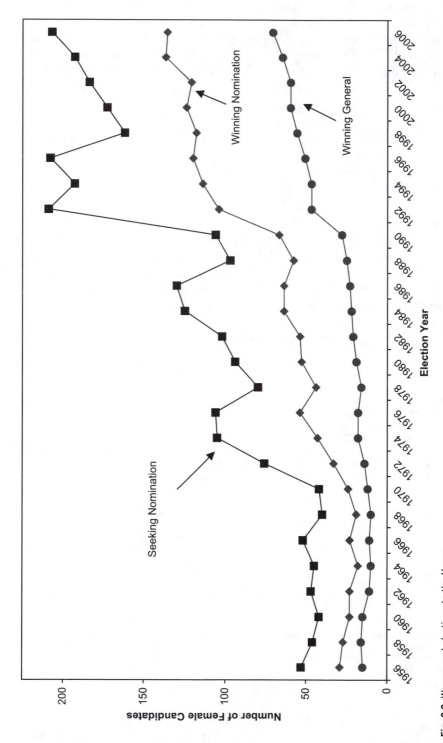

Fig. 2.2 Women and elections to the House.

National Organization for Women exploded from 3,000 in 1970 to 50,000 in 1974.[20] *Ms. Magazine* was launched in 1972. Practical politics was emphasized as well. Organizations dedicated to recruiting and electing women to public office were created for the first time. In July 1971, Bella Abzug, Shirley Chisholm, Gloria Steinem, and Betty Friedan started the National Women's Political Caucus at a conference attended by over 300 women. In 1974, the Women's Campaign Fund was created to provide financial support directly to women candidates, to help women network with other powerful political action committees (PACs), and to make connections with political consultants.[21] Thus, a new financial base for women candidates was established to increase their viability.

Other important events also took place during these years. The issue of abortion achieved national prominence, as *Roe v. Wade* was argued before the U.S. Supreme Court in 1971 and reargued in October 1972. The decision handed down in March 1973 struck down a restrictive Texas law and "prompted extensive, long-lasting national debate."[22] In 1971, the Court also reached its landmark decision in *Reed v. Reed* and for the first time ruled that discriminatory treatment based on sex was a violation of the Equal Protection Clause.[23] That same year, the national Democratic Party approved the recommendations of the McGovern-Fraser Commission, a panel assigned the task of reforming the delegate selection rules. After adopting these reforms, the proportion of female delegates to the Democratic National Convention increased from 13 percent in 1968 to 40 percent in 1972.[24] Watergate and opposition to the Vietnam War mobilized women activists. In 1970, Bella Abzug, founder of Women Strike for Peace, organized Democrats in New York to oppose American foreign policy in Vietnam and also decided to run for Congress. On the day she was sworn in, she introduced a bill demanding that President Nixon withdraw American forces from Vietnam.[25]

The 93rd Congress (1972 session) passed the largest number of bills on the "women's agenda" in congressional history, including Title IX of the Education Amendments.[26] One of the most galvanizing episodes of this

[20] Davis, 1991, 108.

[21] Linda Witt, Karen Paget, and Glenna Matthews, *Running as a Woman: Gender and Power in American Politics* (New York: Free Press, 1995), 136–37.

[22] Karen O'Connor, *No Neutral Ground: Abortion Politics in an Age of Absolutes* (Boulder, Colo.: Westview Press, 1996), 3.

[23] Karen O'Connor, *Women's Organizations' Use of the Courts* (Lexington, Mass.: Lexington Books, 1980).

[24] Stephen Wayne, *The Road to the White House, 2000: The Politics of Presidential Elections* (Boston: St. Martin's Press, 2000), 120.

[25] Two years later, the New York legislature eliminated Abzug's district in their new redistricting plan. She chose to run in a primary in a neighboring district against another incumbent Democrat, Bill Fitts Ryan. Ryan won, but two months before the election, he died. Abzug then was selected by the county Democratic Party to replace him. Ryan's widow had also unsuccessfully sought the seat; Foerstel and Foerstel, 1996, 31.

[26] Costain, 1992, 10.

period was the congressional debate over the proposed Equal Rights Amendment. Consideration of the amendment began on August 10, 1970. Representative Martha Griffiths (D-MI) organized an effort to use the discharge petition, a rarely used parliamentary maneuver, to wrest control of the resolution from the hostile chair of the House Judiciary Committee, Representative Emanuel Celler (D-NY), and bring it to the floor for debate.[27] The effort was successful, and the amendment passed in the House by a vote of 352–15. It was then "amended to death" in the Senate, including, among other things, a provision exempting women from military service and allowing school prayer. As a result, no final vote was taken on the ERA in the 1970 session of the Senate. However, the proponents of the ERA were successful in the 93rd Congress (1971 session), when a new version of the ERA was introduced. Attempts to amend the resolution failed, and bipartisan majorities voted to send the ERA to the states for ratification in March 1972.[28]

These events produced a substantial spike in the media coverage of women's issues in the early 1970s.[29] In effect, these developments constituted a declaration that politics was no longer an arena primarily reserved for men. For the next two decades, the number of women in Congress began a slow, steady climb, until an astonishing turn of events in 1992. As figure 2.2 illustrates, there was a dramatic spike in the number of women candidates. Often referred to as the "Year of the Woman," 1992 saw an unprecedented number of women running for office; 209 women ran in primaries, 104 women won primaries, and 47 women were elected to the House.[30] Only twenty-three of these women were incumbents. Twenty-four new women were sworn in on January 5, 1993, doubling the number of women in the House. Representative Henry Hyde (R-IL) remarked that with all the women now in Congress, the House floor was beginning to look "like a mall."[31]

Initially, there were few who thought that 1992 would become the tremendous victory for women that it did. The ousting of Saddam Hussein's

---

[27] During Celler's House career, he was a champion for the civil rights of blacks. However, during the battle over the Civil Rights Act of 1964, he opposed the addition of women to the list of groups protected in Title VII; the amendment to add women to Title VII was a maneuver by Representative Howard Smith of Virginia, chairman of the House Rules Committee and an opponent of the bill; Steven Gillon, *That's Not What We Meant to Do: Reform and Its Unintended Consequences in Twentieth-Century America* (New York: W.W. Norton, 2000), 122. Celler was instrumental in keeping the proposed Equal Rights Amendment bottled up in committee for most of the 1960s, and his opposition ultimately led to his primary defeat by Elizabeth Holtzman.

[28] Mansbridge, 1986. See also Janet Boles, *The Politics of the Equal Rights Amendment* (New York: Longman, 1979); and Nancy McGlen, Karen O'Connor, Laura Van Assendelft, and Wendy Gunther-Canada, *Women, Politics, and American Society*, 4th ed. (Upper Saddle River, N.J.: Prentice Hall, 2005).

[29] Using the *New York Times*, Costain's analysis shows a significant increase in both the number of issues covered and the number of reports for 1970, 1971, and 1972; see especially chapter 4.

[30] The partisan split was thirty-five Democrats and twelve Republicans.

[31] Foerstel and Foerstel, 1996, 112.

army from Kuwait in the Gulf War of 1990 and early 1991 dominated news coverage. It was assumed that the success of President George Bush, foreign affairs, and military issues would be the top concerns on the political agenda during the election. This changed in the fall of 1991, when President Bush nominated Clarence Thomas, former chair of the Equal Employment Opportunity Commission, to fill a vacancy on the U.S. Supreme Court created by the death of Justice Thurgood Marshall. During the confirmation hearings, it was revealed that Thomas was accused of sexually harassing Anita Hill, an attorney working for the commission when Thomas served as chair. Many women were outraged as they watched the live broadcast of the hearings and saw the all-white male Senate Judiciary Committee badger Hill. Hill became "a symbol of women's status in American life and, in particular, their exclusion from the halls of power."[32] For the first time, the hearings brought national attention to the issue of sexual harassment. Moreover, as the economy slumped, the political agenda fundamentally changed; issues such as education and health care, issues generally associated with women, were now the major problems on the minds of voters.[33]

The Thomas–Hill hearings not only inspired women to run for office; they also inspired them to open their checkbooks. In 1990, PACs that supported women candidates contributed $2.7 million. In 1992, this increased to $11.5 million.[34] Female candidates also did particularly well among voters. Surveys taken in the spring and summer of 1992 showed that male and female voters believed that increasing the number of women in office would benefit the country.[35] Many women ran as "outsiders," which gave them a substantial advantage with the anti-incumbency mood of the electorate that particular year.[36] An exit poll indicated that voters actually preferred female candidates to male candidates.[37] As one journalist explained, "[T]he farther away a woman was from power, the better her position to attain it."[38] Reactions to these events crystallized into the most spectacular success female candidates have ever seen.

---

[32] Witt, Paget, and Matthews, 1995, 1.

[33] Witt, Paget, and Matthews, 1995. According to a Gallup Poll released on September 17, 1992, 27 percent of the issues mentioned by respondents when asked about the most important problem facing the country were "compassion issues," such as poverty, homelessness, health care, and education. Additionally, 7 percent of the responses cited dissatisfaction with government, ethics, and moral decline; *Gallup Poll* (Wilmington, Del.: Scholarly Resources, 1992), 160.

[34] Clara Bingham, *Women on the Hill* (New York: Times Books, 1997), 70.

[35] Carole Chaney and Barbara Sinclair, "Women and the 1992 House Elections," in *The Year of the Woman: Myths and Reality*, ed. Elizabeth Adell Cook, Sue Thomas, and Clyde Wilcox (Boulder, Colo.: Westview Press, 1994), 127.

[36] Kathy Dolan, "Voting for Women in the 'Year of the Woman,' " *American Journal of Political Science* 42 (1998): 272–93.

[37] Elizabeth Adell Cook, "Voter Reactions to Women Candidates," in *Women and Elective Office: Past, Present and Future*, eds. Sue Thomas and Clyde Wilcox (New York: Oxford University Press, 1998), 59.

[38] Bingham, 1997, 28.

The following election cycle, 1994, stood in sharp contrast. Dubbed the "Year of the Angry White Male," the number of women in the House remained the same.[39] This stagnancy, however, masked several cross-cutting trends. The number of women running in primaries dropped, but the number of women winning primaries increased; in other words, women were more likely to win their primaries in 1994 than they were in 1992. Eleven new women were elected to the House, a higher number than usual, but eight female incumbents were defeated, six of whom had just been elected in 1992. As one journalist noted, "Marjorie Margolies-Mezvinsky was gone in less time than it takes to say 'Marjorie Margolies-Mezvinsky.' "[40] Margolies-Mezvinsky, a Democrat from Pennsylvania sometimes referred to as the "3-M Woman," won her first election to the House in 1992 by a margin of only 1,373 votes in a district that was solidly Republican.[41] Her defeat in 1994 is attributed to her vote for President Bill Clinton's budget plan. She had actually voted against Clinton's preliminary budget proposals three times and knew that voting for the budget would be "political suicide."[42] She promised Clinton, however, that she would not let the budget fail and would vote "yes" if hers would be the deciding vote. It was. Just after she cast her vote at the last minute, the Republicans on the House floor chanted, "Bye-bye Marjorie!"[43] She lost her reelection bid by 10,000 votes.[44]

The Year of the Angry White Male got its name in part because of the substantial increase in the gender gap among voters. Since the 1980s, approximately 52 percent of men consistently identified with the Republican Party. In 1994, 62 percent of men voted Republican.[45] In addition, the issues on the national agenda changed from education and health care to crime, which hurt many women candidates.[46] The same anti-incumbency mood that helped women win in 1992 made it difficult for them to retain their seats, as they were now perceived as "insiders."[47] For the first time in four decades, Republicans took control of the House and the Senate. That year, Republican women did very well. Of the eleven women first elected to the House, seven were Republicans. All eight of the female incumbents who lost

---

[39] Witt, Paget, and Matthews, 1995, 285.
[40] Quoted from Foerstel and Foerstel, 1996, 53.
[41] Foerstel and Foerstel, 1996, 53.
[42] Bob Woodward, *The Agenda: Inside the Clinton White House* (New York: Simon and Schuster, 1994), 300.
[43] Woodward, 1994, 300–2.
[44] Foerstel, 1999, 172. See also Marjorie Margolies-Mezvinsky, *A Woman's Place: The Freshmen Women Who Changed the Face of Congress* (New York: Crown, 1994).
[45] Witt, Paget, and Matthews, 1995, 298.
[46] Foerstel and Foerstel, 1996, 50–51.
[47] Foerstel and Foerstel, 1996, 52.

were Democrats.[48] Many pundits felt that a more accurate label for the election would be the "Year of the Republican Woman."[49]

Although the number of women running in primary elections took a dive in 1998, the next several election cycles saw relatively steady growth in the number of women candidates. In 2004, a record number of women, 137, won their primaries, and all fifty-seven of the female incumbents who ran for reelection won. In 2006, 207 women ran in primaries, 136 women were nominated, and a record seventy-one women won in the general election.

The Integration of Women into the Senate

Prior to 1970, only a handful of women ran in Senate primaries, even fewer won their primaries, and hardly any won Senate seats in a general election.[50] For many of the women who have served in the Senate, the political career pipeline was not the route they took. While House seats that become vacant due to unscheduled retirements must be filled by a special election, Senate seats that become vacant can be initially filled by gubernatorial appointment. Then a special election is held in the next election cycle to fill the remainder of the term.

Sixteen of the thirty-five women who have served in the Senate were interim appointments made by governors. Eight of the sixteen were appointed after the death of their husbands. Among these Senate widows, four did not seek service beyond their initial appointment: Jocelyn Burdick (D-ND), Vera Bushfield (R-SD), Muriel Humphrey (D-MN), and Rose Long (D-LA).[51] Maurine Neuberger (D-OR), because of the timing of her husband's death, simultaneously ran in both a special election to serve out the remaining two months of her husband's 1960 term and in the general election for the full term that began in January 1961. She did not seek reelection in 1966.[52]

---

[48] In addition to Margolies-Mezvinsky, four other first-term female Democrats were defeated in 1994: Lynn Schenck (CA), Karen Shepherd (UT), Leslie Byrne (VA), and Maria Cantwell (WA).

[49] Foerstel and Foerstel, 1996, 48.

[50] For a complete list of all the women who served in the Senate, see Center for American Women and Politics, *Women in the U.S. Senate 1922–2005*, 2005.

[51] Long's husband, the notorious former Governor of Louisiana Huey Long, was assassinated after being in the Senate for only three years. Rose was not the first choice of Governor O. K. Allen, but he died before he could make the appointment. Allen's successor selected Rose to avoid infighting in the Democratic Party. Long resigned after her husband's term expired; Foerstal, 1999, 163.

[52] Maurine and her husband, Richard Neuberger (D-OR), were a 1950s version of the political "power couple." When they wed, she was a teacher and he was a journalist. Their partnership included collaborating on magazine articles as well as electoral campaigns. Maurine was the manager of her husband's successful campaign for the Oregon Senate in 1948. Two years later, she was elected to the state house of representatives. In 1954, she managed her husband's successful campaign for the U.S. Senate and left the Oregon legislature to work in his Washington, D.C., office. Following his election to the Senate, Richard wrote an article for *Harper's* entitled "My Wife Put Me in the Senate"; Foerstel, 1999, 201–3.

Three widows attempted to retain their seats and ran in the special elections to complete the remainder of their terms. Only one, Senator Hattie Caraway (D-AR), was successful; after her initial appointment in 1931, she was reelected twice. The other two were not successful. Maryon Allen (D-AL) was initially appointed by Governor George Wallace to the Senate in June 1978 after the death of her husband, Senator James Allen. While it was assumed she would not try to keep the seat, she decided that she would run in the special election that fall to fill the remaining two years of her husband's term.[53] She lost the primary.[54] Her defeat is partially attributed to an interview she did for the Style Section of the *Washington Post* that ran in July. The article described her as a "small, fragile, delicate-looking . . . southern lady," and also noted that she was "startlingly honest."[55] In the interview, Allen said, "I learned one thing in politics. The hardest thing to do is keep your mouth shut. I never have before. Sometimes I just want to scream at some of these people and say 'you goddam idiot.' "[56] Halfway through the interview, Allen asked to borrow a mirror to retouch her lipstick and said that "without a mirror I always end up with lipstick halfway up my nostril."[57] She called the management style of the Carter administration "dumb," noted that conservative activist Phyllis Schlafly was "about as feminine as a sidewalk drill," and described the chief justice of the Alabama Supreme Court, Howell Heflin, as "cuter than Warren Burger," and Robert Byrd, then majority leader of the Senate, as "just a little power nuts and everybody knows it."[58]

The other widow who pursued reelection, Jean Carnahan, became senator after "one of the most unusual elections in U.S. history."[59] Mel Carnahan, the Democratic candidate and governor of Missouri, was killed in a plane crash three weeks before the November election in 2000. It was too late to remove his name from the ballot. Democratic Party leaders convinced Jean to accept the lieutenant governor's appointment if Mel won. He did, making him the

---

[53] Foerstel, 1999, 21.

[54] This particular election was unusual in Alabama politics because there were three statewide elections. In addition to Allen's seat, there was an open race for governor since Governor Wallace was term-limited, and the other Senate seat was open after the retirement of Senator John Sparkman. In Allen's Democratic primary race, she was defeated in a runoff election by Donald Stewart, who was originally among the candidates seeking nomination for the seat vacated by Sparkman. In June 1978, Stewart switched races rather than run against Alabama Supreme Court Chief Justice Howell Heflin, finished second to Allen in the initial primary, won the runoff in what was called a "stunning upset," and defeated Republican James Martin to win the seat; Bill Peterson, "Alabama Senate 'Sleeper' Catches Political Experts Dozing," *Washington Post,* October 3, 1978, A2. See also Michael Barone, Grant Ujifusa, and Douglas Matthews, *Almanac of American Politics, 1980* (New York: E. P. Dutton, 1979), 2–3.

[55] Sally Quinn, "Maryon Allen: The Southerngirl in the Senate," *Washington Post,* July 30, 1978, K1.

[56] Quinn, 1978, K1.

[57] Quinn, 1978, K1.

[58] Quinn, 1978, K1.

[59] "Carnahan, Jean," in *CQ's Politics in America 2002, the 107th Congress* (Washington, D.C.: CQ Press, 2001), http://library.cqpress.com/elections/pia107-0453058594 (accessed July 9, 2005).

first deceased candidate to win a Senate election.[60] He defeated incumbent Republican Senator John Ashcroft, who was later appointed attorney general by President George W. Bush. Two years later, when Jean had to run in a special election to complete the remainder of the term, she was defeated by Republican Representative Jim Talent.

Eight women were appointed after other unscheduled vacancies. Dixie Graves (D-AL), for example, benefited from her husband's political position while he was alive. As the governor of Alabama, Bibb Graves appointed her to complete the term of Senator Hugo Black, who resigned from his Senate seat to become an associate justice on the U.S. Supreme Court.[61] Three women obtained Senate seats due to the death of another senator. Senator Felton, the first woman, was appointed at the age of eighty-seven after the death of Senator Thomas Watson (D-GA). The governor who appointed Felton called her "a noble Georgia woman now in the sunset of a splendid, useful life."[62] Senators Eva Bowring (R-NE) and Hazel Abel (R-NE) completed the term of Senator Dwight Griswold (R-NE). Griswold won his Senate seat in 1952 in a special election to fill a vacancy created by the death of Senator Kenneth Wherry (R-NE). Griswold himself died two years later, and the governor of Nebraska, Robert Crosby, asked Bowring if she would be interested in the appointment in the spring of 1954. She almost turned it down, explaining that she was already serving as the vice chair of the Nebraska Central Republican Committee and herding cattle on her 10,000-acre ranch.[63] She reconsidered, noting that "I've been saying for years that women should get into politics, and so when I got the chance, I just didn't feel I could turn it down."[64] Nebraska election law, however, required her to give up the seat two months before the end of the session and that a special election be held. Bowring decided not to run in the special election. Abel ran, facing a field of fourteen men, and won. She criss-crossed the state in an air-conditioned Cadillac, earning the nickname "Hurricane Hazel."[65] Although she only served the two months left in the unexpired term, she said, "To me it was more than a short term in the Senate. I wanted Nebraska voters to express their approval of a woman in government."[66] Two other women were appointed to the Senate after the death of another senator, Gladys Pyle (R-SD) and Vera Bushfield (R-SD), but they did not take their seats because the Senate was out of session.

Of these eight women, only two sought to retain their seats, and one was not successful. In June 1996, Kansas Governor Bob Graves, a moderate Republican, appointed Sheila Frahm, another moderate Republican, to fill

---

[60] "Carnahan, Jean," 2001.
[61] Foerstel, 1999, 102.
[62] Foerstel, 1999, 87.
[63] Foerstel, 1999, 35.
[64] Quoted from Foerstel, 1999, 35.
[65] Foerstel, 1999, 17.
[66] Quoted from Foerstel, 1999, 17.

the vacancy caused by the resignation of Senator Bob Dole when he became the Republican nominee for president after his thirty-year career in the Senate. Frahm had served as the majority leader in the state senate and as lieutenant governor. In the special primary to fill the remainder of Dole's term, held a few months after her appointment, Governor Graves and Senator Nancy Kassebaum (R-KS) endorsed Frahm. Her opponent, one-term House member Sam Brownback, mobilized the Christian Coalition and criticized her pro-choice position and refusal to endorse term limits. His negative ads targeting Frahm gave him a reputation for "being comfortable with sleaze."[67] The race was characterized as "high noon" between the moderate and conservative blocks of the Republican Party.[68] Although polls showed Frahm with a commanding two-to-one lead three months before the primary, Brownback defeated her, 55 to 42 percent, and then went on to defeat another woman, Democrat Jill Hocking, to win the seat.[69] One campaign observer commented, "I've not seen anything so heated and pointed in Kansas politics in the 25 years I've lived here."[70]

The only woman to successfully retain her Senate seat after initially being appointed without a dead husband was Lisa Murkowski (R-AK). Instead, she benefited from her father's political position. Frank Murkowski had served in the Senate since 1980, and in 2002, he decided to run for governor of Alaska and won. In December of 2002, he appointed his daughter, a two-term state legislator, to complete his term. In 2004, to retain the seat, Lisa easily won the Republican primary against three men, but faced a former Democratic governor, Tony Knowles, in what turned out to be the most expensive Senate race in Alaska history. Knowles made nepotism one of the primary themes of his campaign and also attacked her for giving a $6.5 billion tax break to Exxon Mobile. Murkowski countered by pointing out that the $6.5 billion figure was "made up" by the Knowles campaign and that the legislation she supported would bring jobs to Alaska. During one of their televised debates, the candidates were asked to name something they liked about each other. Knowles said, "Senator Murkowski is a good person with a great family." Senator Murkowski said that her sons really liked his black Labradors.[71] She defeated Knowles 49 percent to 45 percent, proclaiming, "Alaska girls kick ass."[72]

[67] Guy Gugliotta, "In a Republican Redoubt, Doubts on Senate Hopeful: Conservative in Tight Race for Kansas Seat," *Washington Post*, October 29, 1996, A8.
[68] Robert Novak, "Showdown in Kansas a Major Test for GOP," *Chicago Sun-Times*, August 6, 1996, 21. See also William Welch, "Ideology Rocks the Vote in Kansas," *USA Today*, August 2, 1996, A13.
[69] Welch, 1996, A13.
[70] Dirk Johnson, "Race for Dole's Senate Seat Provokes Ideological Split," *New York Times*, August 5, 1996, A11.
[71] Nicole Tsong and Sean Cockerham, "ANWR, tax issue separate debaters," *Anchorage Daily News*, October 29, 2004, A1.
[72] Richard Mauer, Nicole Tsong, and Paula Dobbyn, "Murkowski up; votes to come," *Anchorage Daily News*, November 3, 2004, A1.

In 1948, Senator Margaret Chase Smith (R-ME), after a nine-year career in the House, became the first woman to be elected to the Senate in her own right. Her House career, however, began after her husband died. In 1930, at the age of thirty-three, she married Clyde Smith, who was fifty-four years old. In 1936, Clyde Smith was elected to the House as a Republican representing the 2nd District of Maine. Margaret worked on his staff; she answered constituent mail, wrote his speeches, and researched legislation. She was also part of the leadership hierarchy in the Republican Party of Maine. Just before his death in April 1940, Clyde Smith asked the voters in his district to elect his "partner in public life."[73] She won with almost three times the vote her husband received in his last election. After being elected to the Senate in 1948, she served for twenty-four years, most of it as the lone woman. She departed the Senate fearful that "there is no indication another qualified woman is coming in."[74]

Women and Elections to the Senate

As figure 2.3 shows, the trends in the number of women running in primaries, winning primaries, and winning Senate seats match the trends in the House for the most part.[75] The Senate numbers, however, are much smaller than those of the House. From 1958 to 1968, the number of women running in Senate primaries did double, but the number of women winning their primaries remained constant. After Senator Smith's election in 1948, the only woman to join her for any length of time was Maurine Neuberger (D-OR), who served for one term.[76] After Senator Smith retired in 1973, there were no women in the Senate until Muriel Humphrey (D-MN) was appointed in 1978 to complete the term of her deceased husband, Senator Hubert H. Humphrey (D-MN).

The real increase in the number of female Senate candidates began in the late 1970s and early 1980s. EMILY's List, a PAC that raises money for pro-choice female Democrats, supplied candidates with much-needed funds. The creation of EMILY's List was fostered by Harriett Woods' experience when she ran for Senate in Missouri in 1982. Woods had twenty years of political experience on the city council and in the state senate. Even though

---

[73] Foerstel, 1999, 254.

[74] Foerstel, 1999, 256.

[75] Except for the 1956 and 1958 elections, the data are grouped into six-year periods. For each period, the membership of the Senate is divided into three groups (Class 1, Class 2, and Class 3). In each election cycle, one class—essentially one-third of the membership—stands for reelection. The six-year period we use thus represents the time span required for the entire membership of the Senate to stand for reelection.

[76] Smith had personally encouraged Neuberger to run; Foerstel, 1999, 201. Three other women did briefly serve with her: Eve Bowring (R-NE) for seven months and Hazel Abel (R-NE) for two months in 1954, and Elaine Edwards (D-LA) for three months in 1952.

no male candidates initially expressed interest, Democratic Party leaders told her, "We have to find a man for the job."[77] At the last minute, a lobbyist with no prior political experience filed, but Woods won the primary. Very late in the general election campaign, she received a "token contribution" from the national party.[78] To raise more money, Woods started calling other women, including philanthropist Ellen Malcolm, and raised $50,000, but it was not enough. She lost the general election to John Danforth by less than 1 percent. Woods and Malcolm realized that the $50,000 was "too little, too late," and founded EMILY's List (EMILY is an acronym for "Early Money Is Like Yeast") to provide women with money early in their campaigns when they needed it most.[79] The first race they funded was Representative Barbara Mikulski's 1986 bid for the Senate in Maryland; they raised $250,000 for her primary.[80] Mikulski became the first Democratic woman elected to the Senate in her own right. In the 2006 election cycle, EMILY's List raised over $34 million.[81]

The Year of the Woman also had a notable impact on the number of women in the Senate, with the number of female senators increasing from two in 1990 to six in 1992. The Thomas–Hill hearings, in particular, inspired women to run. Patty Murray, for example, a first-term state senator in Washington, was so angered by the way the fourteen white males on the Judiciary Committee treated Hill that she decided to run for the Senate herself.[82] She challenged first-term Democratic Senator Brock Adams in the primary. The *Seattle Times* called her "the longest of long shots."[83] She received no support from the party or even EMILY's List. But then media reports revealed that Adams sexually harassed and molested eight women. One of his former congressional aides publicly accused him of drugging her drink and taking advantage of her. Adams announced that he would not seek reelection.[84] Throughout her campaign, Murray referred to Anita Hill and became known as the "mom in tennis shoes." After she won the Democratic primary, her Republican opponent, Rod Chandler, mocked her by carrying around a pair of sneakers.[85] By all appearances, Chandler should have cruised to victory: he was outspending Murray two to one, had a great deal of campaign experience after five terms in the House, and was a former television anchor man. During their second televised debate, he hammered

---

[77] Quoted from Witt, Paget, and Matthews, 1995, 137.
[78] Witt, Paget, and Matthews, 1995, 138.
[79] Quoted from Witt, Paget, and Matthews, 1995, 138.
[80] Witt, Paget, and Matthews, 1995, 139.
[81] "EMILY's List 2006 PAC Summary Data," *Opensecrets.org*, http://opensecrets.org/pacs/lookup2.asp?strID=C00193433 (accessed May 10, 2007).
[82] Bingham, 1997, 28–29.
[83] Quoted from Bingham, 1997, 35.
[84] Bingham, 1997, 37.
[85] Bingham, 1997, 43.

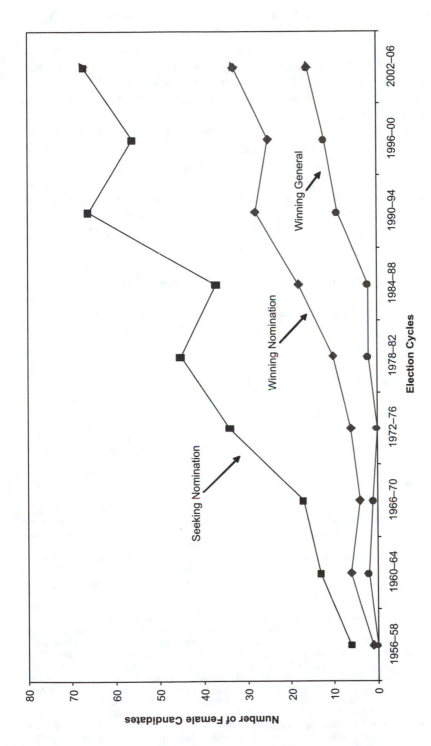

Fig. 2.3 Women and elections to the Senate.

away at a shaky Murray. But instead of a closing statement, he sang a song made famous by Roger Miller: "Dang me, dang me. They ought to take a rope and hang me—hang me from the highest tree. Woman would you weep for me?" He continued singing the song, telling the tale of a philanderer who leaves his wife and child. The audience sat in stunned silence. Murray replied, "That's just the kind of attitude that got me into this race, Rod." She won with 54 percent of the vote.[86]

The number of women running in Senate primaries peaked in 1992, when twenty-eight women ran. In 2004, twenty-three women ran in primaries, with ten women winning their party's nomination. Of these ten women, the five incumbents won.[87] In 2006, twenty-four women ran in Senate primaries and twelve won. The six female incumbents running for reelection all won. Claire McCaskill was the only female Senate candidate to successfully challenge a male incumbent, Republican Senator Jim Talent, in one of the closest races in the country. Stem-cell research became one of the key issues in the race, with a constitutional amendment on the ballot that would have protected all forms of stem-cell research allowed under federal law in the state of Missouri. Michael J. Fox appeared in an ad for McCaskill that ran during the World Series opening game featuring the St. Louis Cardinals. The ad featured Fox, shaking uncontrollably from his Parkinson's disease, endorsing McCaskill, a strong supporter of stem-cell research. Talk radio host Rush Limbaugh jumped into the debate, accusing Fox of "exaggerating the effects of the disease. He's moving all around and shaking and it's clearly

---

[86] Democrat Lynn Yeakel was another Senate hopeful in 1992 and challenged incumbent Republican Senator Arlen Specter in Pennsylvania. One Democratic Party official flippantly remarked to the press that all she had going for her was that she "had breasts." Claire Sargent, who was running for the U.S. Senate in Arizona, quipped, "It's about time we voted for senators with breasts. After all, we've been voting for boobs long enough"; quoted from Witt, Paget, and Matthews, 1995, 20.

[87] The two women challenging incumbents in 2004, Nancy Farmer (D-MO) and Doris R. Haddock (D-NH), both lost. Three women ran in open seats against male opponents: Betty Castor (D-FL), Denise Majette (D-GA), and Inez Tenenbaum (D-SC). The closest of these three races was Betty Castor's campaign against Republican Mel Martinez, the former secretary of Housing and Urban Development (HUD). Martinez ran an ad insinuating that Castor was against the "war on terror." He attacked her for refusing to suspend Professor Sami Al-Arian while she was president of the University of South Florida. Al-Arian was suspected of having ties to Islamic Jihad and was accused of financing terrorism. The Florida Leadership Council, a PAC, attacked Castor's handling of Al-Arian in a newspaper ad asking, "Who would Osama bin Laden prefer?" William March and Keith Epstein, "Bile Flows as Tight Senate Race Heads to End," *Tampa Tribune*, October 29, 2004, 1. Castor countered with her own ads, calling Martinez "unprincipled and nasty;" Jim Rutenberg, "An Idea, with 4 Words, That Was Supposed to Soothe the Tone of Ads but Did Not," *New York Times*, October 30, 2004, 15. She attacked him for authorizing federal grants for nursing homes to refurbish rooms with La-Z-Boy furniture while he was secretary of HUD; after Martinez left HUD, he became a member of La-Z-Boy's Board of Directors. Steve Bousquet and Anita Kumar, "Castor, Martinez Keep Senate Race Attacks Coming," *St. Petersburg (Fla.) Times*, October 29, 2004, 5B. Martinez won with 49.4 percent of the vote to Castor's 48.4 percent, becoming the first Cuban American to be elected to the Senate; Allison North Jones and Ellen Gedalius, "Martinez 'Humbled to Be' U.S. Senator," *Tampa Tribune*, November 4, 2004, 5.

an act."[88] The Republican National Committee ran an ad accusing McCaskill of "exploiting the medical tragedy of others just to get votes," and said her husband allowed "rape, poor care and even wrongful death" to occur in nursing homes that he owned.[89] Although Senator Talent outspent McCaskill, $16.5 million to $11.6 million,[90] she narrowly defeated him by less than 2 percent of the vote.

In sum, our data show that the integration of women into Congress has not been marked by slow, steady growth. In fact, during the 1960s, the number of women running and winning declined. It was not until the early 1970s that relatively consistent increases in the number of women candidates began and continued for the next twenty years. In 1992, there was a dramatic increase in the number of women running in primaries, winning primaries, and winning the general election. In contrast, 1994 saw no net gain in the number of women in Congress. Since then, however, the rate at which women are being integrated into Congress has actually been higher. What explains these trends? While every election cycle features a unique campaign environment, is there a general pattern that can help to explain why there are still so few women in Congress?

The Power of Incumbency

Today, one of the central features of American elections is incumbency.[91] Once candidates win an election and become members of Congress, they have substantial advantages when they run for reelection. For example, incumbents have access to the franking privilege. Since the First Continental Congress in 1775, members of Congress had the right to send mail to every one of their constituents for free; in place of a stamp, they use their signature. The idea was that this would facilitate communication between representatives and their constituents. Members also discovered, however, that this could also help their reelection campaigns. While reforms in the 1990s have substantially reduced abuse, the use of the frank typically doubles during election years. Representative Bill Frenzel (R-MN) commented that newcomers to Congress are taught three rules for getting reelected: "Use the frank. Use the frank. Use the frank."[92] In the 2002 election cycle, use of

---

[88] Sheldon Alberts, "Limbaugh remains defiant after saying Fox faked illness," *Montreal Gazette*, October 26, 2006, A4.

[89] "What to believe: U.S. Senate ads," *St. Louis Post-Dispatch*, November 1, 2006, B5.

[90] Jake Wagman, Matthew Franck, and Virginia Young, "McCaskill prevailed despite cash gap," *St. Louis Post-Dispatch*, December 9, 2006, A11.

[91] See for example Gary Jacobson, *The Politics of Congressional Elections*, 4th ed. (New York: HarperCollins, 1997); and Paul Herrnson, *Congressional Elections: Campaigning at Home and in Washington* (Washington, D.C.: CQ Press, 1998).

[92] Quoted from Roger Davidson and Walter Oleszek, *Congress and Its Members*, 9th ed. (Washington, D.C.: CQ Press, 2004), 145.

the franking privilege gave incumbents a $31 million dollar advantage over their challengers.[93]

In addition, simply by virtue of being a member of Congress, incumbents have more name recognition than challengers. At least half of the people who voted in the last election can recognize the incumbent, while challengers are typically unknown. In the early stages of a campaign, television ads repeatedly mention the candidate's name in an effort to increase recognition.[94] Unless a major scandal develops, the local press is unlikely to provide any coverage of challengers at all, and if they are covered, the stories are usually about how they have no chance of winning. Many newspapers have a policy that if a challenger is running uncontested in the primary, they will not provide any coverage of the candidate until after the primary. If a state's primary is not until September, this means that the challenger only has six weeks to get press coverage.[95] Meanwhile, the incumbent is getting coverage of their legislative accomplishments in Washington.[96] As one political consultant explained, press coverage of incumbents and challengers is so unequal that "the local press is the unindicted co-conspirator" in perpetuating the invincibility of incumbents.[97]

Incumbents also have the added advantage of having a well-established "money machine" at their disposal. Many candidates, regardless of whether they are incumbents, find fundraising not only time consuming but also humiliating. Rather than face his fourth reelection campaign, Senator John Glenn (D-OH) retired in 1998, commenting that "I'd rather wrestle a gorilla than ask anybody for another fifty cents."[98] Running for office requires the creation of a fundraising network, a network that can be used over and over again when candidates run for reelection. The experience that incumbents have in asking people for money makes it easier for them to raise more money. In addition, PACs, a major source of campaign dollars, are much more likely to give to incumbents; in fact, incumbents receive six times the PAC contributions that challengers do.[99] It is also not uncommon for incumbents to have money left from their previous campaigns; this provides the base for building substantial "war chests" to scare off future challengers. As a result, incumbents are able to outspend their challengers by substantial margins. For example, in the 2006 election cycle, House incumbents raised an average of $1.3 million, while their challengers typically raised less than $300,000. Senate incumbents raised an average of $11.3 million, while their

---

[93] Davidson and Oleszek, 2004, 146.
[94] Herrnson, 2004, 216.
[95] Herrnson, 2004, 228–29.
[96] Edward Sidlow, *Challenging the Incumbent: An Underdog's Undertaking* (Washington, D.C.: CQ Press, 2004).
[97] Herrnson, 2004, 228.
[98] Quoted from Davidson and Oleszek, 2004, 69.
[99] Davidson and Oleszek, 2004, 74.

challengers raised $1.8 million; incumbents outspent their opponents by a ratio of six to one.[100]

As a result, incumbents are virtually assured reelection. As table 2.1 shows, for the last fifty years, incumbent House members have a 95 percent success rate. In fact, only once in the last fifty years has their reelection rate dipped below 90 percent; in the Democratic landslide of 1964, it dropped to 88.6 percent.[101] Four years later, however, the rates peaked at 98.8 percent. In 2004, only 7 of 349 House incumbents lost.[102] In the midterm elections of 2006, the Democrats gained thirty seats in the House and recaptured control of the chamber after a twelve-year hiatus. Despite this partisan shift, 94.5 percent of House incumbents were reelected. Democratic incumbents were perfect—all 191 won reelection; 189 of the 211 Republican incumbents won reelection for a victory rate of 89.4 percent.

Table 2.1 illustrates that not only do House incumbents enjoy a high rate of reelection, but over time they have also increasingly won by larger margins. During the 1950s, 79.0 percent of incumbents were reelected with more than 55 percent of the two-party vote. In the three most recent electoral cycles, 92.3 percent of incumbents were reelected with more than 55 percent of the two-party vote. In other words, incumbents have grown more secure electorally; almost all of them come from safe seats.

Table 2.1 also reveals that House elections are uncompetitive, particularly primaries. In an average election year, over 70 percent of incumbents have no opponent in the party primary. They are virtually assured renomination. Since 1956, only 1.2 percent of incumbents lost a primary challenge. On the rare occasion when incumbents lose a primary, it is usually because they are running against another incumbent in the wake of redistricting.[103] In 2002, for example, Michigan lost a House seat. The state legislature redrew the lines, pitting two Democratic incumbents against each other, Representatives Lynn Rivers and John Dingell. In a primary that split the party, Rivers received the support of women's groups, environmentalists, and gun-control advocates, while Dingell relied on a coalition made up of unions, the auto industry, business lobbyists, and the National Rifle Association. He won with 59 percent of the vote.[104] In 2003, the state legislature in Texas did an

---

[100] *2006 Election Overview: Incumbent Advantage,* http://www.opensecrets.org/overview/ incumbs.asp?cycle=2006 (accessed May 10, 2007). For earlier data, see Norman Ornstein, Thomas E. Mann, and Michael Malbin, eds., *Vital Statistics on Congress* (Washington, D.C.: CQ Press, 1998).

[101] In 1964, 39 of 161 Republican incumbents were defeated. Among Democrats, only 5 of 225 incumbents lost their general election races.

[102] Four of the male Democrats were from Texas and were the targets of a partisan gerrymander following the 2002 election. If these four incumbents are eliminated, the incumbency reelection rate for 2004 was 98.9 percent.

[103] Herrnson, 2004, 50.

[104] "Dingell, John D.," in *CQ's Politics in America 2006, the 109th Congress* (Washington, D.C.: CQ Press, 2005), http://library.cqpress.com/congress/pia109-Dingell-John-D (accessed July 15, 2005).

Table 2.1 Incumbents and Elections to the House by Redistricting Period

Redistricting Period	Incumbents Running Who Are Reelected (%)	Incumbents Reelected with a Safe Margin (%)	Incumbents with No Primary Opponent (%)	Incumbents Renominated (%)	Incumbents with No Major Party Opponent (%)	Incumbents Who Get a "Free Pass" (%)
1956–1960	93.2	79.0	73.4	98.8	20.1	13.0
1962–1970	93.6	83.5	68.4	98.6	13.4	7.9
1972–1980	94.1	85.3	66.4	98.5	14.6	8.1
1982–1990	96.7	89.9	70.5	99.4	18.1	12.4
1992–2000	95.4	86.9	71.8	98.6	13.6	9.3
2002–2006	97.3	92.3	77.5	99.5	16.7	12.5
Overall	95.0	86.2	70.7	98.8	15.8	10.2

unprecedented second round of redistricting after partisan control of the state house of representatives changed. Although the Texas case is unusual, it highlights the importance of redistricting for incumbents. Eleven of seventeen Democratic incumbents lost over half of the constituents who elected them in 2002. One incumbent changed parties, one retired, and one lost his primary.[105] Four more were defeated in the general election.[106]

In addition to facing little or no competition in their own primaries, it is not uncommon for incumbents to run uncontested in the general election. Historically, nearly 16 percent of House incumbents face no opponent in the general election. While this phenomenon dropped from its peak in 1956–1960, it increased to 16.7 percent in the three most recent election cycles. In every election cycle, there is a substantial minority of incumbents who have no competition in the general election. For obvious reasons, the most desirable state of affairs for any incumbent is the "free pass"—facing no competition in both the primary and general election. As the last column of table 2.1 shows, between 1956 and 2006, the proportion of "free passes" averaged just over 10 percent of those incumbents seeking reelection. In three of six instances, including the three most recent elections, the proportion exceeds 12 percent.[107] What this shows is that a substantial minority of House incumbents have no competition at all.

While reelection rates are still high, Senate seats are more competitive than House seats. As table 2.2 shows, Senate incumbents are, on average, reelected 84.6 percent of the time. A substantial proportion also come from safe seats, although there is much more variability. In the 1978–1980–1982 sequence of elections, for example, slightly more than half of the Senate incumbents won with more than 55 percent of the two-party vote. In the three most recent election cycles, the proportion has increased to 79.3 percent winning with more than 55 percent of the two-party vote, the most in congressional history. There has been an even more dramatic change in the number of Senate incumbents facing primary challenges. During the period from 1960 to 1964, only 35.3 percent of incumbents had no primary opposition, suggesting there was substantial competition, especially when compared to the rates for the House. In the last three cycles (2002,

---

[105] They were Ralph Hall, Jim Turner, and Chris Bell, respectively; Ronald Keith Gaddie, "The Texas Redistricting, Measure for Measure," in *Extensions: Congressional Redistricting*, ed. Ronald Peters (Norman: University of Oklahoma, 2004), 19–24.

[106] They were Max Sandlin, Nick Lampson, Charles Stenholm, and Martin Frost; Gaddie, 2004, 24.

[107] There is evidence that the "free pass" is disproportionately southern. For example, between 1956 and 1960, 44.0 percent of House elections in the South involved a "free pass"; in nonsouthern congressional districts, the proportion was 2.4 percent. In the elections of 2002, 2004, and 2006, the proportion in the South was 21.2 percent, and in the non-South, 9.5 percent. In the South, the beneficiaries of these passes have changed. Between 1956 and 1960, 98.7 percent (147/149) of the "free passes" in the South went to Democrats. In the last three elections, 56.2 percent (45/80) of the passes went to southern Republicans.

Table 2.2 Incumbents and Elections to the Senate

Election "Class"	Incumbents Running Who Are Reelected (%)	Incumbents Reelected with a Safe Margin (%)	Incumbents Facing No Primary Opponent (%)	Incumbents Renominated (%)	Incumbents with No Major Party Opponent (%)	Incumbents Who Get a "Free Pass" (%)
1956–1958	75.9	59.3	42.0	100.0	9.3	7.4
1960–1964	91.2	60.4	35.3	97.7	6.6	2.2
1966–1970	86.3	65.0	36.1	90.4	7.5	1.1
1972–1976	78.7	60.0	45.2	94.5	6.7	2.5
1978–1982	75.6	53.8	38.3	91.4	2.6	0.0
1984–1988	83.3	71.4	57.5	100.0	1.2	1.2
1990–1994	91.6	71.1	51.8	98.8	7.2	3.6
1996–2000	86.8	64.5	55.2	98.7	2.6	1.3
2002–2006	87.8	79.3	59.0	97.6	9.4	6.0
Overall	84.6	65.3	46.9	96.3	5.6	2.6

2004, 2006), 59 percent of incumbents had no primary opposition; in other words, today most senators run unopposed for renomination by their party. Regardless of the level of primary competition, senators, like House members, are virtually assured of renomination, winning 96.3 percent of their primaries. With a few exceptions (1984–1988, 1996–2000), there have always been a good number of senators who run unopposed in the general election. Free passes, however, are relatively uncommon and do not approach the level found in House elections.

Tables 2.1 and 2.2 suggest, then, that voters are extremely reluctant to oust a House or Senate incumbent. Occasionally, scandal will make incumbents vulnerable.[108] For example, in April 2001, Chandra Levy, an intern working in Washington, D.C., disappeared. Eventually, a connection was made between Levy and seven-term Representative Gary Condit (D-CA). Condit initially refused to cooperate with the police, and the story became a media frenzy. He appeared on *Prime Time Live* and on the cover of *People* magazine with his wife, denying that he was anything but friends with Levy. After four months, Condit admitted to the police that they had a sexual relationship.[109] Although the police never considered him a suspect, the damage was done. He lost his 2002 primary to Dennis Cardoza, 53 to 39 percent.[110]

In many cases, however, scandal has remarkably little effect on incumbents. Eight-term Representative Jim Moran (D-VA) has long had a reputation for being controversial. In 1995, Moran had to apologize to Representative Randy Cunningham (R-CA) after he shoved him off the House floor and into a cloakroom.[111] In 2002, with over two dozen credit cards and $700,000 worth of debt, Moran received a home-refinancing loan from MBNA, the largest loan the company made that year, at a lower interest rate than industry standards suggested. Four days later, Moran cosponsored a bankruptcy bill that MBNA spent millions lobbying for.[112] In March 2003,

---

[108] The campaign of 2006 featured three unusual instances where incumbents, having won their primaries, were "forced" by scandals to withdraw from the general election campaign. All three incumbents were Republicans: Tom DeLay (TX, 22), Bob Ney (OH, 18), and Mark Foley (FL, 16).

[109] Allan Lengel and Petula Dvorak, "Condit Offers Long-Awaited Comment Tonight," *Washington Post*, August 23, 2001, A18.

[110] Cardoza actually worked on Condit's first House campaign and on his congressional staff. Later, when Cardoza served in the California State Assembly, he hired Condit's son and sister to work on his staff; http://nationaljournal.com/pubs/almanac/2004/people/ca/rep_ca18.htm (accessed July 15, 2005). Levy's remains were found over a year after she disappeared in Rock Creek Park; Allan Lengel, "Discovery May Alter Questions for Condit," *Washington Post*, May 24, 2002, A22.

[111] Jim Geraghty, "Moranic Record," *National Review Online*, March 12, 2003, http://www.nationalreview.com/comment/comment-geraghty031203.asp (accessed July 15, 2005).

[112] Even more incredible, Moran gave a speech on the House floor in support of the bankruptcy bill, stating, "Some people are taking these credit cards in, they sign up, they max it out, whatever they can charge. . . . They pile up debt, and then they get themselves relieved from paying off their debt, and oftentimes they can go right back to doing it all over again. It needs to be fixed." Jo Becker and Spencer Hsu, "Credit Firm Gave Moran Favorable Loan Deal," *Washington Post*, July 7, 2002, A1.

he appeared at an antiwar event and stated, "If it were not for the strong support of the Jewish community for this war with Iraq, we would not be doing this."[113] Several Jewish members of the House encouraged him to resign.[114] Despite this behavior, Moran defeated his Republican opponent, Lisa Marie Cheney, winning 62 percent of the two-party vote in 2004, the seventh of eight campaigns in which he was elected with more than 60 percent of the vote. Beyond Moran, "one of the most colorful figures" to serve in Congress is former nine-term Democratic Representative Jim Traficant from Ohio, well known for his colorful suits and bad hairpiece.[115] He once voted for Republican Representative Dennis Hastert for speaker of the House; in response, Democratic Party leaders refused to give Traficant any committee assignments.[116] In 2000, despite an investigation for violating tax laws and accepting illegal gifts, he cruised to reelection, winning 68.7 percent of the two-party vote. Shortly afterwards, he was indicted on ten counts of bribery, tax evasion, and obstruction of justice.[117] During the trial, he represented himself. He admitted he took money from mobsters, but claimed he did it to get evidence against them, and argued that the investigation of him was a "government vendetta."[118] After he was convicted in 2001 on all ten counts, he refused to resign his House seat and ran for reelection as an independent; he vowed to become the first person elected to Congress from a prison cell.[119] The House voted to expel him.[120] Even in jail, he received 15 percent of the vote and had a 30 percent approval rating.[121]

Open Seats in Elections to the House and Senate

Given the tremendous odds against defeating an incumbent, it would appear that the primary opportunity for turnover is open seats. And there is some evidence that women are more likely to run in open seats and win.[122] In fact,

---

[113] Chris Jenkins and R. H. Melton, "Contrite, Combative Moran on the Ropes; Congressman Fights to Survive," *Washington Post*, March 16, 2003, A1.

[114] Jenkins and Melton, 2003, A1.

[115] "Traficant, James A., Jr.," in *CQ's Politics in America 2002, The 107th Congress* (Washington, D.C.: CQ Press, 2001), http://library.cqpress.com/congress/pia107-0453055393 (accessed July 15, 2005).

[116] "Traficant, James A., Jr.," 2001.

[117] "Traficant, James A., Jr.," 2001.

[118] "Traficant, James A., Jr.," 2001; and Steven Patrick, "Traficant Refuses to Go Quietly Despite Calls for His Resignation," *CQ Weekly*, April 13, 2002, 962.

[119] Jack Torry, "From His Cell, Traficant Still a Force in Election," *Columbus Dispatch*, November 2, 2002, 1A.

[120] Ruth Brady and Donna Cassata, "Ohio's Convicted Rep. Traficant May Campaign from Prison," *CQ Weekly*, August 3, 2002, 2110.

[121] Torry, 2002, 1A.

[122] See for example Barbara Burrell, "Women Candidates in Open-Seat Primaries for the U.S. House: 1968–1990," *Legislative Studies Quarterly* 17 (1992): 493–508; Robert Bernstein, "Might Women Have the Edge in Open-Seat House Primaries?" *Women and Politics* 17 (1997): 1–26; and Melinda Mueller and Barbara Poole, "A New Year of the Woman? Women Candidates for U.S. House Seats in 2004" (paper presented at the Southern Political Science Association Annual Meeting, January 2005, New Orleans).

the election to draw the most women candidates was a 1996 Democratic primary for Maryland's 7th District, a safe Democratic black-majority district that covered large sections of Baltimore. Representative Kweisi Mfume (D-MD) resigned in February to become the head of the NAACP, and the state decided to combine the primary for the special and general election. The stampede of candidates included five Republicans and twenty-seven Democrats. Six of the Democrats were women. Elijah Cummings, the speaker pro tem for the Maryland House of Representatives, was the strongest candidate and locked up the primary with 37 percent of the vote. His closest competitor was Reverend Frank Reid, from a large African American church. State Senator Delores Kelley came in third, with 10 percent of the vote.[123] Kelley, also African American, had been in the state legislature since 1991. After her congressional primary loss in 1996, she held on to her state senate seat and eventually became chair of the Joint Committee on Fair Practices and the Joint Committee on the Port of Baltimore.[124]

As figure 2.4 shows, while the number of open Senate seats in an election cycle has remained relatively stable at just over seven, the number of open House seats has fluctuated substantially over the fifty years of our analysis. Once again, the most prominent feature of figure 2.4 is the spike in open House seats in 1992, the election cycle that produced the dramatic increase in the number of women running and winning election to Congress. That year, states had just redrawn their district lines following the 1990 U.S. Census. Typically, redistricting induces a few incumbents to retire rather than face reelection in a redrawn district with a substantial proportion of new constituents; nineteen House seats were reallocated from states losing population in the Northeast and Midwest to states growing in population in the South and West.[125] In addition, 1992 was the last year that members could take advantage of a loophole in campaign finance regulations allowing them to convert leftover campaign funds to personal use; twenty representatives were eligible to take over $500,000 with them if they retired that year.[126] The House check-writing scandal also created an unusually high number of open seats. In 1991, the General Accounting Office discovered that the House bank, run by the sergeant-at-arms, reported 8,331 bounced checks. The bank covered the checks of 269 representatives with no penalties or interest.[127] Many of the worst offenders, such as Representative Dennis

---

[123] "New Member Profile: Elijah E. Cummings, D-Md. (7)," CQ Weekly, April 20, 1996, 1070.

[124] http://mdarchives.state.md.us/msa/mdmanual/05sen/html/msa12170.html (accessed June 5, 2005). The winner of the Republican primary was Kenneth Kondner, a dental technician. After the primary, Cummings beat Kondner in the special election and then again in the regularly scheduled general election in November.

[125] CQ's Guide to 1990 Congressional Redistricting (Washington, D.C.: CQ Press, 1993), 1.

[126] Janet Hook, "Will the Flood of Retirements Arrive in 1992? Maybe Not," CQ Weekly, January 12, 1991, 72.

[127] Phil Kuntz, "Uproar over Bank Scandal Goads House to Cut Perks," CQ Weekly, October 5, 1991, 2841.

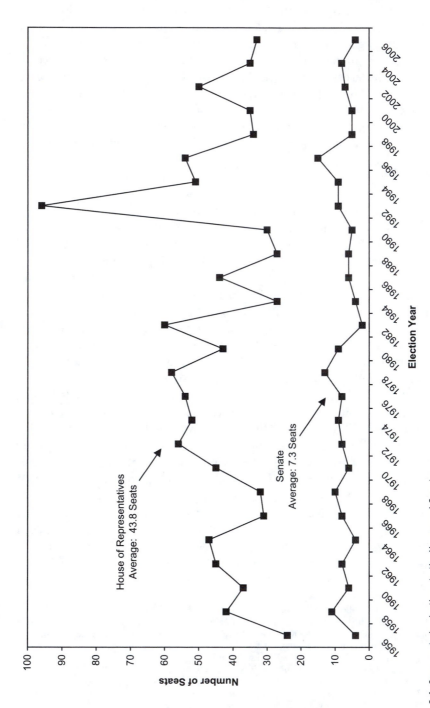

Fig. 2.4 Open seats in elections to the House and Senate.

Hertel (D-MI), who had 547 overdrafts, decided to retire.[128] Ultimately, seventy-seven incumbents who had overdrafts retired or were defeated in primaries or general elections.[129] These events created ninety-one open House seats in 1992.

Consequently, the Year of the Woman was largely a function of women taking advantage of this remarkable number of opportunities.[130] It was "the perfect storm," an election cycle that featured a unique combination of factors: a campaign environment that favored women candidates, a mobilizing event in the Thomas–Hill hearings, and an unusually high number of open seats. Consequently, it is unlikely that anything like the increases in women's success that happened in 1992 will occur again. Ultimately, our analysis thus far shows that there is not much genuine competition in American congressional elections. Incumbents, especially in the House, have very little opposition and are virtually invincible. As former Representative Clem Miller (D-CA) explained, "[F]ew die and none resign."[131]

The Rise of Careerism

It is important to keep in mind, however, that the pursuit of long-term congressional careers is a twentieth-century phenomenon. High reelection rates and low retirement rates are associated with the development of professionalized legislatures.[132] In contrast to "amateur" or "citizen" legislatures, where membership turnover is high, professionalized bodies have a variety of identifiable characteristics that further the careerist aspirations of their

---

[128] Representative Ron Dellums (D-CA) had the most: 851; Kuntz, 1991, 2841.

[129] Phil Kuntz, "Overdrafts Were a Potent Charge," *CQ Weekly*, November 7, 1992, 3575.

[130] Barbara Burrell, *A Woman's Place Is in the House: Campaigning for Congress in the Feminist Era* (Ann Arbor: University of Michigan Press, 1994); Susan Carroll, *Women as Candidates in American Politics* (Bloomington: Indiana University Press, 1994); Chaney and Sinclair 1994; Clyde Wilcox, "Why Was 1992 the 'Year of the Woman'? Explaining Women's Gains in 1992," in *The Year of the Woman: Myths and Reality*, eds. Elizabeth Adell Cook, Sue Thomas, and Clyde Wilcox (Boulder, Colo.: Westview Press, 1994); Elizabeth Adell Cook and Clyde Wilcox, "Women Voters in the Year of the Woman," in *Democracy's Feast: Elections in America*, ed. Herbert Weisberg (Chatham, N.J.: Chatham House, 1995); Ronald Keith Gaddie and Charles Bullock, "Congressional Elections and the Year of the Woman: Structural and Elite Influences on Female Candidates," *Social Science Quarterly* 76 (1995): 749–62; Neil Berch, "The 'Year of the Woman' in Context: A Test of Six Explanations," *American Politics Quarterly* 24 (1996): 169–93; and Georgia Duerst-Lahti, "The Bottleneck: Women Becoming Candidates," in *Women and Elective Office: Past, Present and Future*, eds. Sue Thomas and Clyde Wilcox (New York: Oxford University Press, 1998).

[131] Clem Miller, *Member of the House: Letters of a Congressman*, ed. John Baker (New York: Scribner, 1962), 93.

[132] Nelson Polsby, "The Institutionalization of the U.S. House of Representatives," *American Political Science Review* 52 (1968): 124–43; Samuel Kernell, "Toward Understanding 19th Century Congressional Careers: Ambition, Competition, and Rotation," *American Journal of Political Science* 21 (1977): 669–93; H. Douglas Price, "Congress and the Evolution of Legislative Professionalism," in *Change in Congress*, ed. Norman Ornstein (New York: Praeger, 1975); and Jonathan Katz and Brian Sala, "Careerism, Committee Assignments, and the Electoral Connection," *American Political Science Review* 90 (1996): 21–33.

members.[133] There is a division of labor through a committee system with fixed jurisdictions. In addition, there are formal rules and informal norms that govern member behavior. Within committees, for example, the norm of specialization encourages the development of substantive expertise. Position in the committee hierarchy is determined largely by seniority. Given this, the importance of continuous service becomes obvious: influence in the policy-making process and prestige among colleagues are among the payoffs for the successful careerist. Reelection becomes the most immediate goal, and a necessary condition, for long-term service. Thus, the mindset of the careerist "is not just how to win next time, but how to win consistently."[134] Incumbents run for reelection over and over because they want to. For the first one hundred years of Congress, however, most members of Congress did not want to run for reelection.

Figure 2.5 presents, for the years from 1800 to 1992, the proportion of House members who retired after one or two terms and the proportion of House members who served more than five terms.[135] There are three distinct eras: a period characterized by short careers in the House from 1800 to 1860, a transition era between 1862 and 1914, and a period of substantial growth in careerism beginning in 1916.

Careerism in the House

From 1800 to 1860, nearly one-fourth of all members retired from the House after serving one or two terms; only 5.6 percent served for more than five terms. During these years, it was understandable why long careers were rare. First, there were the physical conditions. The city of Washington, D.C., was not a pleasant place. It was hot, humid, and undeveloped, and "epidemics of fever were chronic."[136] Congress itself could be equally

---

[133] Many state legislatures meet only periodically for short sessions and provide, at best, a modest salary for members. For example, the Texas Legislature meets every other year for 140 days and pays only $600 a month. Of necessity, Texas legislators have other jobs; interview by the authors with Lauren Hutton, press secretary for Texas State Senator Tommy Williams, June 4, 2005. In contrast, for the 109th Congress (2005 session), rank-and-file House members earned $158,100 annually; http://usgovinfo.about.com/library/weekly/aa031200a.htm (accessed June 16, 2005). There is evidence that until the 1970s, women were more likely to serve in part-time, less professionalized legislatures; David Hill, "Political Culture and Female Representation," *Journal of Politics* 43 (1981): 159–68.

[134] Richard Fenno, *Congress at the Grassroots: Representational Change in the South, 1970–1998* (Chapel Hill: University of North Carolina Press, 2000), 8.

[135] In constructing this figure, we relied upon Elaine Swift, Robert Brookshire, David Canon, Evelyn Fink, and John Hibbing, comps., *Database of Congressional Historical Statistics*, Interuniversity Consortium for Political Research Study 3371 (Ann Arbor, Mich.: Interuniversity Consortium for Political Research, 2004). The 6th Congress in 1800 was the first to convene in Washington, D.C. Here, our data end in 1992 because this was the last year provided by the Swift et al. data set.

[136] James Sterling Young, *The Washington Community 1800–1828* (New York: Columbia University Press, 1966), 42. See also "The Battle for America's Front Yard," *National Geographic*, June 2004, 70.

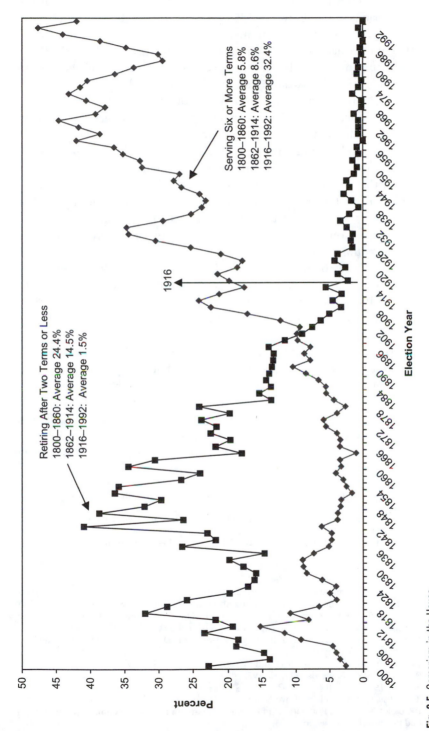

Fig. 2.5 Careerism in the House.

unpleasant—crowded, noisy, smelly, and occasionally violent. One of the most notorious examples was in 1856, when Representative Preston Brooks (D-SC) beat Senator Charles Sumner (R-MA) senseless with a cane on the Senate floor because of their differing views on the issue of slavery.[137] Duels were not uncommon.[138] The norms of comity and reciprocity had yet to arise.[139] There were few social or cultural diversions in the city, no museums, and no monuments, and cows grazed in front of the White House.[140] In fact, the presence of politicians in Washington seemed to act "as a magnet for society's idle and society's unwanted: people sick in mind or body, imagining conspiracies against them."[141] Long-term service was not pursued, largely because it removed most members from both their private occupations and their homes. A political career meant "estrangement from wives and children" and potentially "financial ruin."[142] Second, in the later part of this era, the rise of strong party organizations actually discouraged careerism in the House. Nominations to run for the House were a product of local party conventions, and in many areas of the country, parties adopted a practice of office rotation to prevent infighting.[143] In 1846, for example, Abraham Lincoln was nominated by the Whig Party convention in the 7th District of Illinois after the incumbent of his party declined renomination. After serving for one term, Lincoln stepped aside and ended his career in the House.[144]

The post-Civil War years were an era of transition. From 1862 to 1914, there was a noteworthy decline in early retirements, dropping from a high of 30.5 percent to a low of 5.5 percent. On average, the retirement rate declined from 24.4 percent in the prior era to 13.7 percent. The proportion of members serving lengthy careers in the House increased as well. Initially, the increase was gradual, from 1.1 percent in 1864 to 9.8 percent in 1900, and then became more rapid, peaking in 1910 at 24.1 percent.[145] Emerging

---

[137] Roger Davidson and Walter Oleszek, *Congress and Its Members*, 5th ed. (Washington, D.C.: CQ Press, 1996), 32.

[138] Joanne Freeman, *Affairs of Honor: National Politics in the New Republic* (New Haven, Conn.: Yale University Press, 2001).

[139] Donald Matthews, *U.S. Senators and Their World* (Chapel Hill: University of North Carolina Press, 1960); and Price, 1975.

[140] "The Battle for America's Front Yard," 2004, 70.

[141] Young, 1966, 25.

[142] To reduce this separation and to escape the hot summers in the capital city, Congress adapted its work schedule to the planting and harvest cycle. The 7th Congress, elected in 1800, did not convene until December 7, 1801. The session adjourned in time for the planting season on May 3, 1802. The last congressional session before the onset of the Civil War, the 2nd Session of the 36th Congress, began on December 3, 1860, and ended on March 3, 1861; Young, 1966, 52–53.

[143] Robert Struble, "House Turnover and the Principle of Rotation," *Political Science Quarterly* 94 (1979): 649–67. See also Kernell, 1977, 685–88.

[144] Struble, 1979, 659–60.

[145] This measure is a product of two factors: the desire to serve a lengthy career and success at the ballot box. Thus, fluctuations in this measure are, in part, a reflection of partisan gains and losses in House elections.

national issues, coupled with the legislative agenda forwarded by Presidents Theodore Roosevelt and Woodrow Wilson, made Congress a "more authoritative locus of public policy."[146] As a result, the "job of [a] congressman became more important and probably more prestigious, and the hardships became more endurable."[147] In addition, two Progressive era reforms made it easier for incumbents to pursue a career. First, the direct primary, adopted by numerous states between 1905 and 1910, reduced the influence of local party elites in the nomination of candidates for the House.[148] Second, the introduction of the Australian ballot paved the way for candidate-centered campaigning and the cultivation of a "personal vote."[149] Both of these changes helped to open a path to Congress for entrepreneurial and careerist-oriented candidates.

The last era, from 1916 forward, was marked by substantial growth in careerism.[150] On average, nearly one-third of the House membership served for more than five terms. During the 102nd Congress (1991–1993), nearly half the members, 47.6 percent, were long-term incumbents. The average proportion of members retiring after one or two terms dropped below 2.0 percent. The average length of service for House members in the 110th Congress (2005 session) was just over five terms.[151] In contrast to the first one hundred years of congressional history, individuals retiring after a short period of service became a rarity. This growth in careerism and incumbency had a substantial impact on how the modern Congress operates. It has influenced the structure of the committee system,[152] the committee

---

[146] Kernell, 1978, 674.

[147] Kernell, 1978, 674.

[148] This innovation essentially shifted an incumbent's "primary constituency" from party leaders, the practitioners of office rotation in many states, to the party rank and file; David Brady, Kara Buckley, and Douglas Rivers, "The Roots of Careerism in the U.S. House of Representatives," *Legislative Studies Quarterly* 24 (1999): 489–510.

[149] Under the old system, the "party strip ballot" was a single sheet of paper, often produced and distributed by the local party, that provided only the party's chosen candidate for each office. The names of rival candidates within the party were not included. In many states, voters simply deposited the "party strip" in the ballot box. The character of these ballots not only encouraged straight ticket voting, but also "limited the relevance of any individual candidate's personal reputation for the voter's choice"; Katz and Sala, 1996, 22. In contrast, the Australian ballot listed all candidates running for each office; while a straight ticket option was often maintained, voters now had the ability to express their preference office by office. See for example Jerrold Rusk, "The Effect of the Australian Ballot on Split Ticking Voting: 1876–1908," *American Political Science Review* 64 (1970): 1220–38; and Bruce Cain, John Ferejohn, and Morris Fiorina, *The Personal Vote: Constituency Service and Electoral Independence* (Cambridge, Mass.: Harvard University Press, 1987). Between 1888 and 1910, forty-three of the forty-eight states adopted the Australian ballot; Katz and Sala, 1996, 25.

[150] The installation of air conditioning in the Capitol in the 1930s is often credited with not only making Washington a more comfortable place to be but also actually prolonging the session; Davidson and Oleszek, 2004, 34.

[151] Mildred Amer, *Membership of the 110th Congress: A Profile* (Washington, D.C.: Congressional Research Service, 2007) 1, http://www.senate.gov/reference/resources/pdf/RS22555.pdf (accessed May 15, 2007).

[152] Polsby, 1968.

assignments sought by members,[153] the wave of internal reforms adopted by the House in the 1970s,[154] how members strategically allocate their time, and the way members campaign for reelection.[155]

Recognizing the development of a professionalized Congress with a career-oriented membership is essential for understanding the context in which women emerged as candidates and officeholders. The timing of this development is of particular importance. The movement of women into the electoral arena began in an era when careerism and incumbency rates were climbing to historic highs. In effect, our analysis documents the formation of the political glass ceiling; it was created just as the first women ran for Congress. It was firmly in place by the 1970s, when the number of women seeking election to the House began to steadily increase. Women began entering the electoral arena in an era when the opportunities for success were the lowest.[156]

Conclusion

One of the most compelling explanations for the lack of women in Congress is the power of incumbency.[157] For both genders, crossing the threshold from challenger to officeholder is extremely difficult. Thus, women have a hard time winning seats in Congress not because they are women, but because of incumbency—and most incumbents are men. Since the 1950s, over 95 percent of incumbents seeking reelection were successful. It is important to keep in mind, however, that long congressional careers, especially in the House, are a twentieth-century phenomenon. In fact, it is quite striking that careerism peaked at almost exactly the same time that women first began running for Congress. Just as women were entering the political arena, success in that arena became more difficult. As a result, the phenomenon of incumbents seeking and winning reelection over the long term was firmly entrenched well before social attitudes and gender stereotypes began to change in the 1970s.

---

[153] Richard Fenno, *Congressmen in Committees* (Boston: Little Brown, 1973); and Christopher Deering and Stephen Smith, *Committees in Congress*, 3rd ed. (Washington, D.C.: CQ Press, 1997). See also Katz and Sala, 1996.

[154] Normal Ornstein, ed., *Congress in Change: Evolution and Reform* (New York: Praeger, 1975).

[155] David Mayhew, *Congress: The Electoral Connection* (New Haven, Conn.: Yale University Press, 1974); Morris Fiorina, *Congress: Keystone of the Washington Establishment*, 2nd ed. (New Haven, Conn.: Yale University Press, 1989); and Fenno, 2000.

[156] See also Kristi Andersen and Stuart Thorson, "Congressional Turnover and the Election of Women," *Western Political Quarterly* 37 (1984): 143–56; and R. Darcy and James Choike, "A Formal Analysis of Legislative Turnover: Women Candidates and Legislative Representation," *American Journal of Political Science* 30 (1986): 237–55.

[157] See for example Burrell, 1994; Carroll, 1994; R. Darcy, Susan Welch, and Janet Clark, *Women, Elections, and Representation*, 2nd ed. (Lincoln: University of Nebraska Press, 1994); and Barbara Palmer and Dennis Simon, "Breaking the Logjam: The Emergence of Women as Congressional Candidates," in *Women and Congress: Running, Winning, and Ruling*, ed. Karen O'Connor (Binghamton, N.Y.: Haworth Press, 2001).

There is no doubt that incumbency plays a fundamental role in candidate strategy: the likelihood of success influences the decision to become a candidate.[158] Today, women do not typically offer themselves up as "sacrificial lambs"—running without any hope of winning—any more often than men do.[159] Logically, then, open seats are thought to be the main avenue of access for women. The problem with open seats, of course, is that there are so few of them in a given election cycle. As a result, if women wait for an opportunity to run in an open seat, they may be waiting for a long time. If the average incumbent is now serving four terms, that means the seat is open once every decade. As Melissa Martin, a candidate for northern Virginia's 8th District, explained, "Timing is everything."[160] What we have shown in this chapter is that careerism and the power of incumbency are the foundations for understanding the slow integration of women into Congress. But, as the rest of our analysis will explore, the political glass ceiling is not merely a function of incumbency. Decisions to enter the electoral arena are the products of political ambition, opportunity, and strategic considerations. Once the decision to run is made, success in the electoral arena depends upon the competitive environment in a district, as well as the political geography of the constituency.

---

[158] See for example Wilma Rule, "Why Women Don't Run: The Critical and Contextual Factors in Women's Legislative Recruitment," *Western Political Quarterly* 34 (1981): 60–77; Rosalyn Cooperman and Bruce Oppenheimer, "The Gender Gap in the House of Representatives," in *Congress Reconsidered*, 7th ed., ed. Lawrence Dodd and Bruce Oppenheimer (Washington, D.C.: CQ Press, 2001); and Palmer and Simon, 2001.

[159] Irwin Gertzog and Michele Simard, "Women and 'Hopeless' Congressional Candidacies: Nomination Frequency, 1916–1978," *American Politics Quarterly* 9 (1991): 449–66; Darcy, Welch, and Clark, 1994; and Richard Fox, *Gender Dynamics in Congressional Elections* (Thousand Oaks, Calif.: Sage, 1997); but see Lester Seligman, "Political Recruitment and Party Structure: A Case Study," *American Political Science Review* 5 (1961): 77–86; M. Kent Jennings and Norman Thomas, "Men and Women in Party Elites: Social Roles and Political Resources," *Midwest Journal of Political Science* 12 (1968): 462–92; Peggy Lamson, *Few Are Chosen* (Boston: Houghton Mifflin, 1968); and Raisa Deber, "The Fault Dear Brutus: Women as Congressional Candidates in Pennsylvania," *Journal of Politics* 44 (1982): 463–79.

[160] Interview with Barbara Palmer, Washington, D.C., February 11, 2004. Martin ran for the House for the first time in 2004 as a Republican in a district held by seven-term incumbent, Democrat Jim Moran. Lisa Marie Cheney, another first-time female candidate, won the district Republican convention.

3

Political Ambition and Running for the U.S. House

Why does anyone, male or female, decide to run for political office? Your personal life is fair game for the press. The financial costs are sizeable. You have to ask people for money, and, in some instances, you may have to go into a great deal of personal debt. There are emotional costs as well. Campaigns are grueling, often focused on the personal and trivial, and potentially humiliating. And after all that, you could lose.

Why individuals choose to subject themselves to such experiences is probably best understood by the observation that "ambition lies at the heart of politics."[1] Elective politics is not attractive to everyone. It draws into its arena only those who are willing to demonstrate, in a very public manner, the desire to gain political office. By virtue of being candidates, individuals make a declaration of their ambition for political power and authority. A variety of goals—acquiring personal power and influence, serving communities and constituencies, influencing the content of public policy—can fuel this desire.[2] In spite of the distasteful elements of campaigns, there are, in each election cycle, thousands of people whose political ambition is intense enough that they publicly demonstrate it by choosing to become candidates for political office.

Until relatively recently, the stereotype of the early woman in Congress was the "bereaved widow" who was a "reluctant placeholder" for a deceased husband: "[F]or women aspiring to serve in Congress, the best husband [was] a dead husband."[3] Even women who were not "congressional widows"

---

[1] Joseph Schlesinger, *Ambition and Politics: Political Careers in the United States* (Chicago: Rand McNally, 1966), 1.
[2] See for example Richard Fenno, *Congressmen in Committees* (Boston: Little Brown, 1973).
[3] Diane Kincaid, "Over His Dead Body: A Positive Perspective on Widows in the U.S. Congress," *Western Political Quarterly* 31 (1978): 96–104.

and won elections in their own right were often lumped into this category. As a result, the earliest quantitative studies of political ambition had very little to say about women as office seekers. This silence was largely a function of numbers. Joseph Schlesinger's landmark 1966 study, *Ambition and Politics*, includes all elections from 1914 to 1958. Only 155 of 9,508 (1.6 percent) House elections during this period featured a victorious female candidate.[4] Between 1947 and 1957, there were only 3 women among the 180 members examined in Donald Matthews' seminal study, *U.S. Senators and Their World*.[5] To the extent that they even mention female officeholders, neither of these works concluded that women lacked political ambition. Rather, the relative absence of women as officeholders was attributed to the "hoary rule that politics is a man's game,"[6] where "opportunities to advance have been best for white Anglo-Saxon Protestant males."[7] The exclusion of women, as suggested in chapter 1, was a product of cultural norms about gender roles and restrictions on women's ability to enter both the preparatory professions and the hierarchy of political offices. As we demonstrated in chapter 2, much has changed in American culture and politics since the 1950s. Women are more welcome in party organizations and no longer confined to "lickin' and stickin'" duties. Attitudes toward women in the workplace, particularly the political preparatory professions of law and business, are more accepting. More and more women are in the eligibility pool for political office.

However, we still know little about whether there are differences between men and women in deciding to step beyond the eligibility pool and run for office. In this chapter, we apply Schlesinger's *Ambition and Politics* to explore the political ambitions of women candidates. More specifically, studying congressional widows provides a unique opportunity to explore the differences between "discrete" and "static" ambition. We examine why some congressional widows simply serve out the term of their deceased husbands while others choose to pursue congressional careers and run for office in their own right. Our analysis of the forty widows who served in the House from 1916 to 2006 shows that they are not a monolithic group. Women who stepped down after completing the terms of their husbands have very different backgrounds than the women who ran for reelection. The widows who sought congressional careers were more likely to be younger when they first ran to succeed their husbands. They were also more likely to have substantial political experience, either working as political partners to their husbands or holding political office themselves. In addition, cultural factors

---

[4] The total number of elections is drawn from Schlesinger, 1966, 61. The number of women winning a House election during these years was calculated from our data.
[5] Donald Matthews, *U.S. Senators and Their World* (Chapel Hill: University of North Carolina Press, 1960).
[6] Matthews, 1960, 14.
[7] Schlesinger, 1966, 172.

also play a role: widows who were from outside the South and those who were elected after 1970 were also more likely to run again. These results challenge the stereotype of congressional widows as demure stand-ins. Some were, but many more were not. A substantial proportion of these women, when given the opportunity, were politically ambitious. Moreover, there are identifiable and systematic factors that can predict this ambition.

Deciding to Run for Office

The Citizen Political Ambition Study (CPAS) conducted in 2002 provides some of the best insight available into the initial decision to run for office. This study surveyed approximately 3,000 people in the three fields that tend to produce the most candidates for public office: law, business, and education.[8] In general, only about 12 percent of the people surveyed seriously considered running for office, but men were twice as likely as women to have considered the possibility. Almost two-thirds of the women indicated that they never thought about running for office, while only 46 percent of the men never thought about it. This difference is even more striking, because in other forms of political participation—voting, community involvement, and interest group membership—there were no differences based on gender.[9] Moreover, when asked how they felt about participating in the kinds of activities associated with running for office, such as attending fundraisers, going door-to-door to meet with constituents, and dealing with the press, women were much more likely to feel positive about them. In addition, women had substantially fewer negative feelings about the time-consuming nature of running for office.[10]

The CPAS also revealed substantial differences in how respondents perceived their qualifications. In spite of the fact that there were no gender differences in levels of political participation, the survey found that women were 20 percent less likely than men to rate themselves as qualified or very qualified to run for office. This is quite surprising, especially given that the

---

[8] See Richard Fox, "Gender, Political Ambition and the Decision Not to Run for Office" (New Brunswick, N.J.: Rutgers University, Center for American Women and Politics, 2003), http://www.rci.rutgers.edu/~cawp/Research/Reports/Fox2003.pdf (accessed July 1, 2005); Richard Fox, Jennifer Lawless, and Courtney Feeley, "Gender and the Decision to Run for Office," *Legislative Studies Quarterly* 26 (2001): 411–35; and Jennifer Lawless and Richard Fox, *It Takes a Candidate: Why Women Don't Run for Office* (New York: Cambridge University Press, 2005). The survey was initially mailed to a total of 5,400 people, 2,700 men and 2,700 women, based on randomly drawn samples of lawyers, businesspeople, professors, university administrators, and public school teachers and principals. The samples of men and women were roughly equal with respect to race, residence (urban, suburban, and rural), region, education level, and income, but women were much more likely to be Democrats, while men were more likely to be Republicans and Independents.

[9] Fox, 2003, 4; but see M. Margaret Conway, Gertrude Steuernagel, and David Ahern, *Women and Political Participation* (Washington, D.C.: CQ Press, 1997).

[10] Fox, 2003, 5.

survey respondents largely had the same professional backgrounds; the resumes of the women and men in the study were virtually the same. But, as Representative Loretta Sanchez (D-CA) explained,

> When you ask a man to run, he says, "Okay, but the party is going to have to do this for me, and the party is going to have to do that for me, and you are going to have to throw a fundraiser for me." When you ask a woman to run, she says, "Do you think I'm qualified?"[11]

When a woman thinks about running for office, she considers her qualifications, the impact on her family, and her chances of winning. When a man considers the question, often the only thing that he considers is whether he wants to run.[12]

The survey also revealed that women were told less often that they should consider running for office. They were half as likely to receive suggestions about running for office from party officials, political activists, or other elected officials, and about 10 percent less likely to receive suggestions from friends or coworkers. Even spouses and family members were less likely to suggest that they run for office.[13] The good news is that if women receive a suggestion to run, they are almost equally as likely as men to consider running.[14] Moreover, the suggestion to run from someone else can be quite powerful. For example, Beverly Moore, former mayor of Kalamazoo, Michigan, said that a neighbor who was on the school board talked her into running for a position on the board:

> At that time, I had not even thought of entering into any kind of politics. I had children in the school system. I've always been one that, if it sounds interesting, why not try it?. . . I decided to be on the side of the table that makes the decisions.[15]

After serving for four years on the school board, she ran for city commission and was elected mayor.

Sometimes telling a woman she "can't" will have the opposite effect. Patty Murray was a suburban mom in Seattle with two children who was

---

[11] Personal interview with Barbara Palmer, September 28, 2004.

[12] See for example Virginia Sapiro, *The Political Integration of Women* (Urbana: University of Illinois Press, 1983); and Timothy Bledsoe and Mary Herring, "Victims of Circumstances: Women in Pursuit of Political Office," *American Political Science Review* 84 (1990): 213–23.

[13] Fox, 2003, 9.

[14] Richard Fox and Jennifer Lawless, "The Impact of Sex-Role Socialization on the Decision to Run for Office" (paper presented at the Southern Political Science Association Annual Meeting, January 2002, Atlanta).

[15] Interview by C. Allen Alexander, in *Social Changes in Western Michigan, 1930 to 1990: Alexander Oral History Project*, vol. 2, ed. Henry Vance Davis (Kalamazoo: Western Michigan University, 1997), 123–32.

very active in her children's preschool; in addition to leading sing-alongs, she taught parent education classes on nutrition and child development. In 1980, the Washington State Legislature proposed cutting funds for parent–child preschool programs. Murray took her children with her as she lobbied legislators to fight the cuts. One male state senator told her, " 'You can't do anything. You're just a mom in tennis shoes.' "[16] A friend of Murray's said that this remark, instead of discouraging her, was like " 'wav[ing] a red flag in front of a bull.' "[17] She organized 12,000 families and successfully blocked the funding cuts. Three years later, she ran for the school board. In 1992, when she successfully ran for U.S. Senate, she used the "mom in tennis shoes" message as an integral part of her campaign.[18]

One of the most striking findings of the CPAS was the impact of family arrangements on the decision to run for office. Women in the survey were much less likely than the men to be married and have children. In spite of the progress women have made, studies show that tremendous hostility still exists in the workplace toward women who have children, particularly in the fields of law, business, and higher education. Consequently, many women who reach the highest ranks within these professions are unmarried and childless.[19] Moreover, the women in the survey who were married and had children were nine times more likely than their spouses to be responsible for housework and child care. Only 5 percent of the men responded that they did more housework than their wives and were responsible for child care. For men, there was no relationship between the household division of labor and their likelihood to consider running for office. For women, as housework and child care responsibility increased, the likelihood they would consider running for office declined.

The Citizen Political Ambition Study surveyed women who were accomplished in their fields; they were partners in law firms, business owners, professors, and school principals. Although these women have clearly overcome professional barriers, their family situations still indicate that their attitudes about running for office may be a reflection of more traditional views of women's roles.[20]

Do younger women, who typically do not have the same family time demands, have similar feelings toward running for office? In 2003, the CPAS was replicated on a younger "eligibility pool," college students who participated in the American University Washington Semester Program. Students

---

[16] Quoted from Clara Bingham, *Women on the Hill* (New York: Times Books, 1997), 33.
[17] Quoted from Bingham, 1997, 33.
[18] Karen Foerstel, *Biographical Dictionary of Congressional Women* (Westport, Conn.: Greenwood Press, 1999), 198.
[19] See for example Joan Williams, *Unbending Gender: Why Family and Work Conflict and What to Do about It* (Oxford: Oxford University Press, 2000).
[20] Fox, 2003, table 1.

in the Washington Semester Program come from all over the country to take seminars and intern on Capitol Hill, with political consultants, and with a wide variety of nonprofits. These students chose to come to D.C. and, as a result, were much more interested in politics and government than typical college students. Thus, they offer a unique opportunity to study an emerging "eligibility pool" of twenty- to twenty-one-year-olds.[21] In 2003, two-thirds of the participants in the Washington Semester Program were female, suggesting that they might be more likely than their older counterparts to consider running for office. Unfortunately, these expectations were not borne out. Female students in the college-level eligibility pool were almost 20 percent less likely than their male counterparts to consider running for political office. Like their older counterparts, however, they had equally positive feelings about engaging in campaign activities like fundraising, going door-to-door, meeting with the media, and giving their time.[22]

The study of these eligibility pools leads to a number of conclusions. First, given that they look favorably upon the tasks demanded in a run for office, the women in these samples do not regard campaigning as exclusively a "man's business." Gone are the days, described in chapter 1, when women themselves held these beliefs. Second, for a variety of reasons, women are not conscious or appreciative of the fact that their skills and positions in society make them qualified to run for office. Third, women are as responsive as men when it is suggested or recommended that they run for office. The question, then, is not *whether* women are as ambitious as men, but rather why the process of recruitment—formal and informal—does not call upon women in the eligibility pool more regularly.

Political Ambition Theory

While gender clearly does play a role in whether people consider themselves qualified to run for office, what prompts those who believe in their qualifications to become candidates? Studying what is ultimately a personal decision poses several challenges. For example, it is relatively easy to find people who decided to run and won; there are 535 of them who hold seats in Congress. Those who decided to run and lost at least had to file papers with their state election office and can be tracked down. It is, however, extremely difficult to identify people who may have thought about running and decided not to, or people who may have been viable candidates and simply never thought about it at all. Studying possible candidates can even cause political

---

[21] The average age of the respondents in the CPAS was forty-seven; Fox, 2003, table 1.

[22] Jennifer Drinkard, "The Disparity of Women Running for Congress," American University Washington Semester Program, American University, Washington, D.C., 2003. Drinkard's sample included 127 undergraduates. Her sample was 67 percent female; 62 percent of all Washington Semester Program students were women. Fifty-nine percent of the respondents were political science majors.

controversy. Sandy Maisel and Walter Stone, two political scientists who received a National Science Foundation grant in 1997 to conduct a nation-wide survey regarding the decision to run for office, found themselves embroiled in a major confrontation with Congress. A few members were convinced that this study would actually encourage qualified challengers to run against them. Labeling the project an "affront," a "travesty," and an "embarrassment," they tried to cut the funding and quash the study.[23]

Given the practical restrictions on identifying would-be candidates for the House, we develop an approach for studying ambition that is more indirect. We revisit Schlesinger's theory of ambition, focusing on female members of the House. The point of departure in Schlesinger's theory is the hierarchy of public offices in American politics, or the "political opportunity structure." His analysis shows that pursing a career in politics is a product of ambition, party competition, and the opportunities to enter and to advance in the hierarchy. There are, according to his analysis, three types of ambition: discrete, static, and progressive. "Discrete ambition" refers to an officeholder who serves only briefly and then steps down. "Static ambition" refers to those who are elected to an office and then strive to retain the position for as long as possible. "Progressive ambition" refers to a politician who, after elected to one office, seeks to advance upward in the hierarchy and run for an office perceived as more attractive and prestigious.[24]

Schlesinger suggested that discrete ambition, stepping down after a short term of service, is most common for many local and some state legislative offices;[25] it is easy to envision civic-minded individuals who agree to serve a single elected term on school boards, town councils, and other locally elected offices. Thus, his primary concern was to study the progression of the ambitious through the hierarchy of political offices. In fact, discrete ambition has not been studied in any detail at all. This is especially true for the U.S. House of Representatives, where careerism (i.e., static ambition) and advancement to higher office (i.e., progressive ambition) are now the dominant goals of members. Consequently, to examine the distinction between discrete and static ambition, we focus upon a subset of those women elected to the U.S. House, congressional widows.

Ambition Theory and Congressional Widows

Studying the women who were elected to the House as successors to their husbands provides a novel opportunity to investigate discrete ambition. Of the forty women who have succeeded their husbands in the House, all but

---

[23] Sandy Maisel and Walter Stone, "The Politics of Government-Funded Research: Notes from the Experience of the Candidate Emergence Study," *PS: Political Science and Politics* 31 (1998): 811–17, 815.

[24] Schlesinger, 1966, 10.

[25] Schlesinger, 1966, 10.

one were widows. Katherine Langley (R-KY) is the exception. Her election to the House was not because her husband died, but because he was thrown in jail. Katherine was the daughter of Representative James Gudger (D-NC) and the wife of John Langley, a Kentucky Republican first elected in 1906. John and his father-in-law served together as members of the House during the 62nd and 63rd Congresses (1911–1915).[26] In 1924, Congressman Langley was tried and convicted of "conspiring illegally to transport and sell liquor."[27] He attempted to bribe a Prohibition officer. While his case was under appeal in November 1924, he was reelected to his tenth term in the U.S. House. He had to resign his seat on January 11, 1926, and was subsequently jailed at the federal penitentiary in Atlanta.

In 1926, Katherine won the 10th District seat vacated by her husband with 58.4 percent of the vote.[28] She was, however, hardly a political neophyte. As secretary to her husband throughout his career, she was quite familiar with electoral politics and the ways of Washington, D.C. When she ran for reelection in 1928, she was called the "guardian angel of patronage."[29] President Calvin Coolidge, at Katherine's urging, issued a grant of clemency to her husband; his release was subject to the condition that he would not seek election to any public office. In 1929, a less-than-grateful John declared himself a candidate for his former seat. Katherine, however, refused to give up her seat "for John or anyone else."[30] While there is no record of a primary race between husband and wife, historical accounts refer to a "family feud" and "marital spat" that ultimately led to her 1930 defeat by the Democrat, A. J. May, the same candidate she had defeated in 1926 and 1928.[31]

Like Katherine Langley, many of the first women elected to the House succeeded their husbands. Fourteen of the twenty-eight women (50 percent) elected to the House prior to World War II succeeded their spouses. Between 1942 and 1970, one-third (15/42) of the women elected to the House were widows. Since 1972, the "widow route" has become much less prominent. Of the 143 women elected to the House between 1972 and 2006, only eleven

---

[26] Foerstel, 1999, 155–56.

[27] Hope Chamberlin, *A Minority of Members: Women in the United States Congress* (New York: Praeger, 1973), 63.

[28] In a letter from prison, John Langley appealed to family values, urging voters to " 'send my wife, the mother of our three children, to Washington' because 'she knows better than anyone else my unfinished plans' "; Chamberlin, 1973, 64.

[29] Chamberlin, 1973, 65. The response to Katherine among the capital community elite was less than favorable. Evidently, Washington society regarded the election of a convicted felon's spouse as "gauche"; Chamberlin, 1973, 63.

[30] Chamberlin, 1973, 65.

[31] Little is known about what transpired after Katherine's defeat, but we do know that they were buried in separate cemeteries. John Langley died on January 17, 1932, and was buried in the Langley Cemetery in MiddleCreek, Kentucky. Katherine Langley died on August 15, 1948, and was buried in Johnson Memorial Cemetery in Pikeville, Kentucky; *Biographical Directory of the American Congress* (Washington, D.C.: U.S. Government Printing Office, 1971), 1262.

(7.7 percent) were widows. In the 110th Congress (2007 session), four of the seventy-one female House members were serving in seats held by their deceased husbands: these include Jo Ann Emerson (R-MO), Lois Capps (D-CA), and Mary Bono (R-CA).[32] Doris Matsui (D-CA) was elected in March 2005 in a special election after her husband died from a rare bone marrow disease. She beat eleven other opponents with 71.6 percent of the vote.[33]

As late as the 1970s, much of the attention devoted to women in Congress focused on the widow connection.[34] This was characterized as the primary route to the House and the Senate for women. The prevailing wisdom, particularly in the press, was that women who served in Congress got there "over their husband's dead bodies."[35] In fact, there emerged a "widow stereotype" that included a common plot or storyline describing the widow's journey to elective office: after a member of Congress died, party leaders and

---

[32] Jean Carnahan was the most recent widow to serve in the Senate. Aside from gaining a seat from a spouse, twelve female members of Congress have gained spouses from Congress: they married male members of Congress. Two women married men while they were both serving in Congress together: Representative Susan Molinari (R-NY) married Representative Bill Paxon (R-NY) in 1994, and Representative Martha Keys (D-KS) married Representative Andrew Jacobs (D-IN) in 1975. Three women married members of Congress after they had served together: Representative Olympia Snowe (R-ME) married former Representative John McKernan Jr. (R-ME) in 1989 after he became governor of Maine; Senator Nancy Kassebaum (R-KS) married former Senator Howard Baker (R-TN) in 1996 after he retired; Representative Stephanie Herseth married former Representative Max Sandlin (D-TX) in March of 2007 after he was defeated in 2004. Two other women married members with whom they did not serve: Senator Elizabeth Dole (R-NC, 2003–present) served after her husband, former Senator Bob Dole (R-KS, 1969–1996), and Representative Marjorie Margolies-Mezvinsky (D-PA, 1993–1995) also served after her husband, former Representative Ed Mezvinsky (D-IA, 1973–1977). Representative Emily Taft Douglas (D-IL, 1945–1947) preceded her husband, Senator Paul Douglas (D-IL, 1949–1967). And finally, Representative Ruth McCormick (R-IL, 1929–1931) was married to two members of Congress: before her service in the House, she was married to Medill McCormick (R-IL, House, 1917–1919 and Senate 1919–1925). After he died, she ran for House and met Albert Gallatin Simms (R-NM, 1929–1931), and they married after they both left the House; Mildred Amer, *Women in the United States Congress: 1917–2004* (Washington, D.C.: Congressional Research Service, 2004), http://www.senate.gov/reference/resources/pdf/RL30261.pdf, 5–6 (accessed July 3, 2005); "Representative now known as Stephanie Herseth Sandlin," *Associated Press*, April 1, 2007.

[33] Greg Lucas, "Matsui Wins Election to Late Husband's Seat," *San Francisco Chronicle*, March 9, 2005, B3.

[34] See for example Emmy Werner, "Women in Congress: 1917–1964," *Western Political Quarterly* 19 (1966): 16–30; Martin Gruberg, *Women in Politics: A Source Book* (New York: Academic Press, 1968); Kirsten Amundson, *The Silenced Majority: Women and American Democracy* (Englewood Cliffs, N.J.: Prentice-Hall, 1971); Charles Bullock and Patricia Lee Findley Heys, "Recruitment of Women for Congress: A Research Note," *Western Political Quarterly* 25 (1972): 416–23; Jeane Kirkpatrick, *Political Woman* (New York: Basic Books, 1974); Susan Tolchin and Martin Tolchin, *Clout: Womanpower and Politics* (New York: Coward, McCann, & Geoghegan, 1974); and Irwin Gertzog, "The Matrimonial Connection: The Nomination of Congressmen's Widows for the House of Representatives," *Journal of Politics* 42 (1980): 820–33. See also Irwin Gertzog, *Congressional Women: Their Recruitment, Integration, and Behavior*, 2nd ed. (Westport, Conn.: Praeger Press, 1995).

[35] Kincaid, 1978, 96. See also Gertzog, 1980.

other local elites often recruited the bereaved and politically reluctant widow to run in the special election to fill her departed husband's seat. This served two ends. First, it capitalized on public sympathy to ensure that the party held the seat in the interim. Second, it helped the party avoid internal disputes and provided time to recruit a "real" replacement.[36] In many cases, the understanding, whether explicit or implicit, was that the widow would not try to retain the seat during the next election cycle. For example, Representative Frances Bolton (R-OH) noted that party support for her candidacy to succeed her deceased husband was forthcoming because "they were sure I would get tired of politics in a few months and flit on to something else."[37] Thus, congressional widows were presumed to be the quintessential examples of discrete ambition—dutiful, but temporary, officeholders.

A vivid example of the stereotype was, in fact, the very first congressional widow, Mae Ella Nolan (R-CA). In 1922, Representative John Nolan, chair of the House Labor Committee, died shortly after his fifth reelection to the House. Civic leaders convinced Mae to run in the special election held to fill his seat; she defeated six men in the primary. In addition to securing a spot on the Labor Committee, she became chair of the Committee on Expenditures in the Post Office Department, making her the first woman committee chair. After completing the two-year term, Mae declared that she would not seek reelection, explaining that "[p]olitics is entirely too masculine to have any attraction for feminine responsibilities."[38] Nolan was not alone among the widows to express her distaste for political life. At the beginning of the three months she served to complete her husband's term, Representative Pearl Oldfield (D-AR) announced that she would "gladly retire to where women belong—in the home."[39] Similarly, Representative Florence Gibbs (D-GA), whose term was also three months, left the House because the job was not "to her liking."[40]

Such examples notwithstanding, the problem with the "widow stereotype" is that it rests on several tenuous assumptions. First, it tends to apply the stereotype to all women who served prior to the 1980s, whether they were widows or not. Second, it assumes that all of the widows conform to the examples of Nolan, Oldfield, and Gibbs. Third, it creates the impression that the widow-as-successor is the most common method of filling vacancies. But if one looks at the number of incumbents who died in office, very few wives succeeded their husbands. From 1917 to 1976, for example, 487 members died in office, and widows were the successors only thirty-five times

---

[36] Kincaid, 1978, 97.
[37] Foerstel, 1996, 30.
[38] Foerstel, 1999, 203.
[39] Foerstel, 1999, 212.
[40] Foerstel, 1999, 98.

(7.2 percent).[41] This suggests that the congressional widow is not as common as typically presumed, particularly in light of the number of opportunities for widows to succeed their husbands.[42]

Another assumption of the stereotype is that widows were "given" the seats vacated by their dead husbands. This is simply inaccurate. Although vacant Senate seats can be filled by appointment, vacant House seats must be filled through special elections. Many widows who served in the House faced substantial competition in special primary and general elections; there were several widows who ran for their husbands' seats and were defeated.[43]

More importantly, as table 3.1 illustrates, many widows did not step down after their initial terms expired. Many had lengthy careers. Twelve widows served at least ten years in the House; four of these twelve were elected to ten or more terms. Representative Edith Nourse Rogers (R-MA) won reelection seventeen times, making her the longest serving woman in congressional history (1925–1960). During World War I, she traveled across Europe with her husband, John Jacob Rogers. After he died, she ran for his House seat and made veterans' issues her highest priority. She ultimately became chair of the Veterans Affairs Committee.[44] Cardiss Collins (D-IL) served for nearly twenty-four years (1973–1997) and is the longest serving African American woman in Congress.[45] Representative Leonor Sullivan (D-MO) served for twenty-three years (1952–1975) and became a well-known advocate of consumer protection, chairing the Banking and Currency Subcommittee on the Consumer Affairs Committee and chairing the Merchant Marine and

---

[41] Kincaid, 1978, 97. See also Gertzog, 1980, 1995.

[42] Many men have, of course, also benefited from family connections, George W. Bush and Al Gore being two of the most obvious examples. There is evidence that at least 10 percent of the men in Congress have benefited from a family name that was well known in politics; Joan Hulce Thompson, "Career Convergence: Election of Women and Men to the House of Representatives, 1916–1975," Women & Politics 5 (1985): 69–90. In fact, there have been men who even benefited from the political connections of their mothers. Five women in the House and two women in the Senate had sons serve in Congress. Representative Frances Bolton (R-OH, 1940–1969) served with her son, Representative Oliver Bolton (R-OH, 1953–1957 and 1963–1965). Representative Carrie Meek (D-FL, 1993–2003) was succeeded by her son, Representative Kendrick Meek (2003–present). Representative Katharine Byron (D-MD, 1941–1943) was the mother of Representative Goodloe Byron (D-MD, 1971–1978). Representative Maude Kee (D-WV, 1951–1965) was succeeded by her son, Representative James Kee (D-WV, 1965–1973). Representative Irene Baker (R-TN, 1964–1965) was the stepmother of Senator Howard Baker (R-TN, 1967–1985). Senator Rose McConnell Long (D-LA, 1936–1937) was the mother of Senator Russell Long (D-LA, 1948–1987); Amer, 2004, 7. After Senator Jean Carnahan (D-MO) lost her seat in 2002, her son, Russ (D-MO), was elected to the House in 2004; "New House Member Profile: Russ Carnahan," CQ Weekly, November 6, 2004, 2644. The only sisters to serve are Representatives Loretta (D-CA, 1996–present) and Linda Sanchez (D-CA, 2002–present).

[43] Kincaid, 1978, 101. There is no source that systematically gathers and presents data on these special elections. Additionally, as one goes back in time, information on these elections becomes increasingly sparse. As a result, it would be terribly difficult to determine the number of special elections in which the widow unsuccessfully sought to replace her husband.

[44] Foerstel, 1999, 233.

[45] Foerstel, 1999, 264.

Table 3.1 Women Who Succeeded Their Husbands in the House

Name	Service Begins	Service Ends	Ambition (Terms)
Pre–World War II			
Mae Ella Nolan (R-CA)	1/23/1923	3/3/1925	Discrete
Florence Kahn (R-CA)	5/4/1925	1/3/1937	Static (6)
Edith Nourse Rogers (R-MA)	1/30/1925	9/10/1960	Static (18)
Katherine Langley (R-KY)	3/4/1926	3/3/1931	Static (2)
Pearl Oldfield (D-AR)	1/11/1929	3/3/1931	Discrete
Effigene Wingo (D-AR)	4/4/1930	3/3/1933	Discrete
Willa McCord Eslick (D-TN)	12/5/1932	3/3/1933	Discrete
Marian Clarke (R-NY)	12/28/1933	1/3/1935	Discrete
Elizabeth Gasque (D-SC)	1/13/1938	1/3/1939	Discrete
Clara McMillan (D-SC)	1/3/1940	1/3/1941	Discrete
Margaret Chase Smith (R-ME)	1/3/1940	1/3/1949	Static (5)
Frances Bolton (R-OH)	1/27/1940	1/3/1969	Static (15)
Florence Gibbs (D-GA)	1/3/1940	1/3/1941	Discrete
Katharine Byron (D-MD)	1/11/1941	1/3/1943	Discrete
1942–1970			
Veronica Boland (D-PA)	1/19/1942	1/3/1943	Discrete
Willa Fulmer (D-SC)	1/16/1944	1/3/1945	Discrete
Marguerite Church (R-IL)	1/3/1951	1/3/1963	Static (6)
Maude Kee (D-WV)	7/26/1951	1/3/1963	Static (7)
Vera Buchanan (D-PA)	8/1/1951	11/26/1955	Static (3)
Leonor Sullivan (D-MO)	1/3/1953	1/3/1977	Static (12)
Kathryn Granahan (D-PA)	11/6/1956	1/3/1963	Static (3)
Edna Simpson (R-IL)	1/3/1959	1/3/1961	Discrete
Catherine Norrell (D-AR)	4/18/1961	1/3/1963	Discrete
Louise Reese (R-TN)	5/16/1961	1/3/1963	Discrete
Corrine Riley (D-SC)	4/10/1962	1/3/1963	Discrete
Charlotte Reid (R-IL)	1/3/1963	10/7/1971	Static (5)
Irene Baker (R-TN)	3/10/1964	1/3/1965	Discrete
Lera Thomas (D-TX)	3/26/1966	1/3/1967	Discrete
Elizabeth Andrews (D-AL)	4/4/1971	1/3/1973	Discrete
1972–Present			
Corrine (Lindy) Boggs (D-LA)	3/20/1973	1/3/1991	Static (9)
Cardiss Collins (D-IL)	6/7/1973	1/7/1997	Static (12)
Shirley Pettis (R-CA)	4/29/1975	1/3/1979	Static (2)
Beverly Byron (D-MD)	1/3/1979	1/3/1993	Static (7)

(Continued)

Table 3.1 Women Who Succeeded Their Husbands in the House *(Continued)*

Name	Service Begins	Service Ends	Ambition (Terms)
Jean Ashbrook (R-OH)	*7/12/1982*	*1/3/1983*	*Discrete*
Sala Burton (D-CA)	1/21/1983	2/1/1987	Static (3)
Catherine Long (D-LA)	*4/4/1985*	*1/3/1987*	*Discrete*
Jo Ann Emerson (R-MO)	11/5/1997	Present	Static (5)
Lois Capps (D-CA)	3/17/1998	Present	Static (5)
Mary Bono (R-CA)	4/21/1998	Present	Static (5)
Doris Matsui (D-CA)	3/3/2005	Present	Static (1)

Fisheries Committee.[46] Overall, the average length of service among widows who sought reelection to the House is 13.5 years.

It should also be recognized that, as widows, women do have substantial electoral advantages. These include inherited name recognition, familiarity with potential donors, and a ready-made staff. Many of them worked on their husbands' campaigns and, as a result, knew their districts well. Representative Corrine "Lindy" Boggs (D-LA) is a noteworthy example. She was first elected to the House in 1973 after her husband, Majority Leader Hale Boggs, disappeared in a plane crash in Alaska. After a two-month search for the plane, the House declared the seat vacant, and Lindy won the seat with 81 percent of the vote in the special election. Her political career, however, had begun well before that. Her grandfather was a state legislator, and her cousin was the mayor of New Orleans. For twenty-five years, she served as her husband's campaign manager and worked in his congressional office in Washington. She also chaired the inaugural ball committees for John F. Kennedy and Lyndon Johnson. Boggs served in the House for almost twenty years, retiring in 1991.[47] As her daughter, journalist Cokie Roberts, explained, "Politics is our family business."[48] Her case illustrates that congressional widows can be as politically inclined as their husbands and have access to resources and advantages similar to those enjoyed by incumbents.[49]

It is clear, then, that congressional widows are not a monolithic group. Not all widows conform to the stereotype or its storyline. While some eschew politics, others relish it. While some pursue political careers, others voluntarily forego that opportunity. Congressional widows thus provide us with an ideal "natural experiment" for examining the differences between

---

[46] When she retired at the age of seventy-five, Representative Dick Gephardt won her seat; Foerstel, 1999, 263–64.

[47] Foerstel, 1999, 28.

[48] "Women's History Month: A New Reason to Celebrate Louisiana Women's History Every Day," http://www.senate.gov/~landrieu/whm/boggs.html (accessed March 30, 2005).

[49] R. Darcy, Susan Welch, and Janet Clark, *Women, Elections, and Representation*, 2nd ed. (Lincoln: University of Nebraska Press, 1994), 91–92.

discrete and static ambition among women in the political arena. The question underlying this analysis is straightforward: why do some congressional widows choose to pursue a career in the House while others simply serve out the term of their deceased husbands?

Understanding Discrete and Static Ambition

Because there is very little systematic analysis of discrete ambition, we draw from a wider body of research associated with the recruitment and political ambitions of women. To explore the differences between the widows who exhibit discrete and static ambition, we will examine four factors commonly deemed important to understanding the entry and success of women in the electoral arena: (1) their age, (2) whether they worked outside the home, (3) whether they lived in the South, and (4) whether they were elected in 1972 or later.

Age Women do tend to be older than men when they first run for office.[50] The primary reason, confirmed by the Citizen Political Ambition Study results regarding housework and child care, is that women usually wait until their children are grown before they run for office. Only four women have ever had a child while serving in Congress. The first was Representative Yvonne Brathwaite Burke (D-CA), elected in 1972, who gave birth during her first term. The next birth would not occur until 1995, when Representative Enid Greene Waldholtz (R-UT) had a child during her first year in office. In 1996 Representative Susan Molinari (R-NY) and her husband Representative Bill Paxon (R-NY) became the only congressional couple to have a child while they were both serving.[51] While she was a House member, Blanche Lambert Lincoln (D-AR) became pregnant with twins, and decided not to seek reelection in 1996. She ran for Senate two years later and ran ads with photos of herself with her babies and the voiceover, "Daughter, wife, mother, congresswoman. . . . Living our rock-solid Arkansas values."[52] In

---

[50] See Kirkpatrick, 1974; Irene Diamond, *Sex Roles in the State House* (New Haven, Conn.: Yale University Press, 1977); Gertzog, 1980; Ruth Mandel, *In the Running: The New Woman Candidate* (New Haven, Conn.: Ticknor and Fields, 1981); Virginia Sapiro, "Private Costs of Public Commitments or Public Costs of Private Commitments? Family Roles versus Political Ambition," *American Journal of Political Science* 26 (1982): 265–79; Susan Carroll, "Political Elites and Sex Differences in Political Ambition: A Reconsideration," *Journal of Politics* 47 (1985): 1231–43; Robert Bernstein, "Why Are There So Few Women in the House?" *Western Political Quarterly* 39 (1986): 155–64; Barbara Burrell, "The Political Opportunity of Women Candidates for the U.S. House of Representatives in 1984," *Women and Politics* 8 (1988): 51–68; and Barbara Burrell, *A Woman's Place Is in the House: Campaigning for Congress in the Feminist Era* (Ann Arbor: University of Michigan Press, 1994); but see Kathleen Dolan and Lynne Ford, "Change and Continuity among Women State Legislators: Evidence from Three Decades," *Political Research Quarterly* 50 (1997): 137–51.

[51] Foerstel, 106, 193.

[52] "Senator Blanche Lincoln," *National Journal Almanac*, 2007, http://nationaljournal.com. proxyau.wrlc.org/pubs/almanac/2006/people/ar/ars1.htm (accessed May 14, 2007).

2006, Representative Cathy McMorris Rodgers (R-WA) learned she was pregnant while she was campaigning for her second term. After winning her reelection, she had a boy in April 2007, noting that, "One of the positives about this job is you do have a flexible schedule. . . . Also, I have a spouse. He's excited about being a caregiver."[53]

Women who do run for Congress while they have small children often have to deal with criticism that their male colleagues with small children do not have to face. For example, in her 1964 House campaign, Patsy Mink was accused of "abandoning her children."[54] In 1971, when Barbara Boxer ran in her first race for county supervisor at the age of thirty-two, she sought the advice of her next-door neighbor, who said, "I don't think you should do this. Your kids are young and it doesn't seem right."[55] During her first campaign in 1972, Pat Schroeder was constantly asked how she could run for Congress with two small children. Frustrated at the press for ignoring her position on the Vietnam War and instead focusing on her parenting skills, she finally told one reporter, "Jim and I get up very early—about 6 A.M. We bathe and dress the children and give them a wonderful breakfast. Then we put them in the freezer, leave for work and when we come home we defrost them. And we all have a wonderful dinner together."[56] In the spring of 1998, Mary Bono, who had two children, ages seven and nine, ran for her husband's seat in a special election against Ralph Waite, the actor who played "Pa" on *The Waltons*. Representative Sonny Bono (R-CA), former mayor of Palm Springs and costar of *The Sonny and Cher Show*, had been killed in a ski accident. A week before the election, Mary's mother-in-law, Jean Bono, wrote a letter to the editor of the *Riverside Press Enterprise*, stating, "Sonny Bono cannot rest in peace. . . . It would disturb him greatly that, if you hired her for the job, his children would essentially become orphans open to abuse by strangers."[57] Mary's thirty-nine-year-old stepdaughter, Christy, responded that Mary would probably be a better representative than her father.[58]

There is, however, evidence that these attitudes about the compatibility of motherhood and public office are changing.[59] For example, Representative Shelley Berkley (D-NV) was thirty when she was deciding between running

[53] "Congresswoman Balances Bills with Birth," *CBSNews.com*, April 21, 2007 (accessed April 23, 2007).

[54] Karen Foerstel and Herbert Foerstel, *Climbing the Hill: Gender Conflict in Congress* (Westport, Conn.: Praeger Press, 1996), 113.

[55] Barbara Boxer, *Strangers in the Senate: Politics and the New Revolution of Women in America* (Washington, D.C.: National Press Books, 1993), 83.

[56] Foerstel and Foerstel, 1996, 114.

[57] Mark Henry, "Bono's Mother Doesn't Want His Widow Elected," *Riverside Press Enterprise*, March 28,1998, A1.

[58] Mark Henry, "Phone Call Discouraged Election Run," *Riverside Press Enterprise*, March 31, 1998, B1.

[59] Linda Witt, Karen Paget, and Glenna Matthews, *Running as a Woman: Gender and Power in American Politics* (New York: Free Press, 1995).

for the state assembly and taking time off to have children. She assumed that she would have to choose between one or the other. Her mother told her to "do both."[60] Representative Debbie Wasserman Schultz (D-FL) first ran for the Florida State Legislature at the age of twenty-six in 1992. While in office, she had twins. When she learned that Representative Peter Deutsch's seat was going to be open in 2004, she decided to run for Congress. In August 2003, she had a baby girl, Shelby, whom she took on the campaign trail with her. At one point in her campaign, she brought Shelby with her to a lunch meeting with Susannah Shakow, president of Women Under Forty Political Action Committee. As Shakow explained:

> We met at this really nice restaurant in downtown Washington to talk about how our PAC could help her. She came with her finance director, her campaign manager, and her three-month-old baby. I told a lot of people about that meeting. Some people were shocked that she would bring her baby along to meetings where she was trying to present herself as a serious candidate. But most people I talked to thought it was great that she brought her child. Young women who have children too often feel pressure to hide that fact when they are doing business. Debbie is a role model for proving that a woman can be professional and a mother at the same time.[61]

Many women no longer feel that a political career and raising a family are mutually exclusive. Senator Mary Landrieu (D-LA) said:

> It breaks my heart when I meet older women who once made a choice between career and a family. There was a time, not long ago, when many women *had* to make that choice. Now these women are retired, and they have no children, no grandchildren. In some cases, not all, they were forced to sacrifice one great joy for another. It just doesn't seem right. I want to make sure that picture is changed for good. If I can do it, other women can.[62]

Of the eighty-seven women in the 110th Congress (2007 session), seventy-one are mothers, but very few of them have young children. As Representative Wasserman Schultz explained, "It's important to have moms in Congress. . . . I want to show other young women that it can be done."[63]

---

[60] Interview with Barbara Palmer, March 20, 2002.
[61] Interview with the authors, November 14, 2004.
[62] Barbara Mikulski, Kay Bailey Hutchison, Dianne Feinstein, Barbara Boxer, Patty Murray, Olympia Snowe, Susan Collins, Mary Landrieu, Blanche Lincoln and Catherine Whitney, *Nine and Counting: The Women of the Senate* (New York: William Morrow, 2000), 25.
[63] Richard Cohen, "Member Moms," *National Journal*, April 7, 2007, 14–19.

While attitudes about mothers and children on the campaign trail are changing, the election of young women to congressional offices is still quite uncommon. As table 3.2 shows, only thirty-eight women under forty years old have served in the House. All but nine of these have been elected since 1972. Only one woman under the age of forty has been elected to the Senate; Blanche Lambert Lincoln (D-AR) ran in 1998 at the age of thirty-eight. She ran for the House in 1992 at the age of thirty-two. The first woman to serve in Congress, Representative Jeannette Rankin (R-MT), ran at the relatively young age of thirty-six. The youngest woman to serve in the House was Representative Elizabeth Holtzman (D-NY), elected at the age of thirty-one.[64]

In the 110th Congress (2007 session), the youngest woman was Representative Stephanie Herseth Sandlin (D-SD), age thirty-six.[65] Herseth Sandlin's first attempt at running for Congress was in 2002, when she ran for South Dakota's open at-large seat. Her opponent was Republican Bill Janklow, the state's "larger than life" former governor.[66] Janklow won with 53 percent of the vote, but a few months later he ran a stop sign at over seventy miles per hour and killed a motorcyclist.[67] After Janklow's manslaughter conviction, Herseth Sandlin ran again in the special election held in June 2004, defeating Larry Diedrich, a state legislator. Five months later,

---

[64] There have been two other women who were elected at age thirty-one, Susan Molinari (R-NY) and Olympia Snowe (R-ME), but they are both a couple of months older. Molinari served as the youngest member of the New York City Council at the age of twenty-six and ran for the House seat vacated by her father in 1990. Snowe, who first ran for the state legislature in 1973 at the age of twenty-six, now serves in the U.S. Senate. In 1972, Holtzman, who never held political office before, defeated a twenty-five-term Democratic incumbent, Representative Emanuel Celler, by six hundred votes in the primary. Celler was chair of the House Judiciary Committee and had blocked the Equal Rights Amendment in his committee for twenty years. Holtzman got his seat on the committee and participated in the impeachment hearings against President Richard Nixon. In 1977, she cofounded the Congressional Caucus for Women's Issues; Foerstel, 1999, 123. See also Elizabeth Holtzman with Cynthia Cooper, *Who Said It Would Be Easy? One Woman's Life in the Political Arena* (New York: Arcade Press, 1996).

[65] Representative Gabrielle Giffords (D-AZ) was also thirty-six, but is six months older than Herseth Sandlin, *Biographical Directory of the United States Congress*, http://bioguide. congress.gov/scripts/biodisplay.pl?index=G000554 (accessed May 14, 2007).

[66] Janklow was a fixture in South Dakota politics for over thirty years. As attorney general in 1975, he charged into the capitol with an automatic rifle during a hostage situation. After Jerry Brown, governor of California, refused to extradite Dennis Banks, a prominent member of the American Indian Movement, Janklow said he would pardon criminals in South Dakota if they agreed to move to California; Conrad deFiebre, "Janklow Case: He Did Politics His Way; Roughshod Style Made Him SD Icon," *Minneapolis Star Tribune*, December 14, 2003, 1B.

[67] Janklow had a reputation for speeding. He was stopped by police at least sixteen other times since 1994; "Janklow Trial Begins, Could Shake Up State's Political Scene," *The Bulletin's Front-runner*, McClean, Virginia, December 2, 2003.

Table 3.2 Women under Forty Years Old Who Have Served in the House

Name	Age When First Elected to the House	Dates of Service
Pre-World War II		
Jeannette Rankin (R-MT)	36	1917–1919, 1941–1943
Mae Ella Nolan (R-CA)	36	1923–1925
Katherine Langley (R-KY)	38	1926–1931
Kathryn O'Laughlin McCarthy (D-KS)	38	1929–1931
1942–1970		
Katharine Byron (D-MD)	37	1941–1943
Clare Boothe Luce (R-CT)	39	1943–1947
Winnifred Stanley (R-NY)	33	1943–1945
Patsy Mink (D-HI)	36	1965–1977, 1990–2002
Margaret Heckler (R-MA)	35	1967–1983
1972–Present		
Elizabeth Holtzman (D-NY)	31	1973–1981
Barbara Jordan (D-TX)	36	1973–1979
Patricia Schroeder (D-CO)	32	1973–1997
Mary Rose Oakar (D-OH)	36	1977–1993
Olympia Snowe (R-ME)	31	1979–1995
Claudine Schneider (R-RI)	33	1981–1991
Marcy Kaptur (D-OH)	36	1983–present
Jill Long (D-IN)	37	1989–1995
Ileana Ros-Lehtinen (R-FL)	37	1989–present
Susan Molinari (R-NY)	31	1990–1997
Blanche Lincoln (D-AR)	32	1993–1997
Cynthia McKinney (D-GA)	37	1993–2003, 2005–2007
Nydia Velázquez (D-NY)	39	1993–2005
Maria Cantwell (D-WA)	34	1993–1995
Enid Greene Waldholtz (R-UT)	36	1995–1997
Lynn Rivers (D-MI)	37	1995–2005
Linda Smith (R-WA)	34	1995–1999
Loretta Sanchez (D-CA)	36	1997–present
Diana DeGette (D-CO)	39	1997–present
Mary Bono (R-CA)	36	1999–present
Heather Wilson (R-NM)	37	1999–present
Tammy Baldwin (D-WI)	36	1999–present
Melissa Hart (R-PA)	38	2001–present
Linda Sanchez (D-CA)	34	2003–present

(Continued)

Table 3.2 Women under Forty Years Old Who Have Served in the House *(Continued)*

Name	Age When First Elected to the House	Dates of Service
Stephanie Herseth Sandlin (D-SD)	33	2004–present
Cathy McMorris Rodgers (R-WA)	33	2005–present
Debbie Wasserman Schultz (D-FL)	37	2005–present
Gabrielle Giffords (D-AZ)	36	2007–present
Kirsten Gillibrand (D-NY)	39	2007–present

she defended her seat and defeated Diedrich again with 53 percent of the vote.[68]

There are political consequences to running later in life. Entry into the leadership structure of Congress depends upon longevity and seniority. This is especially true within the committee system where the key positions, chairs and ranking members, are based largely on continuous service on committees and subcommittees. As Shakow explained, "Women need to get in early and stay in, so that more leadership positions are open to them. In Washington, political tenure equal[s] political power."[69]

Until very recently, women have barely been represented in the leadership hierarchy. As table 3.3 shows, in the history of Congress, only seventeen women have chaired standing committees. With the Democrats taking over both chambers in the wake of the 2006 election and Representative Nancy Pelosi (D-CA) becoming Speaker of the House, the 110th Congress (2007 session) has seen a substantial increase in the number of women in leadership positions.[70] In the 109th Congress (2005 session), only two women were committee chairs, Senators Olympia Snowe and Susan Collins, both of Maine; no women chaired committees in the House. In the 110th Congress (2007 session), six women were committee chairs, two in the Senate and four

---

[68] Herseth Sandlin has noted how a recent change in FEC rules might actually help young women: candidates can now draw a salary from their campaign. She explained that running for office is a full-time job and, as a result, quit her lucrative job as an attorney. She saved money to cushion the loss of income, but being allowed to draw a salary from her campaign meant that she did not have to accumulate more debt on top of her student loans. Diedrich actually tried to make this an issue in the campaign. Herseth Sandlin hopes, however, that her successful precedent will make the practice a nonissue and that people with modest means— more young people, particularly women—will be able to run. Speech at WUFPAC event, Washington, D.C., July 20, 2004.

[69] Interview with the authors, July 19, 2004. Women Under Forty Political Action Committee (WUFPAC) is a nonpartisan political action committee that provides financial support to women under forty years old who are running for Congress; see http://www.wufpac.org (accessed July 10, 2005).

[70] "Special Report: CQ's Guide to the Committees," *CQ Weekly*, April 16, 2007.

Table 3.3 Women Who Have Been Chairs of Standing Committees

House

Name	Committee	Dates of Service
Mae Ella Nolan (R-CA)	Expenditures (Post Office Department)	1923–1924
Edith Nourse Rogers (R-MA)	World War Veterans	1947–1948, 1953–1954
Mary Norton (D-NJ)	District of Columbia	1931–1937
Mary Norton (D-NJ)	Labor	1937–1946
Mary Norton (D-NJ)	Administration	1949–1950
Caroline O'Day (D-NY)	Elections	1937–1942
Leonor Sullivan (D-MO)	Merchant Marine and Fisheries	1973–1976
Nancy Johnson (R-CT)	Standards of Official Conduct	1995–1996
Jan Meyers (R-KS)	Small Business	1995–1996
Juanita Millender-McDonald (D-CA)	Administration	2007*
Louise Slaughter (D-NY)	Rules	2007–present
Stephanie Tubbs Jones (D-OH)	Standards of Official Conduct	2007–present
Nydia Velázquez (D-NY)	Small Business	2007–present

Senate

Name	Committee	Dates of Service
Hattie Caraway (D-AR)	Enrolled Bills	1933–1944
Nancy Kassebaum (R-KS)	Labor and Human Resources	1995–1996
Susan Collins (R-ME)	Governmental Affairs	2003–present
Olympia Snowe (R-ME)	Small Business and Entrepreneurship	2003–present
Barbara Boxer (D-CA)	Environment and Public Works	2007–present
Dianne Feinstein (D-CA)	Rules and Administration	2007–present

* *Millender-McDonald served as chair from January of 2007 until her death in April.*

Sources: Karen McCurdy, "The Institutional Role of Women Serving in Congress: 1960–2000," in *Representation of Minority Groups in the U.S.*, ed. Charles Menifield (Lanham, Md.: Austin and Winfield, 2001); Amer, 2004; *Biographical Directory of the United States Congress*, http://bioguide. congress.gov/biosearch/biosearch.asp (accessed July 3, 2005); "Special Report: CQ's Guide to the Committees," *CQ Weekly*, April 16, 2007.

in the House, representing 16.2 percent of all chairs. Women chaired thirty-three subcommittees, fifteen in the Senate and eighteen in the House.[71]

If the younger members of Congress today are the leadership of Congress in the future, women will be substantially underrepresented. It was not until the 108th Congress (2004 session) that there was at least one woman on every committee.[72] In the 110th Congress (2007 session), only seven women were under forty years old. There were eighteen men under forty.[73] The

---

[71] "Special Report: CQ's Guide to the Committees." There are over 200 committees and sub-committees in the House and Senate. Our count of female chairs does not include any select or joint committees and also does not include any Delegates from U.S. Territories.

[72] Michael Hardy and Karen McCurdy, "Representational Threshold: Women in Congressional Committees" (paper presented at the Southern Political Science Association, January 2005, New Orleans).

[73] "Women by the Numbers," *Women Under Forty Political Action Committee*, http://www. wufpac.org/stats.html (accessed May 14, 2007).

importance of starting young becomes particularly apparent given that twelve of the last nineteen presidents first ran for elective office before they reached the age of thiry-five; for example, Teddy Roosevelt was twenty-four when he first ran for state assembly in New York and Lyndon Johnson was twenty-nine when he first ran for the U.S. House.[74]

The 110th Congress (2007 session) is also the oldest in the history of both the Senate and the House; the average age in the Senate is sixty-two, and the average age in the House is fifty-six.[75] Senator Strom Thurmond (R-SC) holds the record as the oldest person to serve. He retired at the age of one hundred in January 2003, after forty-eight years in Congress.[76] Among all women to serve in the House between 1916 and 2006, the average age when they first ran for office was 48.6. The average age of widows was 52.2; for nonwidows, the average was 47.8. In the 110th Congress (2007 session), the average age of male House members when they first ran was 44.9; female House members were 47.9. Given the importance of age in both the hierarchy of offices and in acquiring internal influence, we expect that the likelihood of a widow seeking a career will vary inversely with her age.[77]

Working Outside the Home One of the most consistent predictors of political ambition among women is whether they worked outside the home and whether their jobs helped them to acquire useful political skills.[78] With regard to working outside the home, two aspects are most relevant to our analysis of congressional widows and political ambition. The first involves whether the woman worked closely, in either a paid or unpaid capacity, with her husband when he served as a member of the House. This kind of experience provides a familiarity with the concerns and interests of con-stituents, how to organize an effective campaign, and the responsibilities and routines of running a congressional office. A second aspect of working outside the home pertains to whether a woman was active in politics

---

[74] Ruth Mandel and Katherine Kleeman, *Political Generation Next: America's Young Elected Leaders* (New Brunswick, N.J.: Rutgers University, 2004). See also Marie Wilson, *Closing the Leadership Gap: Why Women Can and Must Help Run the World* (New York: Viking, 2004).

[75] Robin Toner, "Democraphics; New Congress, Older Look," *New York Times.com*, January 9, 2007 (accessed March 26. 2007).

[76] He died a few months later on June 26, 2003; http://www.strom.clemson.edu/strom/bio.html (accessed July 3, 2005).

[77] In the analysis, we use the age of sixty as a cutoff point to create a dummy variable.

[78] Gertzog, 1980; 1995; Janet Clark, Charles Hadley, and Robert Darcy, "Political Ambition among Men and Women State Party Leaders," *American Politics Quarterly* 17 (1989): 194–207; Edmond Constantini, "Political Women and Political Ambition," *American Journal of Politics* 34 (1990): 741–70; Barbara Norrander and Clyde Wilcox, "The Geography of Gender Power," in *Women and Elective Office: Past, Present and Future*, eds. Sue Thomas and Clyde Wilcox (New York: Oxford University Press, 1998), 103–17; and Kathryn Pearson and Eric McGhee, "Strategic Differences: The Gender Dynamics of Congressional Candidacies, 1982–2002" (paper presented at the American Political Science Association Annual Meeting, September 2004, Chicago).

independent of her husband's political career. The nature of this independent experience may include holding elective office or appointive office, or serving in the organization of a local, state, or national party.

One example of a widow who had a great deal of political experience was Sala Burton (D-CA). Her husband, Representative Phillip Burton, was a powerful House member and leader of the liberal wing of the Democratic Party in the 1970s and early 1980s. Although Sala was never formally on his congressional staff, Phillip called her his "political partner," and she was an integral part of his thirty-year political career.[79] Pansy Ponzio, a member of the local Democratic Party, explained that "she knew just about as much about the office and the constituents and the people who live in San Francisco as he did."[80] Phillip and Sala met at a Young Democrats convention in 1950. When her husband was a member of the California State Legislature, she organized the California Democratic Council and then served as vice president. She also served on the San Francisco Fair Housing Committee, served as a member of the state Democratic Party Steering Committee, and chaired the Democratic Women's Forum. After Phillip became a member of Congress, she served on the boards of the National Security Committee, the National Council on Soviet Jewry, and the Women's National Democratic Club.[81] She was also the president of the Democratic Wives of the House and Senate and a delegate to four Democratic presidential conventions.[82] While serving in his tenth term, Phillip died of an embolism in April 1983. Sala announced she would run for his seat eight days after his death and defeated ten other candidates in the special election with 56.9 percent of the vote.[83] Within days of her victory, she announced that she would run for reelection in 1984.[84] She ran again in 1986 and won, but unfortunately was diagnosed with cancer and died shortly after being sworn in for her third term.[85] Because of the independent political experience gained while her husband was alive, she easily won the support of party leaders, knew how to campaign, and became a successful member of Congress in her own right.

With respect to independent experience, there are marked differences between widows and nonwidows. Nonwidows entered their first campaign for a House seat with an average of 9.8 years of experience; almost half

---

[79] James Dickenson and Paul Taylor, "Widow of Burton Will Seek Election to His House Seat," *Washington Post*, April 19, 1983, A7.

[80] Wallace Turner, "Burton's Widow among 4 Considering Race for Congress Seat," *New York Times*, April 18, 1983, A12.

[81] Barbara Gamarekian, " 'The Popular Burton' and Her Mission," *New York Times*, July 29, 1983, A10.

[82] Foerstel, 1999, 43.

[83] Gamerekian, 1983, A10.

[84] "Widow of Rep. Burton Is Elected in California Congressional Race," *New York Times*, June 23, 1983, A16.

[85] Foerstel, 1999, 43.

served in other political offices for over ten years. Widows, on the other hand, averaged 3.7 years of experience, with only 15.4 percent (6/39) holding offices for ten years or more. Thus, we expect those widows with more political experience, whether it was from working with their husbands or their own independent activities, to run for reelection.[86]

The South We have noted that, prior to the 1970s, American culture treated politics as primarily a man's game. In a variety of ways, women were discouraged from entering the electoral arena. The barriers faced by women, however, were even more restrictive in the American South.[87] This is attributed to a uniquely traditionalist culture that "function[ed] to confine real political power to a small and self-perpetuating elite who often inherit their right to govern through family title or social position."[88] This traditionalism also includes "a clear predisposition with regard to social conservatism and particularly women's rights."[89] As one historian explained, in the antebellum South, "even though the master's wife and daughters were white and members of the planter class, 'they were . . . in this rigidly hierarchical society, subjected to male rule.' . . . In fact, an educated and well-bred woman . . . was not even allowed to initiate a political conversation."[90] In spite of the dramatic social and economic changes in the South, these regional distinctions "have shown remarkable resilience."[91] Of the eleven states in the Confederacy, only Texas ratified the Equal Rights Amendment.[92]

The impact of southern traditionalism is particularly noteworthy in the early years of our study. Between 1916 and 1970, only three of the nineteen southern women to serve in the House won their seats in regularly scheduled

---

[86] In this analysis, we use dummy variables to represent these aspects of working outside the home. The first assumes a value of one if the widow worked in partnership with her husband. The second takes on a value of one if the widow had independent political experience of her own. The biographies written by Foerstel (1999) are excellent for making this determination. She reports whether the wife worked with or for her husband and provides a great deal of specificity about the kind of work she did (e.g., organized and ran the Washington office). We also recorded the total number of years that the woman served in elective or appointive offices in her own right. We do not "double count" those years in which a woman served in more than one capacity (e.g., state legislature and member of state party central committee), and we apply a strict rule of independence in making these calculations. Thus, service in the party organization (state, local, or national) is counted while service as an officer in the Congressional Wives Club does not. It should be noted that these two aspects of "working outside the home" are not mutually exclusive.

[87] Deanne Stephens Nuwer, "Southern Women Legislators and Patriarchy in the South," *Southeastern Political Review* 28 (2000): 449–68.

[88] Daniel Elazar, *American Federalism: A View from the States* (New York: Crowell, 1966), 93.

[89] Christina Wolbrecht, *The Politics of Women's Rights: Parties, Positions, and Change* (Princeton, N.J.: Princeton University Press, 2000), 187.

[90] Nuwer, 2000, 450.

[91] John Shelton Reed, *The Enduring South: Subcultural Persistence in Mass Society* (Chapel Hill: University of North Carolina Press, 1986).

[92] Wolbrecht, 2000, 187.

Fig. 3.1 Representative Alice Robertson was the first woman elected from the South and the second woman to serve in Congress. Photo courtesy of the Library of Congress.

House elections.[93] The political careers of these three women are particularly illustrative of southern political culture. Representative Alice Robertson (see figure 3.1), a Republican from Oklahoma and a teacher, farmer, and restauranteur, was the first woman elected from the South and the second

---

[93] Thirteen were widows elected to succeed their deceased husbands. Two women also won special elections to fill a vacancy. In February 1946, Helen Mankin (D-GA) won the seat left open by the resignation of Representative Robert Ramspeck. She served in the House from February 12, 1946, until the end of the term on January 3, 1947. Under the Georgia county unit system, Mankin lost her bid for renomination in 1946 despite a popular vote victory; Foerstel, 1996, 170–71. For over twenty years, Eliza Pratt (D-NC) worked as a "top assistant to a parade of representatives from North Carolina's 8th Congressional District"; Foerstel, 1999, 219. She won a special election in June 1946 to succeed her boss, Representative William Burgin; she did not run in 1948, citing the difficulties of fundraising; Foerstel, 1999, 220.

woman to serve in Congress. In the campaign of 1920, she defeated incumbent Democrat William Hastings by the narrow margin of 48.8 to 48.4 percent. Robertson was an ardent antisuffragist who "incurred the wrath of such groups as the League of Women Voters, the National Women's Party, and the Daughters of the American Revolution."[94] These groups took umbrage at Robertson's opposition to an appropriation for the Children's Bureau in the Department of Labor designed to "promote maternity and infant care."[95] In a floor speech, Robertson dismissed as "absurd" the " 'sob stuff' claim that 680 babies die every day from the failure to enact this bill."[96] In addition, Robertson opposed bills creating a Department of Education, U.S. entry into the League of Nations, and bonuses for veterans of World War I.[97] It was this last transgression that led to her 1922 defeat.[98] William Hastings easily reclaimed his seat by a margin of 57.7 to 41.7 percent.

The second woman from the South, Representative Ruth Bryan Owen (D-FL), was the daughter of three-time presidential nominee and former Secretary of State William Jennings Bryan.[99] At twenty-three, she served as secretary to her father during his unsuccessful 1908 presidential campaign against Republican William Howard Taft. Following the divorce from her first husband, she became a "single mom" and supported her family as a lecturer and newspaper writer. She later married Reginald Owen, a former British military officer. Because of Reginald's illness, they moved to Florida and lived with her parents. Following her father's death in 1925, Owen began her own political career and ran for the House. She narrowly lost the Democratic primary to incumbent William Sears in 1926. After her husband's death in 1927, Ruth again announced her candidacy, defeated Sears to win the primary in 1928, and then went on to an easy victory in the general election, defeating Republican William Lawson by a wide margin, 65 to 35 percent. Lawson, however, challenged the election, arguing that she had forfeited her citizenship and eligibility to run for the House when she married a British citizen. The House upheld her election. Owen was re-elected in 1930 and, during her time in the House, served on the Foreign Relations Committee and was an advocate of mothers' pensions, a program later included in the legislation creating the Social Security System. Owen was defeated in the 1932 Democratic primary where her opponent, J. Mark Wilcox, attacked her support for Prohibition.[100]

---

[94] Foerstel, 1999, 231.

[95] "An Undeleted History of Women," http://www.undelete.org/woa/woa01-02.html (accessed May 15, 2005).

[96] Quoted in Foerstel, 1999, 232.

[97] Foerstel, 1999, 232.

[98] Foerstel, 1999, 232.

[99] Owen was the first woman elected from a state in the Confederacy.

[100] Foerstel, 1999, 213–14; and Steven Gillon, *That's Not What We Meant to Do: Reform and Its Unintended Consequences in Twentieth-Century America* (New York: W.W. Norton, 2000), 43–46.

Twenty-six years would pass until the next southern woman was elected in her own right. In the 1940s, Democrat Iris Blitch became known as the "Queen of the Legislature" during her service as one of the only women in the Georgia House and Senate.[101] While in the Georgia legislature, Blitch supported expanding the "county unit system," an indirect method of determining election results that disproportionately favored sparsely populated rural counties. She argued that this system was "another weapon in opposing the Communistic trend" of determining election results by direct popular vote.[102] In 1954, Blitch defeated four-term incumbent William Wheeler, charging him with disloyalty to the Democratic Party,[103] and ran unopposed in the general election. During her tenure, Blitch was clearly a member of the southern "segregationist" bloc. In 1956, she signed the Southern Manifesto decrying the 1954 U.S. Supreme Court decision in *Brown v. Board of Board of Education* and voted against the Civil Rights Act of 1957. Three years later, she was on the record as opposed to the Civil Rights Act of 1960.[104] In 1961, she opposed the effort led by Democratic Speaker of the House Sam Rayburn to expand the membership of the House Rules Committee, which would have ended the conservative southern lock on the committee and allowed civil rights legislation to progress.[105] A year after her retirement from the House in 1963, she switched parties and announced her support for Republican Barry Goldwater in the presidential election of 1964.

We define the South as the eleven states of the Confederacy plus Oklahoma and Kentucky. Numerous state and regional studies have shown

---

[101] Foerstel, 1999, 27.

[102] Albert Saye, "Georgia's County Unit System of Election," *Journal of Politics* 12 (1950): 93–106, 100. In Georgia during this time, the winner of a primary election was not based upon the popular vote. Rather, each county was assigned a specific number of unit votes (three, two, or one), and the popular vote in that county would determine the winner of the county's unit votes. The system was discriminatory because it diluted the influence of urban counties. For example, by winning four rural counties and getting their four unit votes, a candidate could offset an opponent's victory in an urban county worth three unit votes.

[103] The charge of party disloyalty rendered against her opponent is somewhat baffling. As it turns out, Blitch's and Wheeler's voting records were almost identical.

[104] Officially, Blitch was "paired against" this civil rights bill. Members of Congress are "paired" when there is an "agreement between two lawmakers on opposite sides to withhold their votes on roll calls so their absence from Congress will not affect the outcome of record voting"; *Congress and the Nation, 1948–1964* (Washington, D.C.: CQ Press, 1965), 171a.

[105] The Rules Committee plays a powerful role in the House of Representatives because it controls whether a bill passed by an authorizing committee is sent to the floor. In addition, it establishes the rules (e.g., length of debate, amendment procedures) under which the bill is debated. During the 1950s, the Rules Committee was dominated by a conservative alliance of Republicans and southern Democrats. The successful effort to increase the size of this committee was designed to add three more liberals to the panel and thus break this conservative alliance; Milton Cummings and Robert Peabody, "The Decision to Enlarge the Committee on Rules: An Analysis of the 1961 Vote," in *New Perspectives on the House of Representatives*, 2nd ed., eds. Robert Peabody and Nelson Polsby (Chicago: Rand McNally, 1969).

that southern traditionalism produces proportionally fewer female candidates and officeholders than the rest of the country.[106] And as the examples of Robertson and Blitch show, conservative social attitudes in the South were not limited to men. In fact, many southern women still "maintain a cult-of-domesticity mind frame."[107] Between 1956 and 2004, there were 6,326 nomination opportunities for southern House seats, and women won the nomination only 273 times, a rate of 4.3 percent. The comparable rate outside of the South is nearly double, 8.3 percent (1,285/15,406). Similarly, of the 3,163 general elections for the House in the South, women won 3.6 percent (113/3,021), compared to a rate of 7.5 percent (577/7,703), more than double, outside the South. As a result, we would expect widows from the South to be less likely to pursue congressional careers.[108]

Running after 1970 We use 1972 as the "critical moment"[109] to mark the point at which the Women's Movement began to influence attitudes toward women and their entry into the electoral arena. While dating the rise of any social movement is somewhat arbitrary, the period from 1970 to 1972 is appropriate for several reasons. As we noted in chapter 2, a series of events occurred that fostered the beginning of a fundamental shift in American political culture. The number of women's groups skyrocketed, along with media coverage of women's issues and activism. The Supreme Court handed down two landmark women's rights cases: for the first time in history, the Supreme Court voided a sex-based classification as a violation of the Equal Protection Clause and struck down a state law banning abortion. The Democratic Party changed its rules and dramatically increased the number of female delegates attending the national convention. Congress passed the Equal Rights Amendment and sent it to the states for ratification, and passed other landmark women's rights legislation. Organizations such as the National Women's Political Caucus and the Women's Campaign Fund were created to provide financial support for women candidates.

The unfolding of these events corresponded with an increase in the number of women obtaining public office. Beginning in 1972, more women were running in primaries, winning primaries, and winning congressional seats. Attitudes about women's roles were changing; gradually, the perception that politics was a "man's game" was dissolving. As Senator Barbara Boxer (D-CA) explained, "[I]n 1972 you never mentioned being a woman. You never

---

[106] See for example Constantini, 1990; Clark, Hadley, and Darcy, 1989; Burrell, 1994; Darcy, Welch, and Clark, 1994; Gertzog, 1995; Susan Welch and Donley Studlar, "The Opportunity Structure for Women's Candidacies and Electability in Britain and the United States," *Political Research Quarterly* 49 (1996): 861–74; Norrander and Wilcox, 1998, and Nuwer, 2000.

[107] Nuwer, 2000, 451.

[108] Gertzog, 1980.

[109] Edward Carmines and James Stimson, *Issue Evolution: Race and the Transformation of American Politics* (Princeton, N.J.: Princeton University Press, 1989).

brought it up, and you hoped nobody noticed."[110] Today, as Gilda Morales at the Center for American Women and Politics explained, the presumption that female candidates are "inherently vulnerable 'has disappeared.' "[111] As noted earlier, it was largely assumed that the only way women could obtain elective office was by following a dead husband, whether they actually did or not. The Women's Movement and the events of the early 1970s fostered a shift in attitudes about the capabilities of women running for office in their own right.

As table 3.1 shows, from 1916 to 1940, a twenty-four-year period, fourteen widows were elected to the House. From 1942 to 1970, a twenty-eight-year period, fifteen widows were elected. From 1972 to 2006, a twenty-four-year period, only eleven widows served after the death of their husbands. Moreover, widows as a proportion of the number of women elected dropped considerably; prior to 1970, widows were 41.2 percent of all women elected. After 1972, widows were only 7.7 percent of all women elected. More women were running without the benefit of a dead husband. Consequently, we expect that these cultural shifts about the appropriateness of women running for office will also affect widows themselves and that more of them who were elected after 1970 would pursue careers.

Explaining Discrete and Static Ambition

We expect that the decision of widows to seek a second term in the House will be influenced by these four factors. Widows who are under the age of sixty when they first obtain office will be more likely to run for reelection. Widows who worked outside the home, whether they worked directly for their husbands or had independent political experience of their own, would also be more likely to run for reelection. In addition, women from districts outside the South and those who ran after the rise of the Women's Movement in the early 1970s would also be more likely to run for reelection and exhibit static ambition. There were thirty-nine congressional widows who served in the House between 1916 and 2004.[112] Nineteen (48.7 percent) sought reelection after their initial term. It is our expectation that these four factors will explain the choices made by these widows.

As table 3.4 shows, each of our expectations is met.[113] The table reveals

---

[110] Boxer, 1993, 82.

[111] Allison Stevens, "The Strength of These Women Shows in Their Numbers," *CQ Weekly*, October 25, 2003, 2625.

[112] Our analysis here excludes Doris Matsui, who was elected in March 2005. Her situation will be discussed in the conclusion of this chapter.

[113] The full results of our statistical model are presented in Barbara Palmer and Dennis Simon, "Political Ambition and Women in the U.S. House of Representatives, 1916–2000," *Political Research Quarterly* 56 (2003): 127–38. Our results and discussion here largely reflect the results of this analysis. Additional evidence is presented in Lisa Solowiej and Thomas Brunell, "The Entrance of Women to the U.S. Congress: The Widow Effect," *Political Research Quarterly* 56 (2003): 283–92.

Table 3.4 When Congressional Widows Seek Reelection to the House

Characteristics Predicting Discrete versus Static Ambition among Widows	Percentage of All Widows Who Possess the Characteristic	Percentage of Widows with Characteristic Who Seek Reelection
First elected under the age of sixty	71.8% (28/39)	60.7% (17/28)
Worked with or for husband when he served in the House	46.2 (18/39)	72.2 (13/18)
Had political experience independent of husband	28.2 (11/39)	79.3 (9/11)
Elected from district outside of the South	60.0 (23/39)	79.3 (17/23)
Elected to first term in 1972 or later	28.2 (11/39)	79.3 (17/23)

that age is strongly related to the decision of whether to seek a career in the House. Only two of eleven widows (18.2 percent) age sixty or older sought reelection compared to 60.7 percent (17/28) of those widows younger than sixty years of age. The probability of a widow seeking a second term is strongly related to whether she worked outside the home. First, the likelihood that she will pursue a congressional career increases when she has worked with her husband. Almost half of the widows worked with or for their husbands. And thirteen of the eighteen widows (72.2 percent) who worked with their husbands sought a second term compared to only six of the twenty-one widows (28.6 percent) not actively engaged in their husband's career. In addition, there is a clear relationship between independent political experience and seeking reelection. While only about a quarter of the widows had independent political experience, nine of the eleven (81.8 percent) sought reelection to the House; only 35.7 percent (10/28) of those without this experience sought reelection.

The prevailing political and social culture also has an influence on whether a widow will run again. The probability of seeking a second term decreases if the widow is from the South. In our data, sixteen of the thirty-nine women are from the South. Only two of them pursued a House career: Katherine Langley (R-KY), after her husband's incarceration, and Lindy Boggs (D-LA). Among those widows representing districts outside the South, 79.3 percent (17/23) sought election to a second term. The probability of pursuing a career has also increased since 1972, in the wake of the Women's Movement. Most widows (71.8 percent) were elected before 1972. Of the twenty-eight widows who were first elected to the House before 1972, only eleven (39.3 percent) sought a second term. Of the eleven elected since 1972, eight (79.3 percent) pursued a career in the House. Overall, table 3.4 demonstrates that there are differences between careerist and noncareerist widows. As such, the results reveal that there is a systematic and measurable distinction between discrete and static ambition.

Our analysis correctly predicts the decision of widows to seek a second term in thirty-four of thirty-nine cases.[114] Table 3.5 reports the probability that a widow will seek reelection and pursue a career given combinations of the five measures we use.[115] Probabilities equal to or greater than .50 lead to a prediction of static ambition and the widow seeking a second term; entries below .50 lead to a prediction of discrete ambition and retirement. Several important relationships are clear. The first pertains to the historical time period and region. The first row presents the scenarios associated with women elected from the South prior to 1972. The probabilities of seeking a House career are uniformly low. In fact, the only situation that leads to a probability greater than .50 that the widow will run for reelection is the instance where the woman is under sixty years of age, has worked with her husband, and has also accumulated ten years of independent political experience. Outside of the South, the probabilities also remain low, with six of twelve profiles less than .50. In these instances, running for reelection depends upon either substantial experience or working for or with the husband. In fact, table 3.5 highlights the importance of this wife-husband political partnership, which can be seen by comparing the third and fourth columns of the table. There are seven instances in which, all other factors being equal, a political partnership with the husband moves the probability that the widow will run for reelection over the .50 threshold.

The table also highlights the change that has occurred since 1972. In the South, there are four profiles, compared to one in the years before 1972, associated with a probability greater than .50 (less than sixty years old, with either ten years of experience or working with the husband, regardless of experience). Outside the South, the change is even more pronounced. Of the twelve profiles shown in the fourth row of the table, only two have associated probabilities less than .50 (sixty years or older, with less than ten years

---

[114] Palmer and Simon, 2003, 133.

[115] For a complete explanation of this analysis, see Palmer and Simon, 2003. In our statistical model, political experience is measured as a continuous variable, the total number of years that a woman served in political office. We performed the simulation by first combining the variables to form a set of officeholder profiles (e.g., elected before 1972, from the South, did not work with her husband, and held no office independent of her husband). The set of profiles includes all possible combinations of the binary independent variables in tandem with three values of the experience variable (zero, five, ten). This produced a set of forty-eight officeholder profiles. The estimated coefficients of the model were then used to simulate the probability of seeking reelection for each profile. To obtain these probabilities, we used the Clarify suite of programs (a STATA module) developed in Michael Tomz, Jason Wittenberg, and Gary King, *Clarify: Software for Interpreting and Presenting Statistical Results* (Cambridge, Mass.: Harvard University Press, 2001). See also Gary King, Michael Tomz, and Jason Wittenberg, "Making the Most of Statistical Analyses: Improving Interpretation and Presentation," *American Journal of Political Science* 44 (2000): 341–55. The program was set to perform 1,000 simulations for each profile. The probabilities reported in table 3.5 are the average probabilities over the 1,000 simulations.

Table 3.5 The Probability That Congressional Widows Will Seek Reelection to the House

Time Period and Region	Age and Independent Experience	Did Not Work with or for Husband	Worked with or for Husband
1916–1970 South	60 or Older		
	No independent experience	.00	.01
	Five years of experience	.00	.04
	Ten years of experience	.01	.10
	Less Than 60		
	No independent experience	.02	.26
	Five years of experience	.07	.44
	Ten years of experience	.17	*.62*
1916–1970 Non-South	60 or Older		
	No independent experience	.04	.27
	Five years of experience	.08	.44
	Ten years of experience	.17	*.62*
	Less Than 60		
	No independent experience	.30	*.83*
	Five years of experience	*.51*	*.93*
	Ten years of experience	*.71*	*.98*
1972–2004 South	60 or Older		
	No independent experience	.02	.14
	Five years of experience	.04	.27
	Ten years of experience	.11	.44
	Less Than 60		
	No independent experience	.21	*.63*
	Five years of experience	.35	*.77*
	Ten years of experience	*.51*	*.86*
1972–2004 Non-South	60 or Older		
	No independent experience	.18	*.66*
	Five years of experience	.32	*.82*
	Ten years of experience	*.51*	*.92*
	Less Than 60		
	No independent experience	*.74*	*.97*
	Five years of experience	*.87*	*.99*
	Ten years of experience	*.94*	*.99*

Note: The cell entries represent the probability of seeking reelection to the House and were generated using the Clarify program module; Michael Tomz, Jason Wittenberg, and Gary King, *Clarify: Software for Interpreting and Presenting Statistical Results* (Cambridge, Mass.: Harvard University, 2001). The highlighted and italicized probabilities represent values that would generate a prediction that the widow will run for reelection.

of experience and no association with the husband's career). Regardless of age or experience, a partnership with the husband produces probabilities ranging from .66 to virtual certainty. The probability that a nonsouthern widow less than sixty years old who had worked with her husband would run for reelection is .97. In other words, these women will run again and seek a congressional career.

Conclusion

For much of the twentieth century, it was largely assumed that the typical congressional widow was Veronica Boland (D-PA). After the death of her husband in 1942, she ran unopposed in the special election to fill his seat. She held the office for only forty-five days, did not serve on any committees, and did not make any floor speeches.[116] Our analysis shows, however, that she was hardly the quintessential congressional widow. The more typical story is that of Jo Ann Emerson (R-MO), who ran for Congress for the first time at age forty-six. When her husband, Representative Bill Emerson (R-MO), died of lung cancer in 1996, local and national Republican Party leaders asked her to run in the special election to fill his seat. Given the timing of her husband's death, she technically had to run in two races: as a Republican in the special election to fill the remainder of the current term, and as an Independent in the general election because the filing deadline for running in the Republican primary had passed. Although she never held public office, she had extensive political experience, working as a lobbyist on Capitol Hill and as the deputy communications director for the National Republican Congressional Committee. She actually grew up living next door to House Majority Leader Hale Boggs and his family. Cokie Roberts was her babysitter. Her father was executive director for the Republican National Committee. In 2006, she was elected to her sixth term with 72 percent of the vote.[117]

Representative Doris Matsui (D-CA) is the most recent widow to serve in Congress. She provides an opportunity for us to use our analysis to predict whether she would seek reelection. Matsui was elected in March 2005 to succeed her husband, who served for twenty-six years in the House. She was sixty years old when she ran in the special election and won the seat with 69 percent of the vote. Her closest opponent received 8.5 percent of the vote.[118] Although she never held elective office, she was a member of the Clinton administration from 1992 to 1998, serving as the deputy assistant to the president and as deputy director of public liaison in the White

---

[116] Foerstel, 1999, 30.

[117] "2006 Tip Sheets; Missouri House," *National Journal*, http://nationaljournal.com. proxyau.wrlc.org/members/campaign/2006/house/mo.htm (accessed May 13, 2007).

[118] Kevin Yamamura, "Matsui Set to Be Sworn in Today and Cast First Vote as a Congressman's Widow and Washington Veteran," *Sacramento Bee*, March 10, 2005, A3.

House. From 1998 to her election in 2005, she was a lobbyist for a Washington firm that represented medical technology, telecommunications, and financial organizations.[119] Shortly after her swearing in, Ted Gaebler, city manager of Rancho Cordova, emphasized her experience by stating that "nothing about her is a rookie. I am amazed at her comfort and her ease."[120] In the three months before the special election, she raised over $1.1 million. After the campaign, she had $172,000 left, a sizeable war chest compared to other area House incumbents.[121]

Matsui was a sixty-year-old, nonsouthern widow elected after 1970, with thirteen years of independent experience, although none of it was working with her husband. According to table 3.5, the probability that she would run for reelection is .51. Although it is a "close call," our analysis predicts that she would seek reelection. However, she was exactly sixty years of age when she had to make that decision. Were she below that cutoff, the probability that she would run for reelection jumps to .94, near certainty. In either case, our model suggests that she would exhibit static ambition and pursue a career in the House. Ultimately, in the fall of 2006 Representative Matsui did seek reelection and defeated Claire Yan with 71 percent of the vote.

There has not, as of yet, been a congressional widower, although one husband did try. Representative Patsy Mink (D-HI) died on September 28, 2002, a week after easily winning her primary, but two days after the deadline to replace her name on the ballot. She actually won the general election posthumously. At the end of November, a special election was held for the remaining five weeks of her term, with Democrat Ed Case as the victor. Another special election had to be held to fill her two-year term, and Mink's widower, John, ran in a field of forty-three candidates. Case, however, held on to the seat.[122] Prior to 2007, there was only one woman who had been elected after the death of a female member. Representative Nancy Pelosi (D-CA) was elected in a special election following the death of Representative Sala Burton (D-CA). In May of 2007, the first daughter to ever run for her mother's seat announced her candidacy. Representative Juanita Millender-McDonald (D-CA) died of cancer in April. Her daughter, Valerie McDonald, announced she would run for her mother's seat. Although she had never run for office before, she had helped her mother for years as an "informal advisor" and explained that her mother had often encouraged

[119] *Biographical Directory of the United States Congress,* http://bioguide/congress.gov/scripts/biodispaly.pl?index=M0011163 (accessed May 20, 2005).

[120] David Whitney, "Freshman Matsui Learns Life in Congress Is Hectic," *Sacramento Bee,* March 20, 2005, A3.

[121] David Whitney, "Matsui Has Money in Bank for '06 Race," *Sacramento Bee,* April 27, 2005, A3.

[122] B.J. Reyes, "Case Wins Hawaii's 2nd Congressional District," *Associated Press State and Local Wire,* January 5, 2003.

her to run for the seat after she retired.[123] In a crowded primary with eleven Democrats, five of whom were women, McDonald came in a distant third with 9.4 percent of the vote, behind former state representative Laura Richardson, who won the primary with 37.1 percent of the vote, and former state senator Jenny Oropeza, who received 30.9 percent of the vote.[124]

Studying the decision to run for office poses several challenges. Identifying the eligibility pool and those in the pool who considered but decided not to run are quite difficult; there is also the danger of incurring the wrath of Congress. Studying the decisions of congressional widows, however, provides a unique opportunity to assess how women might make the decision to pursue a congressional career. Rather than being a monolithic group, there are clear differences between those who resigned after completing their husband's terms and those who went on to serve multiple terms in the House. Women who are younger when they first obtain their husband's seat are more likely to run for reelection. Prior political experience, especially if they worked in a political partnership with their husband, has a substantial effect on whether they will seek their own congressional careers. Finally, cultural factors play a role. Women from outside the South and those who ran since the advent of the Women's Movement in 1970 are more likely to be careerists. In fact, widows who share all four of these characteristics are almost certain to run again. Over time, congressional widows have come to look more and more like women who run without the benefit of a dead husband—careerists whose objective is long-term service in the House. In this sense, our analysis challenges the conventional stereotype of the congressional widow as a placeholder or demure stand-in.

[123] Gene Maddaus, "Congress a Family Affair?" *Long Beach Press Telegram*, May 12, 2007.

[124] "Special Election Results, United States Representative in Congress, 37th District, Final Canvass," *California Secretary of State*, June 26, 2007. http://www.sos.ca.gov/elections/elections_cd 37.htm (accessed August 4, 2007).

4

Political Ambition and Running for the U.S. Senate and Beyond

While the distinction between discrete and static ambition was the focus of chapter 3, here we examine the distinction between static and progressive ambition. Why do some women pursue a career in the House while others leave the security of their seat and run for higher office? When faced with the opportunity to run for the Senate, do women respond to the same strategic considerations as men?

The objective of those with static ambition is to retain their seats and acquire the influence that comes with long service. Representative Nancy Pelosi (D-CA) is a classic example of a House careerist who has met this goal.[1] Pelosi first came to Congress in June 1987 after winning a special election to fill the vacancy created by the death of Representative Sala Burton (D-CA). During her second term, she served on the Appropriations Committee, one of the most influential committees in the House. In 1992, Pelosi had the opportunity to run for the Senate in California; both Senate seats were available. Senator Alan Cranston had announced his retirement, and Senator Pete Wilson had resigned in January 1991 after he was elected governor. His appointed successor, Republican John Seymour, had to stand for election again in 1992. Pelosi, however, chose not to enter either of the campaigns that ultimately resulted in the election of Democrats Barbara Boxer and Dianne Feinstein. Instead, Pelosi continued to accumulate seniority in the House. She eventually became ranking member of the

---

[1] Pelosi was born into a political family. Her father, Thomas D'Alesandro, was a member of the House from 1939 to 1947. He also served as mayor of Baltimore, as did her brother; Karen Foerstel, *Biographical Dictionary of Congressional Women* (Westport, Conn.: Greenwood Press, 1999), 216.

Appropriations Subcommittee on Foreign Operations.[2] She was then elected minority whip by the Democratic Caucus during the 107th Congress (2001 session) and rose to the position of minority leader in the 108th Congress (2003 session).[3] In 2006, Pelosi was elected to her eleventh term. When the 110th Congress convened on January 4, 2007, she was elected Speaker of the House. Pelosi's career reflects the payoff for those with static ambition; as she gained seniority, she moved into increasingly visible and powerful leadership positions.

In contrast, politicians with progressive ambition attempt to climb the career ladder by running for more desirable and prestigious offices. Progressive ambition is well illustrated by the career of Margaret Chase Smith (R-ME). Smith was a congressional widow who defied the conventional wisdom. Not only did she seek reelection to the House, but she also ran successfully for the Senate and then pursued the very top rung of the American political career ladder, the presidency. After winning her husband's House seat in a special election in 1940, Smith successfully retained her seat in the regular election that fall and was reelected to the House three more times. When Senator Wallace White, the incumbent Republican, retired in 1948, she decided to run for the Senate. She faced three men in the primary and won with more votes than the combined total of all her competitors, and then won the general election. Smith became the first woman elected to the House and then to the Senate.[4] In 1964, during an event at the Women's National Press Club, she announced her candidacy for president. On the campaign trail, she handed out muffins, which generated so much publicity that one of her opponents, Nelson Rockefeller, tried to capitalize on her success by giving out his fudge recipe.[5] Smith became the first woman to have a major party place her name in nomination for president; she won twenty-seven delegates at the Republican National Convention.[6] Her congressional career ended in 1972 at the age of seventy-four, when she lost a close election for her fifth Senate term. Smith returned to Maine, having served in Congress for more than thirty-two years.

---

[2] Foerstel, 1999, 217.

[3] *Biographical Directory of the United States Congress*, http://bioguide.congress.gov/scripts/biodisplay.pl?index=P000197 (accessed June 24, 2005).

[4] During the campaign, her opponents were not above accusing her of causing her husband's divorce from this first wife, despite the fact that Smith met him three years later; Marcy Kaptur, *Women of Congress: A Twentieth-Century Odyssey* (Washington, D.C.: CQ Press, 1996), 89. As a senator, Smith achieved national attention and acclaim for her "Declaration of Conscience" speech on June 1, 1950. From the Senate floor, she castigated Senator Joseph McCarthy for his reckless accusations and the way his committee conducted its investigations of communist influence. In the wake of this speech, stories in the media suggested her as a possible vice president for Dwight Eisenhower; Foerstel, 1999, 253–56.

[5] Kaptur, 1996, 95.

[6] Kaptur, 1996, 95.

Our analysis in this chapter is designed to explain the different career paths followed by Pelosi and Smith. It is important to keep in mind that congressional careerism—the product of static ambition—is a twentieth-century phenomenon. In fact, the movement of women into the electoral arena began when the desire to pursue long careers in the House reached historic highs. As we pointed out in chapter 2, women were first running for Congress just as the political glass ceiling was being set. In this chapter, we show that the women who overcame this barrier to win a seat in the House are as careerist as their male counterparts. In addition, our analysis of progressive ambition demonstrates that, like men, women are strategic when deciding whether to run for the Senate. This decision systematically varies with the cost of running, the probability of winning, the value of a House seat, and whether the woman is a "risk taker." We then use our analysis of progressive ambition to identify those women currently serving in the House who are most likely to run for the Senate in 2008, 2010, and 2012, and speculate about the presidential prospects of those women currently serving in the Senate.

The Decision to Seek Reelection

We showed in chapter 3 that a substantial proportion of congressional widows exhibited static ambition and sought reelection. Is this true of most women who have served in Congress? How often have the women in Congress exhibited discrete, static, and progressive ambition? Table 4.1

Table 4.1 The Political Ambitions of Female Members of the House

Type of Ambition	Number of Women	Percentage
Discrete		
Retired after one or two terms	8	4.6
Static		
Retired after three or more terms	33	19.1
Died after three or more terms	5	2.9
Defeated in primary or general election	49	28.3
Current members who served three or more terms	51	29.5
Total	138	79.8
Progressive		
Ran for Senate	20	11.6
Ran for or appointed to other office	7	4.0
Total	27	15.6

summarizes the service of those women elected to the House between 1916 and 2002.[7] Of the 173 women included in table 4.1, only eight, less than 5 percent, fall into the noncareerist category of discrete ambition. The two best examples of discrete ambition are Isabella Greenway (D-AZ), who retired in 1937 after two terms to spend more time with her family,[8] and Shirley Pettis (D-CA), who also retired after two terms in 1979. The remaining women are, in one sense or another, special cases. For example, Clare Boothe Luce (R-CT) was elected to the House in 1942 and served two terms. During her second term, she battled the emotional trauma caused by the death of her daughter in an automobile accident. In 1946, Luce announced that she would not seek a third term in the House, converted to Catholicism, and returned to her former career as a writer.[9] Jessica Weis (R-NY) withdrew from her third campaign in 1962 because of illness and died of cancer shortly after completing her second term.[10] Blanche Lincoln (D-AR) was elected to the House in 1992 and reelected in 1994. In January 1996, Lincoln announced that she was pregnant with twins and would not run for re-election in November.[11] Lincoln, however, returned to the political arena in November 1998 when she won the open Senate seat vacated by Democrat Dale Bumpers.

The last woman in this category is Representative Enid Greene (R-UT), who announced her retirement approximately two months after Blanche Lincoln, making her the most recent woman to leave office after a short period of service. In 1992, Greene ran for Congress for the first time and narrowly lost in an open-seat race against Democrat Karen Shepherd. During the campaign, given the conservative constituency, Shepherd ran as a moderate, reform-oriented Democrat and emphasized that "she was a wife and mother while Greene was single."[12] Shepherd outspent Greene $617,000 to $446,000.[13] The campaign of 1994 featured a rematch with Greene, now wed to Joseph Waldholtz, running under her married name. Waldholtz exploited the vulnerabilities of Shepherd as a first-term incumbent, particularly her vote for the Clinton tax increase of 1993.[14] This time, Waldholtz

---

[7] Specifically, this group includes all nonwidows elected to the House between 1916 and 2002. Because they have yet to face the decision to run for a third term, women elected in 2004 and 2006 are not included in the count. The tally also includes the twenty widows who, as we showed in chapter 3, exhibited static ambition by seeking an additional term after their initial election to succeed their husbands.

[8] Foerstel, 1999, 108.

[9] *Women in History: Living Vignettes of Notable Women in U.S. History*, http://www.lkwdpl.org/wihohio/luce-cla.htm (accessed June 16, 2005).

[10] Foerstel, 1999, 277–78.

[11] Alan Greenblatt and Jonathan D. Salant, "Retirement: Out with the Old and the New: Myers, Lincoln Will Retire," *CQ Weekly*, January 13, 1996, 102.

[12] Michael Barone and Grant Ujifusa, *Almanac of American Politics, 1994* (Washington, D.C.: National Journal, 1993), 1289.

[13] Barone and Ujifusa, 1993, 1290.

[14] Michael Barone and Grant Ujifusa, *Almanac of American Politics, 1996* (Washington, D.C.: National Journal, 1995), 1350.

won.[15] But the spending in the 1994 campaign far surpassed that of the previous race. Shepherd spent $1 million. Waldholtz spent almost twice that, with an estimated $1.6 million coming from her "own resources." Shortly after her swearing in, she appeared to be a rising Republican star and was awarded a seat on the prestigious House Rules Committee. In March 1995, she announced that she was pregnant. Later that year, her political career collapsed. Her husband, who served as her campaign manager, had embezzled $4 million from her father through a phony real estate assets scheme.[16] A large portion of this money had been funneled into Waldholtz's campaign. In March 1996, at the behest of Republican leaders in Washington, D.C. and Utah, Waldholtz announced that she would not seek a second term in the House.[17] On June 6, 1996, Joseph Waldholtz pleaded guilty in federal district court to numerous tax, campaign, and banking violations.[18] Enid divorced him the same day. Subsequent investigations cleared her of any legal wrongdoing.[19] "She trusted her husband," noted her attorney. "A lot of people trust their spouses."[20]

As table 4.1 shows, these examples of discrete ambition are the exception, not the rule. Three times as many women can be classified as exhibiting progressive ambition. Twenty of these women ran for the Senate and will be discussed later in this chapter. Four women left the House to run for governor. Representative Ella Grasso (D-CT) was elected governor of Connecticut in 1974 and reelected to a second term in 1978. Representative Barbara Kennelly (D-CT) was the Democratic nominee for governor in 1998 but lost her race to Republican John Rowland. Both Representatives Helen Delich Bentley (R-MD) and Jane Harman (D-CA) lost their nomination races for governor, in 1994 and 1998 respectively. In 2000, Harman regained her seat in the House by defeating the incumbent Republican, Steve Kuykendall, who had succeeded her in 1998. In addition, two women left their House seats to run for other offices. In 1978, Representative Yvonne Brathwaite Burke (D-CA) lost her nomination race for California attorney general. Representative Geraldine Ferraro (D-NY) left her house seat to become the first female vice presidential nominee in 1984. This category also includes one appointee: Representative Charlotte Reid (R-IL) resigned her House seat after Richard Nixon selected her to serve on the Federal Communications Commission.

---

[15] This campaign was actually a three-way race and included Merrill Cook, the president of a mining and explosives company.

[16] Michael Barone and Grant Ujifusa, *Almanac of American Politics, 1998* (Washington, D.C.: National Journal, 1997), 1422; and Foerstel, 1999, 106–7.

[17] Barone and Ujifusa, 1997, 1422.

[18] Dennis Roddy, "Admission of Guilt: Waldholtz Admits Financial Violations, Apologizes to All but Ex-Wife," *Pittsburgh Post Gazette*, June 6, 1996, A6.

[19] Foerstel, 1999, 107.

[20] Roddy, 1996, A6.

Finally, table 4.1 shows that the largest category is static ambition. Nearly 80 percent of the women elected to the House sought long-term careers. This includes thirty-eight women who retired or died after serving three or more terms, and fifty-one women in the 110th Congress (2007 session) who have already been elected to three or more terms. An additional forty-nine women attempted to pursue careers but suffered electoral defeat. The desire for long careers among women in the House is now the norm.

Examining those who have served "super careers," twenty years or more in the House, is also instructive. Representative John Dingell (D-MI) currently holds the record for longest consecutive service, fifty-one years.[21] The longest serving woman was Edith Nourse Rogers (R-MA), who was a House member for thirty-six years after being elected in 1925. As expected, among men, super careers have increased over the past one hundred years. In 1917, corresponding with our earlier measures of careerism, there were only twenty-six men, 6.0 percent, who had served for ten or more terms in the House. In 1971, just before the number of women in Congress began to rise, there were eighty-seven men, 20.0 percent, who had served for ten or more terms in the House.[22] During the 110th Congress (2007 session), there were seventy men, but only five women, who had served for ten or more terms. As table 4.2 shows, few women have enjoyed the opportunity for the super career. In fact, in the history of Congress only sixteen women have served ten or more terms. In the 110th Congress (2007 session), Representative Marcy Kaptur (D-OH) held the title of most senior woman, serving thirteen terms. The paucity of super careers among women is, however, not all that surprising, given that 45 percent of the careerist women to serve in the House were elected in 1992 or later. Among the women serving in the 110th Congress (2007 session), 90 percent (64/71) were elected between 1992 and 2006.

The House committee leadership in the 110th Congress (2007 session) illustrates the value of lengthy careers most dramatically. Among all twenty-two Democratic chairs of the standing House committees, the average number of terms served is 13.7. Among the Republicans who are ranking members on full committees, the average length of service is ten terms. At the outset of the 110th Congress, four female Democrats served as chairs of full committees; their average length of service was 7.5 terms.[23] Additionally, fourteen Democratic women chaired subcommittees in the House with an average of 6.4 terms. On the Republican side, Ileana Ros-Lehtinen, now in

---

[21] Mildred Amer, *Membership of the 110th Congress: A Profile* (Washington, D.C.: Congressional Research Service, 2007), 5.

[22] Charles Bullock, "House Careerists: Changing Patterns of Longevity and Attrition," *American Political Science Review* 66 (1972): 1295–300.

[23] "CQ's Guide to the Committees," *CQ Weekly*, April 16, 2007. This includes Representative Juanita Millender-McDonald (CA), who served as the Chair of the House Administration Committee until her death in April, 2007. She was replaced by Representative Robert Brady (D-PA); Susan Ferrechio, "Brady to Chair House Administration Panel," *CQ Weekly*, May 28, 2007, 1616.

Table 4.2 Women Who Have Served Ten or More Terms in the House

Name	Year First Elected	Terms
Mary Teresa Norton (D-NJ)	1924	13
Edith Nourse Rogers (R-MA)	1925	18
Frances Bolton (R-OH)	1940	15
Leonor Sullivan (D-MO)	1952	12
Edith Green (D-OR)	1954	10
Martha Griffiths (D-MI)	1954	10
Patricia Schroeder (D-CO)	1972	12
Cardiss Collins (D-IL)	1972	12
Marilyn Lloyd (D-MD)	1974	10
Margaret Roukema (R-NJ)	1980	11
Nancy Johnson (R-CT)	1982	12
Marcy Kaptur (D-OH)	1982	13*
Louise Slaughter (D-NY)	1986	11*
Nancy Pelosi (D-CA)	1987	11*
Nita Lowey (D-NY)	1988	10*
Ileana Ros-Lehtinen (R-FL)	1989	10*

*Currently serving in the 110th Congress (2007 session).

her tenth term, is the only woman who served as a ranking member of a full committee. Among the seven Republican women who were ranking members of subcommittees, the average length of service is 4.3 terms.

All of this suggests that the "threshold" for moving into the leadership structure is roughly five terms, or ten years, of service. It also demonstrates that women in the House are as careerist as their male counterparts.

The Decision to Run for Higher Office: The Lure of the Senate

What makes a seat in the Senate attractive to a House member? Why is the Senate considered a "higher step" on the political career ladder? As a smaller chamber whose members are accountable to a statewide electorate, a seat in the Senate is perceived as more prestigious. As an institution, the Senate is less hierarchical. Given the tradition of the filibuster, individual senators have a great deal of power. Not only is there an ethic of "one among equals," but authority within the committee system is more dispersed.[24] Unlike House members, senators need not wait ten years to acquire a position of influence on a committee. In addition, the Senate is less rule-bound than the

---

[24] Lewis Froman, *The Congressional Process* (Boston: Little Brown, 1967); and Walter Oleszek, *Congressional Procedures and the Policy Process*, 6th ed. (Washington, D.C.: CQ Press, 2004).

House. The Senate frequently operates on the basis of unanimous consent agreements so that individual members, regardless of seniority, are given influence in structuring the agenda. Fewer restrictions on amendments and the absence of a germaneness rule in floor proceedings also provide greater opportunities for creative legislating.[25]

While the Senate may be more attractive to ambitious politicians, campaigning and winning a seat are more difficult. Campaigns for the Senate have to reach a much broader constituency and require a shift from "retail politics," cultivating a constituency through personal, one-on-one contact, to "wholesale politics," attracting media attention, continuous fundraising, and running a media campaign.[26] In fact, many House members who ran for Senate have lamented how they missed the intimacy and familiarity of their House district campaigns.[27] As Representative James Abourezk (D-SD), who served in both the House and Senate, explained, "House members have a good sense of what their district is. Senators have a harder time getting a handle on a state."[28]

Moreover, fundraising for a Senate race can be daunting. The average cost of running for the Senate in 2006 was $3.3 million.[29] In the 2006 election cycle, four of the ten most expensive Senate races involved female candidates. Leading the pack was the New York race. In a financial "show of force," Senator Hillary Clinton, the incumbent Democrat, spent $40.8 million defeating Republican John Spencer, who spent $5.7 million.[30] In Missouri, Democratic nominee Claire McCaskill defeated the Republican incumbent, Senator Jim Thune, despite being outspent $23.7 to $16.3 million.[31] Incumbent Senator Maria Cantwell (D-WA) spent $16.7 million in her reelection

---

[25] "Germaneness" requires that amendments be related to the legislation. For example, a school prayer amendment to the ERA is not germane. See for example Oleszek, 2004; and Barbara Sinclair, *Unorthodox Lawmaking* (Washington, D.C.: CQ Press, 1997).

[26] See for example Ross Baker, *House and Senate*, 2nd ed. (New York: W.W. Norton, 1995), 49–50; and Richard Fenno, *Senators on the Campaign Trail* (Norman: University of Oklahoma Press, 1996).

[27] Baker, 1995, 105–6.

[28] Baker, 1995, 115.

[29] Open Secrets, "2006 Election Overview: Stats at a Glance," http://opensecrets.org/overview/stats.asp?cycle=2006 (accessed May 30, 2007).

[30] Open Secrets, "2006 Race: New York Senate," http://opensecrets.org/races/summary.asp?cycle=2006&id=NYS1 (accessed May 30, 2007). The most expensive race in 2004 was the successful effort by Republican John Thune to unseat incumbent Democrat Tom Daschle, the Senate minority leader. The combined cost of the campaign was over $36 million in a state with only 750,000 people. The candidates spent $92.04 per vote; Open Secrets, "2004 Electiom Overview: Stats at Glance," http://opensecrets.org/races/summary.asp?id=SDS1&cycle=2004 (accessed May 30, 2007). The most expensive Senate race in history was the 2000 campaign of Democrat Jon Corzine in New Jersey. He raised and spent over $63 million, the vast majority of which came from his personal fortune, and defeated his Republican opponent, Bob Franks, who raised and spent $6.5 million; Open Secrets, "New Jersey Senate Race: 2000 Campaign Money Profile," http://www.opensecrets.org/races/summary.asp?ID=NJS1&Cycle=2000 (accessed June 17, 2005).

[31] Open Secrets, "2006 Race: Missouri Senate," http://opensecrets.org/races/summary.asp?cycle=2006&id=MOS2 (accessed May 30, 2007).

campaign while her Republican opponent, Michael McGavick, spent $10.8 million.[32] Finally, Republican House member Katherine Harris spent $8.7 million in her ill-fated attempt to unseat Democratic incumbent Senator Bill Nelson, who spent $16.7 million.[33] As these examples suggest, the path to the Senate requires the ability to raise substantial funds.

In chapter 2, we showed that, for many years, the political career path to the Senate for women was almost exclusively through appointment after a death or unscheduled vacancy. Overall, of the thirty-three women who served in the Senate, fifteen were interim appointees; only two of these fifteen senators, Hattie Caraway (D-AR) and Maurine Neuberger (D-OR), were subsequently elected. Table 4.3 lists the twenty women who won election to the Senate, their prior political experience, and the length of their service.

As noted earlier, the first nonwidow elected to the Senate was Margaret Chase Smith in 1948. The next woman, Nancy Landon Kassebaum (R-KS), would not be elected until 1978, thirty years after Smith's initial Senate campaign. Kassebaum is among the least experienced of the women elected to the Senate. She had only two years of nonelective experience on the Kansas governmental ethics commission and had only two years of elective experience on a local school board.[34] Kassebaum did have the advantage of name recognition and the tinge of political celebrity. She was the daughter of Alfred Landon, former governor of Kansas and Republican nominee for president in 1936. This family connection proved useful in the crowded 1978 Senate primary field that included eight men and another woman, future Representative Jan Meyers. Kassebaum won the Republican primary with 31 percent of the vote and easily defeated her Democratic opponent in the general election.[35]

Very few women came to the Senate without prior political experience. The Senate was the first elective office for only three women. Although she never held elective office, Susan Collins (R-ME) gained twenty years of nonelective experience as a congressional staffer. She worked on the staff of Senator William Cohen (R-ME) from 1975 to 1987 and rose to the position of staff director of the Senate Governmental Affairs Subcommittee on the Oversight of Government Management.[36] In addition to holding several administrative positions in Maine, Collins also won the Republican nomination for governor in 1994 but was defeated in the general election.

---

[32] Open Secrets, "2006 Race: Washington Senate," http://opensecrets.org/races/summary.asp?cycle=2006&id=WAS1 (accessed May 30, 2007).

[33] Open Secrets, "2006 Race: Florida Senate," http://opensecrets.org/races/summary.asp?cycle=2006&id=FLS1 (accessed May 30, 2007).

[34] Foerstel, 1999, 143.

[35] Michael Barone, Grant Ujifusa, and Douglas Matthews, *Almanac of American Politics, 1980* (New York: E. P. Dutton, 1979), 318.

[36] *Biographical Directory of Congress*, http://bioguide.congress.gov/scripts/biodisplay.pl?index=C001035 (accessed June 13, 2005).

Table 4.3 Women Elected to the Senate

Name	Prior Experience: Nonelective	Prior Experience: Elective	Terms in the House	Dates of Senate Service
Margaret Chase Smith (R-ME)	4 years	9 years	4	1949–1973
Nancy Landon Kassebaum (R-KS)	2 years	2 years	0	1979–1997
Paula Hawkins (R-FL)	2 years	8 years	0	1981–1987
Barbara Mikulski (D-MD)	None	16 years	5	1987–present
Dianne Feinstein (D-CA)	6 years	18 years	0	1993–present
Barbara Boxer (D-CA)	2 years	16 years	5	1993–present
Carol Moseley Braun (D-IL)	9 years	11 years[a]	0	1993–1999
Kay Bailey Hutchison (R-TX)	3 years	8 years[a, b]	0	1993–present
Patty Murray (D-WA)	6 years	8 years[a]	0	1993–present
Olympia Snowe (R-ME)	4 years	22 years[a]	8	1995–present
Mary Landrieu (D-LA)	None	16 years[a, b]	0	1997–present
Susan Collins (R-ME)	20 years	None	0	1997–present
Blanche Lincoln (D-AR)	3 years	4 years	2	1999–present
Debbie Stabenow (D-MI)	None	24 years[a]	2	2001–present
Hillary Rodham Clinton (D-NY)	18 years	None	0	2001–present
Maria Cantwell (D-WA)	None	9 years[a]	1	2001–present
Lisa Murkowski (R-AK)	5 years	4 years[a]	0	2002–present
Elizabeth Dole (R-NC)	7 years	None	0	2003–present
Amy Klobuchar (D-MN)	0 years	8 years	0	2007–present
Claire McCaskill (D-MO)	0 years	20 years[a, b]	0	2007–present

[a]Service includes election to state legislature.
[b]Service includes election to statewide office.

Hillary Clinton and Elizabeth Dole are both part of contemporary "power couples" and were far from inexperienced. Hillary Clinton served as legal counsel to the House Judiciary Committee during the impeachment proceedings against President Richard Nixon in 1974. She served as first lady of Arkansas for ten years and the first lady of the United States for eight years. As first lady, she headed the administration's task force on health care reform and played a prominent role in shaping the domestic policy agenda of the administration.[37] Elizabeth Dole served as a cabinet member in two presidential administrations. From 1983 to 1987, she was secretary of transportation in the Reagan administration and served in the Bush administration as secretary of labor from 1989 to 1990. In 1999, she campaigned for the Republican presidential nomination but withdrew before the start of the primary season in 2000.[38] Both Clinton and Dole entered their Senate races with widespread name recognition. Clinton defeated four-term House incumbent Rick Lazio (R-NY), and Dole defeated Erskine Bowles, a former chief of staff in the Clinton administration.

Table 4.3 reveals that the eighteen women elected to the Senate since 1980 had substantial prior experience. Collectively, these women accumulated 277 years of political experience before entering the Senate, with an average of 15.4 years. Fifteen of the eighteen served in elective office. The average time in elective office among the fifteen was 12.8 years. Three senators, Olympia Snowe (R-ME), Debbie Stabenow (D-MI), and Maria Cantwell (D-WA), followed the classic pattern of ambition, moving from the state legislature to the U.S. House and then to the Senate.[39] Overall, seven women senators previously served in the U.S. House. What prompted these women to run? Can we predict which female House members will run for the Senate and exhibit progressive ambition?

Understanding Progressive Ambition

In chapter 3, we focused upon the widows of the House to show that there were systematic differences between those who retired and those who sought a career, and thereby illustrated the distinction between discrete and static ambition. Having shown in this chapter that the women of the House are as careerist as their male counterparts, we now come to the question of progressive ambition, the decision to forsake one office to run for a higher and more prestigious position. Here, we build upon the work of political scientist David Rohde. Refining Schlesinger's distinction between static and

---

[37] Bob Woodward, *The Agenda: Inside the Clinton White House* (New York: Simon & Schuster, 1994).

[38] Harold Stanley and Richard Niemi, *Vital Statistics on American Politics 2003–2004* (Washington, D.C.: CQ Press, 2003), 67.

[39] Cantwell's path, however, was not continuous. She was elected to the House in 1992 but defeated for reelection in the 2nd District of Washington in 1994 by Rick White. In 2000, she defeated incumbent Slade Gorton to win her Senate seat.

progressive ambition, Rohde assumes that almost all members of the House possess progressive ambition in the following sense: if a member of the House, "on his first day of service, were offered a Senate seat . . . without cost or risk, he would take it."[40] In other words, all things being equal, most politicians would prefer advancing to a higher office. There are, however, costs and risks. In a given election cycle, House members exhibit static ambition not only because they value their current office, but also because they perceive the costs of running and the risks to their political career as too high. The question then becomes: under what conditions will members forsake a career in the House and run for the Senate?

The Opportunity to Run

First and foremost, the decision to run for the Senate is not an arbitrary choice made by members of the House. Rather, the strategic calculations that underlie this choice depend on whether there is an *opportunity to run*. The concept of opportunity is critical to understanding the movement of politicians through the hierarchy of offices. Opportunities are a function of the party of the incumbent and the electoral calendar: a House member has an opportunity to run for the Senate when there is a scheduled election that involves an incumbent of the opposition party seeking reelection or an open seat vacated by an incumbent of either party. We assume that no opportunity exists when an incumbent of the House member's own party stands for reelection to the Senate. In this situation, the member must challenge the incumbent senator in a primary, must risk alienating party members by instigating an intraparty dispute, and, as we pointed out in chapter 2, would most likely lose. In addition, in order to run for the Senate, House members must surrender their seats.[41] This requires that members consider the costs of giving up their seats as well as the probability of winning the Senate election.

Based on these criteria, we calculated the number of opportunities for the 182 careerist women who were elected to the House between 1916 and 2004.

---

[40] David Rohde, "Risk-Bearing and Progressive Ambition: The Case of Members of the United States House of Representatives," *American Journal of Political Science* 23 (1979): 1–26. Rohde also explores House members who consider running for governor. Our analysis focuses solely on the Senate. As noted earlier, there have only been four women who left the House to run for governor. See also Paul Hain, Philip Roeder, and Manuel Avalos, "Risk and Progressive Candidacies: An Extension of Rohde's Model," *American Journal of Political Science* 25 (1981): 188–92; Paul Brace, "Progressive Ambition in the House: A Probabilistic Approach," *Journal of Politics* 46 (1984): 556–71; and Gary Copeland, "Choosing to Run: Why House Members Seek Election to the Senate," *Legislative Studies Quarterly* 14 (1989): 549–65.

[41] There is one qualification in our definition of "opportunity." If a woman is elected to the House in a special election at any time before a regularly scheduled election (e.g., in March of an election year), the subsequent general election in November, regardless of conditions, is not counted as an opportunity. As Rohde notes, "[B]ecause of the necessity of planning ahead for a statewide race, such congressmen are almost precluded from running and, in fact, no such member did run"; Rohde, 1979, 14.

During this period, the opportunities to run for a Senate seat varied widely. Seventy of the women who served in the House, over one-third, had no opportunity to run for the Senate. In fact, among these seventy, there were twenty-one women who served in the House for ten years or more without an opportunity. Among the remaining women, the number of opportunities ranged from one to nine. Fourteen female House members had four or more opportunities to run over the course of their careers. The opportunity "leaders" were Mary Teresa Norton (D-NJ), with nine opportunities over her thirteen-term career; Edith Nourse Rogers (R-MA), with eight opportunities in eighteen terms; both Marge Roukema (R-NJ; eleven terms) and Nancy Johnson (R-CT; twelve terms) had seven opportunities over the course of their respective careers.

According to Rohde, when faced with an opportunity to run, a member of the House will make a strategic calculation about whether to give up the House seat and seek election to the Senate. This decision will be a function of four factors: (1) the costs of running, (2) the probability of winning, (3) the value of the member's current office, and (4) whether the member is a risk taker.[42]

Costs of Running

As a general indicator of the costs of running, we use the size of the state, which captures several challenges that House members face when running for the Senate. The size of the state reflects the coincidence of House and Senate constituencies; the smaller the state, the more a House district over- laps with the target electorate in a Senate race. The more overlap there is, the more the character and strategy of the campaigns will be similar and the jump from the House to the Senate is easier. In fact, when House members run for the Senate in states with only one or two congressional districts, they use a virtually duplicate campaign strategy.[43] But for House members from large, populous states, running for the Senate requires a "monumental change" in campaign style and tactics in order to reach a larger audience.[44] Like Rohde, we use the number of congressional districts in a state as a measure of size. Small states are those with three or fewer congressional districts, while large states are those with twenty-two or more congressional districts.

Our data show that the opportunities to run are distributed in roughly the same proportion as the women elected from states of different size. Almost 13 percent of the careerist women elected to the House hailed from states with three or fewer congressional districts; 12.5 percent of all

---

[42] Rohde, 1979, 5–12.
[43] Baker, 1995, 106.
[44] Baker, 1995, 105.

opportunities to run occurred in these small states. Similarly, 35.7 percent of the careerist women were elected from large states; large states accounted for 34.5 percent of the opportunities. Our expectation is that the probability of running for a Senate seat, given the opportunity, will vary inversely with the size of the state. The smaller the state, the more likely it is the female House member will run for the Senate.

Probability of Winning

The probability of winning is influenced by incumbency as well as party. Because incumbents are virtually assured reelection, the opportunity to run in an open seat is the most desirable because this presents the highest chance of winning. The next best scenario would be to run against a marginal incumbent of the opposition party. Typically, marginal incumbents are perceived to be vulnerable and often make fundraising by the opposition party easier. Running against a safe incumbent is the least desirable. In our data, 38 percent of the opportunities occurred in open-seat elections; 32.9 percent were in situations where a marginal incumbent, defined as an incumbent who won the previous election with less than 55 percent of the vote, was seeking reelection; and 29 percent involved races in which the opponent was a safe incumbent. Given an opportunity, we expect that female House members will be more likely to run for the Senate in open-seat elections and least likely to run in elections with a safe incumbent.

Value of the Member's Current Office

The value of a House seat to its current occupant is largely determined by seniority. In general, this value grows as the member serves more terms and as both knowledge of the policy process and the internal influence of the member increase. As noted earlier, House members typically rise to a position of influence in the committee system after five terms. Once this point is reached, the House seat substantially increases in value as the member moves upward in the leadership hierarchy. As this occurs, there are greater costs in giving up the House seat that make the Senate seat less attractive. Therefore, House members who have served five or more terms are going to value their seats more than House members who are midcareer. We define "midcareer" members as those who have served between two and five terms during the year in which the opportunity to run occurs. Of the 255 opportunities to run in our data, 57.6 percent (147) fell to those at midcareer. We expect, then, that the women most likely to run for the Senate are House members at midcareer.

Risk Takers

Finally, the decision to run for the Senate depends on the House member's willingness to take risks. As one House member who ran for the Senate put it, "The Senate seat is by definition more precarious politically than the average House seat."[45] We recognize that any campaign for office requires candidates to put a great deal at risk, but the degree of risk is relative. As Rohde explains, "[I]f two House members are presented with similar opportunities to seek higher office, and one is a 'risk taker' and the other is not, then the 'risk taker' will have a greater probability of running for higher office than the other."[46]

Risk taking focuses upon the circumstances in which a member *first* runs, successfully or unsuccessfully, for a seat in the Congress. Risk takers are defined as those who first run for Congress in a campaign where the probability of winning is low. These are races where a member ran (1) against an incumbent of her own party for the nomination in a primary, (2) against an incumbent of the opposition party in the general election, or (3) in an open district where the opposition party had a secure hold on the district.[47] Of the 182 female careerists in the House, sixty-eight, 37.4 percent, are classified as risk takers. In their first campaign for Congress, thirty-eight challenged incumbents in the general election, twelve challenged incumbents of their own party in the primary, and eighteen ran for open seats that previously were secure for the opposition party. Of the sixty-eight risk takers, however, twenty-six, 38.2 percent, had no opportunity to run for the Senate during their House careers. Among those with opportunities, we expect that risk takers will run for the Senate in proportionally greater numbers than non-risk takers.

Explaining Progressive Ambition

There has been little attention devoted to studying the decisions made by female members of the House to run for the Senate.[48] Our core proposition is that women behave in a strategic manner and, therefore, the decisions of women serving in the House to seek a seat in the Senate will be subject to the same systematic influences identified by Rohde. The likelihood that a female member of the House will run for the Senate when she has the opportunity increases when she comes from a small state, the probability of winning is

---

[45] Baker, 1995, 114.

[46] Rohde, 1979, 12.

[47] This is the definition employed by Rohde, 1979. In open districts where the opposition party held the seat, a secure hold is determined by averaging the proportion of the two-party vote won in the three previous elections. By Rohde's definition, those districts where the opposition party averaged 57 percent of the vote or more are labeled "secure."

[48] Rohde's analysis covers the years from 1954 to 1974. Of the 1,463 opportunities examined, only 43 involved an opportunity for a female member to run for the Senate.

high, she is midcareer, and she is a risk taker. Of the 255 opportunities in our data set, there were twenty cases, 7.8 percent, when a female House member actually ran for the Senate. Clearly, this is a "rare event."[49] The rarity of running for the Senate, however, is not confined to women. Rohde's analysis covered the years of 1954 to 1974. Of the 1,463 opportunities for House members to run for a Senate seat, only eighty-five members, about 6 percent, chose to run.[50] Thus, it appears that, overall, women are about as likely as men to pursue the Senate.

As table 4.4 shows, the size of the state is related to the likelihood that a woman will run for the Senate. The proportion of opportunities resulting in a bid for the Senate are 21.9 percent (7/32) in small states and 5.8 percent (13/223) in medium and large states. Two of the candidacies come from the state of Maine. Margaret Chase Smith (R-ME) served in the House when the state had three congressional districts, and Olympia Snowe later served as one of the state's two representatives when she ran for the Senate. The other small state candidates include Representatives Jeannette Rankin, a Republican from Montana; Claudine Schneider, a Republican from Rhode Island; Gracie Pfost, a Democrat from Idaho; and Patsy Mink, a Democrat, and Patricia Saiki, a Republican, both from Hawaii.

The decision to run for the Senate is also clearly based on the probability of winning. The proportion of women pursuing an opportunity is the highest when the odds of winning are the highest, 10.3 percent (10/97) in open-seat contests and 9.5 percent (8/84) in races with a marginal incumbent. Only 2.7 percent of female House members ran for the Senate in states with a safe incumbent; two women out of seventy-four chose to exercise their opportunity when a safe incumbent of the opposition party stood for reelection, Representatives Bobbi Fiedler (R-CA) and Claudine Schneider (R-RI). In 1986, with Democrat incumbent Senator Alan Cranston standing for reelection, Fiedler gave up her House seat to enter the Republican primary. Fiedler was a single-issue candidate who rose in politics as an opponent of busing. She was first elected to the House in 1980, defeating a Democrat incumbent, James Corman.[51] In 1986, she was the only woman among the thirteen candidates seeking the Republican nomination. Fiedler finished in fourth place in a field of candidates that included Arthur Laffer,

---

[49] In addition to its substantive meaning, the term has statistical consequences. The methodological requirements for working with rare events are fully addressed in Palmer and Simon, "Political Ambition and Women in the U.S. House of Representatives, 1916–2000," *Political Research Quarterly* 56 (2003): 127–38. We use three alternative techniques to estimate the statistical model: a probit, a logit, and a logit model adjusted for rare events. See Gary King and Langche Zeng, "Logistic Regression in Rare Events Data," *Political Analysis* 9 (2001): 1–27; and Michael Tomz, Gary King, and Langche Zeng, *RELOGIT: Rare Events Logistical Regression, Version 1.1* (Cambridge, Mass.: Harvard University Press, 1999). The results of estimating these models are consistent with the descriptive statistics reported here.

[50] Rohde, 1979, 18.

[51] Michael Barone and Grant Ujifusa, *Almanac of American Politics, 1986* (Washington, D.C.: National Journal, 1985).

Table 4.4 Progressive Ambition among Female Incumbents in the House

	Percentage of Opportunities in Which Female House Members Ran for the Senate
Cost of Running	
Small state	21.9%
	(7/32)
Medium or large state	5.8%
	(13/223)
Probability of Winning	
Open seat	10.3%
	(10/97)
Marginal incumbent of opposition party	9.5%
	(8/84)
Safe incumbent of opposition party	2.7%
	(2/74)
Value of House Seat	
Midcareer (2–5 terms)	10.2%
	(15/147)
Early or late career	4.6%
	(5/108)
Risk Taking	
Member is a risk taker	11.5%
	(12/104)
Member is not a risk taker	5.3%
	(8/1151)

the advocate of supply-side economics, and Eldridge Cleaver, a former Black Panther and author of *Soul on Ice*.[52] Schneider, serving her fifth term in the House, ran unopposed for the Republican nomination for the Senate in 1990. In November, she faced Senator Claiborne Pell, the incumbent Democrat seeking his sixth term. In what was described as an "exquisitely polite race," Pell defeated Schneider, 62 to 38 percent.[53]

Table 4.4 also shows that the value of the House seat influences the decision to run for the Senate. More than twice as many women who were

---

[52] Jay Matthews, "California's GOP Primary a Free-for-All," *Washington Post,* June 1, 1986, A8; and Eldridge Cleaver, *Soul on Ice* (New York: McGraw-Hill, 1968).
[53] Michael Barone and Grant Ujifusa, *Almanac of American Politics, 1992* (Washington, D.C.: National Journal, 1991), 1103.

midcareer, 10.2 percent, acted on the opportunity to run for the Senate compared to those in their first terms or serving six or more terms, only 4.6 percent. For example, in 1980, Representative Elizabeth Holtzman (D-NY), after serving in the House for four terms, ran for the Senate with the intention of challenging incumbent Republican Jacob Javits, who was seeking his fifth term. The field of Democratic candidates included John Lindsay, a former Republican mayor of New York who switched parties, and Bess Meyerson, a former Miss America and longtime panelist on the television quiz show, *I've Got a Secret*.[54] While Holtzman handily won the Democratic primary, Javits, among the most liberal Republicans in the U.S. Senate, was defeated in the Republican primary by Alfonse D'Amato, a township supervisor and functionary in the Nassau County Republican Party.[55] Javits, however, won the nomination of the New York Liberal Party. As a result, voters in New York could choose among three candidates: the Democrat Holtzman, the Republican D'Amato, and Javits, now listed on the ballot as the candidate for the Liberal Party. In November, D'Amato narrowly defeated Holtzman, 45 to 44 percent. The difference in the contest was Javits; he won over 660,000 votes. Many of these Javits voters probably would have supported Holtzman over D'Amato in a two-candidate race.[56]

It is easy to understand why more senior women did not give up their seats in the House to run for the Senate. For example, when faced with the opportunity to run in 1972, Representative Martha Griffiths (D-MI) was the fourth ranking member of the House Ways and Means Committee. Despite several opportunities during her career, Representative Patricia Schroeder (D-CO) chose to maintain her position as chair of the Armed Services Subcommittee on Military Installations and Facilities.[57] Republican women made similar decisions after their party captured control of the House in 1994, including Representative Marge Roukema (R-NJ), who chaired the Subcommittee on Financial Institutions and Consumer Credit of the House Banking and Financial Services Committee,[58] and Representative Nancy Johnson (R-CT), a high-ranking member of the Ways and Means Committee who chaired its Subcommittee on Health.[59]

Finally, risk taking exerts a noticeable impact on the decision to run. Among those classified as risk takers, 11.5 percent (12/104) of the opportunities resulted in a run for the Senate. The percentage for non–risk takers was less than half, 5.3 percent (8/151). The behavior of risk takers is well

---

[54] See http://bess-myerson.biography.ms (accessed June 20, 2005).
[55] Alan Ehrenhart, ed., *Politics in America, 1982* (Washington, D.C.: CQ Press, 1981), 803.
[56] Ehrenhart, 1981, 803.
[57] Michael Barone and Grant Ujifusa, *Almanac of American Politics, 1990* (Washington, D.C.: National Journal, 1989), 196.
[58] Barone and Ujifusa, 1995, 860.
[59] Michael Barone and Richard Cohen, *Almanac of American Politics, 2004* (Washington, D.C.: National Journal, 2003), 353.

illustrated by the career of Debbie Stabenow (D-MI). After a long career in the Michigan state legislature, Stabenow ran for the House for the first time in 1996 by challenging and defeating a Republican incumbent, Representative Dick Chrysler. After two terms in the House, she decided to run for Senate, once again taking on a Republican incumbent. In 2000, Stabenow won an uncontested Democratic primary and challenged Senator Spencer Abraham. Despite being outspent $13 million to $7.9 million, Stabenow defeated Abraham, winning 50.5 percent of the vote.[60]

Overall, table 4.4 shows that each of our four expectations is met. The decision to run for the Senate is a strategic calculation based on the costs of running, the probability of winning, the value of the member's House seat, and whether the member is a risk taker. Thus, the difference between static and progressive ambition among the women in the House is systematic and predictable. Table 4.5 summarizes the electoral fate of those sitting female House members who gave up their seats to run for the Senate.[61] Four women were defeated in their party's primary, ten won their party's nomination but lost in the general election, and five were elected to the Senate.

The list includes several campaigns that illustrate the intensity and, at times, nasty character of Senate elections. For example, the 1950 contest for the open Senate seat in California ranks as one of the most unusual and bitter campaigns in modern history. The contest featured two members of California's delegation to the House, Democrat Helen Gahagan Douglas, first elected in 1944, and Republican Richard Nixon, first elected in 1946. Nixon had become a national figure through his service on the House Un-American Activities Committee and the celebrated conspiracy and perjury investigation of former State Department official Alger Hiss.[62] The campaign themes emerged during the primary season, when Manchester Boddy, the publisher of the *Los Angeles Daily News* and Douglas's opponent in the Democratic primary, charged her with being "part of a small subversive clique of red-hots" and giving "comfort to the Soviet tyranny."[63] In spite of these attacks, Douglas defeated Boddy, but the divisive Democratic contest provided Nixon with a clear strategy. Using rhetoric that previously appeared in the California newspapers, Nixon commonly referred to Douglas as the "Pink Lady."[64] His campaign organization distributed "the

---

[60] Barone and Cohen, 2003, 815–17.

[61] There are two other women who have served in both the House and Senate, but they were not sitting House members when they ran for the Senate. Blanche Lincoln (D-AR) served in the House from 1992 to 1996; she opted not to run for the House to retain her seat in 1996 because she was pregnant with twins. She ran for the Senate in 1998. Maria Cantwell (D-WA) was elected to the House in 1992 and was defeated in her 1994 reelection bid. She ran for the Senate in 2000.

[62] Stephen Ambrose, *Nixon: The Education of a Politician, 1913–1962* (New York: Simon & Schuster, 1987), 166–96.

[63] Ambrose, 1987, 210.

[64] Greg Mitchell, *Tricky Dick and the Pink Lady: Richard Nixon vs. Helen Gahagan Douglas— Sexual Politics and the Red Scare, 1950* (New York: Random House, 1998).

Table 4.5 Sitting Female House Members Who Ran for Senate

Name	Year	Outcome
Jeannette Rankin (R-MT)	1918	Lost primary to Oscar Lanstrum
Ruth Hanna McCormick (R-IL)	1930	Lost general to James Lewis
Margaret Chase Smith (R-ME)	1948	**Elected to the Senate**
Helen Gahagan Douglas (D-CA)	1950	Lost general to Richard Nixon
Gracie Pfost (D-ID)	1962	Lost general to Len Jordan
Patsy Mink (D-HI)	1976	Lost primary to Spark Matsunaga
Bella Abzug (D-NY)	1976	Lost primary to Patrick Moynihan
Elizabeth Holtzman (D-NY)	1980	Lost general to Alfonse D'Amato
Millicent Fenwick (D-NJ)	1982	Lost general to Frank Lautenberg
Barbara Mikulski (D-MD)	1986	**Elected to the Senate**
Bobbi Fiedler (R-CA)	1986	Lost primary to Ed Zschau
Lynn Martin (R-IL)	1990	Lost general to Paul Simon
Claudine Schneider (R-RI)	1990	Lost general to Claiborne Pell
Patricia Saiki (R-HI)	1990	Lost general to Daniel Akaka
Barbara Boxer (D-CA)	1992	**Elected to the Senate**
Olympia Snowe (R-ME)	1994	**Elected to the Senate**
Linda Smith (R-WA)	1998	Lost general to Patty Murray
Debbie Stabenow (D-MI)	2000	**Elected to the Senate**
Denise Majette (D-GA)	2004	Lost general to Johnny Isakson
Katherine Harris (R-FL)	2006	Lost general to Bill Nelson

pink sheet," fliers critical of Douglas's voting record that were printed on pink paper.[65] In stump speeches, Nixon regularly criticized Douglas by asserting that she was "pink right down to her underwear."[66] For her part, Douglas popularized the term "Tricky Dick" and referred to Nixon as a "pipsqueak" and a "pee wee."[67] Ironically, Douglas's candidacy received the support of Ronald Reagan, who was then serving as president of the Screen Actors Guild, while John F. Kennedy, a member of the House, delivered a $1,000 donation to the Nixon campaign from his father, Joseph P. Kennedy.[68] Capitalizing upon the unpopular Truman administration and the growing fear of communism, Nixon soundly defeated Douglas with 59.2 percent of the vote.

---

[65] Ambrose, 1987, 216.
[66] Ambrose, 1987, 218.
[67] Mitchell, 1998, ch. 1.
[68] Ambrose quotes Kennedy as telling Nixon that "I obviously can't endorse you but it isn't going to break my heart if you can turn the Senate's loss into Hollywood's gain;" Ambrose, 1987, 211.

In 1982, an open Senate seat was created in New Jersey when Democratic Senator Harrison Williams resigned from his seat in the wake of expulsion proceedings stemming from his indictment in the ABSCAM scandal.[69] Representative Millicent Fenwick, a Republican first elected to the House with the "Watergate Class" of 1974, entered the race to succeed Williams. With a reputation as a likeable pipe-smoking eccentric,[70] Fenwick gained notoriety for her resemblance to Congresswoman Lacey Davenport, a character in the *Doonesbury* comic strip by Garry Trudeau.[71] Despite her voting record being attacked as too "liberal," Fenwick defeated Republican Jeffrey Bell in the Republican primary. Frank Lautenberg, the multimillionaire CEO of Automatic Data Processing, surprisingly emerged from the field of ten candidates to win the Democratic nomination. In the fall campaign, Lautenberg questioned Fenwick's fitness for the job, accused her of supporting "voting-rights opponent Strom Thurmond," and outspent her $6.4 million to $2.6 million.[72] During one of their televised debates, Fenwick said, "If my opponent had spent these floods of money on explaining his position, I would have nothing to say. But too much, in my opinion, has been spent attacking falsely my record and my position and my character. I call it outrageous."[73] Despite trailing Fenwick by eighteen points in voter surveys at the start of the campaign, Lautenberg won the general election with 51.5 percent of the vote.[74]

---

[69] Ehrenhart, 1981, 745–46. In 1980, the FBI conducted an elaborate sting operation and caught several House members on videotape taking thousands of dollars from a fake sheik, Kambir Abdul Rahman (actually an ex-convict in disguise), in exchange for promises of influence on the Hill. One of the more infamous images was of Representative Richard Kelly (R-FL), who was taped stuffing $25,000 into his coat and pants as he asked, "Does it show?" Six members of Congress were ultimately sentenced to jail; Shelly Ross, *Fall from Grace: Sex, Scandal, and Corruption in American Politics from 1702 to the Present* (New York: Ballantine Books, 1988), 257–61.

[70] Fenwick began smoking a pipe when her doctor advised her to stop chain-smoking cigarettes. Although there were always two pipes in her purse, she stopped being photographed with them because she believed "it would be a bad influence on the young"; Joseph Sullivan, "U.S. Senate Race Tops Jersey Elections," *New York Times*, October 31, 1982, 40.

[71] Barone and Ujifusa, 1985, 832. One Doonesbury website noted that "Lacy [*sic*] arrived in Congress two years before Mrs. Fenwick did, but the similarities seemed too distinctive to be coincidental. Indeed, so many people assumed Lacey was Millicent, it seemed ungallant to deny it"; see http://www.doonesbury.com/strip/faqs/faq_ch.html (accessed June 20, 2005).

[72] Michael Norman, "Mrs. Fenwick and Lautenberg Meet in Final Debate," *New York Times*, November 1, 1982, B13.

[73] Norman, 1982, B13.

[74] Fenwick was actually quite surprised about her defeat and admitted, "I never thought I would lose. . . . The fascination of that job is that I couldn't wait to get there"; Michael Norman, "Rep. Fenwick Tries to Figure Out Why She Lost," *New York Times*, November 4, 1982, B15. When asked what she would do after leaving Congress, Fenwick replied that she planned on "sleeping late, take up gardening and 'get fat on truffles and veal piccata' "; Norman, 1982, B15. Lautenberg retired in 2000 after three terms in the Senate. In 2002, he reentered electoral politics in circumstances similar to those of 1982. Amidst growing charges of corruption, incumbent Democrat Robert Torricelli withdrew from his reelection campaign in September 2002. The New Jersey Democratic Party won a court victory that allowed the party to substitute Frank Lautenberg for Torricelli on the ballot. Lautenberg went on to defeat his Republican opponent; Barone and Cohen, 2003, 1029–30.

The most recent example of progressive ambition was the 2006 campaign of Representative Katherine Harris. Harris first gained notoriety as Florida's Secretary of State during the controversy over the 2000 presidential election. In 2002, Harris won an open House seat previously held by Republican Dan Miller.[75] During the fall of 2003, Harris "entertained" the idea of running for the Senate seat that came open with the retirement of Democrat Bob Graham. Her decision not to run in 2004 was attributed to a visit from Karl Rove[76] and rumors that "the president did not want to share his re-election ballot with the Florida official so closely associated with his controversial 2000 win."[77] Instead, Harris announced in June of 2005 that she would challenge Democratic incumbent Senator Bill Nelson, who was elected in 2000 with only 52.6 percent of the vote. Her campaign, however, was at best characterized as a political nightmare. The reaction to her candidacy by both national and Florida Republican leaders was lukewarm. For nearly a year, there were efforts to recruit others to challenge Harris in the primary.[78] Harris' management of her campaign organization was chaotic and suffered from a "seemingly endless exodus of staffers."[79] Many of her public statements also got her into trouble. For example, in one interview she stated, "if you're not electing Christians, then in essence you are going to legislate sin."[80] As a result, Harris failed to mount a credible challenge and lost decisively to Nelson, with only 39 percent of the vote.

All of these female representatives ran when the value of their seats was relatively low; none of them were senior members of the House. As we did in chapter 3 to predict which congressional widows would seek House careers, we can calculate the probability that a female member of the House will act on the opportunity to run for the Senate.[81] Probabilities equal to or greater than .50 lead to a prediction of progressive ambition. The top half of table 4.6

---

[75] Michael Barone and Richard Cohen, *The Almanac of American Politics, 2006* (Washington D.C.: National Journal, 2005), 438.

[76] Barone and Cohen, 2005, 438.

[77] Anita Kumar and Joni James, "Harris Announces Run for U.S. Senate," *St. Petersburg Times*, June 8, 2005, 1A.

[78] Jeremy Wallace, "Harris Unfazed by Apparent Party Pressure," *Sarasota Herald-Tribune*, June 25, 2005, A1; "Report: Pensacola Republicans Say Scarborough Courted for Senate," *Associated Press State and Local Wire*, August 16, 2005; Jeremy Wallace, "At Final Hour, 3 Republicans Join Senate Race," *Sarasota Herald-Tribune*, May 13, 2006, B1.

[79] Larry Lipman, "Ex-Harris Aides Reveal Why They Became 'Exes,' " *Palm Beach Post*, August 6, 2006, 1A.

[80] Lipman, 2006, 1A; Daniel Ruth, "Memo to Harris Staff Members: Keep Digging," *Tampa Tribune*, August 31, 2006, 1.

[81] The cell entries represent the probability that a member will run for the Senate (given the opportunity) and were generated using the Clarify program module; Michael Tomz, Jason Wittenberg, and Gary King, *Clarify: Software for Interpreting and Presenting Statistical Results* (Cambridge, Mass.: Harvard University, 2001). This model is presented in Palmer and Simon, 2003, 135, table 3. We update the original simulation by adding the opportunities from the 2004 election cycle. Because running for the Senate is a rare event, the simulated probabilities are low. Nonetheless, they are meaningful, especially in comparing the prospects of one officeholder to another. For example, the average probability of those who ran for the Senate (.24) is three times larger than the probability of those who did not run (.08).

Table 4.6 The Probability That Female House Incumbents Will Run for Senate

Career in the House	Incumbency and State Size	Non-Risk Taker	Risk Taker
Served One Term or More Than 5 Terms	Incumbent is safe, medium state	.00	.01
	Incumbent is safe, large state	.01	.03
	Incumbent is safe, small state	.03	.10
	Incumbent is marginal, medium state	.01	.05
	Incumbent is marginal, large state	.02	.10
	Incumbent is marginal, small state	.09	.33
	Open seat, medium state	.02	.08
	Open seat, large state	.04	.17
	Open seat, small state	.14	.44
Midcareer: Served 2–5 Terms	Incumbent is safe, medium state	.01	.04
	Incumbent is safe, large state	.02	.07
	Incumbent is safe, small state	.07	.26
	Incumbent is marginal, medium state	.03	.13
	Incumbent is marginal, large state	.07	.25
	Incumbent is marginal, small state	.23	.57
	Open seat, medium state	.05	.20
	Open seat, large state	.11	.35
	Open seat, small state	.35	.70

reports the probability of running for those female House members who are not at midcareer. The probabilities are typically small; there are only two situations where the probability of running exceeds .25, risk takers in small states with either an open seat or a marginal incumbent. The bottom half shows that the probability of running increases substantially for those members in midcareer; seven of the profiles equal or exceed .25. Aside from the stage of career, the most noteworthy differences occur between risk takers and non–risk takers. For each situation, the probability of running is substantially greater for risk takers compared to their non–risk taking counterparts. Risk taking, midcareer female representatives facing an open seat in a small state have a .70 probability of running.

Looking to the Future: Running for the Senate

We can use our analysis of progressive ambition to speculate about those women in the 110th Congress (2007 session) who are well situated to run for the Senate in 2008, 2010, and 2012. We first identified those women who will be at midcareer in each of these election cycles. Of the seventy women, twenty-eight will find themselves in midcareer in 2008, thirty-two will be at that stage in 2010, and twenty-five in 2012.[82] Next, we determined which of those women at midcareer will face an opportunity to run in each cycle. In this part of our analysis, "definite" opportunities occur when an incumbent senator of the opposition party is scheduled to face reelection. In addition, we identified a set of "speculative" opportunities based upon the age of the current Senate incumbent. Finally, we used the factors considered in our analysis of progressive ambition and calculated the probability of running for each midcareer female House member who will have an opportunity to run.

Table 4.7 shows that five women will face an opportunity to run for the Senate in 2008. Only one member is from a small state. Representative Shelley Moore Capito (R-WV), a risk taker, was first elected in 2000 and represents a district that reaches all the way across West Virginia's midsection.[83] This would make her transition to a Senate campaign easier than those faced by members from larger states. In addition, she is the daughter of former House member and Governor Arch Moore and thus has name recognition beyond her congressional district. Democratic Senator Jay Rockefeller's term expires in 2008; he will be seventy-one years old. In 2002, Rockefeller was reelected with 63 percent of the vote. If he runs for a fifth term, the probability that Capito would run is .26, the highest probability among the women with opportunities in 2008. Should Rockefeller retire, Capito would face an open seat. According to our simulation, her probability of running would increase to .70.[84]

The other risk taker with an opportunity in 2008 is Representative Candice Miller (R-MI). Miller first ran for the House in 1986 when she challenged Democratic incumbent David Bonior (D-MI) and lost with 34 percent of the vote.[85] Miller later won two statewide elections for Michigan secretary of state in 1994 and 1998. In 2002, she won the seat vacated by

---

[82] Here we excluded Representative Juanita Millender-McDonald.

[83] Representative Capito won the House seat vacated by Democratic incumbent Robert Wise. Wise held the seat for nine terms and chose to run for governor in 2000; Michael Barone and Richard Cohen, *Almanac of American Politics, 2002* (Washington, D.C.: National Journal, 2001), 1640–42. Capito also had an opportunity to run in 2006 when Democratic Senator Robert Byrd, then eighty-nine years old, sought a ninth term in the Senate. Capito was urged to challenge Byrd by the Republican National Committee and Senator Elizabeth Dole (R-NC), chair of the National Republican Senatorial Committee; Peter Savodnik, "Capito, Dole Discuss Senate Bid," *The Hill*, Washington, D.C., June 27, 2005, http://www.hillnews. com/thehill/export/TheHill/News/Campaign/062705 (accessed June 27, 2005). At the same time, there was sentiment in West Virginia that Capito should wait. For example, an editorial ran in May 2005 pleading with Byrd to run again and encouraging Capito to wait until he retired, stating that "this is not Capito's time. . . . Her time will come;" "Will Byrd Run?" *The Journal*, Martinsburg, WV, May 1, 2005, A6.

[84] As of June, 2007, Rockefeller was preparing to seek reelection; Hoppy Kerchival, "Rockefeller Isn't Taking '08 For Granted," *Charleston Daily Mail*, April 27, 2007, 4A. Capito's response to a 2008 Senate candidacy has been somewhat equivocal: "As of today, I plan to run for a fifth term in a year and a half," Jake Stump, "Capito Says She'll Seek Fifth Term in the House," *Charleston Daily Mail*, May 10, 2007, 10A.

[85] Barone and Cohen, 2003, 840–41.

Table 4.7 Women and Progressive Ambition: The 2008, 2010, and 2012 Election Cycles

Women in Midcareer in Year of Opportunity	Risk Taker	State Size	Seat Status	Probability of Running
2008 Definite Opportunity				
Judy Biggert (R-IL)	No	Medium	Safe	0.01
Betty McCollum (D-MN)	No	Medium	Marginal	0.03
Candice Miller (R-MI)[a]	Yes	Medium	Marginal	0.13
Shelley Moore Capito (R-WV)[b]	Yes	Small	Safe	0.26
Marilyn Musgrave (R-CO)	No	Medium	Open	0.05
2008 Speculative Opportunity				
Jo Ann Davis (R-VA)[c]	No	Medium	Open	0.05
Thelma Drake (R-VA)[c]	No	Medium	Open	0.05
Stephanie Herseth Sandlin (D-SD)	**Yes**	**Small**	**Open**	*0.70*
Heather Wilson (R-NM)[d]	No	Small	Open	0.35
2010 Definite Opportunity				
Nancy Boyda (D-KS)	Yes	Medium	Safe	0.04
Gabrielle Giffords (D-AZ)	Yes	Medium	Safe	0.04
Stephanie Herseth Sandlin (D-SD)	**Yes**	**Small**	**Marginal**	*0.57*
Kathy Castor (D-FL)	No	Large	Marginal	0.07
Cathy McMorris Rodgers (R-WA)	No	Medium	Safe	0.01
Marilyn Musgrave (R-CO)	No	Medium	Marginal	0.03
Carol Shea-Porter (D-NH)	Yes	Small	Safe	0.26
Betty Sutton (D-OH)	No	Medium	Safe	0.01
Allyson Schwartz (D-PA)[e]	No	Medium	Marginal	0.03
Debbie Wasserman Schultz (D-FL)	No	Large	Marginal	0.07
2010 Speculative Opportunity				
Mazie Hirono (D-HI)[f]	No	Small	Open	0.35
2012 Definite Opportunity				
Michelle Bachman (R-MN)	No	Medium	Safe	0.01
Ginny Brown-Waite (R-FL)	Yes	Large	Safe	0.07
Thelma Drake (R-VA)	No	Medium	Marginal	0.03
Gabrielle Giffords (D-AZ)	Yes	Medium	Marginal	0.13
Cathy McMorris Rodgers (R-WA)	No	Medium	Safe	0.01
Candice Miller (R-MI)	Yes	Medium	Safe	0.04
Jean Schmidt (R-OH)	No	Medium	Safe	0.01

(Continued)

Table 4.7 Women and Progressive Ambition: The 2008, 2010, and 2012 Election Cycles *(Continued)*

Women in Midcareer in Year of Opportunity	Risk Taker	State Size	Seat Status	Probability of Running
2012 Speculative Opportunity				
Mazie Hirono (D-HI)[g]	No	Small	Open	0.35

a Senator Carl Levin (D-MI) will be seventy-four years old in 2008 and running for his sixth term. If Levin retires, the probability increases to 0.20.

b Senator John D. Rockefeller (D-WV) will be seventy-one years old in 2008 and running for his fifth term. If Rockefeller retires, the probability increases to 0.70.

c Senator John Warner (R-VA) will be eighty-one years old in 2008 and running for his sixth term.

d Senator Pete Domenici (R-NM) will be seventy-six years old in 2008 and running for his sixth term.

e Senator Arlen Specter (R-PA) will be eighty years old in 2010 and running for his sixth term. If Specter retires, the probability increases to 0.05.

f Senate Daniel Inouye (D-HI) will be eighty-four years old in 2010 and running for his ninth term.

g Senator Daniel Akaka (D-HI) will be eighty-eight years old in 2012 and running for his fourth full term.

Bonior.[86] In 2006, Miller decided not to challenge Democratic incumbent Senator Debbie Stabenow.[87] If Democratic incumbent Senator Carl Levin decides to seek reelection in 2008, Miller's situation is identical to her opportunity in 2006—challenging a marginal Democratic incumbent.[88] However, Levin will be seventy-four years old in 2008, and if he retires, the probability of Miller making a run for the Senate would increase to .20.

The remaining definite opportunities to run in 2008 fall to women who are not risk takers and have a low probability of running for the Senate. Representataive Marilyn Musgrave (R-CO) has the most attractive opportunity because of an open seat,[89] Representative Betty McCollum (D-MN) would face marginal incumbent Republican Norm Coleman;[90] Representative Judy Biggert (R-IL) would have to challenge Democrat Richard Durbin who was reelected in 2002 with 61.2 percent of the vote.

---

[86] Bonior decided to run for governor and lost in the primary to Jennifer Granholm.

[87] Like Representative Shelley Moore Capito, Miller faced significant pressure to run in 2006. Stabenow was first elected in 2000 with only 50.5 percent of the vote. During a visit to Michigan in January of 2005, President George W. Bush personally requested that Miller run for Stabenow's seat; "President Bush Nudges Miller to Senate; Bush Wants Rep. Candice Miller to Run against Sen. Debbie Stabenow," *Grand Rapids Press*, January 8, 2005, A7.

[88] On December 4, 2006, Senator Levin announced that he would seek reelection to the Senate; "No Retirement for Levin; Dems Breathe Easier with Senator's Decision to Run," *Grand Rapids Press*, December 5, 2006, B6.

[89] Republican Senator Wayne Allard announced that he would not run for reelection in 2008; Karen E. Crummy and Anne Mulkern, "Allard Won't Try for 3rd;" *Denver Post*, January 16, 2007, A-01.

[90] On Feburary 14, 2007, comedian Al Franken made a "Valentine's Day" announcement that he would run for the Senate in 2008 against Coleman; Rachel E. Stassen-Berger, "Al Franken Says He is Running for U.S. Senate," *St. Paul Pioneer Press*, February 14, 2007.

Four women may face the "speculative opportunity" of an open seat in 2008. Senator John Warner (R-VA) will be seventy-one and completing his fifth term of service. If Warner retires, two Republican women, midway in their House careers, will have an opportunity to run, Representatives Jo Ann Davis and Thelma Drake. Neither is a risk taker and, as a result, their probability of running is low (.06). Unfortunately, Representative Davis died in October, 2007, of breast cancer. Her husband announced that he would run in the special election to fill her seat.

Representative Stephanie Herseth Sandlin (D-SD; see figure 4.1) faces an uncertain situation in 2008. In December 2006, Democratic Senator Tim Johnson underwent surgery after suffering a brain hemorrhage. Although remaining in office as he undergoes therapy, there is uncertainty as to whether Johnson will seek reelection in 2008.[91] Should Johnson retire, Herseth Sandlin is well-positioned for a Senate campaign. South Dakota has one congressional district and, as a result, she currently represents a statewide constituency. She first ran for the House in 2002, attempting to win an open seat that was secure for the Republicans.[92] Herseth Sandlin is thus a risk taker. She won her seat in a special election held in June 2004 to fill the vacancy caused by the resignation of incumbent Bill Janklow, her 2002 opponent. Five months later, Herseth Sandlin successfully defended the seat, winning 53.5 percent of the vote. In the 2006 midterm election, she overwhelmed her Republican opponent, winning 70.4 percent of the vote. As to her future ambitions, Herseth Sandlin has noted that in looking beyond 2006, "Let's just say that while I haven't mapped out any long-term strategy, I'm not ruling anything out." [93]

The political climate in New Mexico is equally uncertain. In 2008, Republican Senator Pete Domenici will be seventy-six years old and completing his sixth term. The conventional wisdom is that Domenici wants to "promote his protégé," Representative Heather Wilson (R-NM), "as his eventual successor." [94] If Domenici retired, Wilson would be presented with an opportunity, and her probability of running in 2008 would be .35. There are, however, two sources of uncertainty. First, Wilson was electorally vulnerable in 2006; she defeated Democrat Patricia Madrid by only 879 of 210,953 votes.[95] Second, both Domenici and Wilson became embroiled in the controversy involving the firing of federal prosecutors by the Bush

---

[91] Jim Abrams, "Ailing Senator Johnson Returns to His Home in District of Columbia," *Associated Press State and Local Wire*, April 30, 2007.

[92] The seat was vacated by three-term incumbent Republican John Thune, who successfully ran for the Senate. In his three House races, Thune averaged 68.7 percent of the vote.

[93] Joe Kafka, "Herseth Feeling More Settled in Washington," *Associated Press State and Local Wire*, January 30, 2005.

[94] Marie Horrigan, "GOP Troubles Reshuffle New Mexico's '08 Deck," *CQ Weekly Online*, March 12, 2007, 708; http://library.cqpress.com/cqweekly/weeklyreport110-000002467101 (accessed May 31, 2007).

[95] See http://edition.cnn.com/ELECTION/2006/pages/results/states/NM/H/01/ (accessed May 31, 2007).

Administration. In October, 2007, Senator Domenici announced his retirement. Shortly thereafter, Representative Wilson announced she would run for his seat.[96]

Ten women will have definite opportunities and one woman has a speculative opportunity in 2010. As table 4.7 shows, six of the ten definite opportunities fall to non-risk takers. There are two instances in which the prospective opponent is a safe incumbent. Representative Betty Sutton (D-OH), first elected in 2006, would face Republican Senator George Voinovich, who won his 2004 contest with 68 percent of the vote. The opponent of Representative Cathy McMorris Rodgers (R-WA) would be Democratic Senator Patty Murray, who won 56.1 percent of the vote in her reelection bid. The probability that Sutton or McMorris Rodgers will run is .01. Four of the non-risk takers with opportunities in 2010 would challenge marginal incumbents. Representative Marilyn Musgrave (R-CO) would face Democratic Senator Ken Salazer in his first bid for reelection; her probability of running is .03. The same probability holds for Representative Allyson Schwartz (D-PA), should she elect to challenge the Republican incumbent Senator Arlen Specter. There is a .07 probability that Representatives Debbie Wasserman Schultz and Kathy Castor, both Democrats from Florida, would challenge first-term Republican incumbent Senator Mel Martinez.

Four risk takers face opportunities in 2010. Representative Stephanie Herseth Sandlin would face Senator John Thune, who won his 2004 race over Democrat Tom Daschle with only 51 percent of the vote. The probability that Herseth Sandlin will challenge Thune, as shown in table 4.7, is .57, again making her the most likely to run. Democratic Representatives Gabrielle Giffords (D-AZ), Nancy Boyda (D-KS), and Carol Shea-Porter (D-NH) gained their House seats in 2006 by winning in traditionally Republican districts. Should they decide to run for the Senate, each would face a safe incumbent in 2010. The probability that Shea-Porter will challenge Republican Senator Judd Gregg is .26. However, both Giffords (versus Senator John McCain) and Boyda (versus Senator Sam Brownback) have only a .04 probability of leaving the House for a run at the Senate.

In the 2012 election, three women will get their second opportunity to run for a Senate seat. Representative Giffords (D-AZ) would face incumbent Senator Jon Kyl. Because Kyl won with less than 55 percent of the vote in 2006, the probability that Giffords would seek this Senate seat is .13. Having declined to challenge Democrat incumbent Senator Debbie Stabenow in 2006, Representative Candice Miller (R-MI) will face the same choice in 2012. Stabenow, however, improved her electoral performance in 2006,

---

[96] Horrigan, 2007, 708. David C. Iglesias, one of the prosecutors who was fired, testified before a congressional committee that he received calls from both Domenici and Wilson, and that the purpose of the calls was to "pressure him to return indictments" against local Democrats. See David Roybal, "Squeaky Clean Images Take a Hit," *Albuquerque Journal*, March 13, 2007, A7.

Fig. 4.1 Representative Stephanie Herseth Sandlin, the youngest woman in the 110th Congress (2007 session), will have the opportunity to run for the Senate in South Dakota in 2010. Photo by Barbara Palmer.

winning 58.2 percent of the vote compared to 50.5 percent in her first run. The second opportunity for Representative Cathy McMorris Rodgers (R-WA) would pit her against incumbent Senator Maria Cantwell. Given that Cantwell won comfortably in 2006 with 58.7 of the vote, the probability that McMorris Rodgers will run is only .01.

Four Republican women will face their first opportunity in 2012. In Florida, Democratic Senator Bill Nelson will stand for reelection. Republican Representative Ginny Brown-Waite comes from one of the larger geographic districts in Florida that lies north of the Tampa Bay area. As a member of the Florida Senate, Brown-Waite ran for the House in 2002, beating incumbent Democrat Karen Thurman by less than 2 percent of the vote, making her a risk taker. According to table 4.7, the probability that Brown-Waite will run in 2012 is .07. The table also reveals that the probabilities of running for Representatives Michelle Bachman (R-MN), Jean Schmidt (R-OH), and Thelma Drake (R-VA) are very low. Bachman would face first-term incumbent Senator Amy Klobuchar (D-MN), who won with 58 percent of the vote in 2006; Schmidt would challenge Senator Sherrod Brown (D-OH), who won with 56 percent of the vote; Drake's opponent would be Senator Jim Webb (D-VA) who narrowly defeated Republican incumbent and then-presidential hopeful George Allen.

Table 4.7 also shows that Representative Mazie Hirono of Hawaii faces the possibility of an open-seat opportunity in both 2010 and 2012. Prior to her election to the House in 2006, Hirono served in the state House of Representatives for fourteen years and as Lieutenant Governor for eight years.[97] Senator Daniel Inouye (D-HI) will be eighty-four years old when his eighth term expires in 2010. Senator Daniel Akaka (D-HI) will be eighty-eight years old when his third full term expires in 2012. Retirement by either senator will present Hirono with an opportunity to seek the open seat; the probability that Hirono will run is .35 in each scenario.

Overall, twenty-one women serving in the 110th Congress will be faced with either a definite or speculative opportunity to run for the Senate in the next three election cycles. Among those with an opportunity, the most probable Senate candidates include Democrats Herseth Sandlin (2010), Shea-Porter (2010), and Giffords (2012), along with Republicans Capito (2008) and Miller (2008).

That only five women in the House will have serious opportunities over the next six years reinforces our analyses in previous chapters. The Senate projections in table 4.7 illustrate how the schedule of Senate elections, the electoral advantages of incumbency, and the longevity of incumbents make advancing through the pipeline quite difficult.[98] This suggests that increases in the number of women in the Senate will also depend on lateral entry and capitalizing upon name recognition gained elsewhere, much like the paths taken by Senators Nancy Kassebaum, Hillary Clinton, and Elizabeth Dole.

The Ultimate in Progressive Ambition: Running for President

At the apex of the political career ladder in the United States is the presidency. While the paths to the presidency are numerous, the Senate has been called "little more than a halfway house for more or less ambitious presidential contenders."[99] Many senators have, in fact, run for president. Of our forty-three presidents, more than one-third (fifteen) have been senators.[100] In the 2004 Democratic presidential primary race, five of the ten major Democratic contenders were senators or former senators. In 1972, ten Democratic senators, almost one-fifth of the Democrats in the Senate, announced that they were considering running against President Richard Nixon.[101]

---

[97] *Biographical Directory of the United States Congress,* http://bioguide.congress.gov/scripts/biodisplay.pl?index=H001042 (accessed May 31, 2007).

[98] Another route to the Senate is from the governorship of a state. While there are a number of men who were elected to the Senate after serving as governor (e.g., Republican Lamar Alexander of Tennessee), there are no women, to date, who followed this path.

[99] Robert Peabody, Norman Ornstein, and David Rohde, "The United States Senate as Presidential Incubator: Many Are Called but Few Are Chosen," *Political Science Quarterly* 9 (1976): 237–58, 237.

[100] Peabody, Ornstein, and Rohde, 1976, 238, and updated by the authors.

[101] Peabody, Ornstein, and Rohde, 1976, 238.

In light of its reputation as an "incubator for presidential candidates,"[102] we can speculate about those women currently serving in the Senate and their prospects for running for president. We have adapted the model created by political scientists Paul Abramson, John Aldrich, and David Rohde to calculate the probability that each woman currently serving in the Senate will enter the race for the presidential nomination in 2008.[103] Two of the same factors that predict whether a House member will run for the Senate also predict whether a senator will run for president: risk taking and low opportunity costs, that is, the senator is not up for reelection during a presidential election cycle. Unlike all House members, most senators, because their reelections are not synchronized with presidential elections, need not give up their seats to run for president. Beyond these two factors, the new concept of "candidate liabilities" is adopted here.[104] These liabilities include age, the first term of service in the Senate, racial and religious minorities, and an unsuccessful prior campaign for the presidency.[105]

Table 4.8 reveals that four female senators in the 110th Congress share the highest probability of running for president: Kay Bailey Hutchison (R-TX), Blanche Lincoln (D-AR), Debbie Stabenow (D-MI), and Maria Cantwell (D-WA). The comparatively high probability is a result of all being risk

---

[102] Peabody, Ornstein, and Rohde, 1976, 237.

[103] Paul Abramson, John Aldrich, and David Rohde, "Progressive Ambition among United States Senators: 1972–1988," *Journal of Politics* 49 (1987): 3–35. Since the 1970s, governors enjoyed more success at winning the presidency. Four of the last five presidents have been governors. In the 108th Congress, several constitutional amendments were proposed to change the citizenship requirements for being president. The main proponents were supporters of California Governor Arnold Schwarzenegger. Senator Orrin Hatch, former chair of the Senate Judiciary Committee, emerged as a leading advocate of the change. However, some women's groups have silently supported this because it would also allow Michigan Governor Jennifer Granholm, who was born in Canada, to run. Representative John Conyers, a Democrat from Michigan, actually introduced an amendment in the House; Joe Matthews, "Maybe Anyone Can Be President," *Los Angeles Times*, February 2, 2005, A1. See also http://amendforarnold.com (accessed June 21, 2005). In the 109th Congress, at least three proposed amendments were referred to subcommittee (HJ RES 2; HJ RES 15, and HJ RES 42); http://www.thomas.loc.gov (accessed June 21, 2005).

[104] Abramson, Aldrich, and Rohde, 1987, 9–11. Age is considered a liability if a senator is younger than forty-two or older than seventy.

[105] The Abramson, Aldrich, and Rohde study covers 1972 to 1988. They assign a liability if the senator is African American, Asian, Hispanic, female, or Jewish. In performing this exercise, we did not treat being female as a liability in order to examine the probability of running under the assumption of no gender bias. Were gender to be included as a liability, the probabilities reported in table 4.8 would be lower. With respect to religious denomination, seven of the sixteen female senators are Catholic (Mikulski, Murray, Landrieu, Collins, Cantwell, Murkowski, and McCaskill), three are Methodist (Stabenow, Clinton, and Dole), two are Episcopalian (Hutchison and Lincoln), two are Jewish (Feinstein and Boxer), one is Congregationalist (Klobuchar), and one is Greek Orthodox (Snowe). Because of flaws in the estimates for Republicans, we relied upon the Democratic equation reported in Abramson, Aldrich, and Rohde, 1987, 17, to generate the probabilities for all the senators. In addition, we assigned risk-taker status to Blanche Lincoln based upon her initial run for the House when she defeated a sitting incumbent of her own party in the primary. For a recent poll on age and religion as liabilities, particularly with regards to the candidacies of Mitt Romney and John McCain, see Jon Cohen and Jennifer Agiesta, "Poll: Age Important to Voters," *Washington Post*, February 27, 2007.

Table 4.8 Progressive Ambition: From the Senate to the Presidential Arena

Name	Year Elected to Senate	Senate Reelection in 2008	Liabilities	Risk Taker	Probability of Running
Barbara Mikulski (D-MD)	1986	No	1	Yes	0.08
Dianne Feinstein (D-CA)	1992	No	2	No	0.01
Barbara Boxer (D-CA)	1992	No	1	No	0.01
Patty Murray (D-WA)	1992	No	0	No	0.06
Kay Bailey Hutchison (R-TX)	1993	No	0	Yes	0.23
Olympia Snowe (R-ME)	1994	No	0	No	0.06
Mary Landrieu (D-LA)	1996	Yes	0	No	0.03
Susan Collins (R-ME)	1996	Yes	0	No	0.03
Blanche Lincoln (D-AR)	1998	No	0	Yes	0.23
Debbie Stabenow (D-MI)	2000	No	0	Yes	0.23
Hillary Clinton (D-NY)	2000	No	0	No	0.06
Maria Cantwell (D-WA)	2000	No	0	Yes	0.23
Elizabeth Dole (R-NC)	2002	Yes	3	No	0.00
Lisa Murkowski (R-AK)	2004	No	1	No	0.01
Amy Klobuchar (D-MN)	2006	No	1	No	0.01
Claire McCaskill (D-MO)	2006	No	2	Yes	0.07

takers, not facing a reelection race in 2008, and having no liabilities. The youngest of the four are Senators Lincoln and Klobuchar, both age 47. Senator Kay Bailey Hutchison (R-TX) is currently the most senior Republican woman in the Senate. Throughout the spring of 2005, there were numerous rumors that she would leave her Senate seat in 2006 to challenge the incumbent governor of Texas, Rick Perry, in the Republican primary. She would then launch her presidential campaign, like George W. Bush, as governor. In June of 2005, Hutchison put the rumors to rest and announced that she would seek reelection to the Senate. Four days later, she announced her candidacy to chair the Senate Republican Policy Committee and continued to serve in that position in the 110th Congress.[106] Although she is not running for president in 2008, she "is frequently on lists as a possible vice-presidential candidate."[107]

Among those with the lowest probability of running are Senators Dianne Feinstein (D-CA) and Elizabeth Dole (R-NC). Neither are risk takers. Feinstein will be seventy-five years old in 2008, and although she has been considered a possible contender in the past, she has expressed her disinterest: "People have talked to me about running for president . . . and I sort of

---

[106] R. G. Ratcliffe, "Hutchison to Run for Senate, Not Governor," *Houston Chronicle*, June 18, 2005, 1.

[107] Ratcliffe, 2005, 1.

laughed at it." [108] Elizabeth Dole has the most liabilities of all the women in the Senate. She will be seventy-two years old in 2008, she is serving her first term, and she has already taken a shot at running for president. In fact, Dole did it "backwards" and ran for the Senate in 2002 after she dropped out of the presidential race in October 1999.[109]

On January 20, 2007, Senator Hillary Clinton (D-NY) ended years of speculation and formally announced her candidacy for president. In her webcast, seated on her living room couch, she stressed her Midwestern middle-class roots and that she was "in it to win." [110] While our analysis suggests that her probability of running for president is low, her prospects for success go far beyond her status as a first-term senator. Clinton is *sui generis*, the only one of her kind. In effect, she does not fit into our model. She is the first spouse of a president to enter electoral politics after serving as first lady. Since the 1992 campaign when Bill Clinton remarked, "Buy one, get one free," it has not been hard to imagine Hillary running in her own right.[111] She has a name recognition rate of 94 percent.[112] On the day of her announcement, polls showed her with a 24 point lead over Senator Barack Obama (D-IL) among Democratic respondents. In what will be the most expensive presidential race in history, for the first quarter of 2007 (the first official fund-raising period of the campaign), Clinton raised a "staggering" $26 million, almost three times as much as any other presidential candidate in history. In addition, she transferred another $10 million left over from her 2006 senate race.[113] In spite of all this, Clinton does face at least one major challenge with regards to her gender. A Gallup poll in October of 2006 found that while over 90 percent of Americans say they would vote for a woman for president, only 61 percent think that the country is "ready to elect a woman as president." [114]

There are three other women who deserve mention. Carol Moseley Braun, the first African American woman to serve in the Senate, ran for

---

[108] Eleanor Clift and Tom Brazaitis, *Madam President* (New York: Scribner, 2000), 168.

[109] Stanley and Niemi, 2003, 67.

[110] Dan Balz, "Hillary Clinton Opens Presidential Bid," *Washington Post*, January 12, 2007, A1.

[111] Eleanor Clift and Tom Brazaitis, *Madam President*, 2nd ed. (New York: Routlege Press, 2003), 149.

[112] Frank Newport, "Update: Hillary Rodham Clinton and the 2008 Election," *Gallup Poll News Service*, June 7, 2005. See also Clift and Brazaitis, 2003, ch. 6.

[113] Anne Kornblut, "Clinton Shatters Record for Fundraising," *Washington Post*, April 2, 2007, A1. A week later, Senator Barack Obama announced that he had raised $23.5 million; Jake Tapper, "Obama Bests Clinton in Primary Fundraising," *ABCNews.com*, April 4, 2007, http://www.abcnews.go.com/print?id=3008821 (accessed June 7, 2007).

[114] Jeffrey Jones, "Six in 10 Americans Think U.S. Ready for a Female President," *Gallup Poll News Service*, October 3, 2006, Most social scientists consider the 61 percent a more accurate measure of how many Americans would actually vote for a woman for president. See Barbara Palmer, "Woman President in the U.S.: Will It Ever Happen?" *The Anniston Star*, Anniston, AL, February 18, 2007, 1E.; Georgia Duerst-Lahti, "Presidential Elections: Gendered Space and the Case of 2004," in *Gender and Elections: Shaping the Future of American Politics*, eds. Susan Carroll and Richard Fox (Cambridge University Press: New York, 2006).

Fig. 4.2 Senator Clinton Campaigns for President in South Carolina. Photo © Tannen Maury/ epa/Corbis.

president in 2004. Moseley Braun served in the Senate for one term and narrowly lost her reelection campaign in 1998, after being plagued by fund-raising and sexual harassment scandals.[115] Following her defeat, she vowed "never to run for public office" again.[116] She was then appointed ambassador to New Zealand and Samoa by President Bill Clinton. Some speculated that she decided to run for president, at least in part, to clear her name.[117] While she was a regular participant in Democratic presidential debates, she only raised $628,000.[118] If we apply our model to her, Moseley Braun would be classified as a risk taker, having taken on and defeated Democratic incumbent Senator Alan Dixon in the primary the very first time she ran for Senate in 1992. She would have, however, at least one liability: being an African American. Moseley Braun felt the sting of racism early in her Senate career, after she single-handedly defeated an amendment proposed by Senator Jesse Helms (R-NC) extending a trademark to the Daughters of the Confederacy on their use of the Confederate flag in their logo. Shortly after the amendment was defeated on the Senate floor, Moseley Braun encountered Helms in the Senate elevator. As she recounted, "He saw me standing there, and he started to sing, 'I wish I was in the land of cotton . . .' And he looked at Senator [Orrin] Hatch and said, 'I'm going to sing Dixie until she cries.' And I looked at him and said, 'Senator Helms, your singing would make me cry if you sang Rock of Ages.' "[119]

---

[115] Foerstel, 1999, 197.

[116] Foerstel, 1999, 197.

[117] Darryl Fears, "On a Mission in a Political Second Act; Bush's Record Forced Her to Run, Braun Says," *Washington Post*, July 13, 2003.

[118] Federal Election Commission, http://herndon1.sdrdc.com/cgi-bin/cancomsrs/ ?_04+P40002552 (accessed June 28, 2005).

[119] Quoted from Foerstel, 1999, 196.

Two female members of the House have also run for president. Representative Patricia Schroeder (D-CO) announced her candidacy in 1987. She had been co-chair of Senator Gary Hart's presidential campaign that year, until Hart dared the press to "go ahead and follow me." They did and reported that he spent the night with Donna Rice, a model who was not his wife.[120] Shortly thereafter, a photograph was published showing Rice sitting on Hart's lap while they cruised on a yacht called *Monkey Business*. After Hart withdrew from the race, Schroeder decided to run "only if I had a good chance of winning."[121] A poll in August 1987 had her running third among the Democratic nominees, but she was not raising enough money to be competitive, so Schroeder withdrew from the race before the start of the primary season.[122] During her final press conference, her tears as she announced the end of her candidacy became infamous enough to be parodied on *Saturday Night Live*.[123] The first African American woman to run for president was Representative Shirley Chisholm (D-NY). Chisholm was first elected to the House in 1968. In 1972, she announced her candidacy for the Democratic nomination for president. Her name appeared on the primary ballot in twelve states. When the other Democratic candidates tried to exclude her from the televised debates because she was not "a real candidate," she went to the Federal Communications Commission and got a federal court order allowing her to participate.[124] On the first roll call at the Democratic National Convention, Chisholm won 151 votes.[125] She said, "I knew I wouldn't be president, but somebody had to break the ice, somebody with the nerve and bravado to do it."[126]

Conclusion

Rohde assumes that all members of the House have progressive ambition, and that given the opportunity they would run for the Senate. But running for this office, especially in a large state, is much riskier and more difficult than running for the House. Not all House members make that transition successfully. For example, in 1980, when Representative John Anderson (R-IL) resigned from the House to launch his third-party presidential campaign, Lynn Martin, a former state senator from his Rockville-based district, decided to run for the open seat, defeating four other candidates in the

---

[120] Larry Sabato, *Feeding Frenzy: How Attack Journalism Has Transformed American Politics* (New York: Free Press, 1991), 13–14.

[121] Pat Schroeder, *Twenty-four Years of House Work and the Place is Still a Mess* (Kansas City, Mo.: Andrews McMeel, 1999), 180.

[122] Foerstel, 1999, 247.

[123] Schroeder, 1999, 187.

[124] Clift and Brazaitis, 2003, xxii.

[125] Foerstel, 1999, 56. In 2004, a documentary of Chisholm's campaign was released, *Chisholm '72: Unbought and Unbossed,* shortly before her death at the age of eighty on January 1, 2005.

[126] Clift and Brazaitis, 2003, xxiii.

primary.[127] Considered a rising star in the Republican Party, she was given a seat on the powerful House Budget Committee. In 1984, Vice President George Bush personally asked her to coach him in a series of practices to prepare him for his televised debate against the Democratic vice presidential nominee, Geraldine Ferraro.[128] In 1986, Martin was elected vice chair of the Republican Conference, making her the first Republican woman to serve in a leadership position.[129] In her House reelection campaigns, Martin received on average well over 60 percent of the vote. After her fifth term, she decided to run for the Senate against the popular incumbent Democratic Senator Paul Simon, well known for his bow ties and unsuccessful presidential bid in 1988. Martin's campaign got off to a rocky start when she referred to southern Illinois voters as "rednecks" and called Simon a "twerp." [130] At the time of her announcement as a Senate candidate, she had raised less than $100,000 while Simon had almost $2 million.[131] Her fundraising was disappointing, and she admitted to running "a terrible campaign." [132]

Very few of the female representatives who have run for the Senate were successful; only five of the twenty, less than one-third, were able to move up the political hierarchy from the House to the Senate. Indeed, very few sitting female House members have made a run for the Senate in the first place, only 20 of 255 opportunities, or 7.8 percent. Our analysis shows that this is largely a function of opportunity: the power of incumbency, the longevity of incumbents, and the electoral calendar largely block the career ladder. Consider the situation in California since 1992, when Democrats Barbara Boxer and Dianne Feinstein were elected to the Senate. Feinstein was reelected in 1994, 2000, and 2006; Boxer was reelected in 1998 and 2004. Between 1992 and 2004, California elected sixteen female Democrats to the House. None of these women have had an opportunity, as we define it, to run for the Senate.

Although it does not happen very often, we can predict which female House members will make a run for the Senate. Women from small states are

---

[127] Martin's very first race for office was actually in the eighth grade for class president. She lost by one vote—her own. She voted for her boyfriend, who had voted for himself. After the election, they broke up; Clift and Brazaitis, 2003, 70. In 1980, in addition to Martin, three other Republican women were elected to the House. This was considered enough of a novelty that they were all asked to appear on Phil Donahue's daytime talk show; Clift and Brazaitis, 2003, 41.

[128] Martin knew Ferraro from serving in the House together, and they had worked as allies on women's issues. In 2000, they started a business, G & L Strategies, that advised companies how to develop women-friendly workplaces; Clift and Brazaitis, 2000, 81.

[129] Known for her quick and sarcastic wit, she was once called the "political version of Joan Rivers"; Foerstal, 1999, 174.

[130] Paul Merrion, "Martin Campaign Lags; Gaffes Raise GOP Doubts, May Imperil Fund-Raising," *Crain's Chicago Business*, October 2, 1989, 4.

[131] "Simon, Martin File Campaign Funding Data," *Crain's Chicago Business*, August 7, 1989, 46. When Bush became president, he asked her to be secretary of labor. In 1995, she ran an exploratory campaign for president, made trips to New Hampshire and Iowa, but after a month decided not to run; Clift and Brazaitis, 2003, 70.

[132] Clift and Brazaitis, 2003, 42.

more likely to take advantage of an opportunity to run for the Senate, given the congruence between their House district and potential Senate constituency. Moreover, women are more likely to run for the Senate when there is an open seat and they have the highest probability of winning. Rather than sacrifice seniority, women are more likely to take a shot at the Senate midcareer. Finally, risk taking is an essential feature of progressive ambition. Those women who ran under politically adverse conditions in their first attempt at a House seat are more likely to take the risk and run for the Senate.

Representative Sue Myrick observed, "Men are raised to play football, to bash their heads and come back for more. Women are raised to stand back. We aren't raised to be risk takers."[133] Our analysis suggests that this is not necessarily true. A substantial proportion of women elected to the House are classified as risk takers; their first run for the office occurred under conditions that were politically perilous. Some women—like some men—are taught or acquire the ability to take electoral risks when entering congressional politics. This attitude helps explain the differences between static and progressive ambition. Studying the decision to run for the Senate thus suggests that, in moving through the hierarchy of offices, women respond to the same systematic factors and share the same goals as their male counterparts: electoral survival, spending a career in Congress, reaping the payoffs that accompany political longevity, and the pursuit of higher office when the right opportunity arises. Some of them even run for president.

---

[133] Foerstal, 1999, 11.

5

Understanding the Glass Ceiling
Women and the Competitive Environment

Chapters 3 and 4 suggest that women make strategic calculations that are basically the same as men's when deciding whether to pursue a congressional career or run for higher office. In this chapter, we focus upon the competitive environment faced by careerists, that is, incumbents seeking reelection to the House. Is the electoral environment the same for men and women, or do gender and incumbency interact to create a different competitive playing field for male and female incumbents? Does the presence of female incumbents draw more women into the electoral arena?

There are examples that suggest that the road to reelection may be more perilous for women. Consider the Democratic women first elected in 1992, the "Year of the Woman." In this election, fifty-two new Democrats won seats in the House, twenty women and thirty-two men. These first-term Democrats were quickly put into a precarious position when the final version of President Bill Clinton's deficit reduction plan came before the House on August 5, 1993.[1] The plan was especially controversial since deficit reduction was achieved, in part, by $250 billion in new taxes.[2] Voting for the plan among the first-term Democrats were twenty-five, or 78 percent, of the new men, and eighteen, or 90 percent, of the new women. The vote to increase taxes made many of these members vulnerable and the target of Republican efforts in the midterm elections of 1994. In fact, Republican primaries were far more competitive in those districts held by female incumbents. There were contested Republican primaries in only eight of the twenty-five districts, 32 percent, held by the first-term male Democrats who

---

[1] "Deficit-Reduction Bill Narrowly Passes," *Congressional Quarterly Almanac, 1993* (Washington, D.C.: CQ Press, 1994), 107.
[2] "Deficit-Reduction Bill Narrowly Passes," 1994, 108.

voted for the bill; there were contested Republican primaries in ten of the seventeen districts, 59 percent, held by the first-term female Democrats who supported the bill.[3] For example, the Republican primary in the 6th District of Arizona featured four Republican candidates, including one woman, competing to challenge incumbent Karen English, who had won a newly created district in 1992 with over 56 percent of the two-party vote. The winner of the Republican primary was J. D. Hayworth, a sports reporter from Phoenix with no prior political experience.[4] In the 49th District of California, Brain Bilbray defeated three opponents in the Republican primary for the opportunity to challenge Democrat Lynn Schenck, who had won her seat in 1992 with 54 percent of the vote.[5] Jon Fox defeated two male and two female competitors in the 13th District of Pennsylvania and won a rematch with Marjorie Margolies-Mezvinsky.[6]

In the general election of 1994, four of the twenty-five first-term male Democrats who supported Clinton's plan were defeated, giving them a reelection rate of 84 percent.[7] Among the first-term female Democrats who supported Clinton's plan, six of the eighteen were defeated, giving them a reelection rate of only 67 percent. The female incumbents who lost their seats were Representatives Leslie Byrne (VA), Maria Cantwell (WA), Karen English (AZ), Marjorie Margolies-Mezvinsky (PA), Lynn Schenck (CA), and Karen Shepherd (UT). Ironically, the disproportionate support women gave to Clinton's deficit plan resulted in a disproportionate number of defeats among the first-year class elected in the "Year of the Woman."

The example of 1994 suggests that the playing field for men and women may not be level. In this chapter, we explore the impact of incumbency and the competitive environment on the electoral fortunes of women. For the most part, because of the near invincibility of incumbents and the fact that most incumbents are male, it has been assumed that open seats were the primary avenue of entry for women into the House.[8] As a result, there has

---

[3] This count excludes the 11th District of Virginia, where the Republican nominee was chosen by party convention.

[4] Michael Barone and Grant Ujifusa, *Almanac of American Politics, 1998* (Washington, D.C.: National Journal, 1997), 58.

[5] Barone and Ujifusa, 1997, 220.

[6] Barone and Ujifusa, 1997, 1162. As we noted in chapter 2, Margolies-Mezvinsky had won the open-seat race against Fox in 1992 by a very narrow margin. He soundly defeated her in 1994.

[7] They were Representatives Don Johnson (GA), Tom Barlow (KY), Ted Strickland (OH), and Eric Fingerhut (OH).

[8] For a discussion of the success of women in open seats, see for example Barbara Burrell, "Women Candidates in Open-Seat Primaries for the U.S. House: 1968–1990," *Legislative Studies Quarterly* 17 (1992): 493–508; Kim Hoffman, Carrie Palmer, and Ronald Keith Gaddie, "Candidate Sex and Congressional Elections: Open Seats Before, During, and After the Year of the Woman," in *Women and Congress: Running, Winning and Ruling*, ed. Karen O'Connor (New York: Haworth Press, 2001); and Robert Bernstein, "Might Women Have the Edge in Open-Seat House Primaries?" *Women & Politics* 17 (1997): 1–26.

been very little analysis of female incumbents and their success rates.[9] But the conventional wisdom is that a "candidate's sex does not affect his or her chances of winning an election."[10] And there is some evidence that this is, in fact, the case. Female incumbents actually have slightly higher reelection rates than male incumbents. Our analysis, however, goes beyond the re-election rates for incumbents and examines several additional measures of the electoral environment in a district. Although there are variations between the parties, we find that female incumbents face a more competitive environment than their male colleagues. Female incumbents are also less likely than male incumbents to run unopposed in both their own primary and the general election; in other words, they are less likely to get a "free pass." In addition, we show that a female incumbent seeking reelection triggers more competition for the nomination within the opposition party and that female incumbents are more likely to face female challengers. These results lead us to conclude that female incumbents have a "hidden influ-ence": while on the surface, women win reelection at rates comparable to those of men, they have to work harder to retain their seats. Their presence also encourages other women to run.

When Women Run against Women

The first time two women faced each other as opponents in a general elec-tion was a House race in 1934, when Democrat Caroline O'Day ran against Republican Natalie Couch for New York's at-large open seat. O'Day was active in Democratic Party politics and was selected as a delegate to each Democratic National Convention between 1924 and 1936. She also worked with Jeannette Rankin, lobbying to give women the right to vote in New York in 1917. Her electoral success in 1934 is attributed to her friendship with Eleanor Roosevelt, who campaigned for her—the first time a first lady campaigned for anyone. In each of her three reelection bids, the Republicans nominated a woman to oppose her.[11] The first time two women ran against each other in a general election for the Senate was in 1960, when incumbent Senator Margaret Chase Smith (R-ME) defeated Lucia Cormier. Cormier served six terms in the Maine House of Representatives and was the Democratic floor leader. During the campaign, Cormier and Smith partici-pated in one of the first televised political debates, the same year as the Kennedy–Nixon debate. Cormier spent $20,000 in the effort to oust Smith,

---

[9] But see Neil Berch, "Women Incumbents, Elite Bias, and Voter Response in the 1996 and 1998 U.S. House Elections," *Women & Politics* 26 (2004): 21–33. Berch found that female incumbents faced better funded challengers than male incumbents.

[10] Richard Seltzer, Jody Newman, and Melissa Voorhees Leighton, *Sex as a Political Variable* (Boulder, Colo.: Lynne Rienner Publishers, 1997), 79.

[11] Karen Foerstel, *Biographical Dictionary of Congressional Women* (Westport, Conn.: Green-wood Press, 1999), 210–11.

who only spent $5,000. Smith won with 62 percent of the vote, the highest vote total of any Republican Senate candidate that year. The race made the cover of *Time Magazine*.[12]

It has only been very recently that women found themselves running against other women candidates with any kind of frequency in primary or general elections, and as a result, there is very little analysis of this phenomenon.[13] Since 1916, only about 3 percent of all primary and general House and Senate races have featured multiple women candidates.[14] In fact, in general elections from 1916 to 2006, this has happened 114 times. Only seven of these races were for the Senate.[15]

Since 1972, there have been ninety-eight general House elections with two women candidates. As table 5.1 shows, unlike the general trends discussed in chapter 2, there is no slow and steady increase in these numbers since 1972. During the 1970s and 1980s, the average number of general elections with two women candidates was two. In 1992, the number jumped to six. One of the races that received a great deal of attention in 1992 was the Democratic primary for the Senate in New York. The primary featured two male candidates, Robert Abrams, the state attorney general, and Al Sharpton, the flamboyant boxing promoter and preacher, along with two female candidates, Elizabeth Holtzman, the youngest woman to serve in the House, and Geraldine Ferraro, a former member of the House and vice presidential candidate. Ferraro and Holtzman targeted their campaigns almost exclusively against each other, and the race became known as "the mother of all cat fights."[16] About a month before the primary, when Ferraro had a commanding lead in the polls, the *Village Voice* ran a story entitled "Gerry

---

[12] Paul Mills, "Mr. Vacationland and Why We Can't Forget the Lady from Rumford," *Lewiston (Maine) Sun Journal*, September 3, 2000, http://members.aol.com/FAWIDIR/cormier.html (accessed June 15, 2005).

[13] The little research that does exist provides conflicting findings. Robert Bernstein's analysis of the 1992 and 1994 elections found that a woman had a substantial edge in winning an open-seat primary when she was the lone female candidate running against two or more men; in primaries with multiple women candidates, a woman was less likely to win; Robert Bernstein, "Why Are There So Few Women in the House?" *Western Political Quarterly* 39 (1986): 155–64. Richard Fox, however, in his assessment of 1992 California congressional races, found just the opposite; in primaries with multiple women candidates, all of the women tended to do better than the men; Richard Fox, *Gender Dynamics in Congressional Elections* (Thousand Oaks, Calif.: Sage, 1997). See also Burrell, 1992; Bernstein, 1997.

[14] Here, it is especially important to note that we are only referring to the two major parties. Prior to the 1950s, many women ran as third-party candidates.

[15] In addition to the Smith–Cormier race in 1960, Democrat Barbara Mikulski (MD) defeated Republican Linda Chavez in an open-seat race in 1986. In 1998, Senator Patty Murray (D-WA) defeated Republican Linda Smith. In 2002, Senator Mary Landrieu (D-LA) defeated Republican Suzanne Terrell, and Senator Susan Collins (R-ME) defeated Democrat Chellie Pingree. In 2006, Senator Olympia Snowe (R-ME) defeated Democrat Jean Hay Bright and Senator Kay Bailey Hutchison (R-TX) defeated Democrat Barbara Ann Radnofsky.

[16] Karen Foerstel and Herbert Foerstel, *Climbing the Hill: Gender Conflict in Congress* (Westport, Conn.: Praeger Press, 1996), 75.

Table 5.1 General Elections in House Races with Two Women Candidates

Year	Female Incumbent Defeats Female Challenger	Female Challenger Defeats Female Incumbent	Open Seats	Total
1972	2	0	0	2
1974	3	0	0	3
1976	1	0	0	1
1978	2	0	0	2
1980	2	0	0	2
1982	1	0	2	3
1984	2	0	0	2
1986	3	0	1	4*
1988	3	0	0	3
1990	0	0	0	0
1992	2	0	4	6
1994	9	2	0	11
1996	3	0	1	4
1998	13	0	1	14
2000	10	0	1	11
2002	7	1	2	10
2004	8	0	3	11
2006	8	0	1	9
Total	79	3	16	98

* This includes a special election in 1987 for an open seat race between Nancy Pelosi and Harriet Ross.
Sources: Data collected by the authors and from the Center for American Women and Politics, *Woman versus Woman Fact Sheet, 2006* (New Brunswick, N.J.: Rutgers University, 2006), http://www.cawp.rutgers.edu/~cawp/Facts/CanHistory/WomVWom.pdf (accessed May 16, 2007).

and the Mob."[17] Part of the story focused on an incident that occurred during her 1984 vice presidential campaign, when it was revealed that Ferraro's husband had rented space to a child pornographer with mob ties. She pledged to evict him, but he remained in the building for three more years. The day after the *Village Voice* article was published, Holtzman held a press

---

[17] The article claimed that she and her husband had ties to twenty-four mafia figures. For example, two of Ferraro's campaign supporters were named "One-Eyed Charlie" and "Billy the Butcher"; Helen Dewar, "NY Senate Primary Gets Muddy Near the Wire," *Washington Post*, August 30, 1992, A3. See also Bruce Frankel, "Anything Goes in NY Primary," *USA Today*, September 11, 1992, 10A.

conference outside the empty building and demanded that Ferraro "come clean."[18] During one of the debates, Holtzman said, "We need someone in the U.S. Senate who knows how to get rid of a child pornographer."[19] Her attack ads became some of the most memorable of the campaign, with one of them stating, "Questions Gerry Ferraro won't answer: collecting $340,000 from a child pornographer—after promising not to."[20] Abrams also attacked Ferraro for her less-than-clean past, but it was Holtzman who was criticized by some women's groups for her tactics.[21] Ultimately, Abrams narrowly won the primary, but was defeated by Republican Alfonse D'Amato in the general election.

Since 1994, the number of races with two women candidates has fluctuated from a minimum of three in 1996 to a maximum of thirteen in 1998. Table 5.1 also reveals that the vast majority of women candidates who face a female opponent are incumbents. Of the races since 1972 featuring two women in the general election, 83.7 percent have been elections with female incumbents facing female challengers. Many of these incumbents have faced female challengers several times. Incumbent Representatives Pat Schroeder (D-CO) and Nancy Johnson (R-CT), for example, faced a female challenger four times. Representatives Nancy Pelosi (D-CA), Carolyn Cheeks Kilpatrick (D-MI), Cynthia McKinney (D-GA), and Jane Harman (D-CA) faced female challengers three times. As expected, the incumbent almost always wins. Only three female challengers have defeated a female incumbent. All were cases in which a Republican challenger defeated a Democratic incumbent. In 1994, Linda Smith (R-WA) defeated incumbent Jolene Unsoeld (D-WA), and, as noted in chapter 2, Enid Greene Waldholtz (R-UT) defeated incumbent Karen Shepherd (D-UT). In 2002, Ginny Brown-Waite (R-FL) defeated incumbent Karen Thurman (D-FL) after redistricting substantially changed the district. As table 5.1 shows, very few general elections for an open House seat feature two women candidates. Since 1972, there have only been sixteen open-seat races with two women candidates. In fact, prior to 1982, there had never been an open-seat House race with two women candidates in the general election.

"Equality" in the Electoral Arena

The conventional wisdom is that once they make the decision to run, women have achieved electoral parity with men. Although women are less likely to consider running for office or to be encouraged to run, when women do

---

[18] Dewar, 1992, A3.

[19] Jay Gallagher and Kyle Hughs, "Dirty Campaign Muddies Senate Contest in NY," *Chicago Sun-Times*, September 12, 1992, 36.

[20] Alessandra Stanley, "In Primary Race for Senate, Ads Are Costly and Caustic," *New York Times*, September 13, 1992, 1.

[21] Foerstel and Foerstel, 1996, 75–76.

run for office, they are as likely to win as men.[22] Women who challenge incumbents are not any more likely to win (or lose) than men who challenge incumbents. Female incumbents are reelected at the same rates as male incumbents. In fact, female House incumbents do slightly better; their over-all reelection rate is 95.8 percent compared to 94.5 percent for men. As table 5.2 shows, over the last five decades, female incumbents have generally outperformed male incumbents. In fact, between 1982 and 1990, female incumbents had a perfect track record, winning all 101 of their campaigns. During this redistricting period, sixty-five male incumbents lost. In 2004, female incumbents also had a perfect record; all fifty-seven female House incumbents won, as did all five female incumbents in the Senate. Eight male House incumbents lost.[23] In the 2006 midterm elections, the victory rates of male (94.7 percent) and female (93.8 percent) incumbents were virtually identical. Thus, as far as winning reelection is concerned, female incumbents have reached electoral parity with men.

Moreover, female incumbents tend to win with larger electoral margins. From 1956 to 2006, slightly more female incumbents earned the status of a safe seat and were likely to win with slightly larger shares of the two-party vote than their male counterparts. On average, female incumbents won 67.3 percent of the vote, almost three percentage points higher than male incumbents, who won 64.5 percent of the vote. In every redistricting period, women won more of the two-party vote than men. During the 1970s, this difference was six percentage points.

This suggests that there is a level playing field for male and female candidates, at least in terms of outcomes. Female incumbents actually do slightly better in terms of reelection rates. They are more likely to come from a safe

---

[22] R. Darcy and Sarah Slavin Schramm, "When Women Run against Men," *Public Opinion Quarterly* 41 (1977): 1–12; Susan Welch, Margery M. Ambrosius, Janet Clark, and Robert Darcy, "The Effect of Candidate Gender on Election Outcomes in State Legislative Races," *Western Political Quarterly* 38 (1985): 464–75; Burrell, 1992; Barbara Burrell, *A Woman's Place Is in the House: Campaigning for Congress in the Feminist Era* (Ann Arbor: University of Michigan Press, 1994); R. Darcy, Susan Welch, and Janet Clark, *Women, Elections, and Representation*, 2nd ed. (Lincoln: University of Nebraska Press, 1994); Ronald Keith Gaddie and Charles Bullock, "Congressional Elections and the Year of the Woman: Structural and Elite Influences on Female Candidates," *Social Science Quarterly* 76 (1995): 749–62; Richard Seltzer, Jody Newman, and Melissa Voorhees Leighton, *Sex as a Political Variable* (Boulder, Colo.: Lynne Rienner Publishers, 1997); Barbara Palmer and Dennis Simon, "Breaking the Logjam: The Emergence of Women as Congressional Candidates," in *Women and Congress: Running, Winning, and Ruling*, ed. Karen O'Connor (Binghamton, N.Y.: Haworth Press, 2001); but see Richard Fox, Jennifer Lawless, and Courtney Feeley, "Gender and the Decision to Run for Office," *Legislative Studies Quarterly* 26 (2001): 411–35; and Richard Fox and Zoe Oxley, "Gender Stereotyping in State Executive Elections: Candidates Selection and Success," *Journal of Politics* 65 (2003): 833–50.

[23] Seven of these men lost House races, while one male Senate incumbent lost; Senate Minority Leader Tom Daschle lost his reelection bid in South Dakota to Republican John Thune. Four of the male House incumbents in Texas lost due to the unprecedented redistricting that occurred in 2003. One of the other male House incumbents, Phil Crane (R-IL), lost to a woman, Melissa Bean.

Table 5.2 Reelection Rates for Male and Female Incumbents in the House, 1956–2006

Redistricting Period	Reelection Rates for Male Incumbents (%)	Reelection Rates for Female Incumbents (%)	Male Incumbents Reelected with Safe Margin (%)	Female Incumbents Reelected with Safe Margin (%)	Average Two-Party Vote for Male Incumbents (%)	Average Two-Party Vote for Female Incumbents (%)
1956–1960	93.1	95.2	79.8	88.1	61.0	63.0
1962–1970	93.6	95.9	84.8	95.9	63.0	67.4
1972–1980	94.0	95.6	86.8	91.2	65.2	71.6
1982–1990	96.5	100.0	90.1	95.0	66.4	68.8
1992–2000	95.6	93.5	88.3	85.5	64.9	66.4
2002–2006	97.4	96.6	93.5	88.1	66.5	66.9
Overall	94.5	95.8	87.2	89.2	64.5	67.3

seat and win with a greater share of the two-party vote. Once in office, it appears that the political glass ceiling is gone. But what does the broader competitive arena look like? Are female incumbents as likely to get a "free pass" as men and face no competition at all? Table 5.1 shows that most of the general elections featuring two women candidates are races with a female incumbent and female challenger. Are female incumbents as likely to face a female challenger as male incumbents? Do women tend to run against women more often than they run against men?

Understanding the Competitive Environment

Despite parity in electoral success, campaigns with women candidates are fundamentally different than those where only men compete for nomination and election. In particular, there are differences in (1) how the media cover the campaigns of female candidates, (2) how voters perceive and evaluate male and female candidates, and (3) how candidates formulate campaign strategy in light of the stereotypes present in media coverage and voter perceptions.

Media Coverage

Reporting on campaigns has been found to vary substantially depending on the gender of the candidate. Media coverage is often "the bane of the political woman's existence."[24] It is still "an artifact of this country's age-old but unresolved debate over the women citizens' proper roles versus 'proper women's' place."[25] As Eleanor Roosevelt put it, "If you're going to be a woman in public life, you've got to have skin as thick as a rhinoceros."[26]

Press secretaries for female members of Congress consistently report that the media tend to stress that their bosses are women first and representatives second. As one press secretary put it, "The next time [our local paper] puts together a story that doesn't mention she's a mom with young children it will be a first."[27] In contrast, press secretaries for male members of Congress generally complain about the way the media cover issues and legislation their representative sponsored. News stories are still substantially more likely to mention a woman's marital status and her age than a man's.[28] Women who run for the U.S. Senate actually receive less media coverage than their male

---

[24] Linda Witt, Karen Paget, and Glenna Matthews, *Running as a Woman: Gender and Power in American Politics* (New York: Free Press, 1995), 184.

[25] Witt, Paget, and Matthews, 1995, 182.

[26] Quoted from David Niven and Jeremy Zilber, " 'How Does She Have Time for Kids and Congress?' Views on Gender and Media Coverage from House Offices," in *Women and Congress: Running, Winning, and Ruling*, ed. Karen O'Connor (New York: Haworth Press, 2001), 149.

[27] Quoted from Niven and Zilber, 2001, 154.

[28] Diane Bystrom, Mary Christine Banwart, Lynda Lee Kaid, and Terry A. Robertson, *Gender and Candidate Communication* (New York: Routledge, 2004), 179.

counterparts.[29] And when they do receive coverage, the content tends to reinforce sex role stereotypes and traditional attitudes about women's roles, particularly in campaigns for higher-level offices.[30]

In fact, media coverage of women in elective office does not appear to have changed much over the last hundred years. Beginning with the first woman to serve in Congress, female candidates have always complained about the "soft news" focus in which their wardrobe, hairstyles, femininity, and family relationships receive more emphasis than their political experience or issue positions.[31] Throughout her career in Congress, Representative Jeannette Rankin (R-MT) was frustrated by her media coverage. She was constantly asked about her wardrobe and often portrayed as "a lady about to faint."[32] Once, when an Associated Press reporter appeared in her office, she told him to "go to hell."[33] The woman who followed Rankin in 1921 was lambasted by the press. There is no doubt that Representative Alice Robertson (R-OK) was very different from Rankin; she was an ardent antisuffragist and made it very clear that she would have voted for the United States' entry into World War I. The press, however, went well beyond comparing their policy positions. The *New York Times*, for example, wrote, "She is no tender Miss Rankin ... [She has] never wore a pair of silk stockings and won't wear high-heeled shoes."[34]

---

[29] Kim Fridkin Kahn and Edie Goldenberg, "Women Candidates in the News: An Examination of Gender Differences in U.S. Senate Campaign Coverage," *Public Opinion Quarterly* 55 (1991): 180–99; and Bystrom et al., 2004. See also Pippa Norris, "Women Leaders Worldwide: A Splash of Color in the Photo Op," in *Women, Media, and Politics*, ed. Pippa Norris (New York: Oxford University Press, 1997); Martha Kropf and John Boiney, "The Electoral Glass Ceiling? Gender, Viability, and the News in U.S. Senate Campaigns," in *Women and Congress: Running, Winning and Ruling*, ed. Karen O'Connor (New York: Haworth Press, 2001); and Niven and Zilber, 2001.

[30] Witt, Paget, and Matthews, 1995; and Niven and Zilber, 2001. See also Kim Fridkin Kahn, "Characteristics of Press Coverage in Senate and Gubernatorial Elections: Information Available to Voters," *Legislative Studies Quarterly* 20 (1995): 23–35; Kim Fridkin Kahn, *The Political Consequences of Being a Woman* (New York: Columbia University, 1996); Susan Carroll and Ronnee Schreiber, "Media Coverage of Women in the 103rd Congress," in *Women, Media, and Politics*, ed. Pippa Norris (New York: Oxford University Press, 1997); Shanto Iyengar, Nicholas A. Valentino, Stephen Ansolabehere, and Adam F. Simon, "Running as a Woman: Gender Stereotyping in Political Campaigns," in *Women, Media, and Politics*, ed. Pippa Norris (New York: Oxford University Press, 1997); Pat Schroeder, *Twenty-four Years of House Work and the Place Is Still a Mess* (Kansas City, Mo.: Andrews McMeel, 1999); and Eleanor Clift and Tom Brazaitis, *Madam President* (New York: Scribner, 2000).

[31] Kathleen Hall Jamieson, *Beyond the Double Bind: Women and Leadership* (New York: Oxford University Press, 1995); Maria Braden, *Women Politicians and the Media* (Lexington: University of Kentucky Press, 1996); Fox, 1997; Niven and Zilber, 2001; Bystrom et al., 2004; Marie Wilson, *Closing the Leadership Gap: Why Women Can and Must Help Run the World* (New York: Viking, 2004); and Julie Dolan, Melissa Deckman, and Michele Swers, *Women and Politics: Paths to Power and Political Influence* (Upper Saddle River, NJ: Pearson Prentice Hall, 2007), 113–18.

[32] Witt, Paget, and Matthews, 1995, 184–85. See also Kevin Giles, *Flight of the Dove: The Story of Jeannette Rankin* (Beaverton, Ore.: Touchstone Press, 1980), 83.

[33] Quoted from Witt, Paget, and Matthews, 1995, 186.

[34] Quoted from Foerstel, 1999, 231.

Even today, examples of this kind of media coverage are not hard to find. During the 1992 Illinois Senate race, the front page of the *New York Times* ran a story contrasting Democrat Carol Moseley Braun with Republican Richard Williamson: "She is commanding and ebullient, a den mother with a cheerleader's smile; he, by comparison, is all business, like the corporate lawyer he is."[35] Buried deep in the story, which was written by a female journalist, readers were told that Moseley Braun was also a lawyer with service as a U.S. attorney.[36] When Elizabeth Dole was running for president in 2000, the *Detroit News* remarked that her "public speaking style looks and sounds like Tammy Faye Baker meets the Home Shopping Network."[37] Alison Roberts, a journalist for the *Sacramento Bee*, covered the 2005 campaign of Doris Matsui (D-CA):

> Doris Matsui, who is 60, is running to succeed her husband in Congress. As she talks about her loss and her new plans less than a week after her husband was buried, her manner is open and energetic. She sits on the edge of her living room couch, looking as though she might jump up at any moment. She is petite, dressed stylishly in a black sweater, a black-and-white nubby wool skirt and fine gold jewelry. Her delicate appearance belies the steadiness of her candidate's stance.[38]

As Representative Susan Molinari (R-NY) explained, "There I'd be, in a war zone in Bosnia, and some reporter—usually female—would comment on how I was dressed, then turn to my male colleague for answers to questions of substance."[39]

In 2005, Secretary of State Condoleezza Rice visited Wiesbaden Army Airfield. Her visit to this military base made headlines, not for what she did there, but because of what she wore. The *Washington Post* ran an article stating:

> As Rice walked out to greet the troops, [her] coat blew open in a rather swashbuckling way to reveal the top of a pair of knee-high boots. The boots had a high, slender heel that is not particularly practical. . . . In short, the boots are sexy . . . Rice looked as though she was prepared to talk tough, knock heads and do a freeze-frame "Matrix" jump kick if necessary.

---

[35] Isabel Wilkerson, "Black Woman's Senate Race Is Acquiring a Celebrity Aura," *New York Times*, July 29, 1992, 1.

[36] Witt, Paget, and Matthews, 1995, 181.

[37] Quoted from Wilson, 2004, 36.

[38] "Electing to Carry On: Grief Fuels Matsui's Bid for Congress," January 22, 2005, E1.

[39] Susan Molinari, *Representative Mom: Balancing Budgets, Bill, and Baby in the U.S. Congress* (New York: Doubleday, 1998), 7.

The article continues, "Rice's coat and boots speak of sex and power," and then refers to her as a "Dominatrix."[40] This label would follow Rice for almost a year. The outfit she wore also earned her the nickname, "Secretary of Style," and in 2006, she earned a spot on Vanity Fair's Best-Dressed List.[41]

Senator Hillary Clinton has also had her share of comments on her appearance. In 1992, during Bill Clinton's first presidential campaign, her headbands were a constant source of comment. In 2007, it was her cleavage. On July 20, an article appeared in the style section of the *Washington Post*, entitled, "Hillary Clinton's Tentative Dip into New Neckline Territory." The article began:

> There was cleavage on display Wednesday afternoon on C-SPAN2. It belonged to Senator Hillary Clinton. She was talking on the Senate floor about the burdensome cost of higher education. She was wearing a rose-colored blazer over a black top. The neckline sat low on her chest and had a subtle V-shape. The cleavage registered after only a quick glance. No scrunch-faced scrutiny was necessary. There wasn't an unseemly amount of cleavage showing, but there it was. Undeniable.

After discussing Clinton's "feminine and stately" wardrobe as first lady, the article, written by the same reporter who called Condoleezza Rice a "dominatrix," concluded that her appearance that day on the Senate floor was something quite different: "With Clinton, there was the sense that you were catching a surreptitious glimpse at something private. You were intruding—being a voyeur."[42] The article caused a firestorm on political blogs. Clinton, however, used the discussion as an opportunity for her presidential campaign, sending an email to supporters with the subject line: "Cleavage." The email called the article "grossly inappropriate," and noted that, "focusing on women's bodies instead of their ideas is insulting." The email went on to ask supporters to "Take a stand against this kind of coarseness and pettiness in American culture. And take a stand for Hillary, the most experienced, most qualified candidate running for president," followed by a link to make a contribution to her campaign.[43]

Kathleen Hall Jamieson, a professor at the Annenberg School of Communications at the University of Pennsylvania, suggested that the focus on

---

[40] Robin Givhan, "Condoleezza Rice's Commanding Clothes," *The Washington Post*, February 25, 2005, C1.

[41] "Moss tops 'Vanity Fair's best-dressed list," *USAToday.com*, July 31, 2006, http://www.usatoday.com/life/people/2006-07-31-vanity-fair-best-dressed_x.htm (accessed May 15, 2007),

[42] Robin Givhan, "Hillary Clinton's Tentative Dip into New Neckline Territory," *Washington Post*, July 20, 2007, C1.

[43] http://www.washingtonpost.com/wp-srv/artsandliving/daily/graphics/hillary_for_president 072807.pdf (accessed September 27, 2007).

fashion with female politicians is "the natural news interest in talking about what changes, and men don't look different. There is a uniform for men in power and we all know what it looks like."[44] Thus, it should come as no surprise that when Representative Nancy Pelosi became Speaker of the House, the wardrobes of the female members of the 110th Congress prompted a wave of media coverage.[45] Moreover, "these women do not altogether fear that their seriousness as politicians will be undermined by speaking aloud about hem lengths or helmet hair." As Representative Debbie Wasserman Schultz explained, her constituents pay attention to the way she looks: "I say to my constituents, 'Give me advice,' and my seniors, everyone, says, 'Debbie, get yourself a haircut.' " As one *New York Times* reporter put it, "the days of the dowdy Washington dress code may be numbered."[46]

Wardrobe aside, women who cry—or even allegedly cry—cause a media frenzy. When Rankin cast her vote against World War I in 1917, the front page of the *New York Times* ran a headline that read, "Miss Rankin—Sobbing—Votes No."[47] (See figure 5.1.) Rankin's biographer did note that as she read her sixteen-word statement on the House floor, "[t]ears wandered down her cheeks."[48] The *New York Times*, however, reported that she "sank back to her seat . . . pressed her hands to her eyes, threw her head back and sobbed,"[49] which was patently false. Moreover, the paper neglected to mention that many of the male members, regardless of how they voted, were also weeping.

Fast-forward seventy years later. In September 1987, Representative Pat Schroeder (D-CO) held a press conference in Denver announcing that she was dropping out of the Democratic presidential primary. When she came to the part of her speech when she said she would no longer be running, tears momentarily ran down her face. (See figure 5.2.) The photo of her crying has become one of the most famous in presidential politics.[50] As Schroeder put it, "Those seventeen seconds were treated like a total breakdown."[51] Her tears were the subject of weeks of media coverage and debate. In fact, she noted that even after all of her years of service in Congress, "Anytime I go to any city to talk, that's the first piece of film the TV stations pull out. They've just decided that's the only thing I've ever done that counted."[52]

---

[44] Annette Fuentes, "Out-of-style thinking," *USAtoday.com*, February 13, 2007, *http://blogs.usa today.com/oped/2007/02/post_28.html* (accessed May 15, 2007).

[45] See for example, Robin Givhan, "Muted Tones of Quiet Authority: A Look Suited To the Speaker," *The Washington Post*, Friday, November 10, C1.

[46] Lizette Alvarez, "Speaking Chic to Power," *New York Times*, January 18, 2007, G1.

[47] "Miss Rankin—Sobbing—Votes No," *New York Times*, April 6, 1917, 1.

[48] Giles, 1980, 83.

[49] "Miss Rankin—Sobbing—Votes No," 1917, 1.

[50] See for example Clift and Brazaitis, 2000; and Schroeder, 1999.

[51] Schroeder, 1999, 185.

[52] Witt, Paget, and Matthews, 1995, 205.

DEBATE LASTED 16 1/2 HOURS
Special to The New York Times.
New: Apr 6, 1917; ProQuest Historical Newspapers The New York Times (1851 - 2001)
pg. 1

DEBATE LASTED 16½ HOURS

One Hundred Speeches Were Made—Miss Rankin, Sobbing, Votes No.

ALL AMENDMENTS BEATEN

Resolution Will Take Effect This Afternoon with the President's Signature.

KITCHIN WITH PACIFISTS

Accession of the Floor Leader Added Others to the Anti-War Faction.

Special to The New York Times.
WASHINGTON, Friday, April 6.—At 3:12 o'clock this morning the House of Representatives by the overwhelming vote of 373 to 50 adopted the resolution that meant war between the Government and the people of the United States and the Imperial German Government.

Fig. 5.1 Press coverage of Jeannette Rankin's WWI vote.

Even in the twenty-first century, a woman candidate crying was big news. In 2002, when Governor Jane Swift (R) announced she would not run for reelection, the front page of the *Massachusetts Telegram and Gazette* featured a photo of her wiping a tear from her eye. (See figure 5.3.) During her entire press conference, which lasted over thirty minutes, Swift teared up for about thirty seconds as she was thanking her staff, yet that was the photo the paper ran above the fold. Even the *Boston Globe* referred to the event as

Miss Rankin Votes "No."

Miss Jeanette Rankin, the woman Representative from Montana, had been absent from the House most of the evening, but took her accustomed place while the roll call was in progress. When her name was called she sat silent. "Miss Rankin," repeated the clerk. Still no answer. The clerk went on with his droning, and floor and galleries buzzed.

On the second roll call Miss Rankin's name was again called. She sat silent as before. The eyes of the galleries were turned on her. For a moment there was breathless silence. Then Miss Rankin rose. In a voice that broke a bit but could be heard all over the still chamber she said:

" I want to stand by my country, but I cannot vote for war. I vote no." The " No " was scarcely audible.

And the maiden speech of the first woman Congressman ended in a sob. She was deeply moved and big tears were in her eyes.

Fig. 5.1 (Continued)

Fig. 5.2 Democratic Representative Pat Schroeder of Colorado prepares to wipe away tears after announcing on September 28, 1987, in Denver that she would not seek the 1988 Democratic presidential nomination. Schroeder served twenty-three years in the U.S. House of Representatives. Photo: AP Photo/Aaron Tomlinson. Reprinted by permission of Associated Press.

her "tearful State House news conference."[53] Swift said she dropped out because of the challenge she would face in the primary from Mitt Romney, former head of the Salt Lake City Olympic Committee. She stated that she could not balance running in a tough primary with her responsibilities as governor and her family; "I am sure there isn't a working parent in America that hasn't faced it, that when the demands of the two tasks you take on both increase substantially, something has to give."[54] Swift had gained national attention as the first woman to give birth while governor and was dogged by bad press during much of her term. When she decided not to run for reelection, citing family reasons, the *Lowell (Mass.) Sun* ran a front-page story entitled "Swift Sent Women a Bad Message."[55]

Over the last thirty years, while cultural attitudes about women running for office have changed substantially, and while more and more women have run for political office, it seems that media coverage of women candidates has remained constant. Female candidates may win at rates equal to their male counterparts, but the media still reinforce sex-role stereotypes and portray them in a way that can disadvantage their campaigns. In other words, except in unusual circumstances like the 1992 election when being a woman was an advantage, they do not receive equal press coverage. In order to achieve equal rates of success, female candidates may have to work harder to counteract the stereotypes typically found in their coverage.

---

[53] Frank Phillips, "Shake-up in the Governor's Race: Swift Yields to Romney Saying 'Something Had to Give,' Exits Race for Governor," *Boston Globe*, March 20, 2002, A1.

[54] Phillips, 2002, A1.

[55] Jennifer Fenn, "Swift Sent Women a Bad Message," *Lowell (Mass.) Sun*, March 22, 2002. Interestingly, with the help of friends and constituents, Schroeder has collected stories of prominent political men crying. She calls it her "sob sister file." It includes the story of George Washington's farewell meeting with his Revolutionary War generals, who all cried around the dinner table. Her file also includes President George H. W. Bush, Russian leader Mikhail Gorbachev, Lieutenant Colonel Oliver North, General Norman Schwarzkopf, President Ronald Reagan, Chile's General Augusto Pinochet, Senator John Sununu, and several male professional athletes, Schroeder, 1999, 186. Thus, crying seems to help men, but just proves that women are too emotional for politics. One exception to this is Edmund Muskie's 1972 Democratic presidential campaign. In late February, a week before the New Hampshire primary, Muskie was leading in the polls by a two to one margin, and was considered the man to beat. The *Manchester (N.H.) Union Leader* then published stories attacking his wife and accusing him of racial slurs against New Hampshire's French Canadian population. Muskie appeared live on the *CBS Evening News* to respond to the charges. Anchor Roger Mudd opened the story, stating, "Senator Edmund Muskie today denounced William Loeb, the conservative publisher of the Manchester, New Hampshire, *Union Leader*, as a 'liar' and a 'gutless coward,' " and then cut to Muskie, standing on a flatbed truck in front of the paper's offices as the snow fell, crying, his voice breaking, barely able to speak. Muskie later explained that the moment "changed people's minds about me. . . . They were looking for a strong, steady man, and here I was weak." He won the primary, but only by nine points. In the wake of this episode, Muskie's campaign floundered. He came in fourth in the next primary in Florida, and by the end of April dropped out of the race; Theodore H. White, *The Making of the President, 1972* (New York: Atheneum Publishers, 1973), 84–87.

Fig. 5.3 Massachusetts acting governor, Jane Swift, wipes a tear from her face after announcing she would not run for governor in the upcoming election, at the Statehouse in Boston on March 19, 2002. Photo: AP Photo/Lawrence Jackson. Reprinted by permission of Associated Press.

Voter Perceptions

Media coverage of campaigns involving female candidates tends to reinforce stereotypes held by voters. Male and female candidates are often perceived as having different leadership traits and different levels of competence in handling issues. Women are viewed as being more compassionate, trustworthy, and willing to compromise. Men are seen as more assertive, aggressive, and self-confident.[56] In addition to personality traits, there are perceived differences in "issue ownership," the issues on which men and women are viewed as more competent.[57] Women candidates are typically seen as more competent on issues such as education, health care, civil rights issues, the

---

[56] Mark Leeper, "The Impact of Prejudice on Female Candidates: An Experimental Look at Voter Inference," *American Politics Quarterly* 19 (1991): 248–61; Deborah Alexander and Kristi Anderson, "Gender as a Factor in the Attribution of Leadership Traits," *Political Research Quarterly* 46 (1993): 527–45; Clyde Brown, Neil Heighberger, and Peter Shocket, "Gender-Based Differences in Perceptions of Male and Female City Council Candidates," *Women & Politics* 13 (1993): 1–17; Leonie Huddy and Nayda Terkildsen, "The Consequences of Gender Stereotypes for Women Candidates at Different Levels and Types of Office," *Political Research Quarterly* 46 (1993): 503–25; Leonie Huddy and Nayda Terkildsen, "Gender Stereotypes and the Perception of Male and Female Candidates," *American Journal of Political Science* 37 (1993): 119–47; Burrell, 1994; David Niven, "Party Elites and Women Candidates: The Shape of Bias," *Women & Politics* 19 (1998): 57–80; and Kira Sanbonmatsu, "Gender Stereotypes and Vote Choice," *American Journal of Political Science* 46 (2002): 20–34.

[57] John Petrocik, "Issue Ownership in Presidential Elections, with a 1980 Case Study," *American Journal of Political Science* 40 (1996): 825–50; Jeffrey Koch, "Gender Stereotypes and Citizens' Impression of House Candidates' Ideological Orientations," *American Journal of Political Science* 46 (2002): 453–62; and Richard Fox and Zoe Oxley, "Gender Stereotyping in State Executive Elections: Candidate Selection and Success," *Journal of Politics* 65 (2003) 833–50.

environment, and welfare, while men are seen as more competent on issues such as taxes, budgets, crime, national defense, and foreign policy.[58]

Voter perceptions of a particular candidate's ideology are also strongly related to the gender of that candidate. Compassion issues such as education, health care, and welfare are largely associated with the Democratic Party and liberal policy positions. In contrast, the Republican Party is generally considered more competent to deal with issues like taxes, national defense, and crime.[59] These general party associations interact with gender. Female Democrats are perceived as more liberal than they actually are, and female Republicans are perceived as less conservative than they actually are.[60]

Thus, like political party labels, the gender of the candidate acts as a cue for voters.[61] Just knowing this small bit of information, voters "make inferences about a candidate's issue positions, policy competencies, ideological leanings, and character traits."[62] Gender provides a shortcut that helps voters "*estimate* the views of candidates."[63] Because women running for office, especially statewide office, are still a rare event, voters are more likely to rely on gender as a cue.[64] Gender cues are especially salient when women are a "novelty," such as in a primary election with a woman candidate running

---

[58] Leeper, 1991; Alexander and Andersen, 1993; Huddy and Terkildsen, 1993, "The Consequences"; Huddy and Terkildsen, 1993, "Gender Stereotypes"; Susan Carroll, *Women as Candidates in American Politics* (Bloomington: Indiana University Press, 1994); Michael Delli Carpini and Ester Fuchs, "The Year of the Woman? Candidates, Voters, and the 1992 Elections," *Political Science Quarterly* 108 (1993): 29–36; Karen Kaufman and John Petrocik, "The Changing Politics of American Men: Understanding the Sources of the Gender Gap," *American Journal of Political Science* 43 (1999): 864–87; Kathy Dolan, "Electoral Context, Issues, and Voting for Women in the 1990s," in *Women and Congress: Running, Winning and Ruling*, ed. Karen O'Connor (New York: Haworth Press, 2001); Sanbonmatsu, 2002, "Gender Stereotypes"; Fox and Oxley, 2003; and Bystrom et al., 2004; but see Kathy Dolan, *Voting for Women: How the Public Evaluates Women Candidates* (Boulder, Colo.: Westview Press, 2004). For a review of this literature, see Michelle Swers, "Research on Women in Legislatures: What Have We Learned, Where Are We Going?" in *Women in Congress: Running, Winning, Ruling*, ed. Karen O'Connor (Binghamton, N.Y.: Haworth Press, 2001).

[59] Petrocik, 1996.

[60] Alexander and Anderson, 1993; Huddy and Terkildsen, 1993, "Gender Stereotypes"; and Jeffrey Koch, "Do Citizens Apply Gender Stereotypes to Infer Candidates' Ideological Orientations?" *Journal of Politics* 62 (2000): 414–29.

[61] Monika McDermott, "Voting Cues in Low-Information Elections: Candidate Gender as a Social Information Variable in Contemporary U.S. Elections," *American Journal of Political Science* 41 (1997): 270–83; Monika McDermott, "Race and Gender Cues in Low-Information Elections," *Political Research Quarterly* 51 (1998): 895–918; Jeffrey Koch, "Do Citizens Apply Gender Stereotypes to Infer Candidates' Ideological Orientations?" *Journal of Politics* 62 (2000): 414–29; Koch, 2002; Richard Lau and David Redlawsk, "Advantages and Disadvantages of Cognitive Heuristics in Political Decision Making," *American Journal of Political Science* 45 (2001): 951–71; Sanbonmatsu, 2002, "Gender Stereotypes"; Lonna Rae Atkeson, "Not All Cues Are Created Equal: The Conditional Impact of Female Candidates on Political Engagement," *Journal of Politics* 65 (2003): 1040–61; and David King and Richard Matland, "Sex and the Grand Old Party: An Experimental Investigation of the Effect of Candidate Sex on Support for a Republican Candidate," *American Politics Research* 31 (2003): 595–612; but see Seth Thompson and Janie Steckenrider, "The Relative Irrelevance of Candidate Sex," *Women & Politics* 17 (1997): 71–92.

[62] Koch, 2000, 414.

[63] McDermott, 1997, 271.

[64] Koch, 2002, 460. See also Atkeson, 2003.

against several male competitors.[65] A 1994 survey found that two-thirds of voters felt that women had a tougher time than men getting elected to public office. Even voters who said they would vote for a woman candidate predicted she would lose.[66] Whether they actually are or not, women candidates may still be perceived as vulnerable by voters. If nothing else, it is clear that gender and party interact and have an impact on voter perceptions of a candidate's qualifications, issue positions, and ideology.

Campaign Strategy

Our discussion suggests that successful female candidates must adapt their campaign strategies to account for gender stereotypes about their character traits, issue competence, and ideology, as well as the media coverage that reinforces sex role stereotypes.[67] In essence, women face particular challenges in their "presentation of self."[68] According to Richard Fenno's classic work, *Homestyle: House Members in Their Districts*, this is the fundamental act of campaigning in which candidates place themselves in the "immediate physical presence of others" and "make a presentation of themselves."[69] In other words, candidates cultivate their images. The presentation of self is both verbal and nonverbal. The nonverbal is critical, particularly for women, since it may enhance or undermine the credibility given to verbal presentations and the level of trust that audiences place in the candidate.[70] For example, Mary Beth Rogers, the campaign manager for Ann Richards' successful run for Texas governor in 1990, explained that the main goal of the campaign was to portray her as a mother, former teacher, and "compassionate outsider" as well as a savvy and tough politician. Television ads featured Richards with her father, promising that she would get tough on insurance companies that were shirking their responsibilities for people like her "daddy."[71]

---

[65] Koch, 2002, 455.

[66] Seltzer, Newman, and Leighton, 1997, 76.

[67] See also Mandel, 1981.

[68] Richard Fenno, *Home Style: House Members in Their Districts* (Boston: Little Brown, 1978), 898.

[69] Fenno, 1978, 898. See for example Dianne Bystrom, "Advertising, Web Sites, and Media Coverage: Gender and Communication Along the Campaign Trail," in *Gender and Elections: Shaping the Future of American Politics*, eds. Susan Carroll and Richard Fox (New York: Cambridge University Press, 2006); and Dolan, Deckman, and Swers, 2007, 159–72.

[70] For example, in her first unsuccessful campaign for the Senate in 1974, Barbara Mikulski realized that "one of my problems is that I don't fit the image of a U.S. senator. You know, an Ivy-League-looking male, over 50 and over six feet tall"; quoted from Mandel, 1981, 36. Instead, she was a "round, short, fuzzy-haired Polish woman from Southeast Baltimore"; Mandel, 1981, 36. So as part of her campaign, she went on a diet. She said, "It showed people I could keep my mouth shut. . . . But it also showed them that when I make up my mind to do something, I can follow a goal"; quoted from Mandel, 1981, 36.

[71] Richards was able to walk this fine line with a great deal of success in 1990. George W. Bush, however, effectively neutralized this in 1994 and was able to portray her as an "insider"; Sue Tolleson-Rienhart and Jeanie Stanley, *Claytie and the Lady: Ann Richards, Gender, and Politics*

It is from this presentation of self that voters draw inferences about the leadership traits of candidates. For the woman who seeks elective office, the challenge is to "craft a message and a public persona" establishing that "she can be as clear and independent a decision maker as any man, but more caring and trustworthy."[72] As one political consultant explained, in appearing before the public, women candidates "can't afford not to be nice, [or they will] immediately be branded as a bitch."[73] Thus, "[T]he woman candidate has to maintain some level of the traditional altruistic and a political above-it-all demeanor expected of a lady, all the while beating her opponents in what sometimes seems the closest thing to blood sport that is still legal."[74]

Women candidates must also account for the "political mood" or temper of the times, both nationally and locally, in formulating their campaign message and issue agendas. There are two important ways that political mood can affect women's success. The first pertains to the problems and issues deemed most important by their constituency and the degree to which these concerns mesh with voter perceptions of issue competency. If the focus rests on compassion issues, as it did in 1992, female candidates will be advantaged. In such circumstances, when women candidates use sex role expectations to their advantage, run on compassion issues, and target women voters, they are substantially more likely to win.[75] To the extent that the political mood and agenda focus on budgets and economic policy or foreign and defense policy, as they did in 2002, women must formulate strategies to weaken the stereotypes and establish perceptions of issue

---

in Texas (Austin: University of Texas Press, 1994); and Jeanie Stanley, "Gender and the Campaign for Governor," in Texas Politics: A Reader, 2nd ed., eds. Anthony Champagne and Edward Harpham (New York: W. W. Norton, 1998). Other women have also attempted to combine these two images, including Dianne Feinstein (D-CA), who ran for governor on the slogan "Tough but Caring"; Celia Morris, Storming the Statehouse: Running for Governor with Ann Richards and Dianne Feinstein (New York: Charles Scribner's Sons, 1992). See also Theodore Sheckels, Jr., "Mikulski vs. Chavez for the Senate from Maryland in 1986 and the 'Rules' for Attack Politics," Communication Quarterly 42 (1994): 311–26; and Julie Dolan, "A Decade after the Year of the Woman: Female Candidates' Success Rates in the 2002 Elections" (paper presented at the Southern Political Science Association Annual Meeting, January 2005, New Orleans).

[72] Witt, Paget, and Matthews, 1995, 214.

[73] Quoted from Witt, Paget, and Matthews, 1995, 214.

[74] Witt, Paget, and Matthews, 1995, 214.

[75] The quintessential example is Patty Murray, who ran as the "mom in tennis shoes." See Witt, Paget, and Matthews, 1995; Iyengar et al. 1997; Leonard Williams, "Gender, Political Advertising, and the 'Air Wars,' " Women and Elective Office: Past, Present and Future, eds. Sue Thomas and Clyde Wilcox (New York: Oxford University Press, 1998); Sanbonmatsu, 2002, "Gender Stereotypes"; Paul Herrnson, J. Celeste Lay, and Atiya Kai Stokes, "Women Running 'as Women': Candidate Gender, Campaign Issues, and Voter-Targeting Strategies," Journal of Politics 65 (2003): 244–55; and Shauna Shames, "The 'Un-Candidates': Gender and Outsider Signals in Women's Political Advertisements," Women & Politics 25 (2003): 115–47; but see Jerry Perkins and Diane Fowlkes, "Opinion Representation versus Social Representation; or Why Women Can't Run as Women and Win," American Political Science Review 74 (1980): 92–103.

competency on these traditional male issues. Second, there are times when the political mood is especially restive toward "politics as usual" and incumbents. Women can take advantage of being perceived as "outsiders" and as more honest during election cycles when events and scandals call into question the trustworthiness of politicians, which became a major theme in 2006.[76] Thus, the campaign strategies employed by female candidates must take these factors into consideration. If they do not, female candidates could be substantially disadvantaged at the polls.

Implications for the Competitive Environment

These three factors—media coverage, voter perceptions, and campaign strategy—suggest important implications for the electoral competition that women might face and lead us to draw several conclusions. Female candidates, including female incumbents, might be perceived as more vulnerable in the electoral arena than male candidates.[77] Despite the increasing presence of women in the electoral arena, a female nominee or incumbent remains a novelty. From 1992 to 2000, a woman won the Democratic nomination for the House at least once in 176 districts (40.5 percent); voters in the remaining 259 districts (59.5 percent) never saw a female Democratic nominee. In other words, during that entire eight-year period, there were no female Democratic candidates in a general election in almost two-thirds of all districts. The nomination of a female Republican is even more of a rare event. For the same period, there were female Republican nominees in only 113 districts (26.0 percent), and no female nominees in 322 districts (74.0 percent). This is particularly important, because reliance on gender stereotypes is stronger in exactly these circumstances, when candidates are perceived as novelties.[78]

Moreover, as much as a candidate's gender serves as a cue for voters, it can serve as a cue for potential opponents. Male candidates typically reformulate their campaign strategies when they run against women, and many plan campaign activities that target women voters.[79] In its August–September 1990 issue, *Campaigns and Elections*, a widely read trade magazine, ran an article entitled "How to Defeat Women and Blacks," advising men to "steal

---

[76] Over the course of the 2006 election cycle, four Republican incumbents resigned their House seats because of scandals: Randy Cunningham of California, Majority Leader Tom DeLay of Texas, Bob Ney of Ohio, and Mark Foley of Florida. Cunningham, DeLay, and Ney were implicated in the investigation of lobbyist Jack Abramoff while Foley was accused of sending illicit computer messages to House pages. The advantages of female candidates during times of scandal are discussed by Burrell, 1994; Kahn, 1996; and Sanbonmatsu, 2002, "Gender Stereotypes."

[77] See for example Allison Stevens, "The Strength of These Women Shows in Their Numbers," *CQ Weekly*, October 25, 2003, 2625.

[78] Koch, 2002.

[79] In a survey of California State Senate campaign managers, Richard Fox found that eighteen of twenty-three (78 percent) campaign managers for male candidates said that they changed their strategy when it became apparent they would face a female opponent; Fox, 1997, 49.

their opponent's rainbow" by quickly and specifically raising women's issues or compassion issues in order to "[b]eat your opponent to her strongest issue."[80] The very next issue of the magazine featured a piece by Sharon Rodine, president of the National Women's Political Caucus, entitled "How to Beat Bubba." Rodine observed, "We know that women are targeted more often due in great part to their perceived vulnerability in raising money and seeking seats which have been held by men for years."[81] She argues that if women "run as women," this can be used against them. If a woman candidate builds her campaign around stereotypes in order to win, this may actually limit her strategic choices and the types of responses she can use effectively. Thus, even though women win elective office as often as men do, women candidates, especially incumbents, may be initially perceived as easier to defeat and may face a more competitive environment.

A second implication is more positive. Conceivably, women candidates may foster competition in a different way, as role models for other women. In states with competitive female candidates, women citizens were more likely to discuss politics, have higher levels of political knowledge, and feel politically efficacious; viable women candidates "represent symbolic and substantive cues to women citizens that increase their political engagement."[82] The logical extension of this is that successful women candidates inspire other women to run. Beyond the role model effect, however, deciding to run against another woman can also be a strategic decision.[83] Against the backdrop of gender stereotypes, it is important to consider what the success of a woman winning a House seat signifies. It demonstrates that the female candidate was able to neutralize the stereotypes or make them work to her advantage. Her victory serves as a cue signaling that a woman can overcome the hurdles and compete successfully in that district.

---

[80] David Beiler, "How to Defeat Women and Blacks," *Campaigns & Elections*, August–September 1990. See also Fox, 1997; and Carole Chaney, "Running against a Woman: Advertising Strategies in Mixed-Sex Races for the United States Senate and Their Impact on Candidate Evaluation" (paper presented at the Western Political Science Association Annual Meeting, 1998, Los Angeles).

[81] Sharon Rodine, "How to Beat Bubba," *Campaigns and Elections Magazine*, October–November, 1990.

[82] Atkeson, 2003, 1042. Research suggests that a female candidate may stimulate more voter participation among women; Susan Hansen, "Talking about Politics: Gender and Contextual Effects on Political Proselytizing," *Journal of Politics* 59 (1997): 73–103; and Angela High-Pippert, "Female Empowerment: The Influence of Women Representing Women," *Women & Politics* 19 (1998): 53–67. See also Jennifer Lawless, "Politics of Presence? Congresswomen and Symbolic Representation," *Political Research Quarterly* 57 (2004): 81–99; and David E. Campbell and Christina Wolbrecht, "See Jane Run: Women Politicians as Role Models for Adolescents," *Journal of Politics* 68 (2006): 233–47.

[83] See for example Wilma Rule, "Why Women Don't Run: The Critical and Contextual Factors in Women's Legislative Recruitment," *Western Political Quarterly* 34 (1981): 60–77; Rosalyn Cooperman and Bruce Oppenheimer, "The Gender Gap in the House of Representatives," in *Congress Reconsidered*, 7th ed., eds. Lawrence Dodd and Bruce Oppenheimer (Washington, D.C.: CQ Press, 2001); Palmer and Simon, 2001; and Barbara Palmer and Dennis Simon, "Political Ambition and Women in the U.S. House of Representatives, 1916–2000," *Political Research Quarterly* 56 (2003): 127–38.

Thus, gender stereotypes may work in a number of ways to stimulate competition. The novelty of female candidates may suggest vulnerability. In addition, female candidates as role models may inspire more women to run. A female incumbent may provide a "strategic signal" to other women about the probability of winning a district. Given all of this, do female incumbents face more competition to retain their House seats than their male counterparts? Do female incumbents face more competition from female candidates?

Explaining the Competitive Environment

On the surface, electoral outcomes for the U.S. House do indicate parity between male and female candidates. As table 5.2 showed, female incumbents actually do slightly better than male incumbents. This does suggest that there is gender equality, at least as far as the final outcome of an election is concerned. We expect, however, given the disparity in press coverage and the way gender can affect voter perceptions and campaign strategies, that female candidates, particularly female incumbents, may be perceived as more vulnerable, and as a result may draw more competition than their male counterparts. In addition, female incumbents may have a "role model" effect and draw more female competition than their male counterparts.

While reelection rates show that there are no differences between male and female incumbents, there are, however, other aspects of the competitive environment that have not been explored. In addition to reelection rates, there are three other indicators of competition: no opponent in the primary, no major party opponent in the general election, and the "free pass" in which the incumbent has no opposition in both the primary and general elections. By examining these additional measures of competition, we produce a more complete and nuanced picture of the electoral environment.[84]

As table 5.3 shows, female incumbents are less likely to enjoy the luxury of having no opponent. In districts where women stand for reelection, there are slightly more contested primaries: 31.7 percent of districts compared to 29.0 percent of districts where men stand for reelection. Female incumbents also have fewer uncontested general elections: 9.8 percent compared to 16.2 percent for men. In fact, female incumbents are approximately half as likely to get the "free pass"; while 12.0 percent of male incumbents had no competition in their primary or general elections, only 6.6 percent of women had no competition.

There are substantial partisan differences as well. Among Democratic incumbents, men and women are equally likely to face competition in their primary, 36 percent of men and 34.6 percent of women, but the parity ends

---

[84] The full statistical tests are available in Barbara Palmer and Dennis Simon, "When Women Run against Women: The Hidden Influence of Female Incumbents in Elections to the U.S. House of Representatives, 1956–2002," *Politics and Gender* 1 (2005): 39–63.

Table 5.3 Uncontested Primary and General Elections among Incumbent Candidates for the House, 1956–2006

	Male Incumbents	Female Incumbents
All Incumbents		
Contested primary election	29.0%	31.7%
	(2,694/9,266)	(202/637)
Uncontested general election	16.2%	9.8%***
	(1,535/9,459)	(64/651)
Uncontested primary and general elections	12.0%	6.6%***
	(1,108/9,268)	(42/637)
Democratic Incumbents		
Contested primary election	36.0%	34.6%
	(1,917/5,325)	(145/419)
Uncontested general election	21.2%	11.5%***
	(1,143/5,386)	(49/425)
Uncontested primary and general elections	14.6%	6.9%***
	(780/5,325)	(29/419)
Republican Incumbents		
Contested primary election	19.7%	26.1%*
	(777/3,941)	(57/218)
Uncontested general election	9.6%	6.6%
	(392/4,073)	(15/226)
Uncontested primary and general elections	8.3%	6.0%
	(328/3,943)	(13/218)

A t-test for the difference in proportions is used for each male–female comparison. *** $p < .001$, ** $p < .01$, and * $p < .05$.

there. Democratic female incumbents are substantially more likely to face major party opposition in the general election; the proportion of uncontested general elections (11.5 percent) is significantly lower than the rate for men (21.2 percent). A similar result holds for the "free pass." Only 6.9 percent of Democratic female incumbents avoid competition throughout the election cycle, compared to 14.6 percent for Democratic males.

It should be noted that, in general, Republican incumbents face a less contentious primary arena than their Democratic counterparts: Democratic incumbents face primary challenges in 35.9 percent of their primaries, whereas the rate for Republicans is only 20.0 percent. But the patterns between Republican men and women are different in two ways. First, in contrast to the parity between men and women in Democratic primaries, female Republican incumbents are more likely to be challenged in a primary than their male counterparts, 26.1 percent versus 19.7 percent. Second, there are only slight differences in the rates of competition that male and female Republican incumbents face in the general election, 9.6 and 6.6 percent respectively. In addition, male and female Republican incumbents are also about equally as likely to receive a "free pass" and face no competition at either stage. Thus, while female Democratic incumbents face more competition in the general election, female Republican incumbents face more competition in their primaries. These results demonstrate that the competitive environment is, in part, a product of an interaction between gender and party.

We also expect that the relationship between incumbent gender and competition should not be confined to contests within the party. If, as we hypothesize, female incumbents are perceived as vulnerable, then there should be greater competition for the nomination within the opposition party as well. As table 5.4 shows, competition for the opposition party nomination is significantly greater in districts with a female incumbent. When a female incumbent is running for reelection, there are contested primaries in the opposition party in 47.3 percent of the districts. When a male incumbent is running for reelection, there are contested primaries in the opposition party in 41.7 percent of the districts. For example, in 2006, Representative Melissa Bean, a Democratic incumbent from the 8th District of Illinois, ran for her second term. She had defeated Republican incumbent Phil Crane two years prior with 51.7 percent of the vote. In her reelection campaign, she ran unopposed in her own primary, but six Republicans, including one woman, ran in the opposition primary. In the general election, she defeated former investment banker David McSweeney with 53.9 percent of the vote.

The relationship holds for both parties, although competition is more intense in Republican districts. When a female Democrat is the incumbent, 43.5 percent of Republican primaries are contested, compared to 38.3 percent of districts where the Democratic incumbent is male. Similarly, when a female Republican holds the House seat, 54.4 percent of the Democratic nominees are chosen in contested primaries, compared to 45.6 percent when the incumbent is a Republican male. Together, tables 5.3 and 5.4 show that female incumbents are associated with a more competitive electoral environment; they face more contested races than their male colleagues and, at the same time, foster more contested primary races within the opposition party.

While this suggests that female incumbents face more competition than male incumbents in general, do they draw other women into the campaign? In other words, are women more likely to run against women than men? Table 5.5 reports the proportion of contested primaries in which women

Table 5.4 Contested Primary Races for the House within the Opposition Party, 1956–2006

	Districts with Male Incumbents	Districts with Female Incumbents
All opposition contests in districts where an incumbent seeks reelection	41.7% (3,259/7,818)	47.3%** (275/581)
Contested Republican primaries in districts with Democratic incumbent seeking reelection	38.3% (1,606/4,197)	43.5%* (163/375)
Contested Democratic primaries in districts with Republican incumbent seeking reelection	45.6% (1,653/3,621)	54.4%** (112/206)

The cell entries represent the proportion of contested primaries. A t-test for the difference in proportions is used for each male-female comparison. ** p < .01 and * p < .05.

challenged an incumbent of their own party and an incumbent of the opposition party. Additionally, to provide a composite picture of female challengers, we combine the first two rows of the table and report the total proportion of women seeking the nomination in districts held by male and female incumbents. The table shows that female incumbents foster additional female candidacies in a district. Among all incumbents, the percentage of female incumbents being challenged by a woman in their own party primary, 15.3 percent, exceeds the rate at which women challenge male incumbents, 11.1 percent. This intraparty gender effect is more pronounced among Democrats than Republicans. Female Democrats are challenged by women in 17.2 percent of contested primaries, while male Democrats are challenged by women in 11.8 percent of the contests. Among Republicans, the pattern still holds, but the difference is not significant. Women challenge female Republicans in 10.5 percent of the contests, while male incumbents face a female opponent in 9.3 percent of the contested Republican primaries.

Table 5.5 also reveals that female incumbents seeking reelection influence the gender distribution of candidates seeking the nomination within the opposition party. Women are significantly more likely to seek the nomination of the opposition party in districts with a female incumbent (23.3 percent) than in districts with a male incumbent (13.5 percent). This relationship holds for both parties. Democratic women are more likely to run in districts held by female Republicans (24.3 percent) than in districts held by male Republicans (17.1 percent). The difference is larger in districts with Democratic incumbents. The presence of Republican women as candidates is greater in districts held by female Democrats (22.7 percent) than in districts held by male Democrats (10.9 percent). Finally, consider the aggregate picture of primary elections for the U.S. House of Representatives, presented in the third row of table 5.5. The presence of additional female candidates is significantly greater in districts where a female incumbent

Table 5.5 Female Competition in Contested Primary Races for the House, 1956–2006

	All Male Incumbents	All Female Incumbents	Male Democratic Incumbents	Female Democratic Incumbents	Male Republican Incumbents	Female Republican Incumbents
Within Incumbent Party						
Incumbent faces a primary challenge from a female candidate	11.1% (298/2,694)	15.3%* (31/202)	11.8% (226/1,917)	17.2%* (25/145)	9.3% (72/777)	10.5% (6/57)
Within Opposition Party						
Female candidate seeks nomination within the opposition party	13.5% (1,296/9,568)	23.3%*** (153/658)	10.9% (594/5,470)	22.7%*** (98/432)	17.1% (702/4,098)	24.3%**** (55/226)
Within Incumbent and Opposition Party (Sum of Rows 1 and 2)						
Proportion of elections with a female challenger for the nomination	13.0% (1,594/12,262)	21.4%*** (184/860)	11.1% (820/7,387)	21.3%*** (123/577)	15.9% (774/4,875)	21.6%*** (61/283)

A t-test for the difference in proportions is used for each male-female comparison. *** $p < .001$, ** $p < .01$, and * $p < .05$.

Table 5.6 Women Winning the Nomination of the Opposition Party in Districts where an Incumbent is Seeking Reelection, 1956–2006

Opposition Party	Districts Held by Male Incumbent	Districts Held by Female Incumbent
All opposition nominations, Democrats and Republicans, in districts where an incumbent seeks reelection	7.5% (715/9,568)	13.7 %*** (90/658)
Democrats running in districts with a Republican incumbent seeking reelection	10.2% (420/4,098)	15.0%** (34/226)
Republicans running in districts with a Democratic incumbent seeking reelection	5.4% (295/5,470)	13.0%*** (56/432)

The cell entries represent the proportion of nomination opportunities won by female candidates. These opportunities include contested primaries, uncontested primaries, and convention nominations. A t-test for the difference in proportions is used for each male-female comparison. *** $p < .001$, ** $p < .01$, and * $p < .05$.

holds the seat. This relationship holds in districts held by Democrats (21.3 versus 11.1 percent), in those controlled by Republicans (21.6 versus 15.9 percent), and in the aggregate (21.4 versus 13 percent). This suggests that female incumbents do provide, as role models or as testaments to the "winability" of the district, a signal that leads other women to run for the seat.

Moreover, within the opposition, not only do women seek the nomination more frequently in districts held by female incumbents, but they win the nomination more frequently in these districts as well. Table 5.6 presents the percentage of nominations won by female candidates in the opposition party. Across all of these opportunities, the success rate for women in districts with a female incumbent is double the rate in districts with male incumbents. The relationship also holds for both Democrats and Republicans. In fact, the Republican difference in success rates, 13.0 percent versus 5.4 percent, is larger than the rate among female Democrats seeking the nomination in Republican-held districts (15 versus 10.2 percent). The results in table 5.6 lend further credence to our earlier observation that the presence of a female incumbent may serve as a signal about the electoral prospects for women in a district. Because more women seek and win nominations in districts with a female incumbent, the presence of a female incumbent is likely to be a salient factor in the strategic decisions women make about where to run.

An additional question that arises from our analysis is whether the effect of female incumbents on the competitive environment varies with the level of electoral security. Table 5.7 presents seven measures of the electoral

Table 5.7 Electoral Competition for Incumbents Seeking Reelection, 1956–2006

	Safe Male Incumbent	Safe Female Incumbent	Marginal Male Incumbent	Marginal Female Incumbent
Uncontested general election	18.7% (1,491/7,967)	11.5%*** (64/556)	2.9% (44/1,493)	0% (0/96)
Incumbent faces contested primary	29.4% (2,297/7,824)	31.5% (172/546)	27.5% (397/1,442)	33.0% (30/91)
Incumbent not contested in primary or general election	13.7% (1,076/7,826)	7.7%*** (42/546)	2.2% (32/1,442)	0% (0/91)
Incumbent challenged by female in party primary	10.2% (260/2,547)	12.3% (27/220)	9.3% (39/418)	11.1% (4/36)
Contested primary in opposition party	38.7% (2,479/6,397)	43.9%* (215/490)	54.8% (780/1,421)	65.9%* (60/91)
Female seeks nomination in opposition party	12.9% (1039/8,050)	20.6%*** (116/562)	16.9% (256/1,517)	39.2%*** (38/97)
Female wins nomination in opposition party	7.3% (589/8,050)	12.6%*** (14/562)	8.1% (123/1,517)	20.6%*** (20/97)

A t-test for the difference in proportions is used for each male-female comparison. *** p < .001, ** p < .01, and * p < .05.

environment for marginal male and female incumbents.[85] There are significant differences between safe female incumbents and their male counterparts on five of the seven indicators. In districts with female incumbents, there are substantially fewer uncontested general elections, (11.5 percent versus 18.7 percent for men) and fewer "free passes" (7.7 percent versus 13.7 percent for men). In this sense, women actually enjoy less of the electoral security that is conventionally attributed to holding a safe seat. While not statistically significant, the table shows that women from safe districts do face more primary challenges and more of these challenges from women than their male counterparts.

Safe female incumbents also stimulate more competition within the opposition party. There were contested primaries in the opposition party in 43.9 percent of the districts with safe female incumbents, while there were contested primaries in the opposition party in 38.7 percent of the districts with safe male incumbents. Safe female incumbents also promote greater participation by women within the opposition party. In 20.6 percent of the districts with safe female incumbents, women ran in the opposition party's primary. This occurred in only 12.9 percent of the districts with male

---

[85] In this analysis, we rely upon the conventional definition of safe and marginal districts. A marginal district is one in which the incumbent won with less than 55 percent of the two-party vote in the previous election.

incumbents. Moreover, women were more likely to win the opposition party primary in these districts; female candidates in opposition party primaries won the nomination in 12.6 percent of the districts with safe female incumbents, while they won in 7.3 percent of the districts with safe male incumbents. Our analysis suggests that, in general elections, not only do safe female incumbents face more competition than safe male incumbents, but also the competition is more likely to be female.

A remarkable illustration is found in the electoral career of Republican Representative Connie Morella. Morella was first elected in 1986 from Maryland's 8th District, which wraps around the northern half of Washington, D.C. A large proportion of her constituents were federal employees, and the district has always leaned Democratic. As a result, throughout her career, Morella was one of the most liberal Republicans in the House. As table 5.8 shows, only in 1996 did she face any major competition for renomination. She was never challenged by a Republican woman. However, there always was a great deal of competition within the Democratic primary. In 1996, for example, there were nine candidates in the Democratic primary, even though Morella won the previous election with over 70 percent of the vote. Several of the challengers in the Democratic primary were women, but none of them ever won the nomination. The level of competition is quite surprising in light of the "safeness" of her district. Despite the fact that Morella was a Republican in a Democratic district, she was quite popular among her constituents. Until 2000, she consistently won reelection with at least 60 percent of the vote. In fact, her average two-party vote for all of her successful reelection campaigns was 65.3 percent, well over the safe

Table 5.8 Representative Connie Morella (R-MD) and her Competition

Year	Her Primary Opponents	Democratic Primary Opponents	Female Democratic Primary Opponents	Her Vote Total in the General Election (%)
1986*	2	7	1	52.9
1988	0	5	1	62.7
1990	1	3	0	76.8
1992	0	8	0	72.5
1994	1	5	0	70.3
1996	3	9	2	61.3
1998	1	7	1	60.3
2000	0	5	3	53.1
2002	0	4	1	48.3

*Open seat.

margin of 55 percent. During the redistricting cycle in the wake of the 2000 U.S. Census, Maryland's state legislature substantially redrew her district, making it even more Democratic. As a result, in 2002, State Senator Chris Van Hollen won a four-way primary that included one woman, and then went on to defeat Morella in one of the most expensive and highly contested races of the year.[86] He won with only 51.7 percent of the vote.

Table 5.7 shows that there have only been forty-two safe female incumbents who enjoyed a "free pass" and had no competition in their primary or general elections. Eleven of these races (26.2 percent) were in 2004 and 2006. In 2006, uncontested primary and general elections were enjoyed by Corrine Brown (D-FL), Diana DeGette (D-CO), Carolyn Cheeks Kilpatrick (D-MI), Hilda Solis (D-CA), and Debbie Wasserman Schultz (D-FL); in 2004, these passes went to Representatives Marsha Blackburn (R-TN), Eddie Bernice Johnson (D-TX), Stephanie Tubbs Jones (D-OH), Sheila Jackson-Lee (D-TX), Hilda Solis (D-CA), and Diane Watson (D-CA). The lone Republican, Representative Blackburn, was running for her second term.[87] Of the nine Democrats to "earn" free passes in these elections, six are African American and one is Latina; they all came from majority-minority districts where the total proportion of blacks, Hispanics, and Asians exceeds 80 percent. All of these districts voted overwhelmingly Democratic in the 2004 presidential election.[88] This suggests that women of color, who tend to come from racially gerrymandered districts, may be more secure electorally than white women. In the aggregate, however, the number of safe female incumbents who face no competition is substantially lower than the number of safe male incumbents.

The environment for marginal female incumbents is even more competitive. As table 5.7 shows, no marginal female incumbent has been unopposed in the general election over the five decades of our study. In contrast, forty-four marginal male incumbents had no opponents. Similarly, there are no marginal female incumbents who enjoyed the "free pass." Thirty-two marginal male incumbents have. While these numbers are small, it is quite surprising that marginal female incumbents *always* have competition.

With respect to competition within the opposition party, there are also substantial differences between men and women from marginal districts. As expected, the data show that marginal districts are more competitive than

---

[86] Jacki Koszczuk and H. Amy Stern, eds., *CQ's Politics in America, 2006* (Washington, D.C.: CQ Press, 2005), 485.

[87] Although the Democratic Party did not field an opponent, she spent over $575,000 on her campaign to fight "those who would oppose freedom and would oppose strengthening democracy," "Marsha Blackburn: Campaign Finance/Money-Contributions-Congressman 2004," http://www.opensecrets.org/politicians/summary.asp?CID=N00003105&cycle=2004 (accessed July 3, 2005); and Bartholomew Sullivan, "Safe Territory: Redrawing of Congressional District Lines Puts Incumbents in Driver's Seat," *Memphis Commercial Appeal,* October 27, 2004, B1.

[88] Koszczuk and Stern, 2005.

safe districts in general, but there is a clear gender effect; 65.9 percent of marginal districts with female incumbents had contested primaries in the opposition party, compared to only 54.8 percent of the marginal districts with male incumbents. Representative Stephanie Herseth Sandlin (D-SD), for example, who won a special election in the summer of 2004 with only 50.6 percent of the two-party vote, saw seven Republicans competing to challenge her reelection in the fall.[89] Moreover, marginal female incumbents were more than twice as likely to draw female candidates into the opposition primary. In 39.2 percent of the districts with marginal female incumbents, women ran in the opposition primary, compared to 16.9 percent of the districts with marginal male incumbents. And women were over twice as likely to win the opposition primary in districts with marginal female incumbents. Women won the opposition primary in 20.6 percent of districts with marginal female incumbents, while they won in only 8.1 percent of districts with marginal male incumbents. As table 5.7 reveals, in marginal districts, female incumbents not only stimulate more competition within the opposition party, but also draw more women of the opposition party into the fray.

Conclusion

In 1986, after serving five terms in the House, Barbara Mikulski (D-MD) won an open Senate seat with 61 percent of the vote. Despite the fact that she won her seat by a margin conventionally considered safe, in her reelection campaign of 1992, fifteen Republicans ran in the opposition primary. Even more astonishing was that six candidates challenged her in the Democratic primary. She won the primary easily with 77 percent of the vote, and then went on to trounce Republican Alan Keyes in the general election with 71 percent of the vote. But even that performance was not sufficient to scare off competition. In 1998, ten Republicans fought for the nomination, and two Democrats challenged her in the Democratic contest. Mikulski won her primary with 84 percent of the vote and won the general election with 71 percent of the vote. Finally, in 2004, "her electoral strength [was] finally beginning to sink in"; she ran uncontested in her own primary, and only one Republican, a little-known state senator, threw his hat in the ring to challenge her.[90]

Chapters 3 and 4 suggest that women make the same strategic calculations as men with regard to pursuing congressional careers. And we began this analysis by showing that male and female incumbents win reelection at equal rates. We also show, however, that if we look more deeply at the competitive environment, the political glass ceiling reappears. While there

---

[89] None of them were women.
[90] Stevens, 2003.

are variations between the parties, women running for reelection face a more competitive environment than their male counterparts in two ways. First, female incumbents face more competition. They foster more competition in the opposition party's primary. They are less likely to face no competition in the general election. They are also less likely to get the "free pass" and face no opposition in the primary and general elections. In fact, female incumbents with the least electoral security, those from marginal districts, *always* face competition.

Second, the presence of a female incumbent encourages more women to run. Female incumbents face more challenges from female candidates in primary elections. Within the opposition party in particular, more women run as challengers. Interestingly, it appears that female incumbents actually help their female opponents. Women running in opposition primaries were more likely to win in districts held by female incumbents. Ultimately, this shows that, despite comparable reelection rates, female incumbents have to work harder than male incumbents to retain their seats.

Our results thus reveal that female incumbents have a "hidden influence." Their presence increases the entry and participation of female candidates in House elections. The more women who serve in the House of Representatives, the more women run. On one hand, this enhances the representative character of House elections. It also has a secondary and salutary effect of increasing awareness and activity among female voters within a district.[91] On the other hand, given where these women are more likely to run—in districts with female incumbents—the overall number of women in the House will not necessarily increase under these circumstances. Female candidacies are disproportionately concentrated in districts already represented by women. Once a woman is elected, she faces higher probabilities of being challenged for renomination by a woman and facing a female opponent in the general election. In House elections from 1956 to 2006, for example, there are seventy-nine instances of female challengers running against female incumbents. In these contests, incumbency maintains its supremacy; female incumbents lost to a female challenger in only four of those seventy-nine elections (5.1 percent).[92] As a result, the increase in competition associated with female incumbents does not trigger changes in the gender composition of the House. While the presence of female incumbents encourages more women to run, incumbency continues to act as a "political glass ceiling," impeding the increase in the number of women who serve in Congress.

---

[91] Hansen, 1997; and Atkeson, 2003.

[92] It is worth noting that female challengers defeated male incumbents in 28 of 680 opportunities for a victory rate of 4.1 percent.

6

Understanding the Glass Ceiling
The "Party Gap"

In 1966, six of the eleven women in the U.S. House of Representatives were Democrats, while five were Republicans; the party distribution among the female members was virtually equal. In 2006, of the seventy-one women elected to the House, fifty, or 70 percent, were Democrats and only twenty-one were Republicans, the biggest difference between the parties in history. Since the early 1970s, as we explored in chapter 2, the number of women running and winning primary and general elections has generally been increasing. But there is something else going on beneath these overall patterns of participation. What accounts for the tremendous gap that has developed between the parties?

In 1920, the 19th Amendment to the U.S. Constitution was ratified, guaranteeing women the right to vote.[1] Prior to its passage, political party leaders "feared the entrance of women onto the voter rolls."[2] They worried that if women had the vote, they would form their own parties or act independently, creating a "petticoat hierarchy which may at will upset all orderly slates and commit undreamed of executions at the polls."[3] When

---

[1] In May of 1919, the House of Representatives passed the 19th Amendment by a vote of 304 to 89. It passed in the Senate two weeks later, 56 to 25. It would take over a year to get the 36 states needed for ratification. The 36th state was Tennessee, where the amendment passed in the state legislature by one vote. The legislator who cast the deciding vote said that he voted in favor because his mother had sent him a telegram urging him to support ratification; Susan MacManus, "Voter Participation and Turnout: It's a New Game," in *Gender and Elections: Shaping the Future of American Politics*, eds. Susan Carroll and Richard Fox (New York: Cambridge University Press, 2006), 46–50.

[2] Barbara Burrell, "Political Parties and Women's Organizations: Bringing Women into the Electoral Arena," in *Gender and Elections: Shaping the Future of American Politics*, eds. Susan Carroll and Richard Fox (New York: Cambridge University Press, 2006a), 145.

[3] William Chafe, *The American Woman: Her Changing Social, Economic and Political Roles*, 1920–1970 (New York: Oxford University Press, 1972), 25; see also Burrell, 2006a, 145.

passage of the amendment looked like a foregone conclusion, both the Republican and Democratic Parties "responded to the imminent granting of suffrage with organizational changes designed to give women nominally equal roles in the party hierarchy and to allow for the efficient mobilization of women voters by women leaders."[4] In 1916, the Democratic National Committee (DNC) established a Women's Bureau. But almost as soon as it started, the party suspended the Bureau during World War I. In the wake of the overwhelming defeat of the Democrats in 1920, the DNC itself was "little more than a skeleton."[5] During the 1920s, the Democratic Party's very survival depended on the women who volunteered through the Women's Division and the National Woman's Democratic Club.[6] In 1918, the Republican Party created a Women's Division as a permanent part of the Republican National Committee (RNC). In addition, the RNC's Executive Committee was expanded to nineteen, in order to add eight women.[7]

Thus far, the forces that we have considered in understanding the political glass ceiling have not been partisan. Neither the events of the 1970s that helped to trigger an increase in the activism of women as candidates, nor the factors that influenced women to pursue careers in elective office are grounded in party differences. In this chapter, however, we show that the glass ceiling does contain a partisan component. The observed change in women seeking and winning office that was highlighted in chapter 2 has not been uniform. Since the early 1990s, the growth of women as candidates and officeholders has occurred disproportionately within the Democratic Party across multiple levels of the political hierarchy. Ultimately, the tremendous gap that has developed between the proportions of Democratic and Republican women in Congress is not particularly well explained by looking at the overall electoral fortunes of the parties or by looking in the "pipeline." There are clues, however, that lie in the perceptions of female candidates held by voters and party leaders.

The Growth of the "Party Gap" in Congress

Shortly after the ratification of the 19th Amendment, one of the ways women quickly became involved in party politics was as delegates to the national conventions.[8] From 1932 to 1968, the proportion of women delegates to the Democratic Party's national convention fluctuated around 12 percent. At the Republican national convention, women gradually

---

[4] Kristi Anderson, *After Suffrage: Women in Partisan and Electoral Politics before the New Deal* (Chicago: University of Chicago Press), 80–81.

[5] Jo Freeman, *A Room at a Time: How Women Entered Party Politics* (New York: Rowman and Littlefield, 2000), 86. See also Anna Harvey, *Votes Without Leverage: Women in American Electoral Politics, 1920–1970* (New York: Cambridge University Press, 1998).

[6] Freeman, 2000, 87.

[7] Freeman, 2000, 97.

[8] Burrell, 2006a, 146.

increased from 6 percent of the delegates in 1928 to 18 percent of the delegates in 1968. However, women activists in each party had pushed the goal of having equal numbers of men and women as delegates beginning in the early 1920s.[9] For the Democrats, this would not happen until reforms advocated by the McGovern-Fraser Commission in the wake of the disastrous 1968 convention in Chicago. The Commission report recommended that women, racial minorities, and youth should be represented in state delegations "in reasonable relationship to their presence in the population of the state."[10] In 1972, 40 percent of the delegates at the national convention were women. In 1980, the Democratic Party changed its rules to mandate gender equity in state delegations, and women have been approximately 50 percent of all delegates to the national convention since then.[11] While the Republican Party did not adopt a similar mandate, the party did yield to pressure for increasing the number of female delegates. In 1972, the proportion of female delegates increased to 30 percent, and in 2004, women were 40 percent of the delegates.[12]

As campaigns have become increasingly candidate-centered over the last thirty years, many argue that political parties have lost much of their power and control over elections.[13] Parties still, however, play a critical role in recruiting and providing assistance to candidates.[14] In 1974, for example, the Democrats created a "Campaign Conference" for women, with the goal of electing more female Democratic candidates. Twelve hundred women attended.[15] In 1982, Senator Richard Lugar, as Chair of the Republican Senatorial Campaign Committee (RSCC), said that, "The full political participation of women is a moral imperative for our society and intelligent political goal for the Republican Party," and vowed to provide the maximum campaign contribution that the RSCC could give to any Republican woman running for Senate in the general election.[16] In 1989, the Lugar Excellence in Public Service Series was created, providing political leadership development programs for Republican women in Indiana.[17] There are now affiliated programs named after prominent Republican women in several other states.[18] The Democrats began a similar training program, Emerge America, in 2002,

---

[9] Freeman, 2000, 180–83.

[10] Quoted from Burrell, 2006a, 147.

[11] Burrell, 2006a, 147.

[12] Burrell, 2006a, 147.

[13] See, for example, Martin Wattenberg, *The Decline of American Political Parties, 1952–1988* (Cambridge, Mass.: Harvard University Press, 1990); Joel Silbey, *The American Political Nation* (Stanford: Stanford University Press, 1991).

[14] See Kira Sanbonmatsu, *Where Women Run: Gender and Party in the American States* (Ann Arbor: University of Michigan Press, 2006a).

[15] Burrell, 2006a, 151.

[16] Quoted from Burrell, 2006a, 151.

[17] http://www.lugarseries.com/objectives.php (accessed July 1, 2007).

[18] The most recent was created in 2007 in Arizona, called the Dodie London Series, named for the only woman to serve as chair of the state Republican party; Mary Jo Pitzl, "GOP Group Formed to Promote Women," *The Arizona Republic*, January 27, 2007.

which runs in six states.[19] For the most part, however, national party commitments to recruiting and running women for public office have been mostly rhetoric.[20]

Given this, what do the patterns in the partisan distributions of female congressional candidates look like? Here we disaggregate the general trends presented in chapter 2 of women running in primaries, winning primaries, and winning general elections. Figure 6.1 shows the proportion of female candidates that ran in each party's primaries. From 1956 to 1988, over thirty years, women were on average 5.1 percent of all Republican primary candidates, and 5.9 percent of all Democratic primary candidates in a given election cycle. In fact, in seven of the seventeen election cycles, the difference between the proportions of female primary candidates in both parties was less than one percent. Beginning in 1990, however, the parties begin to drift apart. By 1996, the gap was significant, with women making up 17.2 percent of Democratic primary candidates and only 9.9 percent of Republican primary candidates. Since then, while the proportion of female Democratic primary candidates continued to increase and reached 19.6 percent in 2006, the proportion of female Republican primary candidates stagnated around 10.8 percent. For the most part, the proportions of women running in Democratic and Republican primaries trend together until the 1990s, when they gradually begin to separate as the proportion of female Republicans running in primaries levels off, and the proportion of female Democrats continues to gradually increase.

The pattern among women winning primaries is similar, but with one noteworthy difference. As figure 6.2 shows, the proportion of Republican and Democratic women who won House primaries was virtually the same from 1956 to 1990, not unlike the pattern for women running in primaries. During these eighteen election cycles, the Republican women won a higher proportion of primaries than Democratic women in eight cycles, and Democratic women won a higher proportion of primaries than Republican women in ten cycles. In 1992, however, the parties suddenly diverge. The proportion of Democratic women winning primaries jumps from 9.5 percent to 16.3 percent, while the proportion of Republican women increased only 1.0 percent, from 7.4 to 8.4. Since 1992, the gap between the parties has averaged 8.9 points. In 2006, the proportion of women nominated by the Democrats was more than twice the proportion nominated by the Republicans, 22.4 percent and 10.8 percent respectively. Since 1992, women running in Republican primaries have not had the same level of success that Democratic women have had. Republican women appear to be having a harder time winning their primaries.

The trends in the proportion of women winning general elections tell

---

[19] http://www.emergeamerica.org/template.php?page=about_us (accessed July 1, 2007).
[20] Burrell, 2006a, 152.

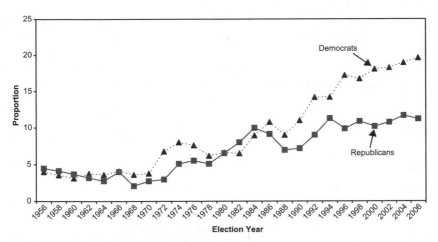

Fig. 6.1 Women as a proportion of candidates seeking their party's nomination for the U.S. House of Representatives, 1956–2006.

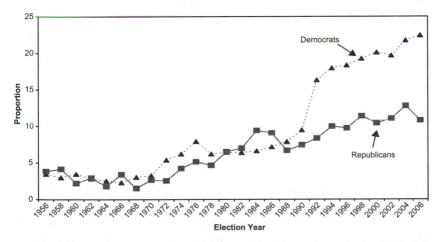

Fig. 6.2 Women as a proportion of candidates winning their party's nomination for the U.S. House of Representatives, 1956–2006.

a remarkably similar story in figure 6.3. Once again, except for 1972, the proportions of Democratic and Republican women successfully running for the House are relatively equal; in twelve of the eighteen election cycles from 1956 to 1990, the difference in the proportion of women that both parties sent to the House is less than 1.0 percent. Once again, we see a spike in the number of Democratic women winning general elections in 1992, with the proportion nearly doubling from 7.1 percent to 13.7 percent, while Republican women increase from 5.4 percent to only 7.3 percent. The proportion of Democratic women continues to climb, and by 2006 women were 21.5 percent of the Democrats in the House. During this period, Republican women made much more modest gains, and in 2006, were only 10.4 percent of their party's delegation in the House, less than half the proportion of the Democrats.

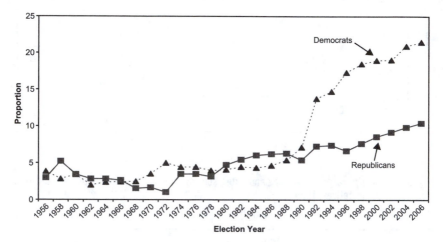

Fig. 6.3 Women as a proportion of their party's members in the U.S. House of Representatives, 1956–2006.

Among women running for the Senate, the familiar pattern emerges again. As figures 6.4 and 6.5 show, until 1990 the average proportions of women running in primaries and winning primaries were relatively equal.[21] The differences in the proportions of Democratic and Republican women were quite small. A gap emerges in the early 1990s, more specifically, in 1992. In fact, in 1990, women were only 5.8 percent of Democratic Senate primary candidates, while they were 14.3 percent of Republican Senate primary candidates. In 1992, the parties switched places, with women as 19.8 percent of Democratic candidates and only 7.0 percent of Republican candidates. This switch was even more extreme among women who won primaries. In 1990, 6.1 percent of the Democrats who won their primaries were women, while an astonishing 18.2 percent of Republicans were women. Two years later, women were 27.8 percent of Democratic Senate primary winners, and a mere 2.8 percent of Republican primary winners. In 2006, the gap between the proportion of Democratic and Republican women winning their party's nomination was 12.9 percent.

---

[21] Here, for continuity and readability, we group our data in six-year periods, except for 1956 and 1958. When the data are disaggregated by year, the same patterns emerge. The proportions reported in figures 6.4, 6.5 and 6.6 are the total proportions across the three election cycles.

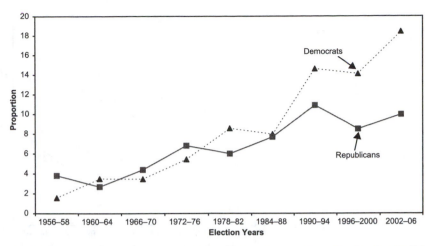

Fig. 6.4 Women as a proportion of candidates seeking their party's nomination for the U.S. Senate, 1956–2006.

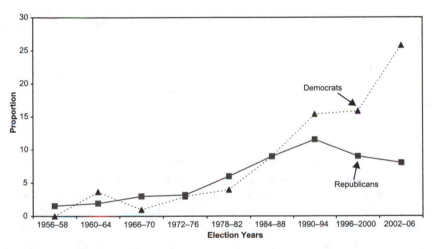

Fig. 6.5 Women as a proportion of candidates winning their party's nomination for the U.S. Senate, 1956–2006.

Figure 6.6 shows the proportion of women in each party's delegation in the Senate. Prior to 1992, while the proportions of Democratic and Republican women were small, Republican women had an edge. In fact, in seventeen of the eighteen election cycles from 1956 to 1990, Republican women were a higher proportion of their party in the Senate than Democratic women. Only in 1976 do Democratic women fare better than Republican women. This changes in 1992, when the proportion of Democratic women once again surges, and Republican women are not able to catch up. In 2006, women were 21.6 percent of Democrats in the Senate, and only 10.2 percent of Republicans.

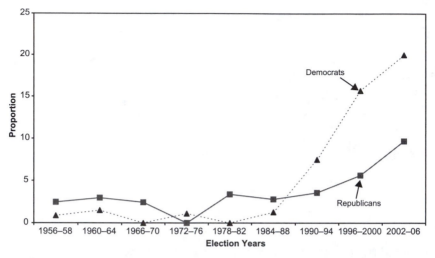

Fig. 6.6 Women as a proportion of their party's members in the U.S. Senate, 1956–2006.

The patterns we have examined suggest that there were two sets of forces operating in the election system. The first, originating in the 1970s, is associated with increasing numbers of Democratic and Republican women entering the electoral arena. The second, emerging in the early 1990s, triggered a separation of the parties. The fortunes of Republican women level off or even decline, while Democratic women see increasing success.

Explaining the Party Gap

As we noted in chapter 2, 1992 became known as the "Year of the Woman," and many analyses have correctly pointed out that the dramatic increase in the number of women winning seats in Congress in this election cycle was largely a Democratic phenomenon.[22] On the other hand, the gap between the parties in the number of women running in congressional primaries pre-dates 1992. And even if Democratic women had an unusually good year in 1992, why would the proportion of Republican women subsequently stall? Having illustrated the emergence and growth of a partisan gap in congressional primary and general elections, we next consider possible factors that may be useful in understanding these partisan trends: the overall success of the parties, the pipeline, and the perceptions of voters and party leaders.

The Success of the Parties

One possible explanation for the changes in the electoral success of women might be changes in the electoral success of the parties. In other words, when

---

[22] See for example *The Year of the Woman: Myths and Reality*, eds. Elizabeth Adell Cook, Sue Thomas, and Clyde Wilcox (Boulder, Colo.: Westview Press, 1994).

the Democratic Party has a good year and increases its delegation in the House, the number of women might increase as well. The same logic would apply to the Republicans. The expectation is that the overall success of a party is correlated with the success of its female delegation.

Figure 6.7 displays the proportion of each party's delegation in the House after each election from 1956 to 2006. Most noteworthy is the fact that the size of the Democratic delegation actually drops in 1992, with a loss of ten seats. The Democratic delegation then declines dramatically in the 1994 midterm election with a loss of fifty-three seats. Yet, in 1992, the proportion of women among Democrats increased from 7.1 percent to 13.6 percent. As figure 6.3 showed, the proportion of women among Democrats continued to grow in the 1990s and 2000s despite the party's minority status in the House. More generally, for the period from 1956 to 2006, the correlation between the proportion of Democrats in the House and women as a proportion of House Democrats is −.76. This suggests that when Democrats fare poorly in the electoral arena, male Democrats absorb the bulk of the electoral losses. The opposite appears to hold for Republicans. As Republicans gained and held majority-party status in the House, the proportion of women in the Republican delegation increased. In fact, for the 1956–2006 period, the correlation between the proportion of Republicans in the House and women as a proportion of Republicans is .58, suggesting that the presence of Republican females depends on the overall success of Republicans at the polls.

The implication is that when Democrats suffer at the polls, incumbent males are the "first to go." When Republicans suffer, the relationship is reversed, with incumbent women being the most likely electoral casualties. Thus, shifts in the partisan makeup of Congress do not exert a uniform impact on the presence of female Democrats and Republicans in their

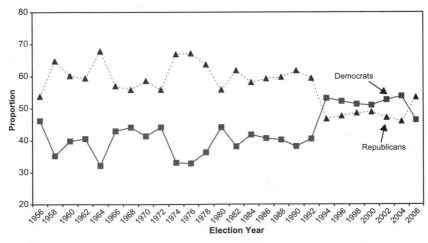

Fig. 6.7 The proportion of Democrats and Republicans in the U.S. House of Representatives, 1956–2006.

party's delegation. In fact, the relationship is the opposite of what was expected for the Democrats.

The Pipeline

If trends in the overall success of the parties do not seem to match the trends in the success of the women within each party, another place to look is in the "pipeline." As we explored in previous chapters, many people aspiring to public office first run and serve at the state or local level before they run for Congress. In other words, there is a "career ladder" in politics; first, candidates run for state house of representatives, then state senate, then the U.S. House of Representatives, then the U.S. Senate. This suggests, for example, that in state legislatures, there might be a spike in the number of Democratic women or a leveling off of Republican women *before* 1992. This is because changes at lower levels of the office hierarchy should pre-date changes at the congressional level. In fact, if we look at the overall numbers of women serving in state legislatures, there was stagnation. It did not, however, occur before 1992. It happened from 1998 to 2004, when the proportion of female state legislators appeared to be stuck at 22.5 percent.[23] In 2006, the number finally took a more noticeable increase to 23.5 percent.[24]

Figure 6.8 shows the proportion of women in state houses of representatives from 1958–2006.[25] Here again, we see the same pattern, with a relatively narrow gap between the parties for the first thirty years of the series. How-ever, one feature that stands out is the remarkable consistency in the higher proportion of Republican women in the lower chamber of state legislatures from 1958 to 1990. The average gap between the two parties is 2.4 percentage points. What is noticeably lacking is a surge in the number of Democratic women before 1992. In fact, Democratic women overtake Republican women in 1992, just as they did in Congress; there is no surge that occurs prior to 1992. Since then, the proportion of Republican women in state houses gradually declined from 21.0 percent in 1992 to 17.5 percent in 2006, while the proportion of Democratic women substantially increased from 22.4 percent to 30.0 percent.

---

[23] See Susan Carroll, "2004 Elections and Women: An Analysis of Statewide and State Legis-lative Election Results," *Spectrum: The Journal of State Government* 78 (2005): 23–25; see also Kira Sanbonmatsu, "Gender Pools and Puzzles: Charting a 'Women's Path' to the Legislature," *Politics & Gender* 2 (2006b): 387–400.

[24] *Women in State Legislatures, 2007*, Center for American Women and Politics (New Bruns-wick: Rutgers University, 2007). Many states hold their elections in odd years. Using CAWP's data, we code the annual percentages of women slightly differently, in that we are looking at when women were elected, not when they were sworn in.

[25] The data from 1958 to 1970 were compiled by the authors from the *Book of the States* series. Unfortunately, data for 1956 is not available. The data from 1972 to 2006 were compiled from data provided by the Center for American Women and Politics, supplemented by the National Council of State Legislators.

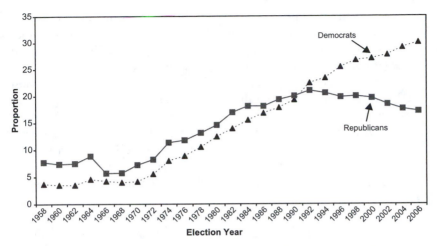

Fig. 6.8 Women as a proportion of their party's members in the lower chamber of state legislatures, 1958–2006.

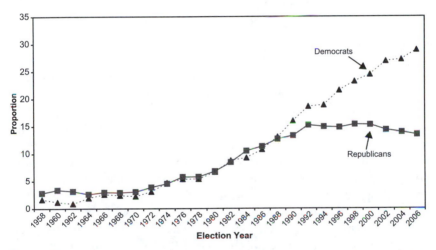

Fig. 6.9 Women as a proportion of their party's members in the upper chamber of state legislatures, 1958–2006.

While the trends for women elected to the upper chambers of state legislatures are similar, there are some differences worth noting. First, as figure 6.9 shows, for the first thirty years, the proportions of Democratic and Republican women in state senates are much closer than the proportions in lower chambers. From 1964 to 1984, the difference is less than 1.0 percentage point. But for the most part, except for 1974 and 1982, Republican women are a higher percentage of their party's delegation than Democratic women. Second, the timing of the party switch is earlier. Democratic women slightly outnumber Republican women in 1988, by less than half a percentage point, but then in 1990, the gap grows to nearly 3 points. In other words, the party switch occurs in the upper chamber before it occurs in the lower chamber. This is not the expected sequence of changes. And the gap becomes even more pronounced than the gap in the lower chamber. By 2006, women were 28.9 percent of Democratic state senators and only 13.4 percent of Republican state senators, a difference of 15.5 percent. The proportion of Democratic women is more than double the proportion of Republican women in state senates.

The analysis suggests that, in the initial years of the twenty-first century, while the proportion of Democratic women in state legislatures was on the rise, it was not enough to counteract the decline in the proportion of Republican women. As a result, the overall proportion of women remained flat. There is no question that the pipeline theory helps us to understand the rates of electoral participation among women.[26] However, there is no sequential appearance in the rise of the gap moving from lower to higher levels in the office hierarchy. In fact, the gap appears in state senates just before it appears in state houses and assemblies. Across the four offices examined, from lower chambers of state legislatures to the U.S. Senate, the actual sequence is best described as nearly simultaneous.

The Perceptions of Voters and Party Leaders

If the differences in the rates of success between Democratic and Republican women cannot be explained by the overall success rates of the parties in Congress or by the pool of candidates moving through the pipeline, another possibility lies in the perceptions of female candidates held by voters and party leaders. As we discussed in chapter 5, voters make assumptions about candidates based on gender. For example, women are seen as more competent on issues of education and health care, while men are seen as more competent on crime and foreign policy. And there is some evidence that gender and party interact as cues in the minds of voters in a way that may help explain development of the party gap.[27] In 1993, the Republican Network to Elect Women (RENEW) sponsored a poll of 820 randomly selected adults. Each respondent was read an identical description of a Republican candidate, but half of the sample was told the candidate was male, and the other half was told the candidate was female. As expected, in the aggregate, substantially more Republican respondents said they would be "very likely" to vote for the candidate (47.1 percent) than Demo-

---

[26] See Sanbonmatsu, 2006b, for a critical analysis of the pipeline, or "social eligibility" theory.

[27] For a review of this literature, see Richard Matland and David King, "Women as Candidates in Congressional Elections," in *Women Transforming Congress*, ed. Cindy Simon Rosenthal (Norman: University of Oklahoma Press, 2002). See also Barbara Burrell, *A Woman's Place Is in the House: Campaigning for Congress in the Feminist Era* (Ann Arbor: University of Michigan Press, 1994); R. Darcy and Sarah Slavin Schramm, "When Women Run against Men," *Public Opinion Quarterly* 41 (1977): 1–12; and David King and Richard Matland, "Sex and the Grand Old Party: An Experimental Investigation of the Effect of Candidate Sex on Support for a Republican Candidate," *American Politics Research* 31 (2003): 595–612.

cratic respondents (19.6 percent).[28] However, the survey also found that Republican female candidates "have serious problems within their own party."[29] Respondents who identified themselves as Republicans were less likely to support the female candidate than the male candidate. When asked to compare identical profiles, male Republican respondents' support for the profile dropped by nearly fourteen percentage points when told the candidate was female.[30] Overall, Republican women candidates actually did better among Democratic and Independent voters.

In 2006, a very real example of this occurred in Idaho's First District, after the retirement of Republican Representative C. L. "Butch" Otter, who decided to run for governor. Six candidates ran in the Republican primary, including state senator Sheila Sorensen, a former nurse practitioner, who was endorsed by Representative Mike Simpson, the incumbent Republican who held Idaho's other House seat, and former Representative Steve Symms, who held the First District seat before Otter.[31] Sorensen came in third. The winner of the primary was conservative state representative William Sali, who had been described by Bruce Newcomb, the Republican Speaker of the Idaho House of Representatives, as an "absolute idiot" without "one ounce of empathy in his whole frickin body."[32] The National Journal called Sali "the most unpopular man elected to Congress this year."[33] In its analysis of the election, the Idaho Lewiston Morning Tribune suggested that the Democratic candidate, Larry Grant, was "a centrist who [could have worked] with members of both parties for the benefit of his district. . . . Republicans had an opportunity to field such a candidate in Sheila Sorensen. But they didn't take it, permitting true believers from the religious right to nominate one of their own."[34] At any rate, all of this suggests at least a partial explanation for why female Republican candidates have not had the kind of success that female Democratic candidates have had.

Moreover, gender acts as a cue for party leaders in much the same way it does for voters; "[c]andidate gender is one piece of information that party leaders may use to weigh the strengths and weaknesses of a potential

---

[28] King and Matland, 2003, 601.

[29] King and Matland, 2003, 604.

[30] King and Matland, 2003, 604.

[31] Peter Savodnik, "Sorensen Heading to D.C., as Fight for Idaho-1 Revs Up," TheHill.com, February 8, 2006, http://thehill.com/campaign-2008/sorensen-heading-to-d.c.-as-fight-for-idaho-1-revs-up-2006-02-08.html (accessed July 1, 2007); Jim Fisher, "Symms gives Sheila Sorensen a Bite from his Apple," Lewiston Morning Tribune (Idaho), January 20, 2006, http://idahoptv.org/idreports/showEditorial.cfm?StoryID=19467 (accessed July 1, 2007).

[32] Jim Fisher, "Why the Bleep Don't We Use the Words We Mean?" Lewiston Morning Tribune (Idaho), November 12, 2006, 3F.

[33] "2006 New Member Profiles: Idaho's First District: Bill Sali," National Journal, http://election.nationaljournal.com/2006/profiles/id01_sali.htm (accessed July 1, 2007).

[34] Jim Fisher, "A Gut Check for Mainstream Republicans," Lewiston Morning Tribune (Idaho), May 25, 2006; see also Barbara Burrell, "Parties, Money, and Sex" (paper presented at the National Symposium on Women and Politics, June 2006b, Berkeley).

candidate."[35] A recent study of state parties showed that in states with strong party systems, in other words, states where parties had substantial control over the recruitment of candidates, women were less likely to run for state legislature and more likely to drop out of campaigns.[36] State party leaders are still overwhelmingly male, and there is increasing evidence that "political elites continue to value men's political leadership more than women's."[37] But even this does not necessarily explain the gap that has developed in the proportions of Democratic and Republican women in elective office. Much like the trend in Congress, the Republican Party has been increasingly successful in winning control of state legislatures, while the proportion of female Republican state legislators has been declining. "At the same time, the Democratic party, which has been losing seats, is seeing women become a larger share of its caucuses around the country."[38] This is particularly puzzling, given that in general, "the two parties exhibit fairly similar levels of recruitment and gate keeping activities." In other words, state Democratic parties, for the most part, have not been putting any more effort into recruiting female candidates than the Republicans.

As it turns out, for state party leaders, "the main criterion driving the recruitment process is finding the candidate who can win. Even among party leaders sympathetic to increasing women's representation, winning remains the primary goal."[39] However, party leaders are not gender-neutral in their assessments of male and female candidates and their ability to win. In fact, they "do not necessarily think that women are electable in all state legislative districts."[40] In some instances, women may have an advantage, because they are perceived by voters as being more honest or better on an issue relevant to a particular constituency. In other instances, women may be at a disadvantage. The bottom line is that party leaders take into account what they believe to be the "hearts and minds" of voters in assessing a candidate's chances of winning.[41] Ultimately, "party leaders commonly believe women might have difficulty winning election to the House from some districts in their state; indeed, some party leaders believe that many such districts exist."[42] Thus, an explanation for the differences in the success rates between Democratic and Republican women may lie in legislative districts.

---

[35] Sanbonmatsu, 2006a, 183.
[36] Sanbonmatsu, 2006a. See also David Niven, "Throwing Your Hat Out of the Ring: Negative Recruitment and the Gender Imbalance in State Legislative Candidacy," *Politics & Gender* 2 (2006): 473–89.
[37] Niven, 2006, 473.
[38] Sanbonmatsu, 2006a, 197.
[39] Sanbonmatsu, 2006a, 196.
[40] Sanbonmatsu, 2006a, 184.
[41] Sanbonmatsu, 2006a, 183.
[42] Sanbonmatsu, 2006a, 183. See also Kira Sanbonmatsu, "Do Parties Know that 'Women Win'? Party Leader Beliefs about Women's Electoral Chances," *Politics & Gender* 2 (2006c): 431–50; Kira Sanbonmatsu, *Democrats, Republicans, and the Politics of Women's Place* (Ann Arbor: University of Michigan, 2004).

Conclusion

It has generally been considered a foregone conclusion that the number of women in elective office would continue to grow at a slow, steady pace. This assumption, however, may not be true. The number of women serving in state legislatures stalled for six years at the turn of the twenty-first century. Chapter 2 showed that the increase in the number of women in Congress has not been linear. As Susan Carroll of the Center for American Women and Politics points out, "there is no invisible hand at work to insure that more women will seek and be elected to office with each subsequent election."[43] Moreover, as we have shown in this chapter, the recent increases in the number of women in Congress are more a Democratic than a Republican development. In fact, of all the women who served in the U.S. House and Senate in history, almost two-thirds of them have been Democrats. Since 1992, of all the new women elected to the House, 67.0 percent (63 of 94) have been Democrats. If only one party provides increasing opportunities for female aspirants to enter Congress, this is a tremendous barrier.

Our analysis here serves as a prelude to the next chapter. We have shown that, in election cycles since the early 1990s, a partisan gender gap has arisen and grown larger. The gap is not confined to a single office, but appears throughout the pipeline, in both chambers of state legislatures and both chambers of the U.S. Congress. At the congressional level, the gap includes those who seek their party's nomination, those who win their primary contests, and those who win a seat in both the House and Senate. We have also shown that the timing in the appearance of this gap cannot be attributed to a party's overall electoral fortunes, nor does it reflect sequential change in the hierarchy of offices. There is, however, some evidence that voters, namely Republican voters, are less sympathetic to female candidates, particularly in primaries. Moreover, party leaders take account of voter perceptions in their predictions and assessments of the success of female candidates. In fact, party leaders believe that particular configurations of voters make it more or less likely that a woman (or a man) can win. In other words, they believe that in some districts women do better, and in some districts men do better. Accordingly, in the next chapter, we turn our attention to the constituency level and ask whether there are differences in the political geography of districts that elect women and men of both parties.

---

[43] Carroll, 2005, 25.

7

Understanding the Glass Ceiling
Women-friendly Districts

Two major conclusions emerge from chapters 5 and 6. First, women face a more competitive environment than men when seeking reelection, and female incumbents are more likely than their male counterparts to face female challengers. Second, there is clearly a partisan dimension to the political glass ceiling. The implication is that female candidates tend to cluster in particular districts. What explains this? Can we identify the districts that are more likely to elect women? Do women run and win elections in districts that are different than those that elect men?

Congressional districts in the United States vary widely in their demographic characteristics. Candidates rely heavily on demographic data to create their campaign strategies, and they often hire consulting firms to provide them with detailed demographic data and suggestions for targeting voters in their districts. However, we know very little about the demographic characteristics of the districts where women have been successful candidates. But even a cursory analysis of the geographic distribution of the current women in Congress suggests that there is a distinct political geography to the districts they represent: twenty-six of the seventy-one female House members elected in 2006, or 36.6 percent, are from California and New York. Female Representatives are not randomly distributed across the country. As we noted in chapter 1, even the women elected in the mid-1950s tended to come from urban districts and large cities.

In this chapter, we draw from the research on the relationship between the demographic character of districts and electoral success. There are particular demographic characteristics that make a House district predictably Democratic or Republican. Democratic districts tend to be liberal, urban, racially diverse, and blue collar or working class; Republican districts tend to be conservative, suburban or rural, and wealthier. Our analysis shows that there are particular demographic characteristics that make a House district more or less likely to elect a woman. In effect, there are districts that are "women-friendly." Moreover, the characteristics that make a district women-friendly are not identical to those associated with party victories. Female Democratic House members tend to win election in districts that are more liberal, more urban, more diverse, more educated, and much wealthier than those won by male Democratic members of the House; they come from much more compact, "tonier," upscale districts than their male counterparts. Female Republican House members tend to win election in districts that are less conservative, more urban, and more diverse than those electing male Republicans; they come from districts that are "less Republican." These results, however, only hold true for white women. The African American women in Congress, all of whom have been Democrats, represent districts that are quite similar to those electing African American men. The districts that elect both black men and women are typically very liberal, compact, relatively poor, urban, and have a high proportion of people of color.

Based upon our analysis of district characteristics, we create an index of women-friendliness. This index helps predict where women will run and the likelihood that they will win. Women are more likely to seek and win the nomination for the House in districts that are women-friendly, particularly female Democrats. Moreover, we show that the number of women-friendly districts has increased over the last three redistricting cycles, suggesting that the opportunities for women are expanding. On the other hand, these opportunities may not be equally shared by women in both parties. The districts that have elected Republican women are strikingly similar to the districts that have elected Democratic men. The districts where Republican women are most likely to win the primary because they are female are the districts where they will have a hard time winning the general election because they are Republican.

Demographic Characteristics and Women Candidates

The use of demographic characteristics in predicting electoral success has been an integral part of the academic study of elections and representation.[1]

---

[1] See for example V. O. Key, *Southern Politics in State and Nation* (New York: A. A. Knopf, 1949); Morris Fiorina, *Representatives, Roll Calls, and Constituencies* (Lexington, Mass.: D. C. Heath, 1974); Jon Bond, "The Influence of Constituency Diversity on Electoral Competition in Voting for Congress, 1974–1978," *Legislative Studies Quarterly* 8 (1983): 201–17; Benjamin I. Page, Robert Y. Shapiro, Paul W. Gronke, and Robert M. Rosenberg, "Constituency, Party, and Representation in Congress," *Public Opinion Quarterly* 48 (1984): 741–56; Robert Erikson, Gerald Wright, and John McIver, *Statehouse Democracy: Public Opinion and Policy in the American States* (New York: Cambridge University Press, 1993); Earl Black and Merle Black, *The Rise of Southern Republicans* (Cambridge, Mass.: Harvard University Press, 2002); John Judis and Ruy Teixeira, *The Emerging Democratic Majority* (New York: Scribner, 2002); and Phillip Ardoin and James Garand, "Measuring Constituency Ideology in U.S. House Districts: A Top-Down Simulation," *Journal of Politics* 65 (2003): 1165–89.

Demographics have been used to explain and predict the outcome of presidential elections.[2] These factors have also taken center stage in the study of redistricting and, in particular, racial and partisan gerrymandering.[3] The first response of House incumbents to questions about their districts is usually a description of the demographics of their constituencies: the boundaries of the district, its socioeconomic and racial makeup, and its partisan and ideological leanings. As Richard Fenno noted in *Home Style*, "Every congressman, in his mind's eye, sees his geographic constituency in terms of some special configuration of such variables."[4] For example, one typical member of Congress described his district this way:

> It's a middle America district. It is poorer than most, older than most, more rural than most. It is basically progressive. It's not a conservative district; it's a moderate district. It is a heavily Democratic district—the third most, or second most, Democratic in the state. It is very concerned with bread and butter issues. It is environmentally conscious as far as rural districts go. . . . It is a basic working-class district with pockets of professional leadership.[5]

Some districts are more homogeneous than others, but no member of Congress sees "an undifferentiated glob" within the district boundaries.[6] Fenno found, in fact, that when describing their districts, the vast majority of members provided demographic information before they described the political leanings of their constituents, if they provided an evaluation of the partisanship of the district at all.[7]

The conventional wisdom among academics, political consultants, and candidates is that there are particular configurations of demographic

---

[2] One early work, *Candidates, Issues, and Strategies*, presented simulations of the 1960 and 1964 presidential elections; Ithiel de Sola Pool, Robert Abelson, and Samuel Popkin, *Candidates, Issues, and Strategies: A Computer Simulation of the 1960 and 1964 Presidential Elections* (Cambridge, Mass.: MIT Press, 1965). The analysis included pooling a large number of national surveys from several organizations and the use of demographic factors to create 480 distinct voter profiles. This book prompted publication of a novel, *The 480*, by Eugene Burdick (New York: McGraw-Hill, 1964), coauthor of William Lederer and Eugene Burdick, *The Ugly American* (New York: Norton, 1958), and Eugene Burdick and Harvey Wheeler, *Fail Safe* (New York: McGraw-Hill, 1962). In *The 480*, Burdick implicitly critiqued the simulated use of voter profiles and warned of future campaigns "when all crucial decisions would be made by a 'people machine' "; John Kessel, "Review of Candidates, Issues and Strategies," *Midwest Journal of Political Science* 10 (1966): 515.

[3] See for example Andrew Gelman and Gary King, "Enhancing Democracy through Legislative Redistricting," *American Political Science Review* 88 (1994): 541–59; Kevin Hill, "Do Black Majority Districts Aid Republicans?" *Journal of Politics* 57 (1995): 384–401; and David Lublin, "Racial Redistricting and African-American Representation," *American Political Science Review* 93 (1999): 183–86.

[4] Richard Fenno, *Home Style: House Members in Their Districts* (Boston: Little Brown, 1978), 2.

[5] Fenno, 1978, 2.

[6] Fenno, 1978, 3.

[7] Fenno, 1978, 3.

characteristics associated with typical Democratic and Republican districts:

> Democrats receive strong support from lower socioeconomic groups, blue collar workers, minority ethnic and religious groups and central city voters, while Republicans receive their largest support from higher socioeconomic groups, white collar workers, whites, Protestants, and suburban voters.[8]

The relationship between the characteristics of a constituency and its voting habits is anchored in electoral history and flows from the strategies that the Democratic and Republican Parties devise for building winning coalitions. Platforms and proposed policies are designed to target and win the loyalties of voting blocs. Since the time of Franklin Roosevelt, a vital part of the Democratic Party's coalition has been ethnic, working-class voters residing in large cities such as Boston, New York, Philadelphia, Pittsburgh, Cleveland, Detroit, Milwaukee, and Chicago. Similarly, Republicans built their coalition by advocating the interests of the business and professional classes as well as rural America. In more recent times, support for the Democrats among African Americans, Hispanics, and women is, in part, a response to the party's advocacy of civil rights, while Republicans have made substantial inroads among social conservatives and Evangelical Christians, particularly in the South.

Given that we can identify "party-friendly" districts, there are two possibilities with respect to the impact of these factors on the success of female candidates. First, those women elected to the House may find success in districts that conform to the conventional party profile of districts. In this instance, there would be nothing unique about districts that elect women to the House. Party would trump gender, in that female and male Democratic members would be elected from demographically similar districts, as would female and male Republican members. Alternatively, women may be elected from districts where one or more characteristics do not conform to the standard partisan profile; female and male Democratic members would be elected from demographically distinct districts, as would female and male Republican members. If this is the case, then "women-friendly" and "party-friendly" denote different kinds of districts.

Is there any theoretical reason to expect that districts electing Democratic and Republican women would be different from the standard partisan profile? As discussed in chapter 5, the gender of a candidate is a critical factor that influences media coverage, how voters perceive candidates, and campaign strategy. Voters assume that men and women are "better" on different

---

[8] William Koetzle, "The Impact of Constituency Diversity upon the Competitiveness of U.S. House Elections, 1962–1996." *Legislative Studies Quarterly* 23 (1998): 562–73.

issues. Women candidates are typically seen as more competent on compassion issues—education, health care, rights issues, the environment, and welfare. Men are seen as more competent on issues such as taxes, budgets, crime, national defense, and foreign policy. Most importantly for our analysis here, voter perceptions of candidates' ideology are strongly related to gender. Female Democrats are perceived as more liberal than they actually are, and female Republicans are perceived as less conservative than they actually are.[9] This implies that party identification and gender interact.

Because there are certain demographic characteristics that predict the partisanship of a district, we explore the extent to which these factors predict whether a woman will win that congressional seat. There is a great deal of partisan and ideological variation across districts. This implies that particular districts, because of their demographic composition, may be more or less receptive to the perceived leadership traits of women, to agendas emphasizing compassion issues, and to a candidate's ideology perceived to be on the more liberal (or less conservative) side of the spectrum.

Understanding the Political Geography of Women's Success

There are surprisingly few analyses of geography and demography and their impact on women's success.[10] As a result, we know very little about the districts *where* women win. To explore the impact of political geography on women's success, we examine four categories of demographics: (1) partisanship and ideology, (2) geographic factors, (3) race and ethnicity, and (4) socioeconomic factors. In chapter 6, we demonstrated that there is a growing gap between the parties with regards to the frequency that Democratic and Republican women enjoy success in running for the House. Here, we build upon that analysis by examining the extent to which the "political geography" of congressional districts helps us to understand how party and gender interact in creating the political glass ceiling.

---

[9] Deborah Alexander and Kristi Anderson, "Gender as a Factor in the Attribution of Leadership Traits," *Political Research Quarterly* 46 (1993): 527–45; Leonie Huddy and Nayda Terkildsen, "Gender Stereotypes and the Perception of Male and Female Candidates," *American Journal of Political Science* 37 (1993): 119–47; and Jeffrey Koch, "Do Citizens Apply Gender Stereotypes to Infer Candidates' Ideological Orientations?" *Journal of Politics* 62 (2000): 414–29.

[10] There is some interesting research on state legislatures; Wilma Rule, "Why Women Don't Run: The Critical and Contextual Factors in Women's Legislative Recruitment," *Western Political Quarterly* 34 (1981): 60–77; Wilma Rule, "Why More Women Are Legislators: A Research Note," *Western Political Quarterly* 43 (1990): 437–48; Carol Nechemias, "Geographic Mobility and Women's Access to State Legislatures," *Western Political Quarterly* 38 (1985): 119–31; Carol Nechemias, "Changes in the Election of Women to U.S. State Legislative Seats," *Legislative Studies Quarterly* 12 (1987): 125–42. See also Richard Fox, "Congressional Elections: Where Are We on the Road to Gender Parity?" in *Gender and Elections: Shaping the Future of American Politics*, eds. Sue Carroll and Richard Fox (New York: Cambridge University Press, 2006).

Partisanship and Ideology

Party is the most important cue in the voting booth: Democratic voters overwhelmingly vote for Democratic candidates, and Republican voters overwhelmingly vote for Republican candidates.[11] For example, in the 2004 presidential election, a national exit poll found that 89 percent of those identifying themselves as Democrats voted for John Kerry, and 93 percent of those identifying themselves as Republicans voted for George W. Bush.[12] Party labels provide voters with a shortcut that is used to infer candidate positions and make evaluations about their willingness to support a candidate.

As a measure of district partisanship, we use the proportion of the two-party vote won by the Republican candidate in the most recent presidential election; higher percentages indicate that the district is more Republican, while lower percentages indicate that the district is more Democratic.[13] Using the 2004 election as an example, the vote for President Bush ranged from 9.1 percent in the 15th District of New York to 79.4 percent in the 3rd District of Utah. The average vote across all congressional districts was 49.1 percent.

We measure the ideology of a district using a composite score created by political scientists Phillip Ardoin and James Garand. A positive score indicates that the district is more conservative, while a negative score indicates that the district is more liberal.[14] For the decade from 1992 to 2000, the most conservative district was the 10th District of North Carolina, with a score of 35.5; the most liberal district was the 16th District of New York, with a score of −46.7. The average score across all congressional districts was 10.7. We expect that female members of Congress are elected in districts that have a different partisan and ideological profile than those that elect males.

---

[11] See for example Angus Campbell, Philip Convers, Warren Miller, and Donald Stokes, *The American Voter* (New York: Wiley, 1960); Richard Lau and David Sears, eds., *Political Cognition* (Hillsdale, N.J.: L. Erlbaum Associates, 1986); Wendy Rahn, "The Role of Partisan Stereotypes in Information Processing about Political Candidates," *American Journal of Political Science* 37 (1993): 472–96; and Richard Lau and David Redlawsk, "Advantages and Disadvantages of Cognitive Heuristics in Political Decision Making," *American Journal of Political Science* 45 (2001): 951–71.

[12] www.cnn.com/ELECTION/2004/pages/results/states/US/P/oo/epolls.0.html (accessed June 10, 2005).

[13] A variety of measures of district partisanship have been used in other studies. See for example R. Darcy and Sarah Slavin Schramm, "When Women Run against Men," *Public Opinion Quarterly* 41 (1977): 1–12; and Barbara Burrell, *A Woman's Place Is in the House: Campaigning for Congress in the Feminist Era* (Ann Arbor: University of Michigan Press, 1994).

[14] District ideology is a composite score that includes the Democratic vote for president in the district, location in the Deep South, and the proportion of district residents who are blue-collar workers, homeowners, and urban residents. The scores are available at http://www1.appstate.edu/~ardoinpj/research.htm (accessed July 20, 2005). Unfortunately, this measure is only available for two of the three redistricting periods we analyze.

Geographic Factors

District size has been hypothesized to affect the success of women candidates. The logic is that the larger the House district, measured in square miles, the harder it is to represent. Because constituents are dispersed in larger districts, more time is required to keep in contact with them. This is a particular problem for women. Women are generally under more time constraints than men because they are usually the primary caregivers of children even when they serve in public office.[15] Women are more likely to juggle the roles of spouse, parent, and elected official than their male counterparts. Thus, women are going to encounter more "geographic immobility" than men.[16] A study done in the early 1980s, for example, found that female state legislators were more likely to run in districts closer to the state capital. It would also follow that women candidates would come from smaller, more geographically compact districts.[17]

In fact, in the 110th Congress (2007 session), the smallest House district in the country is represented by a woman. New York's 11th District in Brooklyn is only twelve square miles. Representative Yvette Clark, an African American Democrat, was elected to her first term in 2006. Apart from those states sending only one representative to the House, the largest district in the nation is the 2nd District of Nevada, at 105,635 square miles, and is represented by a man. Republican Dean Heller was also elected for the first time in 2006. Male House members come from districts that average 1,836 square miles, while female House members come from districts that average only 410 square miles. Thus, we expect that the women in the House will, on average, represent smaller districts than the men in the House.

One of the more consistent findings of past research is that women in Congress are more likely to represent urban districts.[18] Women are more

---

[15] Virginia Sapiro, "Private Costs of Public Commitments or Public Costs of Private Commitments? Family Roles versus Political Ambition," *American Journal of Political Science* 26 (1982): 265–79; Richard Fox, "Gender, Political Ambition and the Decision Not to Run for Office," Center for American Women and Politics, 2003, http://www.rci.rutgers.edu/~cawp/Research/Reports/Fox2003.pdf; and Jennifer Lawless and Richard Fox, *It Takes a Candidate: Why Women Don't Run for Office* (New York: Cambridge University Press, 2005).

[16] Nechemias, 1985. One study found that populous states with small legislatures had smaller proportions of women state legislators, which also suggests that district size acts as a constraint; Emmy Werner, "Women in the State Legislatures," *Western Political Quarterly* 19 (1968): 40–50.

[17] We measure geographic size by the total square miles of the district. These data as well as the other demographic measures used in this analysis were obtained from the U.S. Census and are reported in the data sets compiled by Scott Adler (available at http://socsci.colorado.edu/~esadler/districtdatawebsite/CongressionalDistrictDatasetwebpage.htm) and David Lublin (http://www.american.edu/dlublin/research/data.htm). Data pertaining to the 110th Congress are drawn from the 2000 decennial census available at http://factfinder.census.gov.

[18] Barbara Burrell, "Women Candidates in Open-Seat Primaries for the U.S. House: 1968–1990," *Legislative Studies Quarterly* 17 (1992): 493–508; Darcy and Schramm, 1977; Irene Diamond, *Sex Roles in the State House* (New Haven, Conn.: Yale University Press, 1977); Rule, 1981; Susan Welch, "Are Women More Liberal than Men in the U.S. Congress?" *Legislative*

likely to be recruited to run for office in urban areas because there is a "larger pool of activist women who are potential candidates" than in rural areas.[19] There are also more seats and thus more opportunities to run in areas with higher populations.[20] Democratic women in particular tend to rely on women's groups for campaign support, and these organizations tend to be located in larger urban centers.[21] EMILY's List, for example, has major offices in Washington, D.C. and Los Angeles. The Women's Campaign Fund has offices in Washington, D.C. and New York. In addition, women are more likely to be recruited and do well electorally in urban areas because these constituencies are most receptive to agendas emphasizing social welfare issues. These issues, which include funding for after-school programs, aid to dependent children, and other public assistance programs, are often major concerns in urban districts. Because women are perceived to be "better" on these issues, they are more likely to run and win.[22]

Based upon the 2000 U.S. Census, there are forty-nine House districts in which the proportion of urban residents is 100 percent; there are twenty districts where the proportion of urban residents is less than 40 percent. The 5th District of Kentucky, at 21.3 percent, is the least urban in the country. In the 110th Congress (2007 session), it is represented by Republican Harold Rogers. More generally, in House elections from 1956 to 2002, the average percent of urban residents in districts that elected Republican women was 73 percent, compared to 64.5 percent in districts that elected Republican men. Among Democrats, the averages were 85.7 percent for women and 71.4 percent for men. Given that district size and urbanization are related, we expect that women will have a higher probability of winning in districts that have a larger proportion of their population living in urban areas.

Cultural traditionalism has also been found to be an important predictor of women's success. As we explained in chapter 3, women in the South were especially discouraged from running for office. Historically, the barriers that kept women out of the political arena included the region's non-egalitarian heritage, support for restricting women's political and social roles, and rejection of women's suffrage and the Equal Rights Amendment.[23] In the 110th Congress (2007 session), fourteen of the seventy-one female House members, or 19.7 percent, are from the south; five of these women are from Florida. We expect, then, that regional differences help explain the success of

---

Studies Quarterly 10 (1985): 125–34; and Susan Welch, Margery M. Ambrosius, Janet Clark, and Robert Darcy, "The Effect of Candidate Gender on Election Outcomes in State Legislative Races," *Western Political Quarterly* 38 (1985): 464–75; but see Werner, 1968, 40–50; and Jeane Kirkpatrick, *Political Woman* (New York: Basic Books, 1974).

[19] Darcy and Schramm, 1977, 8.
[20] Rule, 1981, 71.
[21] Darcy and Schramm, 1977, 8.
[22] Rule, 1981, 65.
[23] Rule, 1981, 63.

women.[24] Female candidates will be more likely to seek and to win House seats in districts outside the South.

Race and Ethnicity

Numerous studies of congressional districts have examined the impact of race and ethnicity. One analysis of women in Congress during the 1980s found that the diversity of the district had no impact on the success of women candidates.[25] Another study of women in Congress during the 1970s found, however, that women members tended to win in districts that were more racially and ethnically diverse; their districts had a higher percentage of African Americans and a higher percentage of immigrants.[26] Voter registration among African Americans dramatically increased in the wake of the Voting Rights Act of 1965.[27] In many states, these populations tend to reside in urban areas.

As measures of district diversity, we use the percentage of residents who identified themselves in the U.S. Census as African American, Hispanic or Latino, and foreign-born. Across the time frame of our study, districts that elected women were, on average, 13.5 percent black, 9.3 percent Hispanic, and 10.4 percent foreign-born; the comparable averages for districts electing men were 11.1 percent black, 6.3 percent Hispanic, and 5.7 percent foreign-born. Thus, we expect that female House members will run and be elected in districts that are more racially diverse than those of their male counterparts.

Socioeconomic Factors

Several socioeconomic factors are thought to influence the success of women candidates. Women in Congress tend to be elected in wealthier districts.[28] One line of reasoning suggests that lower incomes make legislative service more attractive to men; because politics is an option for men, it "becomes more relevant when men's opportunities in other occupations [are] limited. . . . When income levels are greater for men, other occupations become more attractive even when state legislative salaries are high."[29] As a measure of income, we use the relative medium income of the congressional

---

[24] Here, we use the same classification of states in the South as we did in chapter 3.

[25] Burrell, 1984.

[26] Welch, 1985.

[27] See Edward Carmines and James Stimson, *Issue Evolution: Race and the Transformation of American Politics* (Princeton, N.J.: Princeton University Press, 1989), 49. Within six months of its passage, over 75,000 African Americans were added to voter registration roles. In 1963, only 43 percent of blacks were registered to vote; by 1968, 62 percent of blacks were registered to vote; Marsha Darling, "African-American Women in State Elective Office in the South," in *Women and Elective Office: Past, Present and Future*, eds. Sue Thomas and Clyde Wilcox (New York: Oxford University Press, 1998), 154.

[28] Rule, 1981; Welch, 1985; Nechemias, 1987; and Burrell, 1994.

[29] Rule, 1981, 69.

district, expressed as a percent of the national median.[30] Values greater than 100 percent represent districts over the national median, and values less than 100 percent are those below the national median. The magnitude of the measure conveys the degree to which a district is rich or poor compared to all congressional districts in a given redistricting period. For example, according to the 2000 Census, the poorest congressional district is the 16th District of New York, with a median income of $19,311, and the wealthiest is the 11th District of Virginia, with a median income of $80,397. Across all congressional districts, median income is $41,060. Using our measure, the relative income in New York's 16th is 47.0 percent of the national average, and in Virginia's 11th it is 196 percent of the national average. We expect that as the median income of a district increases, the likelihood that a female candidate would win should also increase.

Income and education are highly correlated, so it is not surprising that women in Congress tend to be elected in districts that have higher education levels.[31] People with more education are more likely to support a more egalitarian view of women and less likely to hold traditional attitudes about gender roles.[32] In addition, women with more education are more likely to run for office, and consequently districts with higher levels of education should be more fertile recruiting grounds.[33] To measure education, we use the proportion of residents age twenty-five or older who completed four or more years of college. According to the 2000 Census, the proportion of residents with college degrees is lowest in two districts, California's 20th and Texas' 29th. In the 110th Congress (2007 session), both of these districts are represented by men, Democrats Jim Costa and Gene Green, respectively. The district with the highest education level, at 57 percent, is the 14th District of New York, represented by Democrat Carolyn Maloney. We anticipate that as the proportion of residents with college degrees increases in a district, women should be more likely to win a House seat.

---

[30] More specifically, simply using the median income in each district could be problematic given the upward trend in the measure over the decades of our analysis. For example, the median income across all congressional districts was $9,555 in the period 1972–1980; this increased to $19,701 during the period 1982–1990 and increased again to $34,114 for the 1992–2000 districting period. Median income across all congressional districts in the 2000 U.S. Census was $41,060. To control for this drift, we used these national median values from each redistricting period and then divided each district's median by the national median. Thus, the measure expresses median income in the district as a proportion of the median across all districts for each redistricting period. The interpretation of the measure is easy. Values greater than 100 percent represent districts over the national median, and values less than 100 percent are those below the national median. The magnitude of the measure conveys the degree to which a district is rich or poor compared to all congressional districts in a given redistricting period. Over the time frame of our analysis, the values of the relative income measure range from 42.7 to 196.0 percent.

[31] Nechemias, 1987.

[32] See for example Susan Welch and Lee Sigelman, "Changes in Public Attitudes toward Women in Politics," *Social Science Quarterly* 63 (1982): 312–21.

[33] Burrell, 1994.

Related to income and education are indicators of social class. There is evidence that women are likely to be less successful in blue-collar, working-class districts.[34] In particular, the traditionalist and less-than-accepting attitudes toward female candidates among labor leaders and white ethnic groups influential in Democratic political machines have served as a substantial barrier.[35] For example, in his recent memoir, former governor of New Jersey James McGreevey explained that strip clubs are the "fraternal lodges" of New Jersey politics; "We used to order beer after beer at Cheeques, watching the dancers twirl on their poles while debating everything from local policy initiatives and tax ratables to the merits of silicone breast enhancements."[36] Politics in the Garden State, as well as in Massachusetts and Rhode Island, is controlled by party bosses and county chairmen. In October 2007, Massachusetts' 5th District elected Niki Tsongas in a special election. The other two states have no women in their congressional delegation.

Currently, the 17th District of Ohio is among those that are the most blue collar. Historically, the core of this district is Youngtown and surrounding areas in Mahoning and Trumbull Counties.[37] Once the home of numerous steel mills, the district is heavily unionized, with the General Motors Assembly Plant in Lordstown now a major employer. Since 1936, five men have represented the district, four Democrats and one Republican.[38] In constrast, with only 2.8 percent of its residents employed in blue-collar jobs, New York's 14th District has one of the smallest working-class constituencies in the nation. The district includes the Upper East Side of Manhattan and is home to "people with more accumulated wealth than anywhere else in the world."[39] Democrat Carolyn Maloney has represented this district since 1992. Between 1972 and 2000, the proportion of blue-collar workers across all districts ranged from 2.3 to 26.3 percent; the national average was 9.5 percent. Given that social class is correlated with income and education, we expect that women will do better in districts with fewer blue-collar workers.[40]

---

[34] Nechemias, 1987; and Susan Welch and Donley Studlar, "The Opportunity Structure for Women's Candidacies and Electability in Britain and the United States," *Political Research Quarterly* 49 (1996): 861–74.

[35] Rule, 1981, 64; Welch and Studlar, 1996, 869. See also Kira Sanbonmatsu, "Political Parties and the Recruitment of Women to State Legislatures," *Journal of Politics* 64 (2002): 791–809; and Alexandra Starr, "Bada Bing Club," *New Republic,* April 23, 2007, 10–12.

[36] Quoted from Starr, 2007, 10. McGreevey resigned as governor in 2004 and made national headlines when he announced he was gay; James McGreevey, *The Confession* (New York: Harper Collins, 2006).

[37] Michael Barone and Richard Cohen, *Almanac of American Politics, 2004* (Washington, D.C.: National Journal, 2003), 1293–96.

[38] Michael Kirwan (D, 1937–1970), Charles Carney (D, 1970–1979), Lyle Williams (R, 1979–1983), James Traficant (D, 1983–2003), and Tim Ryan (D, 2003–present).

[39] Barone and Cohen, 2003, 1138.

[40] We use the data provided by the U.S. Census in the Adler data set. It should be noted that the proportion of blue-collar workers contained in the Adler data differs from those reported in other sources.

One final demographic characteristic that we add to this mix could cut either way: the school-age population in a district. Given that women candidates are perceived as more competent on issues involving education and children, the parents of school-age children might be more likely to vote for a woman candidate: the more parents in a district, the more likely a woman would win the district. On the other hand, families with school-age children might have more traditional attitudes about women. Women with children are less likely to work outside the home full-time than women without children. There are three districts whose school-age population exceeds 24 percent: the 15th District of Texas, represented in the 110th Congress (2007 session) by Democrat Ruben Hinojosa; the 1st District of Utah, represented by Republican Rob Bishop; and the 3rd District of Utah, represented by Republican Chris Cannon. Among the districts with the lowest school-age population are New York's 14th, represented by Maloney, and Florida's 22nd, represented by Democrat Ron Klein. Overall, the average school-age population across all House districts is 15.5 percent. Because women remain the primary caregivers to children, the number of school-age children in a district should have some impact on women's electoral success.[41]

Explaining the Political Geography of Women's Success

There are particular demographic characteristics that determine whether a district will elect a Democrat or a Republican. Are there particular demographic characteristics that influence whether a district will elect a man or a woman? We expect that the success of female candidates will vary with these four types of demographic measures in a district: its partisanship and ideology, its geography, its racial and ethnic makeup, and its socioeconomic characteristics. Beginning with the 1972 election cycle, district lines are regularly redrawn every ten years in response to the Census.[42] For each redistricting decade, we identified those districts that are reliably Democratic or Republican and those that have the characteristics of swing districts. We defined a core Democratic district as one in which the Democratic candidate for the seat won at least four of the five elections in the ten-year period. Similarly, core Republican districts are defined as those in which the Republican candidate won at least four of five elections in the decade. The remaining districts, where the parties split 3–2 during the decade, are treated

---

[41] The specific measure of school-age children is the proportion of residents enrolled in public elementary and high schools; these data were gathered by the U.S. Census and are contained in the Adler data set.

[42] We begin with the 1972–1980 period for two reasons. First, several measures that we use, including the Hispanic population, were not available for earlier periods. Second, because of the "one person, one vote" rulings of the Supreme Court, the decade from 1962 to 1970 was chaotic as far as district boundaries are concerned. A number of states redrew their boundaries in mid-decade, and a handful of states redrew them two or more times.

as swing districts.[43] Overall, our data encompass thirty years and include 1,305 districts, 153 of these elected women.

Gender, Party, and Race

Like gender and party, the race and ethnicity of a candidate also operate as cues for voters.[44] Moreover, taking the race and ethnicity of the candidate into account is important, especially in light of the 1990s round of districting and the creation of majority–minority districts in several states. In 1982, Congress amended the Voting Rights Act of 1965, mandating that minorities be able to "elect representatives of their choice."[45] The theory was that increasing the number of minorities in a district would increase the number of minorities elected to the House: minority voters are much more likely than white voters to vote for minority candidates.[46] In fact, one study suggests that "only the percentage of blacks and Latinos in the district alters the probability of an African American winning election to the House."[47] Thus, in 1992, the first round of elections under the new mandate, fifteen new districts were created to maximize the number of African American constituents. This produced the largest increase in the number of African Americans elected to the House in history. In addition, ten new districts were created to maximize the number of Hispanic constituents, which also resulted in the largest increase in the number of Hispanics in the House.[48]

---

[43] This exercise entails aggregating our database for each redistricting period. We then have observations for 435 districts in each of these three periods (n = 1,305). Given our definitions, 681 districts are classified as core Democratic and 487 are classified as core Republican. In 989 of the 1,168 (85.0 percent) core districts, the party held the seat for all five elections in the districting period. Of the 179 districts that split 4–1, 158 of them (88.0 percent) involved four consecutive wins for one party or the other. We adopted the 4–1 criterion for defining a core district based on these proportions. It does not seem plausible to define a swing district as one where a party won four consecutive elections in a decade.

[44] See for example David Lublin, *The Paradox of Representation: Racial Gerrymandering and Minority Interests in Congress* (Princeton, N.J.: Princeton University Press, 1997); and Lau and Redlawsk, 2001.

[45] Quoted from David Canon, *Race, Redistricting, and Representation: The Unintended Consequences of Black Majority Districts* (Chicago: University of Chicago Press, 1999), 1.

[46] See for example Bernard Grofman and Lisa Handley, "Minority Population Proportion and the Black and Hispanic Congressional Success in the 1970s and 1980s," *American Politics Quarterly* 17 (1989): 436–45; Lisa Handley and Bernard Grofman, "The Impact of the Voting Rights Act on Minority Representation: Black Office Holding in Southern State Legislatures and Congressional Delegations," in *Quiet Revolution in the South: The Impact of the Voting Rights Act, 1965–1990*, eds. Chandler Davidson and Bernard Grofman (Princeton, N.J.: Princeton University Press, 1994); Lublin, 1997; and Canon, 1999.

[47] Lublin, 1997, 40.

[48] Lublin, 1997, 22–23. See also Carol Swain, *Black Faces, Black Interests: The Representation of African-Americans in Congress* (Cambridge, Mass.: Harvard University Press, 1993); Charles Cameron, David Epstein, and Sharyn O'Halloran, "Do Majority-Minority Districts Maximize Substantive Black Representation in Congress?" *American Politics Science Review* 90 (1996): 794–812. Kenny Whitby, *The Color of Representation: Congressional Behavior and Black Interests* (Ann Arbor: University of Michigan Press, 1997); and Richard Fleisher and Jon Bond, "Polarized Politics: Does It Matter?" in *Polarized Politics: Congress and the President in a Partisan Era*, eds. Jon Bond and Richard Fleisher (Washington D.C.: CQ Press, 2000).

Thus, the race and ethnicity of the candidate, as well as the diversity of the district, must be taken into account. As discussed in chapter 3, until the 1960s, many white women obtained legislative seats at the state and national levels upon the death of a husband. Very few black women have taken this route to office;[49] nearly all won election without the advantages bestowed by a deceased husband.[50] In the wake of the Civil Rights and Women's Rights Movements, black women made much faster gains than white women in obtaining elective office, particularly at the local and state levels.[51]

At the national level, as table 7.1 shows, only thirty-three women of color have served in the House, and most of them were elected very recently. In the 110th Congress (2007 session), there were twelve African American women.[52] The only woman of color to ever serve in the Senate was Carol Moseley Braun (D-IL) from 1992 to 1998. The first African American woman to serve in Congress, Shirley Chisholm, was elected in 1968. (See figure 7.1.) Chisholm had been the second black woman to serve in the New York State Assembly. After two terms in the state legislature, she decided to run for Congress when a constituent who was on welfare visited her home, offered her a campaign donation of $9.62 in change from a bingo game she won, and pledged to raise money for her every Friday night.[53] Chisholm noted, "When I decided to run for Congress, I knew I would encounter both anti-black and antifeminist sentiments. What surprised me was the much greater virulence of the sex discrimination. . . . I was constantly bombarded by both men and women exclaiming that I should return to teaching, a woman's vocation, and leave politics to men."[54] While there have been three

---

[49] Of the widows who won a seat in the House, only one, Representative Cardiss Collins (D-IL), was African American.

[50] Jewel Prestage, "Black Women State Legislators: A Profile," in *A Portrait of Marginality: The Political Behavior of American Women*, eds. Marianne Githens and Jewel Prestage (New York: David McKay, 1977); Jewel Prestage, "The Case of African American Women and Politics," *PS: Political Science and Politics* 27 (1994): 720–21; Gary Moncrief, Joel Thompson, and Robert Schuhmann, "Gender, Race and the State Legislature: A Research Note on the Double Disadvantage Hypothesis," *Social Science Journal* 28 (1991): 481–87; and Carol Hardy-Fanta, ed., *Latina Politics, Latino Politics: Gender, Culture, and Political Participation in Boston* (Philadelphia: Temple University Press, 1993).

[51] Herrington Bryce and Alan Warrick, "Black Women in Electoral Politics," in *A Portrait of Marginality: The Political Behavior of American Women*, eds. Marianne Githens and Jewel Prestage (New York: David McKay, 1977); R. Darcy and Charles Hadley, "Black Women in Politics: The Puzzle of Success," *Social Science Quarterly* 69 (1988): 629–45; Darling, 1998; and Wendy Smooth, "African American Women and Electoral Politics: Journeying from the Shadows to the Spotlight," in *Gender and Elections: Shaping the Future of American Politics*, eds. Sue Carroll and Richard Fox (New York: Cambridge University Press, 2006).

[52] This includes Representative Juanita Millender-McDonald (D-CA).

[53] Karen Foerstel, *Biographical Dictionary of Congressional Women* (Westport, Conn.: Greenwood Press, 1999), 55.

[54] Foerstel, 1999, 54.

Table 7.1 Women of Color Elected to the House

Name	Dates of Service
African Americans	
Shirley Chisholm (D-NY)	1969–1983
Yvonne Brathwaite Burke (D-CA)	1973–1979
Cardiss Collins (D-IL)	1973–1997
Barbara Jordan (D-TX)	1973–1979
Barbara-Rose Collins (D-MI)	1982–1985
Katie Hall (D-IL)	1982–1985
Maxine Waters (D-CA)	1991–present
Eva Clayton (D-NC)	1992–2003
Carrie Meek (D-FL)	1993–2003
Cynthia McKinney (D-GA)	1993–2003; 2005–2007
Corrine Brown (D-FL)	1993–present
Eddie Bernice Johnson (D-TX)	1993–present
Juanita Millender-McDonald (D-CA)	1995–2007
Sheila Jackson-Lee (D-TX)	1995–present
Julia Carson (D-IN)	1997–present
Carolyn Cheeks Kilpatrick (D-MI)	1997–present
Barbara Lee (D-CA)	1997–present
Stephanie Tubbs Jones (D-OH)	1999–present
Diane Watson (D-CA)	2001–present
Denise Majette (D-GA)	2003–2005
Gwen Moore (D-WI)	2005–present
Yvette Clark (D-NY)	2007–present
Asian Pacific Islanders	
Patsy Mink (D-HI)	1965–1977, 1990–2002
Patricia Saiki (R-HI)	1987–1991
Doris Matsui (D-CA)	2005–present
Mazie Hirono (D-HI)	2007–present
Latinas	
Ileana Ros-Lehtinen (R-FL)	1989–present
Lucille Roybal-Allard (D-CA)	1993–present
Nydia Velázquez (D-NY)	1993–present
Loretta Sanchez (D-CA)	1997–present
Grace Napolitano (D-CA)	1999–present
Hilda Solis (D-CA)	2001–present
Linda Sanchez (D-CA)	2003–present

Sources: Center for American Women and Politics, *Women of Color in Elective Office, 2007* (New Brunswick, N.J.: Rutgers University, 2007); and *U.S. Congress Handbook* (Washington, D.C.: Votenet Solutions, 2005).

Fig. 7.1 Shirley Chisholm (D-NY) was the first woman of color to serve in Congress. She ran for president in 1972. Photo courtesy of the Library of Congress.

African American Republican men to serve in Congress since Reconstruction,[55] there has yet to be a black Republican woman.

The first Cuban American to be elected to Congress, Representative Ileana Ros-Lehtinen (R-FL), is also the only female Republican Latina to be elected to Congress. Ros-Lehtinen won a highly contested special election for Democrat Claude Pepper's seat after he died in 1989. Born in Havana, Ros-Lehtinen immigrated to the United States when she was seven. She tends to vote with the conservative wing of the Republican Party in Congress the vast majority of the time and has strong ties with President Bush; she is known for arriving early for the president's State of the Union address so she can greet him as he enters the House chamber.[56] In 2006, she won her tenth term, defeating six-foot-five-inch Democrat David Patlak, who ran with the slogan "Vote Big Dave." During the campaign, Oscar-nominated actress Sally Kellerman, who played "Hot Lips Houlihan" in the original movie

---

[55] Senator Ed Brooke of Massachusetts, who served from 1967 to 1979, Representative Gary Franks, who served from the 5th District of Connecticut from 1991 to 1997, and Representative J. C. Watts, who served from the 4th District of Oklahoma from 1995 to 2002.

[56] Luisa Yanez, "A Venerable Politician—And a Celebrity, Too," *Miami Herald*, August 20, 2006. Her American Conservative Union score in 2005 was 88 percent, www.vote-smart.org/issue_rating_category.php?can_id=26815 (accessed May 27, 2007).

version of M*A*S*H, came to Key West and hosted a fund-raising concert for Patlak.[57] Ultimately, Ros-Lehtinen outspent Patlak $1.4 million to $75,700.[58]

In our analysis, of the 681 districts we classified as core Democratic districts, African American candidates were elected in 11.4 percent (78), and Hispanic candidates were elected in 4.7 percent (32). In swing districts, only three African American candidates were elected—all of them male.[59] Only one Hispanic has won in a swing district. In 1996, Democrat Loretta Sanchez defeated nine-term Republican incumbent, Representative Robert "B-1 Bob" Dornan, by 984 votes. Dornan challenged the results and claimed that "the election was stolen through rampant illegal voting by noncitizens."[60] A fourteen-month investigation by the House Oversight Committee concluded that there were voting irregularities, but not enough to affect the outcome. Dornan challenged Sanchez in her 1998 reelection bid in what turned out to be the most expensive House race of the election cycle.[61] He lost badly, with only 39 percent of the vote. His concession speech turned into a tirade in which he spoke of a "fog of evil that has rolled across our country," and his daughter's boyfriend got into a fistfight with a police officer.[62]

Only two African Americans were elected in core Republican districts, Representatives Gary Franks from Connecticut's 5th District and J. C. Watts from Oklahoma's 4th District. Four Hispanics were elected in core Republican districts, one woman and three men: Representatives Ileana Ros-Lehtinen (R-FL), Lincoln Diaz-Balart (R-FL), Henry Bonilla (R-TX), and Manuel Lujan (R-NM), who served from 1969 until 1989, and thus held the seat during two redistricting periods. Only 6 percent of all minority candidates to serve between 1972 and 2000 were elected in core Republican districts. Thus, the partisan makeup of a district is related to the success

---

[57] Luisa Yanez, "Actress Plans Fundraising Concert for Patlak," *Miami Herald*, September 16, 2006.

[58] "Total Raised and Spent, 2006 Race: Florida District 18," http://www.opensecrets.org/races/summary.asp?id=FL18&cycle=2006 (accessed May 27, 2007).

[59] Democrat Mike Espy won Mississippi's 2nd District in 1986, making him the first African American to be elected from Mississippi since Reconstruction. Republican Gary Franks first won Connecticut's 5th District in 1990 and lost his reelection bid in 1996. Democrat Cleo Fields was first elected in 1992 to Louisiana's 4th District, a district that became known as the "Mark of Zorro" because of its unusual Z-shape. In 1995, the U.S. Supreme Court decided that the district was an unconstitutional racial gerrymander, and Fields decided not to run in the redrawn district in 1996; Joan McKinney, "Reapportionment Reaction," *The Advocate*, Baton Rouge, LA, December 1, 1996, 13B.

[60] Jacki Koszczuk,"Proof of Illegal Voters Falls Short, Keeping Sanchez in House," *CQ Weekly*, February 7, 1998, 330.

[61] The two candidates spent more than $6.4 million. Much of the election centered around the issue of abortion. Dornan, who is of Irish descent, called himself the "true Latino candidate" because of his pro-life position; "Sanchez Claims Victory in Nation's Most Expensive Race," *Associated Press*, November 4, 1998, BC cycle.

[62] Larry Gerber, "Dornan Loses Solidly, Not Quietly," *Associated Press*, November 4, 1998, AM cycle.

Table 7.2 Characteristics of Core Democratic and Republican House Districts, 1972–2000

	Core Democratic Districts Electing Only Males during Decade (521)	Core Democratic Districts Electing a Female during Decade (50)
Partisanship and Ideology		
Republican share of presidential vote	50.8%	40.8%***
Simulated ideology of district[a]	11.0	1.6***
Geography		
District size in square miles	1,836.0	409.5***
Urban residents	76.0%	94.7%**
South	33.0%	10.0%***
Race and Ethnicity		
African American residents	6.4%	7.3%
Hispanic residents	1.5%	3.7%***
Foreign-born residents	3.4%	6.8%***
Socioeconomic		
Relative median income	99.4%	109.7%***
College degrees	12.4%	17.6%***
School-age population	19.9%	16.1%***
Blue-collar workers	9.6%	7.8%***

[a]1982–2000 only. The level of significance is denoted as follows: *** $p < .001$, ** $p < .01$, and

of minority candidates. Minority candidates are almost entirely from core Democratic districts.

Core Democratic districts were also more likely to elect women than core Republican districts, 11.3 percent compared to 7.6 percent, but the percentage of swing districts electing women, 20.4 percent, surpasses both of these. However, when we look at the interaction of race and gender, there were few minority women elected from swing or core Republican districts. Core Democratic districts were far more likely to elect black (29.5 percent) and Hispanic (12.5 percent) women than white women (8.8 percent). This suggests that the partisanship of a district interacts with both the gender and race of the candidate. In other words, minority women come from districts with different partisan leanings than white women.

Given that the race of winning candidates is related to partisanship in the district, our analysis will take race and gender into account. We conduct two separate analyses, examining those core Democratic and Republican districts that elected only non-minority candidates to the House, and those

(Districts Electing African Americans and Hispanics Not Included)

Core Republican Districts Electing Only Males during Decade (444)	Core Republican Districts Electing a Female during Decade (36)	Do Districts Electing Female Democrats Differ from Those Electing Female Republicans?
57.4%	49.9%*	Yes***
18.3	15.5*	Yes***
3,615.0	1,622.0	Yes***
62.6%	72.6%	Yes***
28.8%	8.3%**	No
3.8%	3.4%	Yes**
1.5%	2.4%	No
2.9%	5.4%**	Yes*
101.8%	112.1%***	No
15.4%	19.9%*	No
18.8%	17.5%*	No
8.3%	6.6%*	No

* p < .05.

core districts that elected African Americans.[63] We further divide these sets of districts into two sets again: those that elected a woman at least once during a redistricting period, and those that elected only men during the redistricting period. For each set, we calculated the average of our eleven demographic measures.[64]

White Women in Core Democratic and Republican Districts

As table 7.2 shows, the core Democratic and Republican districts electing white women have different demographic characteristics. In fact, the results

---

[63] Unfortunately, it was not possible to compare Hispanic men and women since only six Hispanic women have been elected to Congress.

[64] We use the median values rather than means, because the distribution of several of the demographic variables is substantially skewed. These include ideology, district size, the measures of diversity (African American, Hispanic, and foreign-born), along with the proportion of residents with a college degree. When data are skewed, the median offers a more satisfactory measure of central tendency in a distribution.

for core Democratic districts are dramatic and clearly demonstrate that the districts electing women are distinct.[65] In core Democratic districts, eleven of the twelve demographic factors are different for districts electing men than districts that elected a woman.

With respect to partisanship and ideology, core Democratic districts that elected a woman lean more to the left than those that elected only men. Given our measure of partisanship, Republican share of the presidential vote, we would expect these numbers to be lower in core Democratic districts compared to core Republican districts. But there is a substantial gender gap; the average Republican share of the presidential vote in districts electing only men was ten percentage points higher than the districts that have elected a woman. A similar gap is evident in the measure of district ideology. The average ideology score of those core Democratic districts electing men is 11.0, nearly identical to the overall mean of 10.7. The mean ideological score in those core Democratic districts electing women, 1.6, is significantly to the left of those electing only men. This suggests that the core Democratic districts that elect women produce greater margins for Democratic presidential candidates and, ideologically, are more liberal than the districts electing only men.

With respect to geography, core Democratic districts electing women are smaller, more urban, and non-southern. In fact, as mentioned earlier, the districts that elected white women are, on average, less than one-fourth the size of the districts that elected white men, only 409.5 square miles compared to 1,836.0 square miles. As table 7.2 shows, core Democratic districts that elected a woman are overwhelmingly the smallest of the four categories of districts. Given this result, it should come as no surprise that core Democratic districts that elected a woman are almost entirely urban, while districts that elected men are only 76.0 percent urban. Core Democratic districts that elected a woman are also less likely to be in the South.

In terms of the racial and ethnic makeup, there are no measurable differences between core Democratic districts with respect to the size of their black populations, but this is also no surprise, given that this analysis focuses on non-minority candidates. But core Democratic districts electing

---

[65] In the table, the asterisk next to the median value of the demographic variable for women denotes that the difference in medians between these groups is statistically significant. We used the Mann-Whitney test, which is the nonparametric counterpart of the difference-in-means test. It is used in the analysis because it involves less stringent assumptions about the distribution of the variables. The conventional difference-in-means test assumes that the data are drawn from a normal distribution. As noted previously, this assumption is not reasonable when dealing with distributions that are skewed. Essentially, the Mann-Whitney procedure tests for differences in the medians of the distribution where the null hypothesis is that the medians are equal; Robert Winkler and William Hays, *Statistics: Probability, Inference and Decision*, 2nd ed. (New York: Holt, Rinehart, and Winston, 1975), 848–55.

white women are more diverse, with larger Hispanic and foreign-born populations. The numbers are small, but they are distinct; core Democratic districts electing a woman have almost twice the proportion of Hispanic and foreign-born residents.

The results thus far show that, while core Democratic districts that have elected a white woman are different from those that have only elected men, these factors conform to characteristically Democratic districts and partisan expectations. In other words, all of these demographic measures are in the expected range for Democratic districts, but white women are elected from "more Democratic" districts than their male counterparts.

However, three of the four indicators listed under the socioeconomic category reveal that women are elected from districts that have characteristics atypical of their party. Core Democratic districts electing white women are wealthier than the districts that elected only men. In fact, there is a ten-point difference in the measure of median income. For example, in the redistricting period from 1992 and 2000, the "income advantage" in districts electing women was $3,500 per year. And although the differences are smaller, women are more likely to come from districts with a larger proportion of college graduates and a smaller blue-collar workforce. Interestingly, core Democratic districts electing men have the highest percentage of school-age children, while core Democratic districts electing women have the lowest percentage of school-age children. Thus, these results reveal that for Democrats, while districts that elect women are more liberal, urban, and racially diverse, as well as smaller, they are also more "upscale."

While the differences are not as sharp as those of the Democrats, core Republican districts electing white men and women are distinct as well. Table 7.2 shows that eight of the demographic characteristics are different for districts electing men from the districts that have elected a woman. In terms of partisanship and ideology, core Republican districts that elected a woman are not as far to the right as those districts that elected only men. There is nearly a ten percentage point gap in average support for Republican presidential candidates. Core Republican districts electing only men exhibit the highest average Republican share of the presidential vote of the four categories of districts, 57.4 percent. Core Republican districts that elected a woman had an average 49.9 percent Republican share of the presidential vote. In this respect, core Republican districts that elect women are remarkably similar in their presidential voting patterns to core Democratic districts that elected only men. This suggests that districts electing Republican women are more moderate and less partisan than Republican districts that elect only men.

Turning to geography, while core Republican districts are larger than core Democratic districts, core Republican districts that elected a woman are less than half the size of the districts that elect only male Republicans, 1,622 square miles compared to 3,615 square miles.[66] Of the nation's one hundred largest districts in the 110th Congress (2007 session), only three were represented by women—all Republicans. Along with Representative Cathy McMorris Rodgers from Washington's 5th District, there were Representative Jo Ann Emerson from Missouri's 8th District and Representative Shelley Moore Capito from West Virginia's 2nd District. Core Republican districts electing a woman have a substantially larger urban population; core Republican districts electing a woman are 72.6 percent urban, while core Republican districts electing men are only 62.6 percent urban. Districts that elected a Republican woman are also primarily outside of the South. Core Republican districts in general are not as racially and ethnically diverse as core Democratic districts. Among the core Republican districts, we find that there are no differences in the proportion of African American and Hispanic residents in districts that have elected only men and districts that have elected a woman. Districts that elected a woman, however, do have larger foreign-born populations, indicating that they are slightly more diverse. This leads to the conclusion that women are elected in core districts that are "less" stereotypically Republican. In fact, there are four measures—the Republican share of the presidential vote, district size, urbanization, and foreign-born residents—where the core Republican districts that elected women look more like the core Democratic districts that elected men.

The socioeconomic factors highlight some interesting differences as well. Like core Democratic districts that elected a white woman, core Republican districts that elected a white woman are significantly wealthier than districts electing only males. As in the case of Democrats, districts electing Republican women are 10 percent wealthier than those electing men. For the 1992–2000 period, the median income in core Republican districts electing women was $38,242 compared to $34,728, a difference of $3,514. Core Republican districts that elected a woman are the wealthiest of the four categories of districts. These districts are also more educated; almost 20 percent of residents have college degrees, also the highest proportion of all four categories. Core Republican districts that elected a woman have smaller school-age populations than districts that have elected only men. They also have a lower proportion of blue-collar workers, once again the smallest of all four categories, only 6.6 percent on average.

Overall, table 7.2 reveals the differences and similarities among core Democratic and Republican districts electing white women. The last column of the table shows that, with respect to partisanship and ideology, women of both parties represent districts that are more liberal than those of their male counterparts, but it is important to keep in mind that core Democratic districts electing a woman are still more Democratic and liberal than core

---

[66] This difference is not statistically significant.

Republican districts electing a woman. And while women of both parties represent districts that are smaller than their male counterparts, core Democratic districts electing women are the smallest, about one-fourth the size of core Republican districts electing women. Core Democratic districts electing women are more urban than core Republican districts electing women and are, albeit slightly, more racially and ethnically diverse. For six of the eight measures, there are differences between the core Democratic districts electing a woman and core Republican districts electing a woman. Thus, with respect to partisanship and ideology, geography, and diversity, the core Democratic and Republican districts electing women are distinct. These distinctions, however, fall in line with the expected partisan characteristics. In other words, on these measures, there are differences between the core Democratic districts electing women and the core Republican districts electing women, but these differences can be explained by "party friendliness."

On the other hand, as the last column of table 7.2 also shows, the socioeconomic makeup of core Democratic and Republican districts electing white women is virtually identical. These districts have the same relative median incomes, the same proportion of the population with college degrees, the same proportion of school-age children, and the same proportion of blue-collar workers. In other words, women are elected in districts that are distinct from the districts men represent. And these particular measures can arguably be thought of as indicators of more progressive attitudes about women's roles. Thus, "party-friendly" and "women-friendly" are not the same concept. Women-friendly districts have their own unique political geographies.

White Women in Swing Districts

Over the three decades included in our analysis, there were 133 non-minority districts where a party won two or three elections in the redistricting period. There are 309 elections where male Democrats won, 33 elections where female Democrats won, 297 elections where male Republicans won, and 20 elections where female Republicans won.

Like core Democratic districts, table 7.3 shows that there are significant differences on eleven of our twelve measures between swing districts that elected white male Democrats and swing districts that elected white female Democrats. Swing districts won by a female Democrat are more supportive of Democratic presidential candidates and are more liberal. Once again, with respect to geography, these districts are substantially smaller: roughly half the size of swing districts electing male Democrats, only 1,348 square miles compared to 2,655 square miles. In addition, they have a higher percentage of urban residents, 72.3 percent compared to 66.8 percent respectively. Swing districts in the South are one-third as likely to elect a Democratic

Table 7.3 Characteristics of Swing Districts in House Elections, 1972–2000 (Districts Electing

	Swing Districts Won by Male Democrats (309)	Swing Districts Won by Female Democrats (33)
Partisanship and Ideology		
Republican share of presidential vote	55.0%	47.3%**
Simulated ideology of district[a]	15.7	9.6***
Geography		
District size	2,655.0	1,348.0**
Urban residents	66.8%	72.3%**
South	30.7%	9.1%***
Race and Ethnicity		
African American residents	4.1%	5.2%
Hispanic residents	1.4%	2.9%***
Foreign-born residents	3.0%	6.0%***
Socioeconomic		
Relative median income	99.5%	121.8%***
College degrees	13.4%	25.3%***
School-age population	21.2%	16.0%***
Blue-collar workers	9.2%	5.4%***

[a] 1982–2000 only. The level of significance is denoted as follows: *** p < .001, ** p < .01, and

woman as they are to elect a Democratic man. With respect to diversity, swing districts where a Democratic woman won have higher percentages of Hispanic and foreign-born residents; they are more diverse. The swing districts that elected female Democrats are "more" Democratic in their partisanship and ideology, geography, and diversity.

The biggest differences among these districts are their socioeconomic characteristics. Swing districts electing a Democratic woman are wealthier than districts electing Democratic men. Again using the national median for 1992–2000, median income in swing districts won by male Democrats is $33,943; for female Democrats, it is $41,551, a difference of $7,608. Swing districts won by a Democratic woman are the wealthiest of all four categories. In addition, the swing districts where Democratic women were elected had almost twice as many residents with college degrees, 25.3 percent compared to only 13.4 percent, once again the highest of all four categories. These districts also have a smaller school-age population and only half as

African Americans and Hispanics Not Included)

Swing Districts Won by Male Republicans (297)	Swing Districts Won by Female Republicans (20)	Do Districts Electing Female Democrats Differ from Those Electing Female Republicans?
55.8%	48.9%**	No
16.2%	9.3***	No
3,712.0	541.0**	No
63.7%	93.6%***	No
28.6%	30.0%	Yes*
4.1%	8.5%	No
1.4%	3.7%	No
2.9%	5.9%	No
99.8%	119.1%**	No
13.3%	19.7%***	No
20.9%	16.5%***	No
9.2%	5.8%***	No

* p < .05.

many blue-collar workers. Thus, the swing districts that elect Democratic men are quite different from those that elect Democratic women; their socioeconomic indicators are "less" Democratic.

In the case of the swing districts that elected Republicans, there are significant differences between the districts that elected white men and women on ten of the twelve measures. Here, swing districts won by a female Republican are less supportive of Republican presidential candidates and are less conservative. Their geographic characteristics are also distinct. Swing districts that elected Republican women are one-sixth the size of the districts that elect their male counterparts, only 541 square miles compared to 3,712 square miles. These districts are also almost entirely urban, while the districts electing male Republicans are only 63.7 percent urban. Republican women are also elected from districts that are more diverse than those electing male Republicans; in fact, the proportions of blacks, Hispanics, and foreign-born in districts electing female Republicans are more than twice the proportions in districts electing male Republicans. This demonstrates that swing districts won by Republican women are "less" Republican on these measures.

The socioeconomic characteristics of the swing districts electing Republican men and women are also quite different. Republican women are elected in swing districts that are wealthier. Using the national median for 1992–2000, the median income in swing districts electing Republican men was $34,046; the median income in swing districts electing Republican women was $40,630, a difference of $6,584. These Republican women are elected in swing districts that have a higher proportion of residents with college degrees, fewer school-age children, and fewer blue-collar workers than the swing districts Republican men come from. Thus, Republican women are elected in swing districts that have more characteristically Republican socioeconomic factors.

As the last column of table 7.3 shows, there are strong similarities among swing districts that elect white women candidates of either party. In fact, in almost all respects, the swing districts that elect Democratic and Republican women are virtually identical. Swing districts that have elected a woman of either party are similar in their partisanship and ideology, their geography, their racial and ethnic makeup, and their socioeconomic characteristics. As such, there are no party-friendly characteristics that separate the kinds of swing districts that elect white Democratic and Republican women. In swing districts, the only differences that matter are those that make a district women-friendly. Combined with our analysis of core Democratic and Republican districts, this provides considerable evidence that districts electing non-minority women to the House are unique and distinct from districts that have elected only men.

African American Women and Core Democratic Districts

African American men were elected in fifty-five core Democratic districts, and African American women were elected in twenty-three core Democratic districts.[67] As table 7.4 illustrates, unlike the findings for white women, there are very few differences in the makeup of these districts. Both African American men and women are elected from districts with very low levels of support for Republican presidential candidates, only 20.4 and 23.4 percent respectively. In addition, the ideological scores demonstrate that these districts are distinctly to the left and among the most liberal. Geographically, these districts are quite small and are 100 percent urban. Male and female African Americans are equally likely to be elected from districts in the South; about one-third of the African Americans in the House are from the South.

---

[67] We do not examine core Republican districts here because, as mentioned earlier, no Republican African American woman has ever been elected to the House, and there have been only two Republican African American men.

Table 7.4 Characteristics of Core Democratic Districts Electing African Americans, 1972–2000

	Core Democratic Districts Electing Only African American Males during Decade (55)	Core Democratic Districts Electing an African American Female during Decade (23)	Do Democratic Districts Electing White Females Differ from Those Electing Black Females?
Partisanship and Ideology			
Republican share of presidential vote	20.4%	23.4%	Yes***
Simulated ideology of district[a]	−18.7	−12.7	Yes***
Geography			
District size in square miles	59.0	104.0	Yes**
Urban residents	100%	100%	Yes***
South	27.3%	34.8%	Yes*
Ethnicity			
African American residents	59.4%	49.4%*	Yes***
Hispanic residents	1.9%	8.2%*	Yes*
Foreign-born residents	4.9%	6.0%	No
Socioeconomic			
Relative median income	85.4%	78.9%	Yes***
College degrees	13.1%	11.1%	Yes**
School-age population	18.4%	18.6%	Yes*
Blue-collar workers	8.2%	9.0%	No

[a] 1982–2000 only. The level of significance is denoted as follows: *** $p < .001$, ** $p < .01$, and * $p < .05$.

Finally, these core Democratic districts have similar socioeconomic profiles with no significant differences in income, education, school-age population, or blue-collar workers.

There are some noteworthy patterns with regard to the race and ethnicity of the constituents in these core Democratic districts. These districts have overwhelmingly larger proportions of people of color compared to the districts that elect white House members. But districts that elected African American men have a substantially larger proportion of black residents than districts that elected African American women, 59.4 percent compared to 49.4 percent, a ten-point gap. African American women, however, represent districts that have much larger Hispanic populations, 8.2 percent compared to 1.9 percent.

The last column of table 7.4 compares core Democratic districts that elected an African American woman to those core Democratic districts electing a white woman.[68] Clearly, black and white women are elected from Democratic constituencies that are quite distinct. There are significant differences between ten of the twelve characteristics, with African American women representing districts that are less Republican in their support for presidential candidates, more liberal, substantially smaller, more solidly urban, more diverse, poorer, less educated, and younger than the districts of their white female counterparts. Our analysis shows that failure to control for the race of the winning candidate would obscure the unique character of the districts that elect African American women and the districts that elect white women. In effect, African American women do not come from districts with the distinctly women-friendly socioeconomic characteristics that white women do. The districts that elect black women are virtually identical to the districts that elect black men. And these districts that African American House members represent are different than the districts electing white Democrats; they are the "most" Democratic districts in the analysis. In other words, they have the "party-friendliest" Democratic demographics.

The Index of Women-Friendliness

To further explore the impact of demographics on women's success, we develop an "index of women-friendliness" for each party based on the results of table 7.2. Here, we use eleven of the twelve demographic characteristics; we do not use the measure of ideology, since it is only available from 1982 to 2000. In core Democratic districts, ten of the eleven remaining demographic characteristics have significantly different values in districts that elected a woman compared to districts that elected only men. Six of these demographic characteristics have greater values in the districts that have elected a woman: urban residents, median income, college graduates, and the proportion of African American, Hispanic, and foreign-born residents. In each congressional district, if the particular factor had a value greater than or equal to the average of the core Democratic districts that elected a woman, it is assigned a one. There are four demographic characteristics that have lower values in the districts that elected a woman: Republican vote for president, size of the district, school-age population, and blue-collar workforce. In each congressional district, if the particular factor had a value less than or equal to the average of the core Democratic districts that elected

---

[68] These are based upon comparing the medians of core Democratic districts electing African American women and core Democratic districts electing white women.

a woman, it is also assigned a one.[69] Districts outside the South are also assigned a one.

The idea is that assigning the value of one to a particular characteristic indicates that the district has that women-friendly attribute; the characteristic is different for districts that elected a woman compared to districts that elected only men. For example, the average size of core Democratic districts that elected a woman is 1,348 square miles. Any districts that are 1,348 square miles or smaller are assigned a one; districts greater than 1,348 square miles are assigned a zero. The average share of urban residents in core Democratic districts that elected a woman is 72.3 percent. Any districts that have 72.3 percent or more urban residents are assigned a one; districts whose urban population is smaller are assigned a zero. We used the same process for core Republican districts.

Our index of women-friendliness is calculated by summing these demographic characteristics and ranges from zero to eleven. Thus, for each congressional district, we have two indicators of the relative friendliness of a constituency—one for Democrats and one for Republicans. Among core Democratic districts, the median number of attributes in districts electing only men is three; for districts electing a woman, it is six. For Republican core districts, the median number of attributes in districts electing only men is four; for districts electing a woman, it is also six. For Democrats in swing districts, the median value of those electing only men is two, and for those electing women, it is six. Among Republicans in swing districts, those electing only men have a median number of four, while those electing women have a median number of seven. In sum, our measures perform well in encapsulating the differences highlighted in tables 7.2 and 7.3.

We can use this index to examine the success of women at all three stages of a campaign: running in a primary, winning a primary, and winning the general election. Table 7.5 reports the results for two electoral contexts: elections for open seats, and elections against an incumbent of the opposition party. The set of open seats includes districts where the sitting incumbent vacates the seat as well as those new seats created as a result of reapportionment. For each party, we collapse the eleven-point index into three categories, low (0–3 attributes), medium (4–7), and high (8–11). Those scoring low on the index are considered "ambivalent" toward women candidates, while those scoring high are "women-friendly." For the entire period of our analysis, there were 433 women-friendly districts, 157 for the Democrats and 276 for the Republicans.

As table 7.5 shows, the results are unambiguous. Where women decide to run in a primary is influenced by the friendliness of the district. For female

---

[69] This index is constructed in a manner similar to building a party-friendly index. See for example Lewis Froman, *Congressmen and Their Constituencies* (Chicago: Rand McNally, 1963); and Koetzle, 1998.

Table 7.5 Women Running in Primaries, Winning Primaries, and Winning General Elections by the Friendliness Index, 1972–2000

Electoral Phase and Women-friendly Index Value	Open Districts, Female Democrats	Open Districts, Female Republicans	Female Democrats in Districts with Republican Incumbents	Female Republicans in Districts with Democrat Incumbents
	Ran in the Primary			
Women-friendly Attributes				
Low: 0–3 attributes	29.5%	17.0%	17.7%	10.8%
	(114/387)	(54/317)	(239/1,353)	(129/1,194)
Medium: 4–7 attributes	40.4%	25.8%	23.2%	12.1%
	(108/267)	(72/279)	(206/889)	(174/1,437)
High: 8–11 attributes	61.2%	36.8%	35.9%	20.9%
	(41/67)	(46/125)	(61/170)	(153/732)
Chi-square	27.71***	20.23***	34.32***	43.98***
	Won the Primary			
Women-friendly Attributes				
Low: 0–3 attributes	9.8%	3.5%	9.6%	5.9%
	(38/387)	(11/317)	(130/1,353)	(71/1,194)
Medium: 4–7 attributes	17.6%	8.6%	15.1%	7.1%
	(37/267)	(26/279)	(134/889)	(102/1,437)
High: 8–11 attributes	29.9%	16.8%	21.8%	11.9%
	(20/67)	(21/125)	(37/170)	(87/732)
Chi-square	21.57***	22.53***	29.11***	23.85***
	Won the General Election			
Women-friendly Attributes				
Low: 0–3 attributes	2.6%	2.2%	0.4%	0.1%
	(10/387)	(7/317)	(5/1,353)	(1/1,194)
Medium: 4–7 attributes	10.1%	3.6%	0.4%	0.5%
	(27/267)	(10/279)	(4/889)	(7/1,437)
High: 8–11 attributes	19.4%	4.8%	3.5%	0.0%
	(13/67)	(6/125)	(6/170)	(0/732)
Chi-square	31.67***	2.18	25.07***	6.70*

The proportions presented are the product of a 2 × 3 cross-tabulation. The test statistic is chi-square with 2 degrees of freedom. The level of significance is denoted as follows: *** $p < .001$, ** $p < .01$, and * $p < .05$.

Democrats in open-seat elections, the proportion of contests in which a woman seeks the party's nomination doubles from 29.5 percent in districts ranked low on the index to 61.2 percent in those districts ranked high. The same pattern is evident for Republicans. In districts with open seats, female Republicans are twice as likely to run in a primary in districts that rank high on the women-friendliness index as they are to run in districts that rank low. There is a similar relationship in districts where an incumbent seeks reelection. When faced with the prospect of running against a Republican incumbent, Democratic women are twice as likely to seek the nomination of their party in districts that rank high on the women-friendliness index compared to those districts that rank low. The proportion of elections in which Democratic women seek the nomination increases from 17.7 percent in the least friendly districts to 35.9 percent in the most friendly. Once again, the same pattern holds for Republican women. In districts with a Democratic incumbent, the likelihood that a Republican woman will run in the primary increases from 10.8 percent in districts that rank low on the index to 20.9 percent in districts that rank high on the index.

Table 7.5 also demonstrates that winning a primary varies with the friendliness of the district. Among Democrats in open districts, the proportion of female nominees increases from 9.8 percent in districts that rank low on the index to 29.9 percent in districts that rank high. The increase among Republicans is from 3.5 to 16.8 percent. In other words, for both parties, the movement from the least friendly to the most friendly districts more than *triples* the likelihood of winning a primary. A similar but less dramatic relationship appears in districts where an incumbent is seeking reelection. The proportion of female Democrats winning the nomination in Republican-held districts increases from 9.6 to 21.8 percent. For Republicans in Democratic districts, the proportion of female primary winners increases from 5.9 to 11.9 percent. In sum, our index reveals that the decision of where to seek the nomination and the results of the resulting primaries systematically vary with the women-friendliness of the district. Women of both parties are more likely to seek and win the nomination in districts that are women-friendly. This holds in districts with open seats and in districts where an incumbent of the opposition party is running for reelection.

The last section of table 7.5 presents the proportion of women who won a general election contest. For female Democrats seeking an open seat, there is a strong association between winning and the value of our index. The proportion increases from 2.6 percent in the least friendly districts to 10.1 percent in the midrange districts and increases again to 19.4 percent in the friendliest districts. Thus, for Democratic women, the probability of winning an open seat depends upon the demographic character of the district. The relationship for Republican women in open seats is much weaker. The proportion increases from 2.2 percent in least friendly districts to only 4.8 percent in the most friendly.[70] The number of cases, however, is quite small. Between 1972 and 2000, only twenty-three Republican women won open seats. The last comparison in table 7.5 is the set of general elections where a woman faced a sitting incumbent. The most striking aspect of these results is the small number of women who won, a testament to the strength of incumbency. Across the entire time frame of our analysis, only thirteen female Democrats and eight female Republicans defeated an incumbent member of the House. For the Democrats, winning is related to the friendliness of the district; the proportion of victories in the least friendly and midrange districts is 0.4 percent, and increases to 3.5 percent in the most friendly districts. There is no such increase for Republican women challenging Democrat incumbents; all of these proportions are less than 1.0 percent.

While women of both parties are more likely to run in and win a primary in districts that are women-friendly, it is important to point out the differences between women in the Democratic and Republican Parties. The proportions running in a primary, winning a primary, and winning a general election are lower among Republican women, although they appear to have more opportunities. There were 67 districts with open seats that scored high on the Democratic women-friendliness index. Female Democrats ran in 41, a rate of 61.2 percent. There were almost double the number of open districts that scored high on the Republican women-friendliness index, 125. But only 46 Republican women ran in these districts, a rate of 36.8 percent, about half the rate for Democratic women. Among districts with Republican incumbents seeking reelection, there were 170 that scored high on the women-friendliness index, and Democratic women ran in 61 of these primaries, 35.9 percent. There were four times as many Democratic incumbents who sought reelection in districts that scored high on the women-friendliness index, but Republican women entered only 153 of these primaries, 20.9 percent. At any rate, what we have shown is that open seats are not uniform in their likelihood to elect women. And female candidates, whether they run in open seats or against incumbents, are more likely to run in districts that are women-friendly.

Looking to the Future: Women-Friendly Districts and Their Implications

Our analysis demonstrates that the districts electing white women to the U.S. House of Representatives are distinct. There are demographic characteristics in a district, captured in our index of women-friendliness, that are related to where women run in primaries, win primaries, and, for female Democrats, win general elections. Although we have not ruled out a "role model effect," our analysis demonstrates that where women choose to run and the success of their campaigns vary systematically with the attributes included in our

---

[70] This relationship is not statistically significant.

index. As a result, we can use our index of women-friendliness to speculate about possible opportunities for women candidates.

The Growth in Women-friendly Districts

One way of assessing opportunities for women is to look at the growth of women-friendly districts. We examined those House districts with high scores on the index of women-friendliness, eight or more demographic characteristics, over the redistricting periods in our analysis. Table 7.6 shows that the number of women-friendly districts has increased over time.[71] In the redistricting period from 1972 to 1980, there were only 11 districts classified as women-friendly for the Democrats and 28 districts for the Republicans.

Table 7.6 The Growth in Women-friendly House Districts

Redistricting Period	Democratic Women-friendly Districts	Republican Women-friendly Districts
All House Districts		
1972–1980	2.5% (11/435)	6.4% (28/435)
1982–1990	12.4% (54/435)	20.9% (91/435)
1992–2000	21.1% (92/435)	36.1% (157/435)
Open Districts (Vacated)		
1972–1980	2.4% (6/246)	3.7% (9/246)
1982–1990	9.7% (16/165)	17.6% (29/165)
1992–2000	15.9% (40/251)	30.3% (76/251)
New Districts		
1972–1980	0% (0/18)	5.6% (1/18)
1982–1990	4.5% (1/22)	13.6% (3/22)
1992–2000	21.1% (4/19)	36.8% (7/19)

---

[71] As we noted in chapter 1, the redistricting that occurred in the 1960s in the wake of the U.S. Supreme Court's rulings in *Baker v. Carr* (1962) and *Wesberry v. Sanders* (1964) created substantially more urban districts. Unfortunately, our demographic data do not go back far enough to fully explore this.

During this decade, only 9.0 percent of all 435 districts could be classified as women-friendly. By the 1992 to 2000 period, women-friendly districts numbered 92 (21.1 percent) for the Democrats and 157 (36.1 percent) for the Republicans. In other words, the proportion of women-friendly districts jumped to 57.2 percent of all districts. Thus, the number of districts that afford women a greater likelihood for electoral success dramatically increased. This suggests that there are now substantial opportunities where women would be successful if they ran.

What explains the increase in women-friendly districts? Five of the demographic variables in our analysis have changed over the last three decades in a direction beneficial to women. Constituencies have grown more racially and ethnically diverse. Across all House districts, the median proportion of Hispanic residents has increased from 1.0 percent in the 1972–1980 period to 3.1 percent in the 1992–2000 period; similarly, the proportion of foreign-born residents has increased from 3.0 to 4.2 percent. In addition, the proportion of residents with college degrees has risen from 9.7 to 18.4 percent. At the same time, the school-age population has dropped from 23.7 to 15.6 percent, and the median proportion of blue-collar workers has declined from 13.3 to 6.7 percent. Thus, the changing demography of the United States has expanded political opportunities for women. As our nation becomes increasingly diverse and educated, women are increasingly likely to be successful as candidates.

At the same time, however, it is important to keep incumbency in mind. It is clear from table 7.7 that the number of opportunities to run in open seats that are women-friendly has dramatically increased. The total number of women-friendly seats that were open increased from 16 (6 percent) during the 1972–1980 period to 127 (47 percent) during the 1992–2000 period. In open seats that were vacated by an incumbent, the proportion of women-friendly districts is relatively low, 15.9 percent for the Democrats and 30.3 percent for the Republicans. Newly created districts are more likely to be women-friendly than those that were vacated, but only nineteen new districts were created in the 1992–2000 redistricting period. And overall, women-friendly open seats were only 5.8 percent of all House seats.

As a result, while demographic changes may be working in favor of

Table 7.7 The Partisan Character of Women-friendly Districts, 1972–2000

Party	Women-friendly Districts that are "Core Democrat"	Women-friendly Districts that are "Swing"	Women-friendly Districts that are "Core Republican"
Democrats (157 total)	72.6% (114)	6.4% (10)	21.0% (33)
Republicans (276 total)	58.7% (162)	9.1% (25)	32.2% (89)

women, incumbency is still a consistent barrier. Moreover, our analysis shows that, although open districts do provide the major electoral opportunity for women to win a seat in the House, the districts that come open in any given election do not afford equal opportunities. Not only does incumbency limit real political opportunities for women, but the seats that do come open may not always be receptive to female candidates. The "political glass ceiling" is a function of not simply incumbency, but also particular district-level characteristics that may discourage women from running and keep them from winning.

The Paradox for Republican Women

According to our index of women-friendliness, there are more districts classified as women-friendly for Republicans than for Democrats. As mentioned earlier, during the entire period of our study, there are a total of 157 districts friendly to female Democrats and 276 friendly to female Republicans. In the aggregate, then, there are almost twice as many Republican women-friendly districts than Democratic women-friendly districts. One reason, as noted in our discussion of table 7.2, is that the demographic differences between core Republican districts that elected only men and those that elected a woman are not as sharp or pronounced as the differences for the Democrats. More important, however, is the direction of the Republican differences. Districts grow more friendly toward Republican women as the Republican presidential vote declines, as ideology moves to the left, as Hispanic and foreign-born residents increase, and as the school-age population declines. In effect, as districts become friendlier to Republican women, they simultaneously grow more characteristic of Democratic districts.

This becomes particularly clear when we examine the partisanship of women-friendly districts. Table 7.7 shows that nearly 73 percent of the districts friendly to Democratic women are core Democratic districts; less than one-fourth fall into the core Republican category. In other words, almost three-quarters of the women-friendly Democratic districts are core Democratic districts. In those districts that are the most likely to elect a woman, party and gender interact to the advantage of Democratic women. The contrast with Republicans is striking. Over 58 percent of the districts friendly to Republican women are core Democratic districts; less than a third are core Republican districts. Thus, for Republican women, their gender is an advantage, but their party is a major disadvantage. These districts are more receptive to women but, at the same time, more likely to vote Democratic. Simply put, the districts where Republican women have the best opportunity to win a primary are the districts where their prospects in the general election are the lowest. This, in turn, helps us understand the partisan gender gap illustrated in chapter 6. In addition to the impediments faced by all female candidates, Republican women face a less hospitable "political geography."

The Paradox for Democratic Women

The question arises as to whether female Democrats face a similar predicament in light of the atypical characteristics associated with women-friendly districts, in particular the higher levels of wealth. Wealthier districts are generally assumed to be more Republican. Thus, are Democratic women likely to have trouble in these districts? Our analysis in this chapter suggests no. In fact, the mixing of upscale congressional districts with Democratic or liberal politics does not appear to be an impediment to the political fortunes of Democratic women at all. Wealthier districts have grown less antagonistic toward Democratic presidential candidates over time. During the presidential elections of 1972, 1976, and 1980, 27.7 percent of those districts with relative median incomes of 110 percent or more gave a majority of the presidential vote to the Democratic candidate. In the presidential elections of 1984 and 1988, the proportion increased to 30.6 percent. For the elections of 1992, 1996, and 2000, the proportion again increased to 46.4 percent.

Moreover, the geographic location of these Democratic women-friendly districts is instructive. Many are located in the wealthier and highly professionalized sections of major American cities, such as New York, San Francisco, Los Angeles, and Chicago. These congressional districts resemble the "ideopolis" described in *The Emerging Democratic Majority* by John Judis and Ruy Teixeira.[72] The "ideopolis" is a label used to describe the emerging political economy of particular cities and metropolitan areas. These places, like Austin, Boulder, and the Silicon Valley, have developed postindustrial economies based on research and development, "soft technology," and "knowledge industries" like telecommunications or pharmaceuticals. Most of these cities include a major research university, such as the Universities of Wisconsin, Stanford, and Northwestern. Ideopolises attract well-paid, nonmanagerial professionals who, as a group, are ethnically diverse and culturally "libertarian and bohemian."[73] This growing "creative class" shares "a common ethos that values creativity, individuality, difference, and merit."[74] They choose to live in places that value tolerance and "diversity" in all its forms: "urban grit alongside renovated buildings, the commingling of young and old, long-time neighborhood characters and yuppies, fashion models and 'bag ladies.' "[75] As a result, the ideopolis has a substantially different political outlook than cities like Muncie, Fresno, or Memphis, which still rely on the manufacturing of cars and other industrial goods.[76] Ideopolises are becoming overwhelmingly Democratic in their voting

---

[72] Judis and Teixeira, 2002.
[73] Judis and Teixeira, 2002, 73.
[74] Richard Florida, "The Rise of the Creative Class: Why Cities without Gays and Rock Bands are Losing the Economic Development Race," *Washington Monthly* 34 (2002): 15–26.
[75] These areas also tend to have very large gay populations; Florida, 2002.
[76] Judis and Teixeira, 2002, 72–73.

patterns. For example, in the 2000 election, the Denver–Boulder area favored Al Gore 56 to 35 percent over George Bush. Overall, ideopolis counties in 2000 voted 58 percent Democratic.[77] If ideopolises continue to grow, then the redistricting process will reflect this growth, at least in part. Thus, we should see the number of districts that are friendly toward Democratic women candidates continue to grow as well.

Conclusion

Between 1972 and 1980, female candidates won a total of 85 elections for the U.S. House of Representatives, but these victories were won in only 32 (7.4 percent) of the 435 congressional districts. After the redistricting cycle following the 1980 Census, the number of female victories increased to 119, with 38 districts (8.7 percent) electing a woman at least once. This proportion more than doubled during the districting regime in place from 1992 to 2000. During those years, women won 260 elections to the House in 83 districts (19.1 percent). More districts are becoming women-friendly, and women are winning in more districts.

There are clear differences, at least among white members of Congress, between the districts that elected a woman and districts electing only men. Democratic women tend to represent districts that are upscale, diverse, and highly urbanized: "bohemian ideopolises." Republican women tend to represent districts that are also upscale, but also less conservative, more urban, and more diverse than their male counterparts: Democratic districts. In fact, the districts electing Republican women are quite similar to the districts electing Democratic men. As a result, Republican women face an uphill battle and thus seem to face a Catch-22: they can run in solidly Republican districts where they have less chance of winning because of their gender, or they can run in more moderate districts where they have less chance of winning because of their party affiliation. This may explain, at least in part, the growing gap between the number of Democratic and Republican women in the House.

Our index of women-friendliness reveals that the political glass ceiling is not simply a function of incumbency, but should also be understood in terms of opportunities. There is no doubt that, in general, women have a better chance of winning open seats than defeating an incumbent. But the number of open seats in a given election cycle is quite small, and once the demographics of these open seats are taken into account, the number of real opportunities for women to win these open seats is even smaller. A substantial number of districts, through 2010, are still unlikely to elect a woman.

---

[77] Judis and Teixeira, 2002, 76.

8

Where We Are
Women of the Twenty-first Century

We began our analysis with a central question: why has the pace of electing women to Congress been so slow? In her study of state legislators, Jeane Kirkpatrick argued that increasing the number of women in political office could only be achieved by changing "[s]ocial goals, beliefs about the identity and the role of men and women, [and] practices concerning socialization, education, political recruitment and family."[1] In other words, "both a cultural and a social revolution is required."[2] In addition to a change in the political culture, our analysis shows that there has been change in the political opportunity structure. While entering the pipeline is easier, the upper portions of the hierarchy are blocked. As demonstrated in chapter 2, just as the first women were running for Congress in the early twentieth century, the development of careerism made it more difficult for women to succeed. The system has evolved to the point where incumbents are typically unbeatable. And as our analysis in chapter 7 shows, even open seats do not necessarily provide an electoral environment where female candidates can be successful.

The Picture Now: The Campaign of 2006 and the Women of the 110th Congress

In 2006, eighty-seven women won election to the 110th Congress (2007 session), seventy-one women in the House and sixteen in the Senate. The midterm campaign of 2006 was most commonly characterized as a referendum on the performance of the incumbent president, George W.

---

[1] Jeane Kirkpatrick, *Political Woman* (New York: Basic Books, 1974), 244.
[2] Kirkpatrick, 1974, 244.

Bush.[3] Accordingly, the strategy of the Democrats was to nationalize the campaign. For example, Representative Rahm Emaneul, Chairman of the Democratic Congressional Campaign Committee, emphasized that "Bush is going to be on the ballot, like Clinton was in '94."[4] Poll numbers certainly recommended this strategy. On the eve of the election, only 38 percent of the public approved of Bush's performance as president, and an even lower 34 percent approved of how the president was handling the war in Iraq. Additionally, 55 percent regarded the war as a mistake and 64 percent were dissatisfied with the general direction of the country.[5]

Exacerbating the problem for the Republicans was a string of scandals. On September 28, 2005, the Majority Leader of the House, Representative Tom DeLay (R-TX), was indicted by a Texas grand jury for violations of the state's campaign finance laws.[6] DeLay subsequently relinquished his role as Majority Leader and resigned from the House on June 9, 2006.[7] In November of 2005, Representative Randy "Duke" Cunningham (R-CA) resigned his seat after pleading guilty in federal district court to charges of tax evasion and accepting bribes.[8] The next incident occurred in early August of 2006, when Representative Bob Ney (R-OH) withdrew from his reelection campaign in the face of charges that he accepted illegal gifts from lobbyist Jack Abramoff.[9] Finally, allegations that Representative Mark Foley (R-FL) sent improper internet messages to high school students in the House page program led to his resignation on September 29, 2006.[10] This chain of events allowed the Democrats to add charges of a "culture of corruption" to their strategy of nationalizing the midterm contests.[11]

---

[3] To illustrate, we used a Lexis-Nexis headline and lead paragraph search across major regional newspapers. Between January 1 and November 6 of 2006, there were 642 stories that contained the words "Bush" and "elections" and "referendum" in the heading or lead paragraph.

[4] James Traub, "Party Like It's 1994," *New York Times Magazine*, March 12, 2006, 43.

[5] PollingReport.com, http://www.pollingreport.com (accessed June 30, 2007).

[6] Wes Allison, "House Leader Hit with Indictment," *St. Petersburg Times*, September 29, 2005, 1A.

[7] Jonathan Weisman, "House Ethics Panel Begins Bribery Probe; Congressmen from Ohio and Louisiana Targeted; DeLay Escapes with Resignation," *Washington Post*, May 18, 2006, 4.

[8] Charles R. Babcock and Jonathan Weisman, "Congressman Pleads Guilty to Bribery, Then Resigns," *Washington Post*, November 29, 2005, 1.

[9] Philip Shenon, "Ohio Republican Tied to Abramoff Abandons Reelection Bid," *New York Times*, August 8, 2006, 15. Ney was first elected in 1994 and was seeking his seventh term in office. Joy Padgett, a member of the state Senate, won a special election to replace Ney on the ballot and was defeated in the general election by Democrat Zack Space; Elizabeth Auster and Sabrina Eaton, "Ohio Voters Key to Power Shift," *Cleveland Plain Dealer*, November 8, 2006, S3.

[10] Bill Adair, Adam C. Smith, and Anita Kumar, "Lawmaker Quits Amid Scandal," *St. Petersburg Times*, September 30, 2006, 1A.

[11] Traub, 2006, 43. It should also be noted that the Democrats were not scandal-free. In August of 2006, federal agents raided the Washington home of Representative William Jefferson (D-LA) as part of a bribery probe. Agents found $90,000 in his freezer; Bill Walsh and Bruce Alpert, "FBI Details Jefferson's Dealings; It Videotaped Meetings, Cash Transactions," *New Orleans Times-Picayune*, May 22, 2006, 1. Jefferson, however, was reelected to the House, defeating state Representative Karen Carter in a runoff election; Joe Gyan, Jr., "Jefferson Wins New Term," *Capital City Press*, December 10, 2006, 1.

The combination of low approval ratings for President Bush and these scandals produced a substantial Democratic victory. The Democrats gained thirty seats in the House of Representatives and six seats in the Senate. In the House elections, no Democratic incumbents were defeated, nor did the Republicans capture any open seats defended by the Democrats. In fact, the Democrats defeated twenty-two Republican incumbents and won eight open seats vacated by the Republicans. Similarly, in the Senate elections, all sitting Democrats won reelection, and the party maintained control of all their open seats. In addition, six Republican incumbents were defeated.[12] As a result, the 110th Congress (2007 session) convened with the Democrats enjoying majorities in both the House (233–202) and Senate (51–49).[13]

The role of female candidates in the 2006 campaign was substantial. For example, of the sixty most competitive House races during the last week of the campaign, twenty-eight, or 46.7 percent, involved female nominees.[14] As a result, the number of women elected to the House, seventy-one, represented a net five-seat gain over the election of 2004.[15] Moreover, as illustrated in chapter 6, the gender gap in the partisanship among female members grew in 2006. Fifty of the female House members elected were Democrats and twenty-one were Republicans; eleven of the female senators were Democrats and five were Republicans.

In fact, the outcome of the 2006 House elections clearly illustrates that the national tide against the Republicans exerted a disproportionate impact on female Republican incumbents. For Republican incumbents, table 8.1 provides the proportion of the two-party vote won, the change in the two-party vote between 2004 and 2006, and the proportion reelected. The measures are presented according to the sex of the incumbent and the women-friendliness of the congressional district. Overall, Republican males won a greater share of the vote, 63.0 percent, than their female counterparts, who received only 57.0 percent of the vote. The vote loss suffered by Republican women, 7.2 percent, was nearly double that of Republican men, 3.8 percent.[16] These gender differences not only hold within each category of the women-friendly index, but grow larger as districts become more women friendly. Thus, the four women representing the most friendly Republican districts averaged only 48.2 percent of the popular vote, compared to 57.5 percent for men,

---

[12] The defeated incumbents were Senators Jim Talent (MO), Conrad Burns (MT), Mike DeWine (OH), Lincoln Chafee (RI), Rick Santorum (PA), and George Allen (VA).

[13] The Democratic count in the Senate includes Joe Lieberman (CT), reelected as an independent after losing the Democratic primary, and Bernie Sanders (VT), elected to an open seat as an independent.

[14] "2006 House Race Rankings," *National Journal*, November 6, 2006, http://www.national journal.com/racerankings/house (accessed June 29, 2007).

[15] This number could easily have been larger. Eleven women running as Democrats lost their elections by less than 2 percent of the vote.

[16] This comparison is based upon those Republican incumbents who faced a Democratic opponent in both 2004 and 2006.

Table 8.1 The Electoral Fortunes of Republican Incumbents in the 2006 House Elections

Woman Friendliness of District	Percent of Two-Party Vote for Male Republicans	Percent of Two-Party Vote for Female Republicans	Change in Two-Party Vote from 2004 for Male Republicans*	Change in Two-Party Vote from 2004 for Female Republicans*	Reelection Rates for Male Republicans	Reelection Rates for Female Republicans
All Districts	63.0% (188)	57.0% (23)	-3.8 (149)	-7.2 (21)	90.4% (170/188)	82.6% (19/23)
Low: 0–3 Attributes	65.5% (82)	60.7% (8)	-2.6 (63)	-3.2 (6)	90.2% (74/82)	100% (8/8)
Med: 4–7 Attributes	63.1% (67)	57.6% (11)	-4.9 (50)	-7.4 (11)	94.0% (63/67)	81.8% (9/11)
High: 8–11 Attributes	57.5% (39)	48.2% (4)	-5.1 (36)	-12.6 (4)	84.6% (33/39)	50.0% (2/4)

* Change in the two-party vote is calculated for those incumbents who faced contested general election races in both 2004 and 2006.

and suffered a 12.6 point decline from the vote won in 2004, compared to a 5.1 point decline for men. Of these women, Representatives Nancy Johnson (CT) and Sue Kelly (NY) lost their reelection bids. Both Representatives Deborah Pryce (OH) and Heather Wilson (NM) faced female challengers and barely won reelection. Pryce defeated Mary Jo Kilroy with 50.9 percent of the vote, and Wilson defeated Patricia Madrid with 50.2 percent of the vote.

The 2006 midterm elections clearly illustrate that Republican women are particularly vulnerable when short-term electoral forces favor the Democrats. Our analysis in chapter 7 emphasized that districts most friendly to Republican women are not stereotypical Republican districts. They are more diverse, more urban, and less conservative. In the face of adverse electoral tides, members who hold these seats become the most vulnerable. It is this subtle interaction between the party-friendliness and the women-friendliness of districts that helps to explain why Democratic gains in 2006 were concentrated in those districts more friendly to Republican women.

Looking beyond partisanship, of the seventy-one women elected to the House in 2006, twelve women, all Democrats, were African American. Six female Democrats and one female Republican were Hispanic. The most senior woman was Representative Marcy Kaptur (D-OH), elected to her thirteenth term. Second in the line of seniority among women were Representatives Nancy Pelosi (D-CA) and Louise Slaughter (D-NY), who were serving their twelfth terms. The most senior Republican woman, Representative Ileana Ros-Lehtinen (FL), was elected to her eleventh term. In total, thirty-three women of the House were beyond the midcareer point of five terms; eight women from the "class of 1992" were serving their eighth term of office.

Our analysis in chapter 4 demonstrated that many of these women have risen to leadership positions in both the party and committee hierarchies. When the 110th Congress (2007 session) convened, Democrat Nancy Pelosi was elected Speaker of the House. Four female Democrats chaired standing committees and fourteen chaired subcommittees. On the Republican side, one woman served as ranking member of a full committee and four acted as ranking members of subcommittees. As we noted in chapter 1, in the 85th Congress (1957 session), the fifteen women who served were regarded as novelties. In the 110th Congress (2007 session), the eighty-seven women, while far from proportionate, constituted a presence, both on the floor and in committee rooms.

The Rules: No Longer a Man's Game

With eighty-seven women elected to the House and Senate in 2006, there is no doubt that progress has been made. Women made up 16.3 percent of Congress. On the other hand, one could still say that women have "a very small share, though a very large stake, in political power."[17] Cultural norms and gender role expectations have changed, but there are still remnants, particularly when it comes to raising children and housework. On the other hand, the political pipeline is now open to women. In addition, redistricting and current demographic trends may actually provide opportunities for women.

Cultural Norms

Without doubt, cultural and social attitudes have changed since the 1950s. A college degree is now regarded as important to the futures of both men and women. In 2004, for example, 57.5 percent of bachelor's degrees awarded went to women.[18] In 2004, only 2 percent of the respondents in the National Election Study believed that a woman's place was in the home, down from 19 percent in 1972.[19] In 2005, the proportion of married women in the civilian workforce was 61 percent, compared to 29 percent in 1956.[20]

Politics is no longer off-limits to women. Since the 1970s, the political participation of women has increased substantially. For the last two decades, voter turnout among women has consistently exceeded turnout among men by two to three percentage points. In the 2004 election, for example, 60.1 percent of women reported voting, compared to 56.3 percent of men; 8.8 million more women than men voted.[21] Women are as likely as men to engage in other kinds of political participation as well, including working on campaigns. In fact, women have more positive feelings than men about participating in campaigns, attending fundraisers, going door-to-door to meet with constituents, and dealing with the press.[22]

Despite these changes, the vestiges of the old cultural norms remain. In chapter 5, we emphasized the continued presence of gender stereotypes in evaluating character traits and issue competence. In addition, female candidates, regardless of party, are perceived as more liberal than male candidates. The effects of socialization remain as well. Women are still sub-

---

[17] Kirkpatrick, 1974, 3.

[18] U.S. Bureau of the Census, http://www.census.gov/compendia/statab/education/higher_education_degrees (accessed June 30, 2007).

[19] http://www.electionstudies.org/nesguide/toptable/tab4c_1.htm (accessed June 30, 2007).

[20] U.S. Bureau of the Census, http://www.census.gov/compendia/statab/labor_force_employment_earnings/labor_force_status (accessed June 30, 2007).

[21] U.S. Bureau of the Census, http://www.census.gov/compendia/statab/elections/votingage_population_and_voter_participation (accessed June 30, 2007).

[22] M. Margaret Conway, Gertude Steurnagel, and David Ahern, *Women and Political Participation* (Washington, D.C.: CQ Press, 1997); Richard Fox, "Gender, Political Ambition and the Decision Not to Run for Office," Center for American Women and Politics, 2003, http://www.rci.rutgers.edu/~cawp/Research/Reports/Fox2003.pdf; Richard Fox, Jennifer Lawless, and Courtney Feeley, "Gender and the Decision to Run for Office," *Legislative Studies Quarterly* 26 (2001): 411–35; and Richard Fox and Jennifer Lawless, "The Impact of Sex-Role Socialization on the Decision to Run for Office" (paper presented at the Southern Political Science Association Annual Meeting, January 2002, Atlanta).

stantially less likely to think about running for office. Even when they have the same resumes as men, women are less likely to think they are qualified to run for office. They are also less likely to be told by others, even members of their own families, that they should run for office. For women, housework and child care still play major roles in their decisions to pursue political careers.[23] In contrast, "Men pursue goals of whatever type with a single-mindedness absent in women"; women tend to consider the impact on their families.[24] This suggests that while women are no longer confined to "lickin' and stickin' " jobs on a campaign staff, they are still primarily responsible for raising children and doing most of the housework, and do not appear to be conscious of the fact that their skills and backgrounds make them qualified to run for office themselves.[25] On the up side, although women are not encouraged to run for office as often as men, when they are encouraged, they are as likely to consider running.[26] Thus, internships, mentoring programs, and other informal recruitment methods—for example, something as simple as telling more women they should run—could have a substantial impact on the number of female candidates.[27] Our results in chapter 5 emphasize a possible "role model" effect as well.

Entry Professions and the Pipeline

Over time, the backgrounds of the men and women who serve in Congress have converged. The career paths of women are becoming more like those of their male counterparts.[28] The entry professions of law and business are no longer blocked.[29] In fact, women have caught up to men in law school admissions. The proportion of law degrees awarded to women in 1956 was

---

[23] Fox, 2003; Fox, Lawless, and Feeley, 2001; and Lawless and Fox, 2005. See also Timothy Bledsoe and Mary Herring, "Victims of Circumstances: Women in Pursuit of Political Office," *American Political Science Review* 84 (1990): 213–23.

[24] Bledsoe and Herring, 1990, 221.

[25] Conway, Steuernagel, and Ahern, 1997.

[26] Fox, 2003.

[27] See for example Mark Rozell, "Helping Women Run and Win: Feminist Groups, Candidate Recruitment and Training," *Women & Politics* 21 (2000): 101–16.

[28] Joan Hulce Thompson, "Career Convergence: Election of Women and Men to the House of Representatives, 1916–1975," *Women & Politics* 5 (1985): 69–90; Irwin Gertzog, *Congressional Women: Their Recruitment, Integration, and Behavior*, 2nd ed. (Westport, Conn.: Praeger Press, 1995); Kathleen Dolan and Lynne Ford, "Change and Continuity among Women State Legislators: Evidence from Three Decades," *Political Research Quarterly* 50 (1997): 137–51; Kathleen Dolan and Lynne Ford, "Are All Women State Legislators Alike?" in *Women and Elective Office: Past, Present and Future*, edited by Sue Thomas and Clyde Wilcox (New York: Oxford University Press, 1998); Nancy McGlen and Karen O'Connor, *Women, Politics and American Society*, 2nd ed. (Upper Saddle River, N.J.: Prentice Hall, 1998); but see Kira Sanbonmatsu, "Gender Pools and Puzzles: Charting a 'Women's Path' to the Legislature," *Politics & Gender* 2 (2006b): 387–400.

[29] Christine Williams, "Women, Law and Politics: Recruitment Patterns in the Fifty States," *Women & Politics* 10 (1990): 103–23; and Cynthia Fuchs Epstein, *Women in Law*, 2nd ed. (Chicago: University of Illinois Press, 1993).

only 3.5 percent. In 2004, the proportion of law degrees awarded to women was 49.4 percent.[30] In 1971, only 3.9 percent of all MBA students were women. By 2004, 41.9 percent of all MBA students were women.[31] Women have substantially increased their numbers in lower-level political offices. For the last three decades, there has been a relatively steady increase in the number of women serving in state legislatures, although the numbers stalled at the turn of the twenty-first century. In 1971, 4.5 percent of state legislators were women. In 2007, 23.5 percent of state legislators were women. The political pipeline is now open to women.

As table 8.2 illustrates, among the eighty-two women elected to the House in the twenty-first century, nineteen women, 23.2 percent, were lawyers. This is considerably greater than the 12.7 percent among the women elected between 1916 and 1956.[32] While women have clearly caught up to men in terms of law school enrollment, this suggests that, as a career, law still weighs

Table 8.2 A Profile of the Eighty-two Women Elected to the House in the Twenty-first Century, 2002, 2004, and 2006

Background	Number of Women	Percentage
Lawyer	19	23.2
Prior Elective Office Experience		
Elected to local office	28	34.1
Elected to state house of representatives	37	45.1
Elected to state senate	21	25.6
Elected to statewide office	5	6.1
Other Political Experience		
Served in appointed administrative office	22	26.8
Served in party organization	12	14.6
Lateral Entry		
Widows	4	4.9
No prior elective office experience	6	7.3

[30] http://nces.ed.gov/programs/digest/d05/tables/dt05_256.asp?referer=list (accessed June 30, 2007)

[31] http://nces.ed.gov/programs/digest/d05/tables/dt05_265.asp?referer=list (accessed June 30, 2007).

[32] Our count of women elected between 2002 and 2006 includes Democrat Patsy Mink (D-HI). Mink died on September 28, 2002, but was posthumously elected to the 108th Congress in November 2002.

less heavily for women entering the hierarchy of elective offices.[33] In fact, in recent elections, many women have been successful precisely because they have come from fields other than law, such as health and education.[34] On the other hand, almost one-third, 34.1 percent, of the women elected in 2002, 2004, and 2006 served in local political offices. Over 45 percent were elected to their state house of representatives, and over one-fourth were elected to their state senate. Among all the women elected between 1916 and 1956, only 10.9 percent had served in local offices, 16.4 percent in the state house of representatives, and 1.8 percent in the state senate. Whereas Iris Blitch (D-GA) was the only woman to serve in both chambers during the 1916–1956 era, twelve women of the twenty-first century followed this route.[35]

Table 8.2 also reveals that 26.8 percent of the women elected in 2002, 2004, and 2006 had prior experience in administrative offices. The comparable figure from the 1916 to 1956 period was 18.2 percent. It also appears that as women gained access to the pipeline, the prominence of the party path to the House declined. From 1916 to 1956, 25.4 percent of the women elected to the House worked in party organizations. Among those elected in the three most recent elections, only 14.6 percent, or twelve of eighty-two, served in party organizations. This suggests that women are now launching their political careers in lower-level elective office rather than serving apprenticeships in party organizations.[36]

Finally, table 8.2 shows that only six women were elected without prior elective or administrative experience. Four of them were relatively young when they launched their political careers. Representatives Stephanie Herseth Sandlin (D-SD) and Linda Sanchez (D-CA) ran for the House in 2002, Sanchez at the age of thirty-three and Herseth Sandlin at the age of thirty-two. Representatives Melissa Bean (D-IL) and Loretta Sanchez

---

[33] In the 110th Congress (2007 session), the proportion of all House members who list law as their profession was 37.2 percent; 54.2 percent of these were men and 26.7 percent were women. The proportion of all senators who cited law as their profession was 58.0 percent; this includes 61.9 percent of the male senators and 37.5 percent of the female senators; Mildred Amer, *Membership of the 110th Congress: A Profile*, Washington, D.C.: Congressional Research Service, January 2007, 2.

[34] McGlen and O'Connor, 1998; see also Sanbonmatsu, 2006b.

[35] These include Republicans Ileana Ros-Lehtinen (FL), Barbara Cubin (WY), and Marilyn Musgrave (CO), along with Democrats Gabrielle Giffords (AZ), Patsy Mink (HI), Carrie Meek (FL), Eddie Bernice Johnson (TX), Julia Carson (IN), Barbara Lee (CA), Hilda Solis (CA), Debbie Wasserman Schultz (FL), and Gwen Moore (WI).

[36] The most recent example, Carol Shea-Porter (D-NH), suggests that the nature of "party work" has changed as well. Shea-Porter first became active politically as a volunteer in the 2004 presidential campaign of Wesley Clark. An ardent critic of the war in Iraq who was once escorted from a venue where President Bush appeared, she went on to become Chairwoman of the Democratic Committee in her home town of Rochester, New Hampshire. To win her seat in 2006, she defeated the outgoing Democratic Leader of the state House of Representatives in the primary, and then went on to defeat two-term Republican incumbent Jeb Bradley, who had won reelection in 2004 with 63 percent of the vote; John DiStaso, "Craig Upset in House Bid," *Manchester Union Leader*, September 13, 2006, A1; "Shea-Porter Once Escorted From Bush Event," *Associated Press State and Local Wire*, September 14, 2006.

(D-CA) pursued careers in business for a decade before running. Sanchez was elected to the House in 1996 at the age of thirty-seven, while Bean won election to the House in 2004 at the age of forty. The fifth woman, Representative Carolyn McCarthy, was elected after a personal tragedy prompted her to run on a gun control platform.[37] Nancy Boyda (D-KS) is the most recent women elected without prior experience. Boyda, a chemist and a former pharmaceutical executive, was a Republican who changed her party identification in the face of numerous factional disputes within the Kansas Republican Party.[38] In 2004, she challenged incumbent and former Olympian, Representative Jim Ryun, and lost by the decisive margin of 56 to 41. In the 2006 rematch, Boyda changed campaign strategies and emphasized personal contact with voters and other forms of "retail politics," connecting Ryun to the adverse national conditions confronting the Republicans.[39] Despite a visit by President Bush late in the campaign urging Ryun's reelection, Boyda defeated the incumbent, winning 52 percent of the vote.[40]

There is some evidence that, in general, lateral entry has increased over time, particularly into the Senate. In other words, the pipeline is becoming less relevant for all congressional candidates. There are increasing numbers of "amateur candidates" who have never run before and who spend a great deal of their own money or capitalize on their celebrity status to obtain high-level offices.[41] For example, some senators have come from prominent political families, such as Senators Robert Kennedy (D-NY), Edward Kennedy (D-MA), and Jay Rockefeller (D-WV). Senator George Murphy (R-CA) starred in four Broadway shows and forty-five motion pictures before he ran for the Senate in 1964.[42] Senator Bill Bradley (D-NJ) played professional basketball for the New York Knicks and then ran for the Senate in 1978. Two astronauts have served in the Senate, John Glenn (D-OH) and Harrison Schmidt (R-NM). Before his Senate bid in 1994, Fred Thompson

---

[37] In 1993, her husband was killed and her son injured in the Long Island Railroad massacre when a gunman opened fire on the passengers of a commuter train. In the wake of the incident, McCarthy lobbied Representative Dan Frisa (R-NY) to support stricter gun control measures. Frisa was not interested. In 1996, after contemplating a run against Frisa as a Republican, McCarthy was approached by the Democratic Party and encouraged to run as a Democrat. She defeated Frisa in the general election by sixteen percentage points; Karen Foerstel, *Biographical Dictionary of Congressional Women* (Westport, Conn.: Greenwood Press, 1999), 176–77.

[38] Thomas Frank, *What's the Matter with Kansas?* (New York: Metropolitan Books, 2004). See also John Milburn, "Parkinson's Switch Unlikely to Send Other 'RINOS' Charging Toward the Democrats," *Associated Press State and Local Wire*, June 4, 2006; and Barbara Hollingsworth, "Moderates Leading State Races," *Topeka Capital-Journal*, August 2, 2006, 3.

[39] Dawn Borman, "Boyda Won it Her Way," *Kansas City Star*, November 9, 2006.

[40] Tim Carpenter, "Bush Focuses on Larger Picture in Last Big Push," *Topeka Capital-Journal*, November 6, 2006, 1.

[41] David Canon, *Actors, Athletes and Astronauts* (Chicago: University of Chicago Press, 1990).

[42] *Biographical Directory of the United States Congress*, http://bioguide.congress.gov/scripts/biodisplay.pl?index=M001092 (accessed July 20, 2005).

had a long career as an actor, with roles in *The Hunt for Red October, Cape Fear*, and *Die Hard II*, and guest appearances on *China Beach* and *Matlock*.[43] Thompson resigned from the Senate in 2002 and landed the role of District Attorney Arthur Branch on *Law and Order*.[44] None of these men ever ran for office before their Senate bids.

Among all eighteen women who were elected in their own right to the Senate, there are only two who bypassed the pipeline and ran for Senate as the first elective office they sought. Both of them are examples of political "celebrities." Senator Nancy Kassebaum (R-KS) was the daughter of former governor and presidential nominee Alf Landon (R-KS). Senator Hillary Clinton (D-NY) was a former first lady. Her experience on her husband's two presidential campaigns no doubt helped prepare her. A third woman, Senator Elizabeth Dole (R-NC), was also able to take advantage of her national name recognition when she ran for the Senate in 2002. The first political office she ever ran for was president, two years prior. In other words, 83.3 percent of all the women elected to the Senate had run for a lower-level office before they ran for the Senate. Of the sixteen women in the 110th Congress (2007 session), six, or 37.5 percent, were former House members. This suggests that lateral entry for women is still relatively rare. On the other hand, increasing numbers of women are entering the traditional political pipeline.

The stereotype of the early women in Congress was the "bereaved widow," drafted out of a sense of duty to squelch intra-party disputes and expected to step aside after completing her husband's term. Women who were not widows were also lumped into this category. Thus, until relatively recently, the conventional wisdom was that the path to Congress for a woman was by stepping over her husband's dead body.[45] Our analysis shows, however, that even among widows, this stereotype did not apply to many women. Most congressional widows, especially those who pursued congressional careers, had a great deal of political experience either independently or with their husbands. In other words, a large proportion of widows had political ambitions of their own. Over time, congressional widows have come to look more like the women who ran without the benefit of a dead husband. Those widows who were reelected in 2002, 2004, and 2006 provide a case in point. Representatives Mary Bono (R-CA), Lois Capps (D-CA), and Jo Ann Emerson (R-MO) are serving their sixth terms in the 110th Congress (2007 session). As we noted in chapter 3, the most recent widow,

---

[43] "Thompson, Fred," in *CQ's Politics in America 2002, the 107th Congress* (Washington, D.C.: CQ Press, 2001), http://library.cqpress.com/congress/pia107-0453055379 (accessed July 25, 2005).

[44] http://www.nbc.com/Law_&_Order/bios/Fred_Thompson.html (accessed July 25, 2005).

[45] Diane Kincaid, "Over His Dead Body: A Positive Perspective on Widows in the U.S. Congress," *Western Political Quarterly* 31 (1978): 96–104.

Representative Doris Matsui (D-CA), was reelected in 2006 to her first full term in the House.

Our analysis has also shown that women are as politically ambitious as their male counterparts: once elected, they are as careerist as men. The average length of service in the House is longer for men than women, but the difference can be explained by the fact that most women were elected in 1992 or later. The vast majority of women in Congress now seek long careers and are gradually accumulating the leadership roles and influence that come with long-term service. Some, however, decided to seek higher office. These women are quite strategic in deciding whether to run for the Senate, and they consider many of the same factors that men do. For both men and women, the decision to pursue a Senate seat systematically varies with the cost of running, the probability of winning, the value of a House seat, and whether they are "risk takers." Very few sitting female House members have made a run for the Senate, but very few sitting male House members make the attempt. We argue that, for both men and women, this is largely a function of opportunity: the power of incumbency, the longevity of incumbents, and the electoral calendar block the career ladder. This suggests that women in Congress have career goals and make strategic decisions that are similar to those of men.

The Politics of Redistricting

The pipeline theory is a "bottom-up" approach to explaining the integration of women into Congress; growth in the number of women in the preparatory professions will eventually cause growth in the number of women running for state and local offices, which will eventually cause growth in the number of women running for Congress. This implies a relatively steady and sequential pattern. And, as suggested above, there is evidence that the pipeline matters, especially for women candidates.[46] This approach, however, does not take into account opportunity—or lack thereof. Our analysis shows that the structure of elections, electoral context, and partisanship matter a great deal. Movement through the pipeline is constricted not only by incumbency but also by district-level factors that make a constituency more or less likely to elect a woman. This suggests that the way district lines are drawn can have a substantial impact on the success of female candidates.

---

[46] Given that women are more likely to consider themselves as unqualified to run for office, it makes sense that they might be more likely to go through the traditional political pipeline more often than men and that we would see less lateral entry among women; Kathryn Pearson and Eric McGhee, "Strategic Differences: The Gender Dynamics of Congressional Candidacies, 1982–2002" (paper presented at the American Political Science Association Annual Meeting, September 2004, Chicago).

While the documented examples are few, there is one very direct way in which the drawing of district lines can affect women's success. If female (or male) state legislators are interested in running for Congress, they can serve on the committee in the state legislature responsible for redrawing district lines. This gives them the opportunity to create a House district that largely overlaps their current constituency, making the transition from state legislature to Congress much easier. For example, Eddie Bernice Johnson was elected to the Texas State Senate in 1986, the first African American to serve in that chamber since Reconstruction. She chaired the Committee on Reapportionment and drew herself a House district that she ran for and won in 1992 with 72 percent of the vote.[47] Cynthia McKinney was elected to the Georgia House in 1988. She served on the Reapportionment Committee, drew herself a House district that was 60 percent black, and won the seat in 1992.[48] Having allies on these committees can also help. Ginny Brown-Waite, for example, served in the Florida State Senate for ten years and moved up the leadership ladder to become Republican whip. The Republican-controlled Redistricting Committee substantially changed the lines of incumbent Democratic Representative Karen Thurman's House district. The new district included all of Brown-Waite's state senate district and excluded the more liberal part of the district around the University of Florida.[49] Brown-Waite narrowly defeated Thurman by 1.7 percent. Ironically, Thurman played a key role in drawing the district ten years earlier in the previous round of redistricting. Thurman also served in the Florida State Senate and chaired the Committee on Congressional Reapportionment in 1990. Florida had gained a House seat, and Thurman was instrumental in making sure the new seat included most of her state senate district.[50]

The impact of redistricting on the political fortunes of female candidates has received very little, if any, systematic attention.[51] As we discussed in

---

[47] Foerstel, 1999, 135.

[48] Foerstel, 1999, 181. This district was then the subject of a lawsuit filed by white voters challenging the constitutionality of "racial gerrymandering" and, according to the Supreme Court in *Miller v. Johnson*, had to be redrawn. In 1996, she was reelected in her new district, which was now 65 percent white; J. L. Moore, "Majority-Minority District," in *Elections A to Z* (Washington, D.C.: CQ Press, 2003), http://library.cqpress.com/elections/elaz2d-156-7490-402760 (accessed July 25, 2005).

[49] "Brown-Waite, Ginny," in *CQ's Politics in America, 2006, the 109th Congress* (Washington, D.C.: CQ Press, 2005), http://library.cqpress.com/congress/document.php?id=pia109-Brown-Waite.

[50] Foerstel, 1999, 270.

[51] Interestingly, in 2001, Virginia State Senator Virginia Byrne accused the state legislature of "gender gerrymandering" and making it tougher for the women who had been elected in the northern part of the state to get reelected. Her colleague, Senator Linda Puller, agreed and said that in the latest round of redistricting, "They were harsher on us. It's still good ol' boys"; R. H. Melton, "Byrne Strikes a Nerve in Richmond; Fairfax Senator Says Colleagues Are Trying to Force Out Democratic Women," *Washington Post*, April 15, 2001, C5.

chapter 1, redistricting controversies in the 1960s focused on malapportionment and the resulting rural dominance in state legislatures. Debates in the 1990s focused upon racial gerrymandering and its impact on the representation of people of color in Congress.[52] In 1990, states were mandated to redraw congressional district lines to comply with the Justice Department's new rules regarding the creation of "majority–minority districts." A record number of African Americans and Hispanics were elected to Congress in 1992. There is evidence, however, that racial gerrymandering has also had an unintended consequence: helping Republicans. One study found that four of the nine districts that switched from Democratic to Republican control in 1992 did so because of the creation of majority–minority districts.[53] In fact, some argue that racial gerrymandering actually gave Republicans the opportunity to take control of the House in 1994.[54] To create majority–minority districts, large numbers of African Americans are "packed" into a district. Because African Americans disproportionately vote Democratic, these seats elect Democratic House members by extremely large margins that, in essence, waste Democratic votes. Packing Democratic voters into one district creates opportunities for Republicans in other districts.[55] As a result, according to Michael McDonald, a professor at George Mason University and a redistricting consultant, racial gerrymandering has created an "unholy alliance" between minority and Republican House members.[56] Our analysis in chapter 7 showed that male and female African American representatives come from the most Democratic districts. There are, in fact, few differences between the districts that elect black male Democrats to the House and those that elect black female Democrats. This suggests that racially gerrymandered districts are equally as likely to elect men and women of color.

The latest round of redistricting after the 2000 U.S. Census has refocused the debate on incumbent protection. In fact, "[T]he nationwide theme of

---

[52] See for example David Lublin, *The Paradox of Representation: Racial Gerrymandering and Minority Interests in Congress* (Princeton, N.J.: Princeton University Press, 1997); David Lublin, "Racial Redistricting and African-American Representation: A Critique of 'Do Majority-Minority Districts Maximize Substantive Black Representation in Congress?'" *American Political Science Review* 93 (1999): 183–86; David Canon, *Race, Redistricting, and Representation: The Unintended Consequences of Black Majority Districts* (Chicago: University of Chicago Press, 1999); and David Epstein and Sharyn O'Halloran, "A Social Science Approach to Race, Redistricting, and Representation," *American Political Science Review* 93 (1999): 187–91.

[53] Kevin Hill, "Do Black Majority Districts Aid Republicans?" *Journal of Politics* 57 (1995): 384–401.

[54] See for example Charles Bullock, "Affirmative Action Districts: In Whose Face Will They Blow Up?" *Campaigns and Elections* 16 (1995): 22–23; Lani Guinier, "Don't Scapegoat the Gerrymander," *New York Times Magazine*, January 8, 1995, 36; and Hill, 1995.

[55] Hill, 1995.

[56] Interview with Barbara Palmer, Washington, D.C., March 17, 2004.

congressional line drawing was incumbent protection."[57] In 1992, eighty House members won their seats with less than 55.0 percent of the vote. In 2002, thirty-seven—fewer than half as many—House members won their seats with less than 55.0 percent of the vote. In 2000, the election cycle before the redistricting, there were fifty-seven House members who came from marginal seats. In 2002, after the redistricting, only three of these incumbent House members lost.[58] Incumbent protection plans are typically the product of bipartisan negotiations. For example, Republican Representative and then Speaker of the House Dennis Hastert and Democratic Representative William Lipinski, both from Illinois, brokered a deal that "protected the reelection prospects of almost every Illinois incumbent."[59] In 2001, their proposal sailed through a state legislature that was under divided control of the parties.[60] Even in California, where Democrats controlled the state legislature, incumbent protection was the goal. In addition to protecting almost all of the safe Democratic House members, the seven marginal Democratic House members were given safe seats, and nineteen of the twenty Republicans in the California House delegation were also protected.[61]

Seats are made safer by adding more constituents who identify with the House member's party; Democratic members are given more Democratic voters, and Republican members are given more Republican voters, typically until they reach the 55 to 60 percent range. In addition to being used in racial gerrymandering, "packing" is a technique in which seats are made overly safe (that is, beyond the 55 to 60 percent range) by the opposition party in an effort to waste votes in one district while creating opportunities for themselves in other districts.[62] This "partisan gerrymandering" became a flashpoint in Texas. In 2000, the state legislature was under divided party control and passed an incumbent protection plan. The state's congressional delegation was seventeen Democrats and fifteen Republicans, in spite of the fact that in the aggregate, voters in the state leaned Republican. In 2002, the Republicans gained control of both chambers and also held the governor's seat. In an unprecedented move, in May 2003, House Majority Leader Tom DeLay and Karl Rove, one of President Bush's closest advisors, proposed a

[57] Gregory Giroux, "Remaps' Clear Trend: Incumbent Protection," *CQ Weekly*, November 3, 2001, 2627; Bob Benenson, Gregory Giroux, and Jonathan Allen, "Safe House: Incumbents Face Worry-free Election," *CQ Weekly*, May 17, 2002, 1274; and Richard Scammon, A. V. McGillivray, and R. Cook, "Analysis of the Elections of 2002," in *America Votes, 25* (Washington, D.C.: CQ Press, 2003), http://library.cqpress.com/elections.amvt25-181-9622-602649 (accessed July 25, 2005). See also Gary Cox and Jonathan Katz, *Elbridge Gerry's Salamander: The Electoral Consequences of the Reapportionment Revolution* (New York: Cambridge University Press, 2002).

[58] Connie Morella (R-MD), Bill Luther (D-MN), and Jim Maloney (D-CT); Scammon, McGillivray, and Cook, 2003, 2.

[59] Giroux, "Remaps'," 2001, 2627.

[60] Giroux, "Remaps'," 2001, 2627.

[61] Gregory Giroux, "California Democrats' Remap Puts Two of Their Own in Tough Spots," *CQ Weekly*, September 22, 2001, 2224.

[62] Kenneth Jost, "Redistricting Disputes," *CQ Researcher*, March 12, 2004, 221–47.

new redistricting plan that would create twenty-two Republican seats. Historically, no state had redrawn its district lines at this point in the ten-year cycle unless under orders from the federal courts. In response to this re-redistricting plan, Democrats in the state legislature walked out and took up temporary residence in Oklahoma, out of reach of the state troopers and Texas Rangers. After a bitter fight, which included another walkout to New Mexico by Senate Democrats, the new map passed.[63] In 2004, the Texas congressional delegation included twenty Republicans and twelve Democrats.

What is the impact of incumbent protection or partisan gerrymandering on female candidates? Incumbent protection plans make it harder for any kind of turnover. If more incumbents are running for reelection in safe seats, it further limits opportunities for challengers, male or female. But whether seats are made safer for incumbents or even packed, the result is the same: districts become more extreme and less competitive. They have larger proportions of Democrats or Republicans. Our analysis in chapter 7 showed that female Democratic candidates do better in districts that have more Democratic voters than the districts that elect male Democratic candidates. Thus, female Democratic candidates can benefit from this kind of redistricting, provided that those additional elements that make a district women-friendly are included. On the other hand, the opposite is true for Republican women. The more Republican voters in a district, the less likely it is that a female Republican candidate will run and win. Female Republican candidates do better in more moderate or swing districts. If these districts are disappearing, our analysis suggests that opportunities for Republican women might disappear as well.

Another Option: Women-friendly Districts

These redistricting strategies—the creation of majority–minority districts, incumbent protection, and partisan gerrymandering—potentially have indirect consequences for female candidates. On the other hand, it seems possible that "gender gerrymandering" could be a more direct method of increasing opportunities for women. In chapter 7, we found that women are more likely to run and win in districts that are women-friendly, districts that have particular demographic characteristics. Thus, another way of increasing the number of women in Congress might be to draw district lines taking into account these characteristics. Our analysis of women-friendly districts in chapter 7 focused on three redistricting periods, ending in 2000. Since states redrew their lines in 2002, we can use our index to determine the most and least friendly districts for women in the 2002–2010 period and look for potential opportunities for women candidates.

---

[63] Ronald Keith Gaddie, "The Texas Redistricting, Measure for Measure," in *Extensions: Congressional Redistricting*, ed. Ronald Peters (Norman: University of Oklahoma, 2004); and Jost, 2004.

Table 8.3 provides a list of the districts with high scores, defined as eight or more characteristics, on both the Democratic and Republican women-friendly indices. There were thirty-two districts that fit this criterion; these then are the districts in the nation that are the most friendly to both Democratic and Republican women candidates. Representative Nancy Pelosi (D-CA), the Speaker of the House, represents the district that scored the highest on both indices. In fact, eleven of the districts are in California and another seven are in New York; 56 percent of these districts are in two states.

But, as the table shows, not all women-friendly districts are held by women. In fact, twenty of these districts, 62.5 percent, are occupied by men. These are districts, however, where women would have a good chance of winning. There are two possible routes to these seats. Our earlier analysis

Table 8.3 The Friendliest Districts in the 110th Congress (2007 Session)

State & District	D Index	R Index	2007 Occupant	Party	Sex	Age
CA-8	11	10	Nancy Pelosi	D	Female	66
CA-9	9	9	Barbara Lee	D	Female	60
CA-12	9	11	Tom Lantos	D	Male	78
CA-14	8	11	Anna Eshoo	D	Female	64
CA-15	8	11	Mike Honda	D	Male	65
CA-30	8	10	Henry Waxman	D	Male	67
CA-33	8	8	Diane Watson	D	Female	73
CA-36	9	11	Jane Harman	D	Female	61
CA-46	8	10	Dana Rohrabacher	R	Male	59
CA-48	8	10	John Campbell	R	Male	51
CA-53	8	9	Susan Davis	D	Female	62
CO-1	8	9	Diana DeGette	D	Female	49
FL-20	8	8	Debbie Wasserman Schultz	D	Female	40
Ill-5	9	11	Rahm Emanuel	D	Male	47
Ill-9	9	10	Jan Schakowsky	D	Female	62
MD-8	8	10	Chris Van Hollen	D	Male	47
MA-7	8	10	Edward Markey	D	Male	60
MA-8	10	9	Michael Capuano	D	Male	54
MN-5	8	8	Keith Ellison	D	Male	43
NJ-8	8	10	Bill Pascrell	D	Male	69
NJ-9	8	10	Steven Rothman	D	Male	54
NY-4	8	9	Carolyn McCarthy	D	Female	62
NY-5	10	10	Gary Ackerman	D	Male	64
NY-8	9	10	Jerrold Nadler	D	Male	59
NY-9	8	10	Anthony Weiner	D	Male	42
NY-14	9	10	Carolyn Maloney	D	Female	58
NY-17	8	8	Eliot Engel	D	Male	59
NY-18	8	10	Nita Lowey	D	Female	69
TX-7	9	8	John Culberson	R	Male	50
TX-32	9	8	Pete Sessions	R	Male	51
VA-8	9	9	Jim Moran	D	Male	61
WA-7	8	9	Jim McDermott	D	Male	70

Note: Women are in bold.

emphasizes that while open seats are conventionally seen as the primary opportunities for women, open seats vary in their friendliness to women. The districts listed in table 8.3, should the incumbents retire, would be most receptive to female candidates. It is worth noting that in eight of the twenty districts held by men, 40.0 percent, the age of the sitting incumbent is sixty or more. A second route to office is defeating the sitting incumbent. Here, our index of women-friendliness suggests that there are male incumbents who might be vulnerable against a female candidate. In other words, these districts may offer two kinds of opportunities for women, opportunities that have, for the most part, been largely overlooked.

Aside from the significant male presence in these women-friendly districts, what is most striking is the partisanship of the occupants. Twenty-eight of the thirty-two districts, 87.5 percent, are held by Democrats. Table 8.3 makes the challenges faced by Republican women all too clear. The districts that are friendliest to Republican women are Democratic districts. These are districts where a Republican woman is most likely to win a primary because she is a woman, but she will have trouble winning the general election because she is a Republican. This helps to understand the growing partisan gap among women and why, in the 110th Congress (2007 session), the Democrats enjoy a 50 to 21 advantage in female representation in the House.

While there were thirty-two districts with high scores on both the Democratic and Republican women-friendly indices, there were 136 districts with low scores on both indices. In effect, 31.3 percent of the current House districts are unlikely to be receptive to women candidates through the 2010 elections. Table 8.4 lists the "lowest of the low," the twenty districts with a maximum score of one on the women-friendliness indices. Three districts have a score of zero on both Democratic and Republican indices. Only one of these twenty seats is held by a woman. Representative Virginia Foxx was first elected to represent the 5th district of North Carolina in 2004. Prior to running for the House, she served in the North Carolina Senate and on her local school board.[64] Her campaign for the House was particularly nasty. She ran in a crowded Republican primary that featured eight candidates competing to fill the open seat vacated by Republican Representative Richard Burr. She finished second to Winston-Salem City Councilman Vernon Robinson, an African American Republican, and faced him in a runoff election. Robinson ran television ads featuring a Pakistani man, Kamran Akhtar, who was caught by police in downtown Charlotte filming office buildings and charged with immigration violations. In the ad, Robinson states, "I'm Vernon Robinson and I approve this message because Akhtar

---

[64] *Biographical Directory of the United States Congress,* http://bioguide.congress.gov/scripts/biodisplay.pl?index+F000450 (accessed July 2, 2005).

Table 8.4 The Most Unfriendly Districts in the 110th Congress (2007 Session)

State and District	D Score	R Score	2005 Occupant	Party	Sex
AL-1	1	0	Josiah Bonner	R	Male
AL-2	1	0	Terry Everett	R	Male
AL-4	0	0	Robert Aderholt	R	Male
GA-1	1	0	Jack Kingston	R	Male
GA-10	1	0	Nathan Deal	R	Male
KY-1	0	1	Ed Whitfield	R	Male
KY-2	0	0	Ron Lewis	R	Male
KY-4	0	1	Geoff Davis	R	Male
LA-4	1	0	Jim McCrery	R	Male
LA-5	1	0	Rodney Alexander	R	Male
LA-7	1	0	Charles Boustany	R	Male
MS-1	1	0	Roger Wicker	R	Male
MS-3	1	0	Charles Pickering	R	Male
MS-4	1	0	Gene Taylor	D	Male
NC-5	1	0	**Virginia Foxx**	**R**	**Female**
OK-3	0	1	Frank Lucas	R	Male
OK-4	0	0	Tom Cole	R	Male
SC-5	1	0	John Spratt	D	Male
TX-4	1	0	Ralph Hall	R	Male
VA-4	1	0	Randy Forbes	R	Male

Note: Women are in bold.

didn't come here to live the American dream. He came here to kill you."[65] In another ad, he compared Foxx to Hillary Clinton: "Hillary Clinton voted for racial quotas, higher taxes, gay rights and the abortion bills. So did Virginia Foxx."[66] His aggressive tactics backfired, and Foxx won the runoff by ten points. She then easily defeated her Democratic opponent, Jim Harrell, in the general election. More generally, it is noteworthy that all twenty of these low-scoring districts are southern. Republicans represent eighteen of these districts, or 90.0 percent.

The Political Glass Ceiling

The American electoral arena is unique: it is the only place in the United States where women and men engage in direct, public competition.[67] Sports are segregated by sex. Even the Academy Awards are segregated by sex. But in a campaign, men and women go head to head, winner-take-all. Once women decide to enter the arena, they are as strategic as men in their decisions about where to run, whether to pursue a long career in the House, or whether to

---

[65] Quoted from "Robinson Accuses Arrested Pakistani of Terrorism in New Ad," *Associated Press State and Local Wire*, August 15, 2004, BC cycle.
[66] Quoted from Rob Christensen, "Candidate's Zeal Divides," *(Raleigh, N.C.) News and Observer*, August 13, 2004, A1.
[67] Bledsoe and Herring, 1990, 213.

seek higher office. For both men and women, these strategic choices are fundamentally shaped by the power of incumbency. But even incumbency status is not equal among men and women in Congress. While female incumbents are reelected at slightly higher rates than male incumbents, they face more competition and have to work harder to maintain their seats.

Because of the overwhelming effect of incumbency on the political opportunity structure, open seats are obviously one avenue of change. The problem is, of course, that there are relatively few of these in a given election cycle. Moreover, as we have shown, not all open seats are alike. Women are more likely to run and be successful in districts that are women-friendly. And there are a number of House districts currently held by male Democrats that, under the right circumstances, would elect a woman of either party. These are the kinds of opportunities that have been, for the most part, overlooked in each election cycle. The political glass ceiling is not simply a function of incumbency: it is about districts and their receptivity to female candidates. Further, this receptivity is not party neutral which, in turn, helps us to understand the partisan gender gap in the U.S. House of Representatives.

In her exploration of the paucity of women in elective office, Kirkpatrick called for a revolution in cultural expectations and sex role socialization, and, clearly, attitudes about the role of women in politics have changed. Our analysis demonstrates, however, that cultural change is a necessary but not sufficient condition for accelerating the entry of women into Congress. The political glass ceiling is still unbroken and continues to slow the integration of women into the national political arena.

Bibliography

Abrams, Jim. "Ailing Senator Johnson Returns to His Home in District of Columbia." *Associated Press State and Local Wire*, April 30, 2007.

Abramson, Paul, John Aldrich, and David Rohde. "Progressive Ambition among United States Senators: 1972–1988." *Journal of Politics* 49 (1987): 335.

Adair, Bill, Adam C. Smith, and Anita Kumar. "Lawmaker Quits Amid Scandal." *St. Petersburg Times*, September 30, 2006.

Alberts, Sheldon. "Limbaugh Remains Defiant after Saying Fox Faked Illness." *Montreal Gazette*, October 26, 2006.

Alexander, C. Allen. "Interview with Beverly A. Moore." In *Social Changes in Western Michigan, 1930 to 1990: Alexander Oral History Project*, vol. 2, edited by Henry Vance Davis. Kalamazoo: Western Michigan University, 1997.

Alexander, Deborah, and Kristi Anderson. "Gender as a Factor in the Attribution of Leadership Traits." *Political Research Quarterly* 46 (1993): 527–45.

Allison, Wes. "House Leader Hit with Indictment." *St. Petersburg Times*, September 29, 2005.

Alpern, Sara. "Center Stage: Helen Gahagan Douglas, A Life." *American Historical Review* 98 (1993): 967–68.

Alvarez, Lizette. "Speaking Chic to Power." *New York Times*, January 18, 2007.

Ambrose, Stephen. *Nixon: The Education of a Politician, 1913–1962*. New York: Simon & Schuster, 1987.

Amer, Mildred. *Women in the United States Congress: 1917–2004*. Washington, D.C.: Congressional Research Service, 2004. http://www.senate.gov/reference/resources/pdf/RL30261.pdf.

———. *Membership of the 109th Congress: A Profile*. Washington, D.C.: Congressional Research Service, 2005. http://www.senate.gov/reference/resources/pdf/RS22007.pdf.

———. *Membership of the 110th Congress: A Profile*. Washington, D.C.: Congressional Research Service, 2007. http://www.senate.gov/reference/recources/pdf/RS22555.pdf.

Amundson, Kirsten. *The Silenced Majority: Women and American Democracy*. Englewood Cliffs, N.J.: Prentice-Hall, 1971.

Anderson, Kristi. *After Suffrage: Women in Partisan and Electoral Politics before the New Deal*. Chicago: University of Chicago Press, 1996.

Andersen, Kristi, and Stuart Thorson. "Congressional Turnover and the Election of Women." *Western Political Quarterly* 37 (1984): 143–56.

Ardoin, Phillip, and James Garand. "Measuring Constituency Ideology in U.S. House Districts: A Top-Down Simulation." *Journal of Politics* 65 (2003): 1165–89.

Associated Press. "Swift Steps Out of Race." *Worcester (Mass.) Telegram and Gazette*, March 20, 2002.

Atkeson, Lonna Rae. "Not All Cues Are Created Equal: The Conditional Impact of Female Candidates on Political Engagement." *Journal of Politics* 65 (2003): 1040–61.

Auster, Elizabeth, and Sabrina Eaton. "Ohio Voters Key to Power Shift." *Cleveland Plain Dealer*, November 8, 2006.

Babcock, Charles R., and Jonathan Weisman. "Congressman Pleads Guilty to Bribery, Then Resigns." *Washington Post*, November 29, 2005.

Baker, Ross. *House and Senate*, 2nd ed. New York: W. W. Norton, 1995.

Balz, Dan. "Hillary Clinton Opens Presidential Bid." *Washington Post*, January 12, 2007.

Barone, Michael, and Richard Cohen. *Almanac of American Politics, 2002.* Washington, D.C.: National Journal, 2001.

———. *Almanac of American Politics, 2004.* Washington, D.C.: National Journal, 2003.

———. *Almanac of American Politics, 2006.* Washington, D.C.: National Journal, 2005.

Barone, Michael, and Grant Ujifusa. *Almanac of American Politics, 1986.* Washington, D.C.: National Journal, 1985.

———. *Almanac of American Politics, 1990.* Washington, D.C.: National Journal, 1989.

———. *Almanac of American Politics, 1992.* Washington, D.C.: National Journal, 1991.

———. *Almanac of American Politics, 1994.* Washington, D.C.: National Journal, 1993.

———. *Almanac of American Politics, 1996.* Washington, D.C.: National Journal, 1995.

———. *Almanac of American Politics, 1998.* Washington, D.C.: National Journal, 1997.

Barone, Michael, Grant Ujifusa, and Douglas Matthews. *Almanac of American Politics, 1980.* New York: E. P. Dutton, 1979.

"The Battle for America's Front Yard." *National Geographic*, June 2004.

Becker, Jo, and Spencer Hsu. "Credit Firm Gave Moran Favorable Loan Deal." *Washington Post*, July 7, 2002.

Beiler, David. "How to Defeat Women and Blacks." *Campaigns & Elections*, August–September 1990.

Benenson, Bob, Gregory Giroux, and Jonathan Allen. "Safe House: Incumbents Face Worry-free Election." *CQ Weekly*, May 17, 2002.

Berch, Neil. "The 'Year of the Woman' in Context: A Test of Six Explanations." *American Politics Quarterly* 24 (1996): 169–93.

———. "Women Incumbents, Elite Bias, and Voter Response in the 1996 and 1998 U.S. House Elections." *Women & Politics* 26 (2004): 21–33.

Bernstein, Robert. "Why Are There So Few Women in the House?" *Western Political Quarterly* 39 (1986): 155–64.

———. "Might Women Have the Edge in Open-Seat House Primaries?" *Women & Politics* 17 (1997): 1–26.

Bingham, Clara. *Women on the Hill.* New York: Times Books, 1997.

Biographical Directory of Congress. http://bioguide.congress.gov.

Biographical Directory of the American Congress. Washington, D.C.: U.S. Government Printing Office, 1971.

Black, Earl, and Merle Black. *The Rise of Southern Republicans.* Cambridge, Mass.: Harvard University Press, 2002.

Bledsoe, Timothy, and Mary Herring. "Victims of Circumstances: Women in Pursuit of Political Office." *American Political Science Review* 84 (1990): 213–23.

Boles, Janet. *The Politics of the Equal Rights Amendment.* New York: Longman, 1979.

Bond, Jon. "The Influence of Constituency Diversity on Electoral Competition in Voting for Congress, 1974–1978." *Legislative Studies Quarterly* 8 (1983): 201–17.

Borman, Dawn. "Boyda Won it Her Way." *Kansas City Star*, November 9, 2006.

Bousquet, Steve, and Anita Kumar. "Castor, Martinez Keep Senate Race Attacks Coming." *St. Petersburg (Fla.) Times,* October 29, 2004.

Boxer, Barbara. *Strangers in the Senate: Politics and the New Revolution of Women in America.* Washington, D.C.: National Press Books, 1993.

Brace, Paul. "Progressive Ambition in the House: A Probabilistic Approach." *Journal of Politics* 46 (1984): 556–71.

Braden, Maria. *Women Politicians and the Media.* Lexington: University of Kentucky Press, 1996.

Brady, David, Kara Buckley, and Douglas Rivers. "The Roots of Careerism in the U.S. House of Representatives." *Legislative Studies Quarterly* 24 (1999): 489–510.

Brady, David, and Edward Schwartz. "Ideology and Interests in Congressional Voting: The Politics of Abortion in the U.S. Senate." *Public Choice* 84 (1995): 25–48.

Brady, Ruth, and Donna Cassata. "Ohio's Convicted Rep. Traficant May Campaign from Prison." *CQ Weekly,* August 3, 2002.

Brown, Clyde, Neil Heighberger, and Peter Shocket. "Gender-Based Differences in Perceptions of Male and Female City Council Candidates." *Women & Politics* 13 (1993): 1–17.

"Brown-Waite, Ginny." In *CQ's Politics in America, 2006, the 109th Congress.* Washington, D.C.: CQ Press, 2005. http://library.cqpress.com/congress/document. php?id=pia109-Brown-Waite.

Bryce, Herrington, and Alan Warrick. "Black Women in Electoral Politics." In *A Portrait of Marginality: The Political Behavior of American Women,* edited by Marianne Githens and Jewel Prestage. New York: David McKay, 1977.

Bullock, Charles. "House Careerists: Changing Patterns of Longevity and Attrition." *American Political Science Review* 66 (1972): 1295–3000.

———. "Affirmative Action Districts: In Whose Face Will They Blow Up?" *Campaigns and Elections* 16 (1995): 22–23.

Bullock, Charles, and Patricia Lee Findley Heys. "Recruitment of Women for Congress: A Research Note." *Western Political Quarterly* 25 (1972): 416–23.

Burdick, Eugene. *The 480.* New York: McGraw-Hill, 1964.

Burdick, Eugene, and Harvey Wheeler. *Fail-Safe.* New York: McGraw-Hill, 1962.

Burrell, Barbara. "The Political Opportunity of Women Candidates for the U.S. House of Representatives in 1984." *Women & Politics* 8 (1988): 51–68.

———. "Women Candidates in Open-Seat Primaries for the U.S. House: 1968–1990." *Legislative Studies Quarterly* 17 (1992): 493–508.

———. *A Woman's Place Is in the House: Campaigning for Congress in the Feminist Era.* Ann Arbor: University of Michigan Press, 1994.

———. "Political Parties and Women's Organizations: Bringing Women into the Electoral Arena." In *Gender and Elections: Shaping the Future of American Politics,* edited by Susan Carroll and Richard Fox. New York: Cambridge University Press, 2006a.

———. "Parties, Money, and Sex." Paper presented at the National Symposium on Women and Politics, June 2006b, Berkeley.

Bystrom, Dianne. "Advertising, Web Sites, and Media Coverage: Gender and Communication Along the Campaign Trail." In *Gender and Elections: Shaping the Future of American Politics,* edited by Susan Carroll and Richard Fox. New York: Cambridge University Press, 2006.

Bystrom, Dianne, Mary Christine Banwart, Lynda Lee Kaid, and Terry Robertson. *Gender and Candidate Communication.* New York: Routledge, 2004.

Cain, Bruce, John Ferejohn, and Morris Fiorina. *The Personal Vote: Constituency Service and Electoral Independence.* Cambridge, Mass.: Harvard University Press, 1987.

Cameron, Charles, David Epstein and Sharyn O'Halloran. "Do Majority-Minority Districts Maximize Substantive Black Representation in Congress?" *American Political Science Review* 90 (1996): 794–812.

Campbell, Angus, Philip Converse, Warren Miller, and Donald Stokes. *The American Voter.* Chicago: University of Chicago Press, 1960.

Campbell, David E. and Christina Wolbrecht. "See Jane Run: Women Politicians as Role Models for Adolescents." *Journal of Politics* 68 (2006): 233–47.

Canon, David. *Actors, Athletes and Astronauts.* Chicago: University of Chicago Press, 1990.

——. *Race, Redistricting, and Representation: The Unintended Consequences of Black Majority Districts.* Chicago: University of Chicago Press, 1999.

Carmines, Edward, and James Stimson. *Issue Evolution: Race and the Transformation of American Politics.* Princeton, N.J.: Princeton University Press, 1989.

"Carnahan, Jean." In *CQ's Politics in America 2002, the 107th Congress.* Washington, D.C.: CQ Press, 2001. http://library.cqpress.com/elections/pia107-0453058594.

Carpenter, Tim. "Bush Focuses on Larger Picture in Last Big Push." *Topeka Capital-Journal,* Novermber 6, 2006.

Carroll, Susan. "Political Elites and Sex Differences in Political Ambition: A Reconsideration." *Journal of Politics* 47 (1985): 1231–43.

——. *Women as Candidates in American Politics.* Bloomington: Indiana University Press, 1994.

——. "2004 Elections and Women: An Analysis of Statewide and State Legislative Election Results." *Spectrum: The Journal of State Government* 78 (2005): 23–25.

Carroll, Susan, and Ronnee Schreiber. "Media Coverage of Women in the 103rd Congress." In *Women, Media, and Politics,* edited by Pippa Norris. New York: Oxford University Press, 1997.

Center for American Women and Politics. *Women in Elective Office, 2005.* New Brunswick, N.J.: Rutgers University, 2005.

——. *Women in the U.S. Senate 1922–2005.* New Brunswick, N.J.: Rutgers University, 2005.

——. *Woman versus Woman Fact Sheet, 2006.* New Brunswick, N.J.: Rutgers University, 2006.

——. *Women in State Legislatures, 2007.* New Brunswick, N.J.: Rutgers University, 2007.

——. *Women of Color in Elective Office, 2007.* New Brunswick, N.J.: Rutgers University, 2007.

Chafe, William. *The American Woman: Her Changing Social, Economic and Political Roles, 1920–1970.* New York: Oxford University Press, 1972.

Chamberlin, Hope. *A Minority of Members: Women in the United States Congress.* New York: Praeger, 1973.

Chaney, Carole. "Running against a Woman: Advertising Strategies in Mixed-Sex Races for the United States Senate and Their Impact on Candidate Evaluation." Paper presented at the Western Political Science Association Annual Meeting, 1998, Los Angeles.

Chaney, Carole, and Barbara Sinclair. "Women and the 1992 House Elections." In *The Year of the Woman: Myths and Reality,* edited by Elizabeth Adell Cook, Sue Thomas, and Clyde Wilcox. Boulder, Colo.: Westview Press, 1994.

Chisholm, Shirley. *Unbought and Unbossed: An Autobiography.* New York: Houghton Mifflin, 1970.

Christensen, Rob. "Candidate's Zeal Divides." *(Raleigh, N.C.) News and Observer,* August 13, 2004.

Clark, Janet, Charles Hadley, and Robert Darcy. "Political Ambition among Men and Women State Party Leaders." *American Politics Quarterly* 17 (1989): 194–207.

Cleaver, Eldridge. *Soul On Ice.* New York: McGraw Hill, 1968.

Clift, Eleanor, and Tom Brazaitis. *Madam President.* New York: Scribner, 2000.

——. *Madam President,* 2nd ed. New York: Routledge, 2003.

Cohen, Jon and Jennifer Agiesta. "Poll: Age Important to Voters." *Washington Post,* February 27, 2007.

Cohen, Richard. "Member Moms." *National Journal*, April 7, 2007.

Congress and the Nation, 1948–1964. Washington, D.C.: CQ Press, 1965.

Congress and the Nation, 1973–1976. Washington, D.C.: CQ Press, 1977.

"Congresswoman Balances Bills With Birth." *CBSNews.com*, April 21, 2007.

Constantini, Edmond. "Political Women and Political Ambition." *American Journal of Politics* 34 (1990): 741–70.

Conway, M. Margaret. *Political Participation in the United States*, 3rd ed. Washington, D.C.: CQ Press, 2000.

Conway, M. Margaret, Gertrude Steuernagel, and David Ahern. *Women and Political Participation*. Washington, D.C.: CQ Press, 1997.

Cook, Elizabeth Adell. "Voter Reactions to Women Candidates." In *Women and Elective Office: Past, Present and Future*, edited by Sue Thomas and Clyde Wilcox. New York: Oxford University Press, 1998.

Cook, Elizabeth Adell, and Clyde Wilcox. "Women Voters in the Year of the Woman." In *Democracy's Feast: Elections in America*, edited by Herbert Weisberg. Chatham, N.J.: Chatham House, 1995.

Cook, Elizabeth Adell, Sue Thomas, and Clyde Wilcox, eds. *The Year of the Woman: Myths and Reality*, Boulder, Colo.: Westview Press, 1994.

Cooperman, Rosalyn, and Bruce Oppenheimer. "The Gender Gap in the House of Representatives." In *Congress Reconsidered*, 7th ed., edited by Lawrence Dodd and Bruce Oppenheimer. Washington, D.C.: CQ Press, 2001.

Copeland, Gary. "Choosing to Run: Why House Members Seek Election to the Senate." *Legislative Studies Quarterly* 14 (1989): 549–65.

Costain, Anne. *Inviting Women's Rebellion: A Political Process Interpretation of the Women's Movement*. Baltimore: Johns Hopkins University Press, 1992.

Cox, Gary, and Jonathan Katz. *Elbridge Gerry's Salamander: The Electoral Consequences of the Reapportionment Revolution*. New York: Cambridge University Press, 2002.

"CQ's Guide to Committees." *CQ Weekly*, April 11, 2005.

"CQ's Guide to Committees," *CQ Weekly*, April 16, 2007.

CQ's Guide to 1990 Congressional Redistricting. Washington, D.C.: CQ Press, 1993.

Crummy, Karen, and Anne Mulkern, "Allard Won't Try for 3rd." *Denver Post*, January 16, 2007.

Cummings, Milton, and Robert Peabody. "The Decision to Enlarge the Committee on Rules: An Analysis of the 1961 Vote." In *New Perspectives on the House of Representatives*, 2nd ed., edited by Robert Peabody and Nelson Polsby. Chicago: Rand McNally, 1969.

Darcy, R., and James Choike. "A Formal Analysis of Legislative Turnover: Women Candidates and Legislative Representation." *American Journal of Political Science* 30 (1986): 237–55.

Darcy, R., and Charles Hadley. "Black Women in Politics: The Puzzle of Success." *Social Science Quarterly* 69 (1988): 629–45.

Darcy, R., and Sarah Slavin Schramm. "When Women Run against Men." *Public Opinion Quarterly* 41 (1977): 1–12.

Darcy, R., Susan Welch, and Janet Clark. *Women, Elections, and Representation*, 2nd ed. Lincoln: University of Nebraska Press, 1994.

Darling, Marsha. "African-American Women in State Elective Office in the South." In *Women and Elective Office: Past, Present and Future*, edited by Sue Thomas and Clyde Wilcox. New York: Oxford University Press, 1998.

Davidson, Roger, and Walter Oleszek. *Congress and Its Members*, 5th ed. Washington, D.C.: CQ Press, 1996.

——. *Congress and Its Members*, 9th ed. Washington, D.C.: CQ Press, 2004.

Davis, Flora. *Moving the Mountain: The Women's Movement in America since 1960*. New York: Simon & Schuster, 1991.

Deber, Raisa. "The Fault Dear Brutus: Women as Congressional Candidates in Pennsylvania." *Journal of Politics* 44 (1982): 463–79.

Deering, Christopher, and Stephen Smith. *Committees in Congress*, 3rd ed. Washington, D.C.: CQ Press, 1997.

"Deficit-Reduction Bill Narrowly Passes." In *Congressional Quarterly Almanac, 1993*. Washington, D.C.: CQ Press, 1994.

deFiebre, Conrad. "Janklow Case: He Did Politics His Way; Roughshod Style Made Him SD Icon." *Minneapolis Star Tribune*, December 14, 2003.

Delli Carpini, Michael, and Ester Fuchs. "The Year of the Woman? Candidates, Voters, and the 1992 Elections." *Political Science Quarterly* 108 (1993): 29–36.

Dewar, Helen. "NY Senate Primary Gets Muddy Near the Wire." *Washington Post*, August 30, 1992.

Diamond, Irene. *Sex Roles in the State House*. New Haven, Conn.: Yale University Press, 1977.

Dickenson, James, and Paul Taylor. "Widow of Burton Will Seek Election to His House Seat." *Washington Post*, April 19, 1983.

"Dingell, John D." In *CQ's Politics in America 2006, the 109th Congress*. Washington, D.C.: CQ Press, 2005. http://library.cqpress.com/congress/pia109-Dingell-John-D.

DiStaso, John. "Craig Upset in House Bid." *Manchester Union Leader*, September 13, 2006.

Dolan, Julie. "A Decade after the Year of the Woman: Female Candidates' Success Rates in the 2002 Elections." Paper presented at the Southern Political Science Association Annual Meeting, January 2005, New Orleans.

Dolan, Julie, Melissa Deckman, and Michele Swers. *Women and Politics: Paths to Power and Political Influence*. Upper Saddle River, N.J.: Pearson Prentice Hall, 2007.

Dolan, Kathy. "Voting for Women in the 'Year of the Woman.'" *American Journal of Political Science* 42 (1998): 272–93.

——. "Electoral Context, Issues, and Voting for Women in the 1990s." In *Women and Congress: Running, Winning and Ruling*, edited by Karen O'Connor. New York: Haworth Press, 2001.

——. *Voting for Women: How the Public Evaluates Women Candidates*. Boulder, Colo.: Westview Press, 2004.

Dolan, Kathleen, and Lynne Ford. "Change and Continuity among Women State Legislators: Evidence from Three Decades." *Political Research Quarterly* 50 (1997): 137–51.

——. "Are All Women State Legislators Alike?" In *Women and Elective Office: Past, Present and Future*, edited by Sue Thomas and Clyde Wilcox. New York: Oxford University Press, 1998.

Drinkard, Jennifer. "The Disparity of Women Running for Congress." American University Washington Semester Program, Washington, D.C., 2003.

Duerst-Lahti, Georgia. "The Bottleneck: Women Becoming Candidates." In *Women and Elective Office: Past, Present and Future*, edited by Sue Thomas and Clyde Wilcox. New York: Oxford University Press, 1998.

——. "Presidential Elections: Gendered Space and the Case of 2004." In *Gender and Elections: Shaping the Future of American Politics*, edited by Susan Carroll and Richard Fox. Cambridge University Press: New York, 2006.

Ehrenhart, Alan, ed. *Politics in America, 1982*. Washington, D.C.: CQ Press, 1981.

Elazar, Daniel. *American Federalism: A View from the States*. New York: Crowell, 1966.

Epstein, Cynthia Fuchs. *Women in Law*, 2nd ed. Chicago: University of Illinois Press, 1993.

Epstein, David, and Sharyn O'Halloran. "A Social Science Approach to Race, Redistricting, and Representation." *American Political Science Review* 93 (1999): 187–91.

Erikson, Robert, Gerald Wright, and John McIver. *Statehouse Democracy: Public Opinion and Policy in the American States*. New York: Cambridge University Press, 1993.

Fears, Darryl. "On a Mission in a Political Second Act; Bush's Record Forced Her to Run, Braun Says." *Washington Post*, July 13, 2003.

Fenn, Jennifer. "Swift Sent Women a Bad Message." *Lowell (Mass.) Sun*, March 22, 2002.

Fenno, Richard. *Congressmen in Committees*. Boston: Little Brown, 1973.

——. *Home Style: House Members in Their Districts*. Boston: Little Brown, 1978.

——. *Senators on the Campaign Trail*. Norman: University of Oklahoma Press, 1996.

——. *Congress at the Grassroots: Representational Change in the South, 1970–1998*. Chapel Hill: University of North Carolina Press, 2000.

Ferrechio, Susan. "Brady to Chair House Administration Panel." *CQ Weekly*, May 28, 2007.

Fiorina, Morris. *Representatives, Roll Calls, and Constituencies*. Lexington, Mass.: D.C. Heath, 1974.

——. *Congress: Keystone of the Washington Establishment*, 2nd ed. New Haven, Conn.: Yale University Press, 1989.

Fisher, Jim. "Symms gives Sheila Sorensen a Bite from his Apple." *Lewiston (Idaho) Morning Tribune*, January 20, 2006. http://idahoptv.org/idreports/showEditorial.cfm?StoryID=19467.

——. "A Gut Check for Mainstream Republicans." *Lewiston (Idaho) Morning Tribune*, May 25, 2006.

——. "Why the Bleep Don't We Use the Words We Mean?" *Lewiston (Idaho) Morning Tribune*, November 12, 2006.

Fleisher, Richard. "Explaining the Change in Roll-Call Voting Behavior of Southern Democrats." *Journal of Politics* 55 (1993): 327–41.

Fleisher, Richard, and Jon Bond. "Polarized Politics: Does It Matter?" In *Polarized Politics: Congress and the President in a Partisan Era*, edited by Jon Bond and Richard Fleisher. Washington D.C.: CQ Press, 2000.

Florida, Richard. "The Rise of the Creative Class: Why Cities without Gays and Rock Bands Are Losing the Economic Development Race." *Washington Monthly* 34 (2002): 15–26.

Foerstel, Karen. *Biographical Dictionary of Congressional Women*. Westport, Conn.: Greenwood Press, 1999.

Foerstel, Karen, and Herbert Foerstel. *Climbing the Hill: Gender Conflict in Congress*. Westport, Conn.: Praeger Press, 1996.

Fowlkes, Diane, Jerry Perkins, and Sue Tolleson Rinehart. "Gender Roles and Party Roles." *American Political Science Review* 3 (1979): 772–80.

Fox, Richard. *Gender Dynamics in Congressional Elections*. Thousand Oaks, Calif.: Sage, 1997.

——. "Gender, Political Ambition and the Decision Not to Run for Office." Center for American Women and Politics, 2003. http://www.rci.rutgers.edu/~cawp/Research/Reports/Fox2003.pdf.

——. "Congressional Elections: Where Are We on the Road to Gender Parity?" In *Gender and Elections: Shaping the Future of American Politics*, edited by Sue Carroll and Richard Fox. New York: Cambridge University Press, 2006.

Fox, Richard, and Jennifer Lawless. "The Impact of Sex-Role Socialization on the Decision to Run for Office." Paper presented at the Southern Political Science Association Annual Meeting, January 2002, Atlanta.

Fox, Richard, Jennifer Lawless, and Courtney Feeley. "Gender and the Decision to Run for Office." *Legislative Studies Quarterly* 26 (2001): 411–35.

Fox, Richard, and Zoe Oxley. "Gender Stereotyping in State Executive Elections: Candidate Selection and Success." *Journal of Politics* 65 (2003): 833–50.

Francis, Wayne, and Lawrence Kenny. *Up the Political Ladder: Career Paths in U.S. Politics*. Thousand Oaks, Calif.: Sage, 2000.

Frank, Thomas. *What's the Matter with Kansas?* New York: Metropolitan Books, 2004.

Frankel, Bruce. "Anything Goes in NY Primary." *USA Today*, September 11, 1992.

Freeman, Jo. *The Politics of Women's Liberation*. New York: David McKay, 1975.
——. *A Room at a Time: How Women Entered Party Politics*. New York: Rowman and Littlefield, 2000.
Freeman, Joanne. *Affairs of Honor: National Politics in the New Republic*. New Haven, Conn.: Yale University Press, 2001.
Friedman, Sally. "House Committee Assignments of Women and Minority Newcomers, 1965–1994." *Legislative Studies Quarterly* 21 (1996): 73–81.
Froman, Lewis. *Congressmen and Their Constituencies*. Chicago: Rand McNally, 1963.
——. *The Congressional Process*. Boston: Little, Brown, 1967.
Fuentes, Annette. "Out-of-style thinking." http://www.usatoday.com, February 13, 2007.
Gaddie, Ronald Keith. "The Texas Redistricting, Measure for Measure." In *Extensions: Congressional Redistricting*, edited by Ronald Peters. Norman: University of Oklahoma, 2004.
Gaddie, Ronald Keith, and Charles Bullock. "Congressional Elections and the Year of the Woman: Structural and Elite Influences on Female Candidates." *Social Science Quarterly* 76 (1995): 749–62.
Gallagher, Jay, and Kyle Hughes. "Dirty Campaign Muddies Senate Contest in NY." *Chicago Sun-Times*, September 12, 1992.
Gallup Poll. Wilmington, Del.: Scholarly Resources, 1992.
Gallup Poll, 1935–1971. Wilmington, Del.: Scholarly Resources, 1973.
Gamarekian, Barbara. " 'The Popular Burton' and Her Mission." *New York Times*, July 29, 1983.
Gelman, Andrew, and Gary King. "Enhancing Democracy through Legislative Redistricting." *American Political Science Review* 88 (1994): 541–59.
Geraghty, Jim. "Moranic Record." *National Review Online*, March 12, 2003. http://www.nationalreview.com/comment/comment-geraghty031203.asp.
Gerber, Larry. "Dornan Loses Solidly, Not Quietly." *Associated Press*, November 4, 1998.
Gertzog, Irwin. "The Matrimonial Connection: The Nomination of Congressmen's Widows for the House of Representatives." *Journal of Politics* 42 (1980): 820–33.
——. *Congressional Women: Their Recruitment, Integration, and Behavior*, 2nd ed. Westport, Conn.: Praeger Press, 1995.
Gertzog, Irwin, and Michele Simard. "Women and 'Hopeless' Congressional Candidacies: Nomination Frequency, 1916–1978." *American Politics Quarterly* 9 (1991): 449–66.
Giles, Kevin. *Flight of the Dove: The Story of Jeannette Rankin*. Beaverton, Ore.: Touchstone Press, 1980.
Gillon, Steven. *That's Not What We Meant to Do: Reform and Its Unintended Consequences in Twentieth-Century America*. New York: W.W. Norton, 2000.
Giroux, Gregory. "California Democrats' Remap Puts Two of Their Own in Tough Spots." *CQ Weekly*, September 22, 2001.
——. "'Remaps' Clear Trend: Incumbent Protection." *CQ Weekly*, November 3, 2001.
Givhan, Robin. "Condoleezza Rice's Commanding Clothes." *The Washington Post*, February 25, 2005.
——. "Muted Tones of Quiet Authority: A Look Suited To the Speaker." *The Washington Post*, November 10, 2005.
——. "Hillary Clinton's Tentative Dip Into New Neckline Territory." *Washington Post*, July 20, 2007.
Greenblatt, Alan, and Jonathan D. Salant. "Retirement: Out with the Old and the New: Myers, Lincoln Will Retire." *CQ Weekly*, January 13, 1996.
Grofman, Bernard, and Lisa Handley. "Minority Population Proportion and the Black and Hispanic Congressional Success in the 1970s and 1980s." *American Politics Quarterly* 17 (1989): 436–45.
Gruberg, Martin. *Women in Politics: A Source Book*. New York: Academic Press, 1968.

——. "Defeated Rep. Franks Accused of 'Uncle Tomism.'" *Washington Post*, November 21, 1996.

Gugliotta, Guy. "In a Republican Redoubt, Doubts on Senate Hopeful: Conservative in Tight Race for Kansas Seat." *Washington Post*, October 29, 1996, A8.

Guinier, Lani. "Don't Scapegoat the Gerrymander." *New York Times Magazine*, January 8, 1995.

Gyan, Joe, Jr., "Jefferson Wins New Term." *Capital City Press*, December 10, 2006, 1.

Haga, Chuck. "'Come Home,' Coya Dies." *Minneapolis Star Tribune*, October 11, 1996.

Hain, Paul, Philip Roeder, and Manuel Avalos. "Risk and Progressive Candidacies: An Extension of Rohde's Model." *American Journal of Political Science* 25 (1981): 188–92.

Handley, Lisa, and Bernard Grofman. "The Impact of the Voting Rights Act on Minority Representation: Black Office Holding in Southern State Legislatures and Congressional Delegations." In *Quiet Revolution in the South: The Impact of the Voting Rights Act, 1965–1990*, edited by Chandler Davidson and Bernard Grofman. Princeton, N.J.: Princeton University Press, 1994.

Hansen, Susan. "Talking about Politics: Gender and Contextual Effects on Political Proselytizing." *Journal of Politics* 59 (1997): 73–103.

Hardy, Michael, and Karen McCurdy. "Representational Threshold: Women in Congressional Committees." Paper presented at the Southern Political Science Association, January 2005, New Orleans.

Hardy-Fanta, Carol, ed. *Latina Politics, Latino Politics: Gender, Culture, and Political Participation in Boston*. Philadelphia: Temple University Press, 1993.

Harrison, Cynthia. *On Account of Sex: The Politics of Women's Issues, 1945–1968*. Berkeley: University of California, 1988.

Harvey, Anna. *Votes Without Leverage: Women in American Electoral Politics, 1920–1970*. New York: Cambridge University Press, 1998.

Henry, Mark. "Bono's Mother Doesn't Want His Widow Elected." *Riverside (Calif.) Press Enterprise*, March 28, 1998.

——. "Phone Call Discouraged Election Run." *Riverside (Calif.) Press Enterprise*, March 31, 1998.

Herrnson, Paul. *Congressional Elections: Campaigning at Home and in Washington*. Washington, D.C.: CQ Press, 1998.

——. *Congressional Elections: Campaigning at Home and in Washington*, 4th ed. Washington, D.C.: CQ Press, 2004.

Herrnson, Paul, J. Celeste Lay, and Atiya Kai Stokes. "Women Running 'as Women': Candidate Gender, Campaign Issues, and Voter-Targeting Strategies." *Journal of Politics* 65 (2003): 244–55.

High-Pippert, Angela. "Female Empowerment: The Influence of Women Representing Women." *Women & Politics* 19 (1998): 53–67.

Hill, David. "Political Culture and Female Political Representation." *Journal of Politics* 43 (1981): 159–68.

Hill, Kevin. "Do Black Majority Districts Aid Republicans?" *Journal of Politics* 57 (1995): 384–401.

Hoffman, Kim, Carrie Palmer, and Ronald Keith Gaddie. "Candidate Sex and Congressional Elections: Open Seats Before, During, and After the Year of the Woman." In *Women and Congress: Running, Winning and Ruling*, edited by Karen O'Connor. New York: Haworth Press, 2001.

Hole, Judith, and Ellen Levine. *Rebirth of Feminism*. New York: Quadrangle Books, 1971.

Hollingsworth, Barbara. "Moderates Leading State Races." *Topeka Capital-Journal*, August 2, 2006.

Holtzman, Elizabeth, with Cynthia Cooper. *Who Said It Would Be Easy? One Woman's Life in the Political Arena*. New York: Arcade Press, 1996.

Hook, Janet. "Will the Flood of Retirements Arrive in 1992? Maybe Not." *CQ Weekly*, January 12, 1991.

Horrigan, Marie. "GOP Troubles Reshuffle New Mexico's '08 Deck." *CQ Weekly Online*, March 12, 2007.

Huddy, Leonie, and Nayda Terkildsen. "The Consequences of Gender Stereotypes for Women Candidates at Different Levels and Types of Office." *Political Research Quarterly* 46 (1993): 503–25.

——. "Gender Stereotypes and the Perception of Male and Female Candidates." *American Journal of Political Science* 37 (1993): 119–47.

Inskip, Leonard. "A Revival of Sorts for Minnesota's Knutson." *Minneapolis Star Tribune*, February 4, 1997.

Iyengar, Shanto, Nicholas A. Valentino, Stephen Ansolabehere, and Adam F. Simon. "Running as a Woman: Gender Stereotyping in Political Campaigns." In *Women, Media, and Politics*, edited by Pippa Norris. New York: Oxford University Press, 1997.

Jacobson, Gary. *The Politics of Congressional Elections*, 4th ed. New York: HarperCollins, 1997.

Jamieson, Kathleen Hall. *Beyond the Double Bind: Women and Leadership*. New York: Oxford University Press, 1995.

"Janklow Trial Begins, Could Shake Up State's Political Scene." *Bulletin's Frontrunner (McClean, Virginia)*, December 2, 2003.

Jenkins, Chris, and R. H. Melton. "Contrite, Combative Moran on the Ropes: Congressman Fights to Survive." *Washington Post*, March 16, 2003.

Jennings, M. Kent, and Norman Thomas. "Men and Women in Party Elites: Social Roles and Political Resources." *Midwest Journal of Political Science* 12 (1968): 462–92.

Johnson, Dirk. "Race for Dole's Senate Seat Provokes Ideological Split." *New York Times*, August 5, 1996.

Jones, Jeffrey. "Six in 10 Americans Think U.S. Ready for a Female President." *Gallup Poll New Service*, October 3, 2006.

Jones, Woodrow, and Albert Nelson. "Correlates of Women's Representation in Lower State Legislative Chambers." *Social Behavior and Personality* 1 (1981): 9–15.

Jost, Kenneth. "Redistricting Disputes." *CQ Researcher*, March 12, 2004.

Judis, John, and Ruy Teixeira. *The Emerging Democratic Majority*. New York: Scribner, 2002.

Kafka, Joe. "Herseth Feeling More Settled in Washington." *Associated Press State and Local Wire*, January 30, 2005.

Kahn, Kim Fridkin. "Characteristics of Press Coverage in Senate and Gubernatorial Elections: Information Available to Voters." *Legislative Studies Quarterly* 20 (1995): 23–35.

——. *The Political Consequences of Being a Woman*. New York: Columbia University Press, 1996.

Kahn, Kim Fridkin, and Edie Goldenberg. "Women Candidates in the News: An Examination of Gender Differences in U.S. Senate Campaign Coverage." *Public Opinion Quarterly* 55 (1991): 180–99.

Kaptur, Marcy. *Women of Congress: A Twentieth-Century Odyssey*. Washington, D.C.: CQ Press, 1996.

Kardiner, Abram. *Sex and Morality*. Indianapolis, Ind.: Bobbs-Merrill, 1954.

Katz, Jonathan, and Brian Sala. "Careerism, Committee Assignments, and the Electoral Connection." *American Political Science Review* 90 (1996): 21–33.

Kaufman, Karen, and John Petrocik. "The Changing Politics of American Men: Understanding the Sources of the Gender Gap." *American Journal of Political Science* 43 (1999): 864–87.

Kerchival, Hoppy. "Rockefeller Isn't Taking '08 For Granted." *Charleston Daily Mail*, April 27, 2007.

Kernell, Samuel. "Toward Understanding 19th Century Congressional Careers: Ambition, Competition, and Rotation." *American Journal of Political Science* 21 (1977): 669–93.

Kessel, John."Review of Candidates, Issues and Strategies." *Midwest Journal of Political Science* 10 (1966): 515–18.

Key, V. O. *Southern Politics in State and Nation*. New York: A. A. Knopf, 1949.

Kincaid, Diane. "Over His Dead Body: A Positive Perspective on Widows in the U.S. Congress." *Western Political Quarterly* 31 (1978): 96–104.

King, David, and Richard Matland. "Sex and the Grand Old Party: An Experimental Investigation of the Effect of Candidate Sex on Support for a Republican Candidate." *American Politics Research* 31 (2003): 595–612.

King, Gary, and Langche Zeng. "Logistic Regression in Rare Events Data." *Political Analysis* 9 (2001): 1–27.

King, Gary, Michael Tomz, and Jason Wittenberg. "Making the Most of Statistical Analyses: Improving Interpretation and Presentation." *American Journal of Political Science* 44 (2000): 341–55.

Kirkpatrick, Jeane. *Political Woman*. New York: Basic Books, 1974.

Koch, Jeffrey. "Do Citizens Apply Gender Stereotypes to Infer Candidates' Ideological Orientations?" *Journal of Politics* 62 (2000): 414–29.

——. "Gender Stereotypes and Citizens' Impression of House Candidates' Ideological Orientations." *American Journal of Political Science* 46 (2002): 453–62.

Koetzle, William. "The Impact of Constituency Diversity upon the Competitiveness of U.S. House Elections, 1962–1996." *Legislative Studies Quarterly* 23 (1998): 561–73.

Komarovsky, Mirra. "Cultural Contradictions and Sex Roles." *American Journal of Sociology* 52 (1946): 184–89.

Kornblut, Anne. "Clinton Shatters Record for Fundraising." *Washington Post*, April 2, 2007.

Koszczuk, Jacki. "Proof of Illegal Voters Falls Short, Keeping Sanchez in House." *CQ Weekly*, February 7, 1998.

Koszczuk, Jacki, and H. Amy Stern, eds. *CQ's Politics in America, 2006*. Washington, D.C.: CQ Press, 2005.

Kropf, Martha, and John Boiney. "The Electoral Glass Ceiling? Gender, Viability, and the News in U.S. Senate Campaigns." In *Women and Congress: Running, Winning and Ruling*, edited by Karen O'Connor. New York: Haworth Press, 2001.

Kumar, Anita, and Joni James, "Harris Announces Run for U.S. Senate." *St. Petersburg Times*, June 8, 2005.

Kuntz, Phil. "Uproar over Bank Scandal Goads House to Cut Perks." *CQ Weekly*, October 5, 1991.

——. "Overdrafts Were a Potent Charge." *CQ Weekly*, November 7, 1992.

Lamson, Peggy. *Few Are Chosen*. Boston: Houghton Mifflin, 1968.

Lane, Robert. *Political Life*. Glencoe, Ill.: Free Press, 1959.

Lau, Richard, and David Redlawsk. "Advantages and Disadvantages of Cognitive Heuristics in Political Decision Making." *American Journal of Political Science* 45 (2001): 951–71.

Lau, Richard, and David Sears, eds. *Political Cognition*. Hillsdale, N.J.: L. Erlbaum Associates, 1986.

Lawless, Jennifer. "Politics of Presence? Congresswomen and Sybolic Representation." *Political Research Quarterly* 57 (2004): 81–99.

Lawless, Jennifer, and Richard Fox. *It Takes a Candidate: Why Women Don't Run for Office*. New York: Cambridge University Press, 2005.

Lederer, William, and Eugene Burdick. *The Ugly American*. New York: Norton, 1958.

Leeper, Mark. "The Impact of Prejudice on Female Candidates: An Experimental Look at Voter Inference." *American Politics Quarterly* 19 (1991): 248–61.

Lengel, Allan. "Discovery May Alter Questions for Condit." *Washington Post*, May 24, 2002.

Lengel, Allan, and Petula Dvorak. "Condit Offers Long-Awaited Comment Tonight." *Washington Post*, August 23, 2001.

Lipman, Larry. "Ex-Harris Aides Reveal Why They Became 'Exes.' " *Palm Beach Post*, August 6, 2006.

Lopach, James, and Jean Luckowski. *Jeannette Rankin: A Political Woman*. Boulder, CO: University Press of Colorado, 2005.

Lublin, David. *The Paradox of Representation: Racial Gerrymandering and Minority Interests in Congress*. Princeton, N.J.: Princeton University Press, 1997.

———. "Racial Redistricting and African-American Representation: A Critique of 'Do Majority–Minority Districts Maximize Substantive Black Representation in Congress?' " *American Political Science Review* 93 (1999): 183–86.

Lucas, Greg. "Matsui Wins Election to Late Husband's Seat." *San Francisco Chronicle*, March 9, 2005.

Luce, Clare Boothe. *Stuffed Shirts*. New York: Liveright, 1933.

McCurdy, Karen. "The Institutional Role of Women Serving in Congress: 1960–2000." In *Representation of Minority Groups in the U.S.*, edited by Charles Menifield. Lanham, Md.: Austin and Winfield, 2001.

McDermott, Monika. "Voting Cues in Low-Information Elections: Candidate Gender as a Social Information Variable in Contemporary U.S. Elections." *American Journal of Political Science* 41 (1997): 270–83.

———. "Race and Gender Cues in Low-Information Elections." *Political Research Quarterly* 51 (1998): 895–918.

McGlen, Nancy, and Karen O'Connor. *Women, Politics and American Society*, 2nd ed. Upper Saddle River, N.J.: Prentice Hall, 1998.

McGlen, Nancy, Karen O'Connor, Laura Van Assendelft, and Wendy Gunther-Canada. *Women, Politics, and American Society*, 4th ed. Upper Saddle River, N.J.: Prentice Hall, 2005.

McGreevey, James. *The Confession*. New York: Harper Collins, 2006.

McKinney, Joan. "Reapportionment Reaction." *The Advocate (Baton Rouge, Louisiana)*, December 1, 1996.

MacManus, Susan. "Voter Participation and Turnout: It's a New Game." In *Gender and Elections: Shaping the Future of American Politics*, edited by Susan Carroll and Richard Fox. New York: Cambridge University Press, 2006.

Maddaus, Gene. "Congress a Family Affair?" *Long Beach Press Telegram*, May 12, 2007.

Maisel, Sandy, and Walter Stone. "The Politics of Government-Funded Research: Notes from the Experience of the Candidate Emergence Study." *PS: Political Science and Politics* 31 (1998): 811–17.

Mandel, Ruth. *In the Running: The New Woman Candidate*. New Haven, Conn.: Ticknor and Fields, 1981.

Mandel, Ruth, and Katherine Kleeman. *Political Generation Next: America's Young Elected Leaders*. Rutgers, N.J.: Eagleton Institute of Politics, 2004.

Mansbridge, Jane. *Why We Lost the ERA*. Chicago: University of Chicago, 1986.

March, William, and Keith Epstein. "Bile Flows as Tight Senate Race Heads to End." *Tampa Tribune*, October 29, 2004.

Margolies-Mezvinsky, Marjorie. *A Woman's Place: The Freshmen Women Who Changed the Face of Congress*. New York: Crown, 1994.

Matland, Richard, and David King. "Women as Candidates in Congressional Elections." In *Women Transforming Congress*, edited by Cindy Simon Rosenthal. Norman: University of Oklahoma Press, 2002.

Matthews, Donald. *U.S. Senators and Their World*. Chapel Hill: University of North Carolina Press, 1960.

Matthews, Jay. "California's GOP Primary a Free-for-All." *Washington Post*, June 1, 1986.

Matthews, Joe. "Maybe Anyone Can Be President." *Los Angeles Times*, February 2, 2005.

Mauer, Richard, Nicole Tsong, and Paula Dobbyn. "Murkowski Up; Votes to Come." *Anchorage Daily News*, November 3, 2004.

Mayer, William. *The Changing American Mind*. Ann Arbor: University of Michigan Press, 1992.

Mayhew, David. *Congress: The Electoral Connection*. New Haven, Conn.: Yale University Press, 1974.

Melton, R. H. "Byrne Strikes a Nerve in Richmond: Fairfax Senator Says Colleagues Are Trying to Force Out Democratic Women." *Washington Post*, April 15, 2001.

Merrion, Paul. "Martin Campaign Lags; Gaffes Raise GOP Doubts, May Imperil Fund-Raising." *Crain's Chicago Business*, October 2, 1989.

Mikulski, Barbara, Kay Bailey Hutchison, Dianne Feinstein, Barbara Boxer, Patty Murray, Olympia Snowe, Susan Collins, Mary Landrieu, Blanche Lincoln, and Catherine Whitney. *Nine and Counting: The Women of the Senate*. New York: William Morrow, 2000.

Milburn, John. "Parkinson's Switch Unlikely to Send Other 'RINOS' Charging Towards the Democrats." *Associated Press State and Local Wire*, June 4, 2006.

Miller, Clem. *Member of the House: Letters of a Congressman*, edited by John Baker. New York: Scribner, 1962.

Mills, Paul. "Mr. Vacationland and Why We Can't Forget the Lady from Rumford." *Lewiston (Maine) Sun Journal*, September 3, 2000.

"Miss Rankin—Sobbing—Votes No." *New York Times*, April 6, 1917.

Mitchell, Greg. *Tricky Dick and the Pink Lady: Richard Nixon vs. Helen Gahagan Douglas: Sexual Politics and the Red Scare, 1950*. New York: Random House, 1998.

Molinari, Susan. *Representative Mom: Balancing Budgets, Bill, and Baby in the U.S. Congress*. New York: Doubleday, 1998.

Moncrief, Gary, Joel Thompson, and Robert Schuhmann. "Gender, Race and the State Legislature: A Research Note on the Double Disadvantage Hypothesis." *Social Science Journal* 28 (1991): 481–87.

Moore, J. L. "Majority-Minority District." In *Elections A to Z*. Washington, D.C.: CQ Press, 2003. http://library.cqpress.com/elections/elaz2d–156–7490–402760 (accessed July 25, 2005).

Morris, Celia. *Storming the Statehouse: Running for Governor with Ann Richards and Dianne Feinstein*. New York: Charles Scribner's Sons, 1992.

"Moss tops 'Vanity Fair's best-dressed list,'" *USAToday.com*, July 31, 2006. http://www.usatoday.com/life/people/2006–07–31-vanity-fair-best-dressed_x.htm.

Mueller, Melinda, and Barbara Poole. "A New Year of the Woman? Women Candidates for U.S. House Seats in 2004." Paper presented at the Southern Political Science Association Annual Meeting, January 2005, New Orleans.

Nechemias, Carol. "Geographic Mobility and Women's Access to State Legislatures." *Western Political Quarterly* 38 (1985): 119–31.

———. "Changes in the Election of Women to U.S. State Legislative Seats." *Legislative Studies Quarterly* 12 (1987): 125–42.

"New House Member Profile: Russ Carnahan." *CQ Weekly*, November 6, 2004.

"New Member Profile: Elijah E. Cummings, D-Md. (7)." *CQ Weekly*, April 20, 1996, 1070.

Newport, Frank. "Update: Hillary Rodham Clinton and the 2008 Election." *Gallup Poll News Service*, June 7, 2005.

Niven, David. "Party Elites and Women Candidates: The Shape of Bias." *Women & Politics* 19 (1998): 57–80.

———. "Throwing Your Hat Out of the Ring: Negative Recruitment and the Gender Imbalance in State Legislative Candidacy." *Politics & Gender* 2 (2006): 473–89.

Niven, David, and Jeremy Zilber. " 'How Does She Have Time for Kids and Congress?' Views on Gender and Media Coverage from House Offices." In *Women and*

Congress: Running, Winning and Ruling, edited by Karen O'Connor. New York: Haworth Press, 2001.

"No Retirement for Levin; Dems Breathe Easier with Senator's Decision to Run." *Grand Rapids Press,* December 5, 2006.

Norman, Michael. "Mrs. Fenwick and Lautenberg Meet in Final Debate." *New York Times,* November 1, 1982.

——. "Rep. Fenwick Tries to Figure Out Why She Lost." *New York Times,* November 4, 1982.

Norrander, Barbara, and Clyde Wilcox. "The Geography of Gender Power." In *Women and Elective Office: Past, Present and Future,* edited by Sue Thomas and Clyde Wilcox. New York: Oxford University Press, 1998.

Norris, Pippa. "Women Leaders Worldwide: A Splash of Color in the Photo Op." In *Women, Media, and Politics,* edited by Pippa Norris. New York: Oxford University Press, 1997.

North Jones, Allison, and Ellen Gedalius. "Martinez 'Humbled to Be' U.S. Senator." *Tampa Tribune,* November 4, 2004.

Novak, Robert. "Showdown in Kansas a Major Test for GOP." *Chicago Sun-Times,* August 6, 1996.

Nuwer, Deanne Stephens. "Southern Women Legislators and Patriarchy in the South." *Southeastern Political Review* 28 (2000): 449–68.

O'Connor, Karen. *Women's Organizations' Use of the Courts.* Lexington, Mass.: Lexington Books, 1980.

——. *No Neutral Ground? Abortion Politics in an Age of Absolutes.* Boulder, Colo.: Westview Press, 1996.

Oleszek, Walter. *Congressional Procedures and the Policy Process,* 6th ed. Washington, D.C.: CQ Press, 2004.

Open Secrets. "New Jersey Senate Race: 2000 Campaign Money Profile." http://www.opensecrets.org/races/summary.asp?ID=N.J.S1&Cycle=2000.

——. "Total Raised and Spent, 2006 Race: Florida District 18." http://www.opensecrets.org/races/summary.asp?id=FL18&cycle=2006.

——. "2004 Election Overview: Stats at Glance." http://opensecrets.org/races/summary.asp?id=SDS1&cycle=2004.

——. "2006 Election Overview: Stats at a Glance." http://opensecrets.org/overview/stats.asp?cycle=2006.

——. "2006 Race: Florida Senate." http://opensecrets.org/races/summary.asp?cycle=2006&id=FLS1.

——. "2006 Race: Missouri Senate." http://opensecrets.org/races/summary.asp?cycle=2006&id=MOS2.

——. "2006 Race: New York Senate." http://opensecrets.org/races/summary.asp?cycle=2006&id=NYS1.

——. "2006 Race: Washington Senate." http://opensecrets.org/races/summary.asp?cycle=2006&id=WAS1.

Ornstein, Norman, ed. *Congress in Change: Evolution and Reform.* New York: Praeger, 1975.

Ornstein, Norman, Thomas E. Mann, and Michael Malbin, eds. *Vital Statistics on Congress.* Washington, D.C.: CQ Press, 1998.

Page, Benjamin I., Robert Y. Shapiro, Paul W. Gronke, and Robert M. Rosenberg. "Constituency, Party, and Representation in Congress." *Public Opinion Quarterly* 48 (1984): 741–56.

Palmer, Barbara. "Woman President in the U.S.: Will it Ever Happen?" *The Anniston Star (Anniston, Alabama),* February 18, 2007.

Palmer, Barbara, and Dennis Simon. "Breaking the Logjam: The Emergence of Women as Congressional Candidates." In *Women and Congress: Running, Winning, and Ruling,* edited by Karen O'Connor. Binghamton, N.Y.: Haworth Press, 2001.

——. "Political Ambition and Women in the U.S. House of Representatives, 1916–2000." *Political Research Quarterly* 56 (2003): 127–38.

——. "When Women Run against Women: The Hidden Influence of Female Incumbents in Elections to the U.S. House of Representatives, 1956–2002." *Politics and Gender* 1 (2005): 39–63.

Patrick, Steven. "Traficant Refuses to Go Quietly Despite Calls for His Resignation." *CQ Weekly*, April 13, 2002.

Peabody, Robert, Norman Ornstein, and David Rohde. "The United States Senate as Presidential Incubator: Many Are Called but Few Are Chosen." *Political Science Quarterly* 9 (1976): 237–58.

Pearson, Kathryn, and Eric McGhee. "Strategic Differences: The Gender Dynamics of Congressional Candidacies, 1982–2002." Paper presented at the American Political Science Association Annual Meeting, September 2004, Chicago.

"Pelosi becomes first woman House speaker." *CNN.com*, January 5, 2007. http://www.cnn.com/2007/POLITICS/01/04/congress.rdp/index.html.

Perkins, Jerry, and Diane Fowlkes. "Opinion Representation versus Social Representation: Or Why Women Can't Run as Women and Win." *American Political Science Review* 74 (1980): 92–103.

Peterson, Bill. "Alabama Senate 'Sleeper' Catches Political Experts Dozing." *Washington Post*, October 3, 1978.

Petrocik, John. "Issue Ownership in Presidential Elections, with a 1980 Case Study." *American Journal of Political Science* 40 (1996): 825–50.

Phillips, Frank. "Shake-up in the Governor's Race: Swift Yields to Romney Saying 'Something Had to Give,' Exits Race for Governor." *Boston Globe*, March 20, 2002.

Pitt, Leonard. "Mrs. Deeds Goes to Washington." *Reviews in American History* 21 (1993): 477–81.

Pitzl, Mary Jo. "GOP Group Formed to Promote Women." *The Arizona Republic*, January 27, 2007.

Polsby, Nelson. "The Institutionalization of the U.S. House of Representatives." *American Political Science Review* 52 (1968): 124–43.

Pool, Ithiel de Sola, Robert Abelson, and Samuel Popkin. *Candidates, Issues, and Strategies: A Computer Simulation of the 1960 and 1964 Presidential Elections.* Cambridge, Mass.: MIT Press, 1965.

"President Bush Nudges Miller to Senate; Bush wants Rep. Candice Miller to Run against Sen. Debbie Stabenow." *Grand Rapids Press*, January 8, 2005.

Prestage, Jewel. "Black Women State Legislators: A Profile." In *A Portrait of Marginality: The Political Behavior of American Women*, edited by Marianne Githens and Jewel Prestage. New York: David McKay, 1977.

——. "The Case of African American Women and Politics." *PS: Political Science and Politics* 27 (1994): 720–21.

Price, H. Douglas. "Congress and the Evolution of Legislative Professionalism." In *Change in Congress*, edited by Norman Ornstein. New York: Praeger, 1975.

Quinn, Sally. "Maryon Allen: The Southerngirl in the Senate." *Washington Post*, July 30, 1978.

Rahn, Wendy. "The Role of Partisan Stereotypes in Information Processing about Political Candidates." *American Journal of Political Science* 37 (1993): 472–96.

Ratcliffe, R. G. "Hutchison to Run for Senate, Not Governor." *Houston Chronicle*, June 18, 2005.

Reed, John Shelton. *The Enduring South: Subcultural Persistence in Mass Society.* Chapel Hill: University of North Carolina Press, 1986.

"Report: Pensacola Republicans Say Scarborough Courted for Senate." *Associated Press State and Local Wire*, August 16, 2005.

"Representative now known as Stephanie Herseth Sandlin." *Associated Press State and Local Wire*, April 1, 2007.

Reyes, B. J. "Case Wins Hawaii's 2nd Congressional District." *Associated Press State and Local Wire,* January 5, 2003.

Roberts, Alison. "Electing to Carry On: Grief Fuels Matsui's Bid for Congress." *Sacramento Bee,* January 22, 2005.

"Robinson Accuses Arrested Pakistani of Terrorism in New Ad." *Associated Press State and Local Wire,* August 15, 2004.

Rodine, Sharon. "How to Beat Bubba." *Campaigns & Elections,* October–November 1990.

Roddy, Dennis. "Admission of Guilt: Waldholtz Admits Financial Violations, Apologizes to All but Ex-Wife." *Pittsburgh Post Gazette,* June 6, 1996.

Rohde, David. "Risk-Bearing and Progressive Ambition: The Case of Members of the United States House of Representatives." *American Journal of Political Science* 23 (1979): 1–26.

Ross, Shelly. *Fall from Grace: Sex, Scandal, and Corruption in American Politics from 1702 to the Present.* New York: Ballantine Books, 1988.

Roybal, David. "Squeaky Clean Images Take a Hit." *Albuquerque Journal,* March 13, 2007.

Rozell, Mark. "Helping Women Run and Win: Feminist Groups, Candidate Recruitment and Training." *Women & Politics* 21 (2000): 101–16.

Rule, Wilma. "Why Women Don't Run: The Critical and Contextual Factors in Women's Legislative Recruitment." *Western Political Quarterly* 34 (1981): 60–77.

——. "Why More Women Are Legislators: A Research Note." *Western Political Quarterly* 43 (1990): 437–48.

Rusk, Jerrold. "The Effect of the Australian Ballot on Split Ticking Voting: 1876–1908." *American Political Science Review* 64 (1970): 1220–38.

Rutenberg, Jim. "An Idea, with 4 Words, That Was Supposed to Soothe the Tone of Ads but Did Not." *New York Times,* October 30, 2004.

Ruth, Daniel. "Memo to Harris Staff Members: Keep Digging." *Tampa Tribune,* August 31, 2006.

Sabato, Larry. *Feeding Frenzy: How Attack Journalism Has Transformed American Politics.* New York: Free Press, 1991.

Sanbonmatsu, Kira. "Gender Stereotypes and Vote Choice." *American Journal of Political Science* 46 (2002): 20–34.

——. "Political Parties and the Recruitment of Women to State Legislatures." *Journal of Politics* 64 (2002): 791–809.

——. *Democrats, Republicans, and the Politics of Women's Place.* Ann Arbor: University of Michigan, 2004.

——. *Where Women Run: Gender and Party in the American States.* Ann Arbor: University of Michigan Press, 2006a.

——. "Gender Pools and Puzzles: Charting a 'Women's Path' to the Legislature." *Politics & Gender* 2 (2006b): 387–400.

——. "Do Parties Know That 'Women Win'? Party Leader Beliefs about Women's Electoral Chances." *Politics & Gender* 2 (2006c): 431–50.

"Sanchez Claims Victory in Nation's Most Expensive Race." *Associated Press,* November 4, 1998.

Sapiro, Virginia. "Private Costs of Public Commitments or Public Costs of Private Commitments? Family Roles versus Political Ambition." *American Journal of Political Science* 26 (1982): 265–79.

——. *The Political Integration of Women.* Urbana: University of Illinois Press, 1983.

Savodnik, Peter. "Capito, Dole Discuss Senate Bid." *The Hill,* June 27, 2005.

——. "Sorensen Heading to D.C., as Fight for Idaho-1 Revs Up." *TheHill.com,* February 8, 2006. http://thehill.com/campaign-2008/sorensen-heading-to-d.c.-as-fight-for-idaho-1-revs-up-2006-02-08.html.

Saye, Albert. "Georgia's County Unit System of Election." *Journal of Politics* 12 (1950): 93–106.

Scammon, Richard, A. V. McGillivray, and R. Cook. "Analysis of the Elections of 2002." In *America Votes, 25*. Washington, D.C.: CQ Press, 2003. http://library.cqpress.com/elections.amvt25-181-9622-602649.

Schlesinger, Joseph. *Ambition and Politics: Political Careers in the United States*. Chicago: Rand McNally, 1966.

Schroeder, Pat. *Twenty-four Years of House Work and the Place Is Still a Mess*. Kansas City, Mo.: Andrews McMeel, 1999.

Scobie, Ingrid Winther. *Center Stage: Helen Gahagan Douglas, A Life*. New York: Oxford University Press, 1992.

Seligman, Lester. "Political Recruitment and Party Structure: A Case Study." *American Political Science Review* 5 (1961): 77–86.

Seltzer, Richard, Jody Newman, and Melissa Voorhees Leighton. *Sex as a Political Variable*. Boulder, Colo.: Lynne Rienner Publishers, 1997.

"Senator Blanche Lincoln." *National Journal Almanac*, 2007. http://nationaljournal.com.proxyau.wrlc.org/pubs/almanac/2006/people/ar/ars1.htm.

Shames, Shauna. "The 'Un-Candidates': Gender and Outsider Signals in Women's Political Advertisements." *Women & Politics* 25 (2003): 115–47.

"Shea-Porter Once Escorted From Bush Event." *Associated Press State and Local Wire*, September 14, 2006.

Sheckels, Theodore, Jr. "Mikulski vs. Chavez for the Senate from Maryland in 1986 and the 'Rules' for Attack Politics." *Communication Quarterly* 42 (1994): 311–26.

Shenon, Philip. "Ohio Republican Tied to Abramoff Abandons Reelection Bid." *New York Times*, August 8, 2006.

Sidlow, Edward. *Challenging the Incumbent: An Underdog's Undertaking*. Washington, D.C.: CQ Press, 2004.

Silbey, Joel. *The American Political Nation*. Stanford: Stanford University Press, 1991.

Simon, Dennis. "Electoral and Ideological Change in the South: The Case of the U.S. House of Representatives, 1952–2000." Paper presented at the Southern Political Science Association Annual Meeting, January 2004, New Orleans.

Simon, Dennis, and Barbara Palmer. "Gender, Party, and Political Change: The Evolution of a Democratic Advantage." APSAnet eSymposium, "An Open Boundaries Workshop: Women in Politics in a Comparative Perspective." *PS Online* 37 (2004): http://www.apsanet.org/imgtest/EvolutionDemocraticAdvan-Palmer.pdf.

Simon, Dennis, Barbara Palmer, and David Peterson. "Women in the Political Hierarchy: A Time Series Analysis." Paper presented at the Southern Political Science Association Annual Meeting, January 2004, New Orleans.

"Simon, Martin File Campaign Funding Data." *Crain's Chicago Business*, August 7, 1989.

Sinclair, Barbara. *Unorthodox Lawmaking*. Washington, D.C.: CQ Press, 1997.

Smooth, Wendy. "African American Women and Electoral Politics: Journeying from the Shadows to the Spotlight." In *Gender and Elections: Shaping the Future of American Politics*, edited by Sue Carroll and Richard Fox. New York: Cambridge University Press, 2006.

Solowiej, Lisa, and Thomas Brunell. "The Entrance of Women to the U.S. Congress: The Widow Effect." *Political Research Quarterly* 56 (2003): 283–92.

"Special Election Results, United States Representative in Congress, 37th District, Final Canvass." *California Secretary of State*, June 26, 2007. http://www.sos.ca.gov/elections/elections_cd37.htm (accessed August 4, 2007).

"Special Report: CQ's Guide to the Committees." *CQ Weekly*, April 16, 2007.

Stanley, Alessandra. "In Primary Race for Senate, Ads Are Costly and Caustic." *New York Times*, September 13, 1992.

Stanley, Harold, and Richard Niemi. *Vital Statistics on American Politics 2003–2004*. Washington, D.C.: CQ Press, 2003.

Stanley, Jeanie. "Gender and the Campaign for Governor." In *Texas Politics: A Reader*, 2nd ed., edited by Anthony Champagne and Edward Harpham. New York: W.W. Norton, 1998.

Starr, Alexandra. "Bada Bing Club." *New Republic*, April 23, 2007.

Stassen-Berger, Rachel. "Al Franken Says He is Running for U.S. Senate." *St. Paul Pioneer Press*, February 14, 2007.

Stevens, Allison. "The Strength of These Women Shows in Their Numbers." *CQ Weekly*, October 25, 2003.

Struble, Robert. "House Turnover and the Principle of Rotation." *Political Science Quarterly* 94 (1979): 649–67.

Stump, Jake. "Capito Says She'll Seek Fifth Term in the House." *Charleston Daily Mail*, May 10, 2007.

Sullivan, Bartholomew. "Safe Territory: Redrawing of Congressional District Lines Puts Incumbents in Driver's Seat." *Memphis (Tenn.) Commercial Appeal*, October 27, 2004.

Sullivan, Joseph. "U.S. Senate Race Tops Jersey Elections." *New York Times*, October 31, 1982.

Swain, Carol. *Black Faces, Black Interests: The Representation of African-Americans in Congress*. Cambridge, Mass.: Harvard University Press, 1993.

Swers, Michelle. "Research on Women in Legislatures: What Have We Learned, Where Are We Going?" In *Women in Congress: Running, Winning, Ruling*, edited by Karen O'Connor. Binghamton, N.Y.: Haworth Press, 2001.

Swift, Elaine, Robert Brookshire, David Canon, Evelyn Fink, and John Hibbing, comps. *Database of Congressional Historical Statistics*. Interuniversity Consortium for Political Research Study 3371. Ann Arbor, Mich.: Interuniversity Consortium for Political Research, 2004.

Tapper, Jake. "Obama Bests Clinton in Primary Fundraising." *ABCNews.com*, April 4, 2007.

"Thompson, Fred." In *CQ's Politics in America 2002, the 107th Congress*. Washington, D.C.: CQ Press, 2001. http://library.cqpress.com/congress/pia107-0453055379.

Thompson, Joan Hulce. "Career Convergence: Election of Women and Men to the House of Representatives, 1916–1975." *Women & Politics* 5 (1985): 69–90.

Thompson, Seth, and Janie Steckenrider. "The Relative Irrelevance of Candidate Sex." *Women & Politics* 17 (1997): 71–92.

Tolchin, Susan, and Martin Tolchin. *Clout: Womanpower and Politics*. New York: Coward, McCann & Geoghegan, 1974.

Tolleson-Rienhart, Sue, and Jeanie Stanley. *Claytie and the Lady: Ann Richards, Gender, and Politics in Texas*. Austin: University of Texas Press, 1994.

Tomz, Michael, Gary King, and Langche Zeng. *RELOGIT: Rare Events Logistical Regression, Version 1.1*. Cambridge, Mass.: Harvard University Press, 1999.

Tomz, Michael, Jason Wittenberg, and Gary King. *Clarify: Software for Interpreting and Presenting Statistical Results*. Cambridge, Mass.: Harvard University, 2001.

Toner, Robin, "Demographics; New Congress, Older Look." *New York Times.com*, January 9, 2007. http://query.nytimes.com/gst/fullpage.html?res=9E04EFD 9153OF93AA35752COA9619C8B638n=Top%Reference%2fTimes%20Topics% 2fPeople%2fT%2FToner%2c%20Robin.

Torry, Jack. "From His Cell, Traficant Still a Force in Election." *Columbus Dispatch*, November 2, 2002.

"Traficant, James A., Jr." In *CQ's Politics in America 2002, The 107th Congress*. Washington, D.C.: CQ Press, 2001. http://library.cqpress.com/congress/pia107-0453055393.

Traub, James. "Party Like It's 1994." *New York Times Magazine*, March 12, 2006.

Tsong, Nicole, and Sean Cockerham. "ANWR, Tax Issue Separate Debaters." *Anchorage Daily News*, October 29, 2004.

Turner, Wallace. "Burton's Widow among 4 Considering Race for Congress Seat." *New York Times*, April 18, 1983.

U.S. Bureau of the Census. *Historical Statistics of the United States*. Washington, D.C.: U.S. Department of Commerce, Bureau of the Census, 1975.

——. *Statistical Abstract of the United States, 2004–2005*. http://www.census.gov/prod/www/statistical-abstract-04.html.

U.S. Congress Handbook. Washington, D.C.: Votenet Solutions, 2005.

Wagman, Jake, Matthew Franck, and Virginia Young. "McCaskill prevailed despite cash gap." *St. Louis Post-Dispatch*, December 9, 2006.

Wallace, Jeremy. "At Final Hour, 3 Republicans Join Senate Race." *Sarasota Herald-Tribune*, May 13, 2006.

——. "Harris Unfazed by Apparent Party Pressure." *Sarasota Herald-Tribune*, June 25, 2005.

Walsh, Bill, and Bruce Alpert. "FBI Details Jefferson's Dealings; It Videotaped Meetings, Cash Transactions." *New Orleans Times-Picayune*, May 22, 2006.

Wattenberg, Martin. *The Decline of American Political Parties, 1952–1988*. Cambridge, Mass.: Harvard University Press, 1990.

Wayne, Stephen. *The Road to the White House, 2000: The Politics of Presidential Elections*. Boston: St. Martin's Press, 2000.

Weisman, Jonathan. "House Ethics Panel Begins Bribery Probe; Congressmen from Ohio and Louisiana Targeted; DeLay Escapes with Resignation." *Washington Post*, May 18, 2006.

Welch, Susan. "Recruitment of Women to Public Office." *Western Political Quarterly* 31 (1978): 372–80.

——. "Are Women More Liberal than Men in the U.S. Congress?" *Legislative Studies Quarterly* 10 (1985): 125–34.

Welch, Susan, and Lee Sigelman. "Changes in Public Attitudes toward Women in Politics." *Social Science Quarterly* 63 (1982): 312–21.

Welch, Susan, and Donley Studlar. "The Opportunity Structure for Women's Candidacies and Electability in Britain and the United States." *Political Research Quarterly* 49 (1996): 861–74.

Welch, Susan, Margery M. Ambrosius, Janet Clark, and Robert Darcy. "The Effect of Candidate Gender on Election Outcomes in State Legislative Races." *Western Political Quarterly* 38 (1985): 464–75.

Welch, William. "Ideology Rocks the Vote in Kansas." *USA Today*, August 2, 1996.

Werner, Emmy. "Women in Congress: 1917–1964." *Western Political Quarterly* 19 (1966): 16–30.

——. "Women in the State Legislatures." *Western Political Quarterly* 19 (1968): 40–50.

"What to Believe: U.S. Senate Ads." *St. Louis Post Dispatch*, November 1, 2006.

Whitby, Kenny. *The Color of Representation: Congressional Behavior and Black Interests*. Ann Arbor: University of Michigan Press, 1997.

White, Theodore H. *The Making of the President, 1972*. New York: Atheneum Publishers, 1973.

Whitney, David. "Freshman Matsui Learns Life in Congress Is Hectic." *Sacramento Bee*, March 20, 2005.

——. "Matsui Has Money in Bank for '06 Race." *Sacramento Bee*, April 27, 2005.

"Widow of Rep. Burton Is Elected in California Congressional Race." *New York Times*, June 23, 1983.

Wilcox, Clyde. "Why Was 1992 the 'Year of the Woman'? Explaining Women's Gains in 1992." In *The Year of the Woman: Myths and Reality*, edited by Elizabeth Adell Cook, Sue Thomas, and Clyde Wilcox. Boulder, Colo.: Westview Press, 1994.

Wilkerson, Isabel. "Black Woman's Senate Race Is Acquiring a Celebrity Aura." *New York Times*, July 29, 1992.

"Will Byrd Run?" *The Journal (Martinsburg, West Virginia)*, May 1, 2005.

Williams, Christine. "Women, Law and Politics: Recruitment Patterns in the Fifty States." *Women & Politics* 10 (1990): 103–23.

Williams, Joan. *Unbending Gender: Why Family and Work Conflict and What to Do about It.* Oxford: Oxford University Press, 2000.

Williams, Leonard. "Gender, Political Advertising, and the 'Air Wars.'" *Women and Elective Office: Past, Present and Future,* edited by Sue Thomas and Clyde Wilcox. New York: Oxford University Press, 1998.

Wilson, Marie. *Closing the Leadership Gap: Why Women Can and Must Help Run the World.* New York: Viking, 2004.

Winkler, Robert, and William Hays. *Statistics: Probability, Inference and Decision,* 2nd ed. New York: Holt, Rinehart, and Winston, 1975.

Witt, Linda, Karen Paget, and Glenna Matthews. *Running as a Woman: Gender and Power in American Politics.* New York: Free Press, 1995.

Wolbrecht, Christina. *The Politics of Women's Rights: Parties, Positions, and Change.* Princeton, N.J.: Princeton University Press, 2000.

Women in History: Living Vignettes of Notable Women in U.S. History. http://www.lkwdpl.org/wihohio/luce-cla.htm.

Woodward, Bob. *The Agenda: Inside the Clinton White House.* New York: Simon & Schuster, 1994.

Yamamura, Kevin. "Matsui Set to Be Sworn in Today and Cast First Vote as a Congressman's Widow and Washington Veteran." *Sacramento Bee,* March 10, 2005.

Yanez, Luisa. "A Venerable Politician—And a Celebrity, Too." *Miami Herald,* August 20, 2006.

——. "Actress Plans Fundraising Concert for Patlak." *Miami Herald,* September 16, 2006.

Young, James Sterling. *The Washington Community 1800–1828.* New York, Columbia University Press, 1966.

Index

Page numbers in italics refer to figures and tables; "n" indicates note).